Corporate versus National Interest in US Trade Policy

Richard L. Bernal

Corporate versus National Interest in US Trade Policy

Chiquita and Caribbean Bananas

palgrave
macmillan

Richard L. Bernal
Office of Global Affairs
University of the West Indies
Kingston, Jamaica

ISBN 978-3-030-56949-5 ISBN 978-3-030-56950-1 (eBook)
https://doi.org/10.1007/978-3-030-56950-1

This Palgrave Macmillan imprint is published by the registered company Springer Nature Switzerland AG.
The registered company address is: Gewerbestrasse 11, 6330 Cham, Switzerland

Acknowledgements

A loving family is the ultimate good fortune in life. I have certainly been so blessed throughout my life. The example and unconditional support of my parents is evident in everything I have done. There has been no greater inspiration than the pride in my sons, Brian and Darren and the unlimited joy of my grandchildren, Nile and Elle make me glad for each and every day of life. There is so much to thank my wife Margaret for that it would fill a very long book.

My teachers have the right to expect more and better. I unreservedly express my appreciation to them. My professors at the University of the West Indies, Trevor Munroe, Orlando Patterson, Clive Thomas, Douglas Hall, Adlith Brown, Rex Nettleford, and George Beckford. My exposure to David Gordon, Gita Sen, and Anwar Shaikh was enjoyable and enlightening. I have benefitted immeasurably from the invaluable advice and consistent support of Sir George Alleyne, Prof. Franklin Knight, Prof. Edward Greene, Richard Fletcher, Douglas Fletcher, Dudley Clarke, Dr. W. Astor Kirk, Prof. Vishnu Persaud, and Prof. Donald J. Harris.

Ambassador Donald Mills was such an inspirational example who was always willing to share his experience. My mentor Sir Alister McIntyre always provided sage advice, indeed, I was wiser after every conversation. A very special appreciation must go to Professor Norman Girvan, teacher, mentor, and friend who contributed immeasurably to my intellectual growth and from whom I learnt much about being a professional economist and policy advisor and who provided opportunities for my development. I learnt a great deal from working with Michael Manley on the

South Commission and the various reports of the Socialist International Committee. During these meetings, I had a chance to interact with Julius Nyerere, Manmohan Singh, Jan Pronk, Stuart Holland, and Jorge Sol. I was fortunate to have met Willi Brandt, Carlos Andres Perez, and Rajiv Gandhi and to imbibe diplomacy by osmosis from Michael Manley, P.J. Patterson, David Coore, and Dudley Thompson. What I learnt I had a chance to develop and deploy because of the assignments and opportunities given to me by Michael Manley, P.J. Patterson, David Coore, and Bruce Golding to serve Jamaica and the Caribbean. Starting with my appointment as Jamaica's ambassador to the United States and continuing in subsequent positions.

Exposure and experience contribute imperceptibly to personal development. I have been in meetings too numerous to recount with presidents and prime ministers and heads of international and regional organizations. Among the most memorable interactions were those with President George Bush, President Carter, President, Clinton, President Fidel Castro, Prime Minister Tony Blair, Secretary of State General Colin Powell, Congressman Charles Rangel, Harry Belafonte, Enrique Iglesias, and Pascal Lamy. Especially inspirational was my conversation with Professor Sir W. Arthur Lewis.

My tenure at the Workers Savings and Loan Bank was a period of significant professional development encouraged and fully supported by E. Lloyd Taylor, trade unionist, who had unlimited confidence in me and from whom I learnt a great deal. Managing in the banking and financial sector afforded me an enhanced understanding of the market and private enterprise while not losing sight of the role of the state.

A special word of gratitude to Professor Anthony Payne of Sheffield University for assuring me of the importance of the project and that I should write it and did so with an eloquence of writing that I am still striving to emulate. The very earliest draft was written and dictated during the struggle over the banana issue dating back to the 1990s. During this period, I was fortunate to have the skills of Janice Rowe-Barnwell. The editors Palgrave must be thanked for readily accepting my proposal and for their initiative, courtesy, encouragement, and patience. They would have had a more difficult task had it not been for the very thorough proofreading and careful editing of Stephanie Cain and work of Lisa Hamilton-Braithwaite. The anonymous reviewer made useful suggestions. Hugh Small's wise counsel was much appreciated.

Many people helped in the fight to dissuade the United States government from dismantling the European Union banana regime. Praiseworthy were the ambassadors of the Caribbean countries including those that represented countries that did not export bananas. They were gallant and tireless in their efforts. Vigorous and sustained support was provided by Congresswoman Maxine Waters, Randall Robinson of TransAfrica and advice on lobbying by Hazel Ross-Robinson and George Dalley. Among the stalwart supporters were the hard-working staff of the Embassy of Jamaica in Washington DC and Jamaica's Permanent Mission to the Organization of American States during the time when I was Ambassador to the United States and Permanent Representative to the OAS.

The book is based on notes, statements, and analyses written by me during the events related and reworked in the years since then. I retained extensive and detailed material in my personal files and I was able to draw on letters and correspondence meticulously preserved and filed by my secretary at the time, Mrs. Diane Smith-Brown. I kept the material because while the EU banana was ruled incompatible with the rules of the World Trade Organization in 1997, it was not replaced until 2010. During this time, I retained a feeling that an injustice had been perpetuated which was not in the interest of the USA and it was harmful to the small Caribbean islands that exported bananas. The passage of time had the advantage of allowing me to observe the implications in the Caribbean of the dismantling of the EU banana regime. I decided in 2019 to revisit the issue initially for my own clarification and in the course of writing, I felt that the story was worth sharing with the public in the form of a book. I approached Palgrave Macmillan who had published one of my earlier books and they agreed to publish. This provided the impetus to finish the manuscript.

The process was long and arduous but fortunately, I imbibed a Calvinist work ethic and persistence from my father, Franklin and calmness from my mother, Kathleen. They facilitated my unlimited reading of anything and everything and Franklin set the example of writing books and the fondness for writing. The opportunity to complete the text was afforded me by the lock-down period following the global pandemic of the COVID-19 which saved much commuting time.

I have dedicated previous books to my parents, wife, children, and grandchildren, all of whom have enriched my life and made this book possible. In case this is my last book I do not want to miss the opportunity to dedicate this book solely to my late brother, Robert Franklin Bernal. I express my appreciation to the Rt. Hon. Professor Owen Arthur, former Prime Minister of Barbados for agreeing to write the foreword for this book. Unfortunately he died before completing the foreword.

Contents

1 Objective and Organization 1

2 Corporate Influence in US Trade Policy 13

3 The Importance of Bananas in the Caribbean 41

4 The EU Banana Regime 63

5 Chiquita and Its Influence on US Trade Policy 99

6 Chiquita Overwhelms the Small Caribbean States 117

7 Impact of US Banana Policy on the Caribbean 179

8 Implications for US National Interest in the Caribbean 207

Bibliography 237

Index 269

Abbreviations

AAFA	American Apparel & Footwear Association
ACP	Africa, the Caribbean, and the Pacific
ACTPN	Advisory Committee for Trade Policy and Negotiations
AFL	American Federation of Labor
ALBA	Bolivarian Alliance for the Peoples of Our America
BECO	Banana Export Company of Jamaica
BFA	Banana Framework Agreement
CARIBCAN	Caribbean-Canada Trade Agreement
CARICOM	Caribbean Common Market and Community
CBEA	Caribbean Banana Exporters Association
CBERA	Caribbean Basin Economic Recovery Act
CBI	Caribbean Basin Initiative
CBTPA	Caribbean Basin Trade Partnership Act
CET	Common External Tariff
CIA	Central Intelligence Agency
CIO	Congress of Industrial Organizations
COHA	Council on Hemispheric Affairs
CSME	CARICOM Single Market and Economy
DDA	Doha Development Agenda
DEA	Drug Enforcement Agency
DNC	Democratic National Committee
DSS	Dispute Settlement System
DSU	Dispute Settlement Understanding
EC	Eastern Caribbean
ECCU	Eastern Caribbean Currency Union
ECM	European Common Market

EEC	European Economic Community
EIF	Enhanced Integrated Framework
ESC	English-speaking Caribbean
EU	European Union
FAO	Food and Agriculture Organization
FCFS	First Come First Served
FDI	Foreign Direct Investment
FTAA	Free Trade Area of the Americas
GATT	General Agreement on Tariffs and Trade
GDP	Gross Domestic Product
GSP	Generalized System of Preferences
HIPC	Heavily Indebted Poor Countries
IIE	Institute for International Economics
ILO	International Labour Organization
IMF	International Monetary Fund
JAMCO	Jamaica Marketing Company Limited
LDC	Least Developed Countries
MFN	Most Favoured Nation
MNC	Multinational Corporation
MNE	Multinational Enterprise
MTRV	Metric Tonne Raw Value
NAFTA	North American Free Trade Area
NATO	North Atlantic Treaty Organization
NBER	National Bureau of Economic Research
NCBR	National Council of Black Republicans
NCOCA	National Coalition on Caribbean Affairs
NDC	National Democratic Committee
NGO	Non-governmental Organisation
OAS	Organization of the American States
OECS	Organization of Eastern Caribbean States
PAC	Political Action Committee
PTA	Preferential Trade Agreement
RTA	Regional Trade Agreement
SDE	Small Developing Economies
SDT	Special and Differential Treatment
SEC	Securities and Exchange Commission
SIDS	Small Island Developing States
TIM	Trade Integration Mechanism
TPA	Trade Promotion Authority

TQR	Tariff Rate Quotas
UFC	United Fruit Company
UK	United Kingdom
UPEB/UBEC	Union of Banana Exporting Countries
US	United States
USTR	United States Trade Representative
WINBAN	Windward Island Banana Growers Association
WTO	World Trade Organization

List of Tables

Table 3.1	Land area, population, gross domestic product (GDP), GDP per capita of Caribbean banana exporting countries, and the United States of America (1999)	43
Table 6.1	Lindner's campaign contributions (1991–99)	128
Table 8.1	Status of US National interests during and after the EU banana regime	226

CHAPTER 1

Objective and Organization

Introduction

From antiquity, trade has been dominated by private individuals or groups of individuals in the form of companies. When governments decided to regulate trade and to implement the codification of the rules as national trade policies, the private sector exerted influence. In the modern world, the private sector and corporations, in particular, are the drivers of trade policies. This is the first fact to note about trade policy. The second fact is that throughout history, the state has actively and consistently supported private corporations including defending their property abroad, forcing foreign governments to open access to their markets, subsidizing their costs, and compelling governments to give concessions, inter alia. In mobilizing state support for their activities, corporations have always been able to count on the common belief that in a capitalist economy what is good for corporations is good for the government and the country, that is, in the national interest. This is not necessarily true because what a corporation wants or is doing is often in contradiction to the national interest. In a modern democracy with mechanisms for transparency, an active press, and competing political parties, such a contradiction should be uncovered and be part of the debate over public policy. Such debate is a reflection of society consisting of a variety of groups with different interests, and in a democracy, what is determined to be in the national interest is the outcome of the resolution of these differing interests. The idea of a policy based on a consensus resulting from a reconciliation of different

R. L. Bernal, *Corporate versus National Interest in US Trade Policy*, https://doi.org/10.1007/978-3-030-56950-1_1

perspectives of interest groups is not always realized. When this does not happen, it is the case that a particular interest group and sometimes a single corporation or institution has prevailed in the competition to influence public policy. The public and media find trade issues complex and the beneficiary corporations spend considerable sums to influence public opinion, politicians, and policymaking officials.

Objectives

The objectives of this book are:

First, to document and explain how Chiquita, a large US-owned multinational corporation, succeeded in having the Clinton administration pursue a trade policy of forcing the European Union to dismantle its preferential banana import regime[1] for exports from small Caribbean countries. Chiquita was able to induce the US government to engage in a trade war with the European Union (EU) including the imposition of increased tariffs over a product not produced in the United States and that was equivalent in value to only about 10 percent of US-EU bilateral trade.[2] It is, therefore, a case study of how corporate interest, in this case, an American multinational corporation, influenced US trade policy and, hence, is illustrative and instructive on the process of trade policy formulation in the United States.

Second, to explain that the United States' success in having the EU banana regime dismantled was not in the national interest because of the harmful repercussions for the Caribbean banana exporting countries which experienced a very significant decline in production and exports. The export of bananas was critically important to the economic viability of the Eastern Caribbean islands. The decline put in jeopardy the social and economic basis for their prosperity, peace, and democracy. Subsequent to and accompanying the decline in the banana industry, these tiny monosectoral economies became more vulnerable to drug trafficking, social instability, crime, and the temptation to indulge in policies such as citizen investment schemes, which were in the national security interest of the United States. The national interest of the United States is to have Caribbean neighbors that are peaceful, democratic, and prosperous. The experience indicates that Chiquita's success in having the United States dismantle the EU regime was not in the United States' national interest indeed and was detrimental to US national security interests in the Caribbean. Chiquita's success in having the United States support its cause is in keeping with an American tradition. Maurer documents several instances in which "American domestic interests trumped strategic concerns again and again, for small economic gains relative to the US economy and the potential economic losses."[3]

Methodology

The research methodology examines international trade policy as the outcome of the interaction of competing interests by an application of a nuanced modification of the well-known interest group approach to politics.[4] International trade policy of the United States, like its foreign policy, is the result of complex, constantly shifting interactions among competing interests[5] which are not necessarily groups, but are actors which can take the form of political parties, corporations, business associations, individuals, government departments, think tanks, non-government organizations and even foreign governments.[6] Economic interests dominate the motivations of the interest groups that seek to influence US trade policy. How these goals and efforts translate into trade policy is affected by ideas about trade[7] and approach to overall foreign policy. A disproportionate influence is exerted among the competing interest groups by what Dreiling and Darves explain as the "class agency of business leaders"[8] representing corporations.

Organization

Chapter 2 outlines the process of the formulation and implementation of US international trade policy and explains the role of corporations in this process. Ideally, trade policy is a blend and synthesis of competing societal interests working through the governmental system of Congress, the White House, and federal bureaucracy. The end result, as far as possible, is supposed to be a trade policy that reflects a national consensus, the goals which are regarded as in the national good of the United States. This is often not the outcome in reality. On the contrary, the review of trade policy formation reveals that corporations have always exerted a strong influence on US public policy[9] inclusive of trade policy. This arises from the financial resources that they are able and willing to deploy in support of the objectives. An additional advantage has been the technical complexity of some trade issues, the nature of which often make it difficult for civil society to navigate the arcane and specialized jargon to clearly articulate their respective positions. That corporate interests have always influenced US trade policy is to be expected in a private sector, market-driven economy. After all, it is firms that trade not countries. The predominance of corporate interests in US trade policy is substantiated by a review of the history of international trade policy formulation in the United States citing a substantial number of instances of the powerful influence of corporate interests.

Chapter 3 provides (a) an overview of the Caribbean for readers unfamiliar with the region, and concentrates on (b) explaining and documenting the former vital importance of banana exports to the economies of the banana exporting countries, as reflected in the contribution of the industry to gross domestic product (GDP), exports, and employment. The chapter documents conclusively that banana was the single most important economic activity and that banana exports were the engine of economic growth in the smaller Caribbean islands of Dominica, Grenada, St. Lucia, and St. Vincent and the Grenadines and an important contributor, Jamaica. Banana production and export was by far the most important export, the largest source of foreign exchange earnings, and the largest source of employment. Prime Minister P. J. Patterson tried to convey the importance of the industry to President Clinton when he said: "For many of our countries bananas are what cars are to Detroit."[10]

The United States could not have failed to be aware that the dismantling of the EU banana regime would result in serious economic collapse–although a US embassy official denied that there would be a possible collapse of the banana industry calling that prediction "perhaps the biggest fallacy". "We continue to be perplexed by assertion from regional officials and media that U.S. efforts to ensure (European Union) compliance with international trade rules ... will lead to the demise of the banana industry and the collapse of regional economies."[11] The economic shock to the Caribbean was seen in the United States as collateral damage that the Caribbean could manage. Bad enough to avoid addressing the issue, worse was when President Clinton told Caribbean leaders that "the target of the U.S. was the discriminatory European system, not the Caribbean."[12]

Essential to the viability of the banana export industry in the Caribbean was the EU banana regime. The EU banana regime is explained in Chapter 4. The regime was a preferential market access arrangement restricted to the former European colonies in Africa and the Caribbean which were banana exporting countries. The banana regime consisted of a combined system of tariffs, quotas, and import licenses. It was designed to continue preferential arrangements dating back to the colonial period. The outline of the EU banana regime is set out against the background of an overview of the rationale and operation of preferential trade arrangements employed as development aid mechanisms to assist developing countries. Examples of the provision of preferential trade arrangements to developing countries inclusive of the small island developing states (SIDS) of the Caribbean by Britain, France, Canada, and the United States are cited. Recording this fact is important in the case of the United States because it demonstrates that the US approach to facilitating exports from the Caribbean was by the provision of preferential market access arrangements emblematic of which was the Caribbean Basin Economic Recovery Act (CBERA). The approach to the banana regime in the 1990s, therefore, represented an aberration and not so much a change in policy.

The corporate actor driving the US approach to the EU banana regime was Chiquita Brands International Corporation (Chiquita). Chiquita was a US-owned producer and global distributor of bananas under the brand "Chiquita". It was the largest distributor of bananas in the United States and dominated one of the largest global markets. Reference is also made to the fact that Chiquita is a corporate successor of the United Fruit Company (UFC).[13] The sordid history of the rise of the UFC to dominance in the banana trade[14] and its conduct in Central America[15] is briefly outlined, as it has parallels with the conduct of Chiquita in exerting influence over US foreign policy. Chiquita's influence on US policy is a continuation of those of UFC[16] revealing a continuity of corporate culture. It is illustrative of the extent to which the US government, at the behest of an American corporation, will go to protect/promote the interests of that corporation[17] in the fulfillment of the responsibility to protect American lives and property within the borders of the United States and anywhere in the world.

Chapter 5 provides an overview of Chiquita, its operations, and influence on US trade policy and shows the truly remarkable ability throughout its corporate history to have the US government do whatever it deemed necessary to secure its property and maximize its profits. It is well documented that in the early 1950s, the United States took action to remove a government in Guatemala which it deemed inclined to communism, the proof being that government's policy of land reform. The UFC would have had to yield some of its then vast landholdings for compensation. As astonishing, Chiquita was prepared for the United States to engage in a "trade war" with the European Union to secure additional market share and profits for the corporation, but which would do enormous damage to both the United States, the European Union, and possibly irreparably damage the newly established World Trade Organization (WTO) as well as the smallest banana exporting countries in the world. It is an amazing level of selfishness that Chiquita could so conveniently conflate its corporate interest with that of the national interest of the United States. It is also an indication of the extent of Chiquita's influence on US trade policy, the disregard for the wider American national interests, and the lack of empathy for the possible harmful implications for the very small banana exporting islands. Interestingly, the lobbying and public relations campaign which Chiquita employed to achieve their ends did not have to involve any illegal activities because lobbying is an accepted part of the formulation of US foreign trade policy. This is just the way the process works in the United States.

Chiquita used its financial resources to mobilize political influence in several ways, but most notably in financial contributions to get the Clinton administration to pursue a policy in its interest. Such was the power of Chiquita that it defeated the strenuous opposition of Caribbean governments and the steadfast resistance of the European Union led by the United Kingdom and France. The victory of Chiquita was highly detrimental to US national security interests in the Caribbean. The collapse of the banana industry caused serious economic dislocation and thereby made these small island developing states more vulnerable to narcotics trafficking and the associated transnational crime.

Chapter 6 examines the impact of the dismantling of the EU banana regime on the Caribbean. Barbara Welch writing in the late 1990s describes the dilemma of the Eastern Caribbean banana producing islands as: "They share a long and chequered colonial past, a precarious present and an uncertain future."[18] A July 2019 paper from the International Monetary Fund (IMF) states that the unemployment rates in the small developing economies of the Eastern Caribbean have persistently been among the highest in the world. The analysis concludes that "while available statistics confirm that agricultural employment in many (Eastern Caribbean) countries continuously declined after the collapse of the banana and sugar industries, unemployment rates remained stable amidst contracting agricultural employment, as fast growing employment in tourism and public sector employment considerably offset the impact of the banana and sugar industries collapse."[19] The situation could be seen very differently, that is, if there had not been the collapse of employment in the banana industry, the growth in employment in other sectors such as tourism would have ensured significantly lower unemployment than currently obtains nearly twenty years after the dismantling of the EU banana regime at the instigation of the United States. The Chiquita instigated US trade policy left the small banana exporting islands of the Caribbean a substantially retarded economic present and a precarious future. This is a situation that is not in the national interest of the United States.

US trade policy towards the Caribbean since the early 1980s was the non-reciprocal opening of the US market to imports which did not damage or disrupt American production. Products which could suffer from imports from the Caribbean were omitted from the CBERA legislation. The United States had no need to press the Caribbean governments to open their markets because the United States was the main supplier of imports into these markets. In addition, these markets were so small that they did not matter to any particular American industry nor did the United States face significant competition because it had the advantage of geographic proximity. The policy pursued on bananas was at variance to that embodied in the Caribbean Basin Initiative (CBI) and the measures which constitute the CBERA. The Clinton administration's action on bananas was a deviation from this policy framework despite protestations from the governments of the Caribbean banana exporting countries and the European Union.

The US action on the EU banana regime was diametrically opposed to the approach of the European Union towards the developing countries of the African, Caribbean, and Pacific Group. EU policy was premised on the provision of preferential trade arrangements, supported with financial development aid as a mechanism for export-propelled economic development. It was an efficacious policy because it was financed by European consumers who paid a small unnoticed extra cost for bananas and sugar, and the revenue from exports went directly to farmers and not to governments. There was, therefore, a divide between the United States and the European Union on the approach of bananas from the Caribbean going into the European Union. Chiquita was able to create and exploit this difference.

Chiquita influenced the Clinton administration to vigorously and relentlessly pursue a policy of dismantling the EU's preferential banana import regime, claiming that it was a discriminatory regime which damaged their company. Chiquita's objective was to gain the minute share of the world market supplied by the small states of the Caribbean. This chapter documents how US trade policy was driven at the behest of Chiquita Corporation and how Chiquita successfully combatted the attempts of European and Caribbean governments, as well as corporate interests, to persuade the US government not to force the dismantling of the EU banana regime because such a course of action would be detrimental to the Caribbean banana exporting countries. An integral aspect of Chiquita's campaign was financial contributions to both the Republican and Democratic political parties.

US policy on bananas in the 1990s was a major contributing factor in setting in motion the economic crisis in the Caribbean which continues to the present. It must be stated clearly and categorically that US policy resulting in the dismantling of the EU banana regime was not the only factor, but it set in motion the economic difficulties of the small banana exporting Caribbean islands. Chapter 7 discusses the adverse impact of eliminating the EU preferential market and pricing arrangements and the deterioration in the Caribbean's export earnings, tax revenues, and employment. This made these countries more vulnerable to narcotics trafficking and the associated transnational crime, and that, in turn, has been associated with violence. The economic malaise has not been in the national interest of the United States because the countries affected became less robust trade partners; sought aid from countries through enhanced diplomatic relations with Cuba, Venezuela, and China; and saw increased out-migration. There was also an expansion of drug trafficking activities in the region and an increase in the amount of drugs entering the United States and the accompanying money laundering and human trafficking. All of these cannot be attributed entirely or directly to the decline in banana exports. US policy instigated by Chiquita precipitated the contraction of the banana industry and the resulting negative impact on the overall economy increased the economic and vulnerability of these tiny islands. Hence, while Chiquita got what it wanted, it caused events that were harmful to the Caribbean and certainly not in the national security interest of the United States.

Chapter 8 provides an overview of US national interests in the Caribbean and an evaluation of the impact which the dismantling of the EU banana regime had on those interests. Basically, the United States viewed its national interest in the Caribbean as having neighbors that are peaceful, democratic, prosperous, and pro-American in the conduct of their foreign policy; hence minimizing/eliminating the perceived threats to national security entails the prevention of the emergence of governments that were seen as communist-inclined and less favorable to the United States and the reduction in the flow of narcotics and migrants into the United States. The United States pursued the attainment of these goals by a combination of (1) promoting its neighbors' economic growth as the foundation for democracy, vibrant trade partners and (2) counter-narcotics cooperation in the forms of technical assistance, financial aid, and logistics support to the local security forces. Regarding economic growth, the United States regards the Caribbean countries as middle-income developing countries that do not need developing aid but should rely on foreign direct investment and within a private sector-led, market-driven macro-economic strategy along the lines of the Washington Consensus. The CBI operationalized by the CBERA was motivated by heightened security concerns at a time of the Sandinistas in Nicaragua, Bishop and the New Jewel Movement in Grenada, and administrations in Guyana and Jamaica professing cooperative socialism and Democratic Socialism respectively. This was the genesis of the CBI of 1983 which was designed to assist in the promotion of economic development in Caribbean countries by providing preferential access to the US market, increased financial aid, and debt relief. This was implemented through preferential trade arrangements embodied and legislated in the CBERA. The rationale for the CBERA was that it was in the national security interests of the United States to promote the economic development of the Caribbean and Central American countries by allowing them better access for their exports to the US market. The US provision of preferential access to its market was a deliberate means of assisting the Caribbean's economic development supported by some financial aid. This has remained the template for US policy in the Caribbean.

Conclusion

Chiquita was the successor to UFC, which since the inception of its involvement in the banana trade wielded almost unrestrained power in Central America and enormous influence on the US government. Kepner and Soothill describe United Fruit's operations in 1935 as "economic imperialism",[20] and indeed its history is dramatic, literally a fiction-like "thriller". The text resists the temptation to regale the reader with the flamboyant exploits, devoting only enough attention as is necessary to establish nature and continuation of a corporate culture habituated to having its way with the US government. Chiquita's engagement in US international trade policy continued that tradition established earlier by the UFC. At the time that it was able to persuade the US government to dismantle the EU banana regime, it was controlled by majority owner American businessman, Carl Lindner. The dismantling of the EU banana regime allowed the company to attempt to capture the part of the EU market formerly supplied in part by the small countries of the Caribbean. This opportunity to do so did not prevent Chiquita from entering Chapter 11; however, Carl Lindner's majority ownership of the company ended when Chiquita Brands International completed Chapter 11 bankruptcy proceedings on March 19, 2002. On October 24, 2014, the shareholders of Chiquita accepted the $611 million offer of acquisition by Brazilian companies Cutrale and Safra Group. There ended the infamous saga of Chiquita, the successor of the notorious United Fruit Company which pushed the US government to pursue a trade policy detrimental to US national interest in the Caribbean.

Notes

1. The rationale and evolution of banana policy in Europe is described in Peter Glegg, the Caribbean Banana Trade from Colonialism to Globalization (New: York Palgrave, 2002).
2. John P. Sweeney, The High Cost of Clinton's Trade War with the European Union (Washington DC: The Heritage Foundation Executive Memorandum No. 584, March 26, 1999).
3. Noel Maurer, The Empire Trap: The Rise and Fall of U.S. Intervention to Protect American Property Overseas, 1893–2013 (Princeton: Princeton University Press, 2013) pages 2–3.
4. Arthur Bentley, The Process of Government (Cambridge: Belnap Press of Harvard University, 1967) and Jeffrey M. Berry and Clyde Wilcox, The Interest Group Society (New York: Routledge, 5th ed., 2008).
5. Claude Barfield, "The role of interest groups in the design and implementation of U.S. trade policies" in A. V. Deardorff and R. M. Stern (eds.), Social Dimensions of U.S. Trade Policies (Ann Arbor: University of Michigan Press, 2000) pages 271–280, Robert E. Baldwin, Trade Policy in a Changing World (Chicago: University of Chicago Press, 1988) and Gene M. Grossman and Elhanan Helpman, Interest Groups and Trade Policy (Princeton: Princeton University Press, 2002).
6. E. E. Schattschneider, Politics, Pressures and the Tariff (New York: Prentice-Hall, 1935), Alan Verne Deardorff and Robert Mitchell Stern, Constituent Interests and U.S. Trade Policies (Ann Arbor: University of

Michigan Press, 1998) and Gene M. Grossman and Elhanan Helpman, Interest groups and trade policy (Princeton, NJ: Princeton University Press, 2002).

7. Judith L. Goldstein (ed.), Ideas, Interests and American Trade policy (Ithaca: Cornell University Press, 1994).
8. Michael C. Dreiling and Derek Y. Darves, Agents of Neoliberal Globalization. Corporate Networks, State Structures and Trade Policy (New York: Cambridge University Press, 2016).
9. Lewis Anthony Dexter, Raymond A. Bauer and Ithiel de Sola Pool, American Business and Public Policy: The Politics of Foreign Trade (New York: Aldine Transaction; 2nd ed., 2007).
10. James Bennett, "Clinton In Caribbean: No Bananas Today", The New York Times, May 11, 1997. See also P.J. Patterson, My Political Journey. Jamaica's Sixth Prime Minister (Kingston: University of the West Indies Press, 2019) page 316.
11. "U.S. official: Changes in banana preferences would not hurt Caribbean", March 10, 1999. Associated Press.
12. Ray Sanchez, "Summit's Issue: Bananas/In the Caribbean, trade dispute tops for Clinton", May 11, 1997. http://.newsday.com/mainnews/rnmi0207.htm.
13. Dan Koeppel Banana: The Fate of the Fruit That Changed the World (Plume: 2008) and Peter Chapman, Bananas: How the United Fruit Company Shaped the World (Cannongate: 2009).
14. Rick Cohen, The Fish That Ate the Whale: The Life and Times of America's Banana King (London: Picador, 2013).
15. Stephen Schlesinger and Stephen Kinzer, Bitter Fruit: The Story of the American Coup in Guatemala, Revised and Expanded (David Rockefeller Center for Latin American Studies, 2006). Paul J. Dosal, Doing Business with the Dictators: A Political History of United Fruit in Guatemala, 1899–1944 (Lanham: Rowman & Littlefield Publishers, 1995) and Aviva Chomsky, West Indian Workers and the United Fruit Company in Costa Rica, 1970–1940–1995 (Baton Rouge: Louisiana State University Press, 1995).
16. Jason M. Colby, The Business of Empire: United Fruit, Race, and U.S. Expansion in Central America (Ithaca: Cornell University Press, 2011).
17. Marcelo Bucheli, "Multinational Corporations, Totalitarian Regimes, and Economic Nationalism: United Fruit Company in Central America, 1899–1975", Business History, Vol. 50, No. 4 (July, 2008) pages 433–454.
18. Barbara M. Welch, Survival by Association. Supply Management Landscapes of the Eastern Caribbean (Montreal: McGill-Queen's University Press, 1996) page 16.

19. Ronald James, Jemma Lafeuillee, Mike Xin Li, Gonzalo Salinas, and Yevgeniya Savchenko, Explaining High Unemployment in ECCU Countries, IMF Working Paper, WP/19/144 (July, 2019) pages 25–26.
20. Charles D. Kepner and Jay Soothill, The Banana Empire. A Case Study of Economic Imperialism (New York: Vanguard Press, 1935).

CHAPTER 2

Corporate Influence in US Trade Policy

Introduction

In the US political system, international trade policy is the outcome of competing interests influencing the interagency process of trade policy formulation. In this process, the White House, the Congress, and the US Trade Representative's (USTR) office are particularly important in determining the outcome. Traditionally the private sector, in particular, large corporations have been able to exert considerable influence on trade policy. The influence of corporations emanates from the large sums of money they are able to spend. This chapter explains the influence of corporations on US trade policy.

Objectives

The trade policy of the United States, like that of other countries, represents the government's synthesis of the ideas and the views of stakeholders which can and indeed should include all interest groups. The overall objectives being primarily economic without jeopardizing national security and other goals. The economic objectives are (1) the promotion of economic growth, more specifically, to increase employment, investment, production and exports, and reduce imports, (2) securing an adequate and predictable supply of oil, (3) the protection of certain industries orsupplies of strategic raw materials, (4) to contribute to the economic development of developing countries and strategic allies, and

R. L. Bernal, *Corporate versus National Interest in US Trade Policy*, https://doi.org/10.1007/978-3-030-56950-1_2

(5) contributing to the expansion of global trade and shaping the rules constituting the multilateral trading system and its governance.

Philosophies

While the objectives of US trade policy have remained fairly constant over time, how they are given expression in policy and the respective weighting in actual policy is affected by the prevailing trade philosophy.[1] US trade policy has been molded by the complex dialectic between protectionism and liberalization. When a country is internationally competitive, is a fervent advocate of free trade and this coincides with when they are in a position of global hegemon, then they seek to impose free trade on the world economy (e.g., Britain in the late nineteenth century until World War I and the United States from 1944 until 2008). However, when a country is not internationally competitive, it easily turns to protectionist trade policy and if that country is important in global trade then its policy can and usually does set off retaliation as other countries whose exports are adversely affected resort to protectionism. Protectionism tends to be operationalized unilaterally to gain an advantage at the expense of trade partners. This type of "beggar-thy-neighbor" policy can set in motion retaliatory protectionist actions that can lead to a downward spiral in international trade.

The United States, from its very inception, has experienced bouts of protectionism reflecting the influence of both domestic, political, and economic factors as well as the international context. Among the domestic factors are the currents of isolationism and mercantilism and it contends with impulses towards free trade.[2] The most notorious and ultimately destructive was the passage of the Smoot-Hawley Tariff Act of 1930 which raised tariffs on 20,000 imported goods and contributed to the downward spiral in international trade and intensified the contractionary momentum which resulted in the Great Depression.[3] Protectionism emerged right after independence when Treasury Secretary Alexander Hamilton (1789 to 1795) wrote his infamous tract "Report on the Manufactures, 1792" which called for customs barriers to protect "infant industries". Since the global economic crisis began in 2008, the United States along with other G-20 countries has steadily increased protectionist measures.[4]

When countries are internationally competitive, they are vociferous advocates of free trade forcing the liberalization of international trade to the extent that they are able to exert their hegemonic position in world affairs. They are also capable of a double standard of practicing protectionism while pressuring other countries to dismantle protectionism and move towards greater liberalization of trade. After the consolidation of the first Industrial Revolution, Britain vigorously advocated free trade as an international order while maintaining mercantilism in its empire. After the exhaustion of the Great Depression of the 1930s and the destruction of World War II, Britain was systematically pushed from the role of global hegemon by the United States.[5] Pax Americana replaced Pax Britnnicaa. The United States, without being confronted by competitors, quickly repositioned into the role of global hegemon, led and managed a liberal international economic order in which the liberalization of international trade was a central tenet. The United States enjoyed an advantage in international competitiveness until the early twenty-first century. The latter half of the twentieth century was an era of unprecedented prosperity and steady globalization. But during this period of economic growth, the United States practiced a dual policy of pressing for liberalization of international trade while simultaneously subsidizing production, particularly in agriculture, some of which was exported. The rationale for managing a liberal international economic order was neoliberalism[6] based on the supposed infallibility of the market so eloquently rationalized by the law of comparative advantage at the core of the edifice of neoclassical economics.

Policy Formulation as a Synthesis

The trade policy of a country emerges from the actions and interactions of interested actors and is brought together by the government in an interagency consultative process. Then the trade policy has to be made consistent with the foreign policy of the country which itself consists of several aspects and goals which may vary over time and across different regions and countries. Therefore, trade policy cannot be considered in isolation from all the other goals and interests which comprise the amalgam referred to as "national interest". The national interest of a country involves a composite of economic, political, diplomatic, and security considerations and these, in turn, inform the foreign policy of a country. The foreign policy of the United States is a composite with the weighting varying over time and in response to changing circumstances including the actions of other states.

Trade policy like all public policy is the result of a synthesis of the interests of various groups and the assumption that the state conducts the views and produces a synthesis which maximizes the welfare of the collective of groups which constitutes the nation. In reality, what emerges as a synthesis is not necessarily in the best interest of all concerned because of the way in which end result policy reflects the differentiated influence of groups generally indicating the amount of money spent on influencing the process directly or indirectly by the mobilization of public opinion.

Policy Implementation

At any given time, trade policy is an amalgam of these objectives and the policy measures which are employed to give effect to them. The objectives and implementing policies are given effect in different ways: (1) unilaterally; for example, the imposition of higher tariffs, quotas, or sanctions (2) bilaterally; for example, signing a bilateral trade agreement, or (3) multilaterally; for example, subscribing to the rules of the WTO. The initiative to establish or revise the objectives of trade policies and the policies which seek to give effect to these objectives can emanate from any stakeholder or from within the administration or from in the Congress. Usually, all three have to work together to transform an initiative into an actual policy; for example, a stakeholder proposes an idea which the administration accepts and adopts and proposes it to Congress where a bill has to be drafted and approved by both chambers of Congress in a process involving consultations with stakeholders and the administration.

White House

The overall political philosophy of government depends on which political party, Republican or Democratic is in the presidency and the particular views of the person who is president. The president determines the amount of attention devoted to trade policy and the goals of trade policy; and this, in turn, reflects the state of the economy, in particular the persistent and ever-widening trade deficit. Trade policy is an aspect of US politics that is often overshadowed by domestic issues and about which the general public has only a rather rudimentary understanding, which often does not go beyond generalities like foreign countries are cheating the United States by the use of unfair trade practices. The president does not have specific authority over trade, but the president does have the power to negotiate treaties with other countries, and Congress has delegated authority to adjust tariff rates and implement trade policy. Section 301 of the Trade Act of 1974 is the principal statutory authority under which the United States may impose trade sanctions on foreign countries, empowers the president to impose sanctions, increase tariffs, and refer issues to the WTO dispute settlement process.

The White House has four channels of influence on trade policy: First, to suggest trade legislation through the USTR's office; second, to request investigations into trade issues by Congress and/or the International Trade Commission; third, to initiate trade negotiations under the terms of Trade Promotion Authority (TPA) approved by Congress; and fourth, to impose tariffs. The US Constitution authorizes Congress to impose tariffs but since the Reciprocal Trade Agreements of 1934, it has devolved to the Executive which has responsibility for foreign policy, which encompasses international trade policy.

Congress[7]

Based on authority granted in the Constitution, the US Congress (House of Representatives and Senate) has the responsibility for regulating trade. All trade agreements and commitments are passed into law in Congress because international trade agreements are not treaties in the US system. Congress sets the terms and conditions which constitute the parameters of the negotiating mandate which guides US officials in each international trade negotiation. This is known as Trade Promotion Authority[8] and any draft agreement which conforms to the dictates of the TPA must be voted yes or no with no amendments allowed. Congress exercises generalized suasion on the thinking on trade policy by the oversight and investigative powers of various committees, which hold hearings on issues and propose trade legislation and by requesting and/or receiving annual reports from various departments and agencies of the Federal government. Congress may also request reports be conducted by the Congressional Research Service.

USTR and Interagency Process

US trade policy merges the interaction of several actors. At the center of the process is the Office of the USTR which is responsible for international trade policy. The Office of the USTR is "the government agency responsible for developing and recommending United States trade policy to the President of the United States". Founded in 1962, it is headed by a Cabinet-level official, the USTR is supported by a staff of about 200.[9] Given that the staff is small in relation to the workload, it makes for a situation in which specialized technical and legal expertise can play an enlarged role, in many instances acting on behalf of corporate employers. Amy Skonieczny explains "the U.S. administration often relies on interested corporate parties to provide it with both the expertise that shapes the agreement itself and the political case for trade liberalization that shapes the public pro-trade campaign."[10]

The interagency process policy involves several Federal government departments; prominent among the participants is the Department of Agriculture and the Treasury whose concern is the state of the overall economy, the fiscal implications of trade policy, the balance of payments deficit, and the implications for the exchange rate of the US dollar. The State Department which handles foreign policy is an integral part of the deliberations that bring to bear the perspective of the implications of trade policy for foreign countries and governments. The assessment of the State Department is more encompassing of the consequences and uses of trade policy than the more technical narrow perspective of the USTR. The Department of Commerce weighs in regarding the promotion of exports and assisting US businesses engaged or seeking to engage in international trade and foreign investment. The National Security Council monitors the possible repercussions for national security and strongly influences the prohibition of the export of certain technologies and goods and can block direct foreign investment in certain industries considered too sensitive to allow foreign involvement. The interagency process must take account of the White House which ultimately decides on trade policy in both its direction and application. Consultation with stakeholders takes place through a variety of committees up to the President's Advisory Committee for Trade Policy and Negotiations (ACTPN).

Interest Groups

Interest groups can influence trade policy by lobbying Congress or directly writing to the White House or various government departments and making their case in the media thereby mobilizing public opinion. Interest groups vary widely, and their issue-focused alliances are continually shifting. Holyoke aptly describes these alliances as "friends and foes of convenience".[11] Interest groups often cannot match the financial capacity of their competitors and rely on the mobilization of public opinion[12] through the media in support of their cause. The media has had a major impact on the President and Congress regarding foreign policy issues.[13] Among the most influential actors in trade policy formulation are industry associations that advocate for particular economic sectors, for example, the American Apparel & Footwear Association (AAFA). The AAFA is an industry trade group representing hundreds of clothing, footwear, and sewn products companies and their suppliers. It was established in August 2000 through the merger of the American Apparel Manufacturers Association and Footwear Industry America.[14]

Interest groups, especially those with limited financial capacity, often use the media to get their message out to the public in general, particularly if their point of view is favorably covered in respected publications such as The Wall Street Journal, the Financial Times, the Washington Post, the New York Times, and The Economist. They also seek coverage and information from specialist trade publications such as Inside U.S. Trade. The case of any interest group or trade association is bolstered if supporting argumentation, analysis, or empirical evidence appears in reports from the International Trade Commission and/or the Congressional Research Service.

Lobbyists

Lobbying is an inherent part of the formulation of trade in democratic countries and can be a useful source of information and conversely self-interested corporate misinformation. Lobbying is well developed in both the European Union[15] and the United States. Lobbyists operating at both the federal and state levels are an integral part of US policymaking[16] and their number and level of activity have risen steadily from the 1960s.[17] The number of registered lobbyists overwhelmingly concentrated in Washington DC is estimated to be from 12,000[18] to approaching 14,000, but it is generally agreed that the regularly active full-time lobbyists number about 300.[19] It is estimated that collectively, lobbyists spend $3 billion[20] to $3.5 billion.[21] The advantage of hiring lobbyists[22] is that they have the experience, expertise, and contacts over long periods, sometimes over 40 years. They may be specialists in a single issue (e.g., sugar) or a company with a team with a variety of skills providing services across a range of issues. If they are a large company (e.g., a large law firm), they may contain all the requisite skills but smaller outfits may collaborate or subcontract other expertise (e.g., public relations). Lobbyists are particularly of value to those who are not familiar with how "Washington" works, this is particularly the case for foreign governments. Corporations and business associations are able to spend very large amounts of money. In fact, of the 100 organizations that spend the most money on lobbyists, 95 represent business interests.[23] Corporations outspend other groups when it comes to the services of lobbyists. For every US$1 spent on lobbyists by labor unions and public interest groups, corporations and business associations spent US$34.[24]

Think Tanks

The effectiveness of the mobilization of public opinion is considerably strengthened when its demands and arguments are bolstered by the reports and policy briefs of think tanks.[25] Among the most influential are the Council on Foreign Relations[26] on foreign policy, the Center for Strategic and International Studies on national security, the Brookings Institution, and the Institute for International Economics on trade policy. An important aspect of their reach and influence is that they have on staff many very senior former officials of the state bureaucracy who have retired but continue to be "players" or are awaiting recall to the senior levels of the Federal government and even the Cabinet. The think tanks are also a launching platform for those aspiring to senior posts in the state bureaucracy. Policy briefs, speaking engagements, media appearances and best of all, a book, timed for the run-up to the presidential elections. Their existence depends on fundraising and sometimes this depends on their perspective on issues. Some were established and are focused on advocacy of a particular perspective or a specific subject, for example, the American Enterprise Institute, the Heritage Foundation, the Cato Institute, and the Hudson Institute. Liberal think tanks include the Brookings Institution, National Bureau of Economic Research (NBER), and the Institute for International Economics (IIE). There are no radical or left-wing think tanks but there are a few liberal ones.

Several think tanks at one time or another and depending on the topic, issue briefing papers and studies and host seminars on international trade issues such as the North American Free Trade Area (NAFTA), the TPA, and the WTO. The Institute for International Economics founded in 1981 by C. Fred Bergsten, and as 2006, the Peterson Institute for International Economics produced excellent technical publications led by

Jeffrey Schott[27] and Gary Clyde Hufbauer.[28] Unfortunately, the banana issue was not one that engaged the attention of the IIE.

Nongovernmental Organizations and Universities

The policy environment is also influenced by publications and pronouncements of nongovernmental organizations (NGO) and universities. Some NGOs concentrate on trade as part of their focus on public policy and others intervene when it related to the region of the world which is their priority. Public Citizen founded by Ralph Nader in 1971 is a nonprofit organization with over 500,000 members and supporters which, by its own description, is a consumer advocacy organization that "champions the public interest in the halls of power. We defend democracy, resist corporate power, and work to ensure that government works for the people–not for big corporations."[29] One of its five divisions is Global Trade Watch led by the knowledgeable, astute, and articulate Lori Wallach.[30]

The Council on Hemispheric Affairs (COHA) founded in 1975 seeks to promote interest in inter-American relations, in particular the foreign policy of the United States towards Latin America and the Caribbean. COHA is made up of representatives of trade unions, NGOs, civic activists, and academics. It did raise its "voice" against US policy on bananas even after the WTO settlement pointing to the "normalcy of abuse" in the banana industry in Honduras[31] and Guatemala.[32] Research institutes and prominent academics contribute to public debates through books, articles,[33] and opinion editorials. For example, the John F. Kennedy School of Government at Harvard produced a paper on the banana issue.[34] Some NGOs have become globally influential most notably, OXFAM, which has done a considerable amount of work on issues of aid and trade as they affect developing countries and the poor of the world.

Labor Organizations

Trade unions and other labor organizations have always engaged in attempts to influence international trade policy. Their focus has been on promoting trade policies which encourage increased jobs and more so to prevent loss of American jobs due to imports. The American Federation of Labor (AFL) and Congress of Industrial Organizations (AFL-CIO) have been very active on behalf of the organized labor movement. The position advocated has varied from liberalization of trade to protectionism depending on the state of the US economy and the perception of the impact of various proposed trade agreements and policies.[35] There is empirical evidence that campaign contribution from labor interests influenced the voting of members of Congress on trade legislation.[36] The influence of organized labor has declined in recent years in parallel with the decline in the percentage of the labor force which is unionized. In 1983, union membership was 20.1 percent of the labor force but has declined to 10.3 percent in 2019.[37]

Media

The banana dispute was covered in the print media in the United States, Europe, Latin America, and the Caribbean in every form from newspapers (i.e., the Financial Times, the Guardian, The Wall Street Journal, the New York Times, and the Washington Post) to news magazines (i.e., Time, Newsweek, Fortune, and The Economist). All the major print media covered the "story" at one time or another throughout the prolonged dispute but it never aroused much attention in television coverage. Coverage in these widely read media did not create a high level of awareness of the banana dispute in the public. The banana dispute did not become a public political issue possibly because bananas continued to be available at inexpensive prices. The banana issue was covered weekly in specialized trade newsletters such as Americas Trade, Washington Trade Daily, and Inside U.S. Trade. Special publications were intended for trade specialists and assumed a certain level of specialized trade knowledge. They are not for the average reader but save the specialist the time to consult many sources. They are very thorough in vetting the information and often rely on confidential sources to provide accurate information and informative analysis. This is indispensable to their survival because they are available by expensive subscription only.

Foreign Actors in US Trade Policy

Foreign governments and multinational corporations (MNCs) that are affected by and seek to influence US trade policy are players in trade policy formulation and application. The US government system is remarkable and perhaps uniquely open to the activity of foreign governments and corporations in engaging if trying to influence US trade policy. Because of the "openness" of the US political system, foreign governments and corporations can openly engage in influencing policy in ways which might be considered interference in the internal affairs of a country.[38] Foreign entities usually hire lobbyists including former senior officials of the federal government to assist them in articulating their interests, for example, the Government of Mexico hired 33 former US officials in the course of lobbying for NAFTA.[39] Canada, Japan, and Mexico are among the most active[40] countries seeking to influence US foreign policy. Foreign governments can have an impact especially if they have an internal American "constituency" that share their views (e.g., a diaspora such as that in support of Israel)[41] or where there are complementary US corporate interests that can influence US trade policy.[42] There have even been cases where small developing countries acting in concert have been able to influence US trade policy.[43]

Influence of Corporations on Trade Policy

Throughout history, the state, merchants, investors, and large firms have worked in tandem to pursue economic goals. This collaboration was initially based on the conviction that what was good for a national firm, merchant, or investor was good for the government and the country. The validity of this nexus was easy to discern when merchants and firms were nationally owned. Indeed, the government in the form of the monarchy even financed commercial ventures for a share of the profits. Later in the period of mercantilism, the state used its political and naval forces to monopolize trade in prescribed colonial empires. The British went to extremes in providing exclusive charter to companies, most notably the East India Company,[44] and that corporations came to rule that huge country in lieu of a government. The dominance of the UFC in Guatemala is analogous in several respects with that of the East India Company regarded by some as the forerunner of the modern multinational corporation.[45] The British government used military and naval force to compel China to open a specified number of ports to facilitate the trade in opium, a narcotic drug.[46] The British could not find anything that the Chinese wanted to import from them in order to pay for their imports of Chinese tea and silk and forced China to allow the importation of opium from British-owned plantations in India. It served the British economic interests but created millions of Chinese opium addicts.

The emergence of the MNC meant that what was good for an MNC was not necessarily good for the country in which its headquarters is domiciled. The benefits of the profit maximizing across the global operations of an MNC do not accrue to the home country of the MNC. However, the corporate sector dominated by MNCs has skillfully managed to perpetuate the myth that corporate and national interests are synonymous and even if they are not exactly consonant it would be unpatriotic of any government not to support an MNC or any firm for that matter, whose owners are citizens of that country. Government defense of or rescue of their companies is mandatory when their assets, property, profits, or operations are in jeopardy in foreign countries. Because of the vast resources available to corporations and the permissiveness of the American political system regarding campaign contributions, corporations wield tremendous influence over the formulation and implementation of US policy. President Eisenhower felt compelled in his final speech as president to warn against the overweening influence of the "military-industrial complex".[47] Ledbetter explains that the military-industrial complex is not an arms-length relationship, it is "a network of public and private forces that combine a profit motive with the planning and implementation of strategic policy. The overlap between private military contractors and the federal government is usually presumed to include, in addition to the military itself, areas of both the executive branch (Defense Department contractors and appointments of military contractors to government positions) and the legislative branch (lobbying by military contractors, campaign contributions, and the desire of the members of Congress to protect and expand military spending that benefits their districts)."[48]

Once the analysis goes beyond the conventional economics textbook and seeks policy measures for real world problems, the simplifying assumptions necessary for the formulation of economic theory must give way. The concept of markets in which there is perfect competition is a theoretical construct that does not conform to economic reality. There is no perfect competition, but conventional neoclassical economics policy prescription is to take steps to achieve this ideal and that the closer reality can be made approximate to the perfect competition the better for all concerned. In the quest for perfectly competitive markets, there are times when striving for perfection can become the enemy of the good. For example, to achieve a competitive market it might involve eliminating preferential arrangements for small producers or affirmative action for vulnerable firms but when the pros and cons of the externalities are calculated, the economy as a whole may be worst off. Furthermore, achieving a competitive market for one product may not maximize overall welfare in an economy much less the society or country in which the market is embedded. Therefore, there are even situations in which the cure can be more harmful than the disease or malady, for example, inequality is repugnant and undesirable in a macroeconomic sense but redistribution to correct inequities may have an even more detrimental effect. The complexities of the welfare calculus are even more complicated when applying the perfect competition model to the world economy where markets are comprised of a myriad of national barriers and the existence of MNCs, the logic of whose operations in many instances is inimical to the economic development[49] of their host economies and their countries of origin.

The reality is that cartels and MNCs including state-owned enterprises dominate international trade and investments and global markets and, therefore, many global markets are not genuinely competitive markets. When MNCs engage the intervention of their home governments on the basis that a particular global market is not competitive, this is usually a façade for the fight for market share or entry to a particular national market. In the struggle for market share and the changing reallocation of market share, the producers are often unaffected, and in some instances adversely affected depending on which MNC gains or loses market share.

Wiarda opines: "Business influence over foreign policy extends far beyond traditional lobbying efforts. It now includes business largely running or controlling large areas of foreign economic policy."[50] Indeed, the very wealthy exert a strong influence over corporate and government policy.[51] Business organizations have constantly brought pressure to bear on the state, urging it to play a role supportive of US business abroad. The importance of economic interests and the intimate involvement and influence of business in foreign policy is documented comprehensively in the Open Door policy,[52] New Deal diplomacy,[53] and US policy towards Cuba.[54] Typical of business sector attitudes is a US Chamber of Commerce spokesman's 1982 statement: "The full force of the US Government should be lent to expanding our exports and foreign investments. Ambassadors and cabinet members should intervene to support major transactions when necessary."[55] The history of US policy in Latin America, Central America, and the Caribbean is replete with interventions at the behest of individual corporations (e.g., United Fruit [now Chiquita] in Guatemala[56] and ITT in Chile).[57]

Corporate Executives in the Cabinet

There is a long tradition of corporate executives being selected to serve in the Cabinet. The assumption is that their managerial experience would make them ideally qualified to oversee a large federal government department. It does, however, mean and it would be naiveté to believe otherwise, that they bring with them their values and perspectives[58] on private enterprise, markets, and regulation. It is almost a "rule" that the Secretary of the Treasury is a banker/investment bank from Wall Street, for example, Robert Rubin (1995–1999), Hank Paulson (2006–2009), Tim Geithner (2009–2013), and Steve Mnuchin from 2017. In some instances, appointees were owners of banks (e.g., Andrew W. Mellon who served as Secretary of the Treasury from 1921 to 1932). Some notable appointments were Robert McNamara as Secretary of Defense (1961–1969) and former ExxonMobil CEO Rex Tillerson as Secretary of State[59] during the early period of the administration of President Trump. This appointment continued a tradition of close working relations between oil companies and US foreign policy.[60] Curious that President Hugo Chavez nationalized ExxonMobil's $10 billion worth of assets and, in turn, Tillerson came to direct US foreign policy towards Venezuela. Meanwhile, ExxonMobil explored and drilled in a deal with the Government of Guyana in coastal waters claimed by Venezuela.[61]

The link between government, government policy, and the private sector reaches its apogee in the "military-industrial complex" which President Eisenhower declared in his farewell[62] address on demitting office. Corporations that are leading military contractors such as Lockheed Martin, Boeing, General Dynamics, Northrop Grumman, and Raytheon exert significant influence on US policy.[63] These corporations spend large amounts of money on lobbying and make contributions to both Republican and Democratic parties and selected congressional representatives, senators, and candidates. The objectives are to influence the size of the defense budget, its allocations, and winning contracts. Companies involved in the defense industry spent $132 million in 2012 on more than 900 lobbyists representing nearly 266 clients.[64] Corporations also lobby through industry associations and private sector umbrella organizations such as the National Association of Realtors and the US Chamber of Commerce.[65] There is no guaranteed direct correlation between the amount of money spent and the achievement of the objectives to which it is devoted[66] but money usually makes a difference, and the more money spent the more likely to achieve the goal. Corporations either individual or with or through industry associations attain their goals because they outspend their competitors and opponents. "For every dollar spent on lobbying by labor unions and public interest groups together, large corporations and their associations now spend $34. Of the 100 organizations that spend the most on lobbying, 95 consistently represent business".[67]

Revolving-Door: Federal Bureaucracy and Corporate America

There is a "revolving door" in which former Federal government officials on leaving office become part of the staff of law firms, lobbyists, or firms having or seeking contracts with the Federal government. This is particularly pronounced at the very senior levels from secretary on down to a few of the highest tiers which are usually filled by political appointees. Several retiring senior officers from the army, navy, and air force as well as retiring senior officials from the Pentagon and Department of Defense move seamlessly into executive jobs in corporations supplying the US government. Lockheed Martin advertises: "At Lockheed Martin, veterans are at the center of everything we do—in fact, one in five of our employees has served in uniform. We are proud to help men and women like you successfully transition into civilian careers. Join us and you will find opportunities to take on the same kind of long-term challenging assignments you tackled while in the military."[68] In trade policy, the Cabinet-level post of USTR is always a political appointee. Typical of this prototype were the three persons who served as US Trade Representatives during the banana dispute. Carla A. Hills, lawyer, during 1989–1993 at which time she was the principal US negotiator of NAFTA. She previously served as Secretary of the United States Department of Housing and Urban Development.[69] Michael Kantor, lawyer, during 1993–1996. He practiced law before and after USTR and was active in Democratic Party politics and fundraising. Charlene Barshefsky, lawyer, during 1997–2000. She practiced law before and after USTR. Her clients include Fortune 100 companies and foreign multinational corporations. Charlene Barshefsky was named as one of the most influential lawyers by The National Law Journal and BusinessWeek.[70]

Influence of Money in US Politics

In American capitalism, it has long been recognized that the wealthy acting in concert can exercise considerable influence in politics and the public policy in general.[71] C. Wright Mills[72] speaks of the "power elite" and William Domhoff refers to the "ruling class"[73] within which there is what Useem calls the "inner circle".[74] The cohesion of this group derives from interlocking directorates[75] which forms what Useem calls a "transcorporate network"[76] that provides an overall corporate overview and is the basis for coalitions across industries[77] and the formation of cohesion in political views.[78] While there may be differences between the ownership and managerial classes as pointed out by Berle,[79] they have a common interest in the profitability of the corporation. This concentration of economic power is extended through the MNCs according to Korten.[80] Money is used in the US political system to win support and influence policy, either for or against, by influencing politicians and policymakers at both the Federal and State.[81] The use of money is pandemic, prompting some observers to pun on American democracy as "dollarocracy".[82] It is used to finance campaigns, issue advertising, employ family members and paramours, take all-expense-paid trips, entertain, shop, and solicit special loans.[83] Politicians and political parties need money to pay for their election campaigns and maintain their offices and staff. The need for financial contributions has intensified and increased as the cost of elections has escalated.[84] Money is raised and spent through Political Action Committees (PACs). PACs are also used by interest groups to fund campaigns in support of their interest and causes. While it has not been proven, it is generally accepted that the more money spent the more influence is generated. In the competition for influence, those who spend the most tend to prevail over competing or opposing interests. Corporations and interest groups usually hire lobbyists on a full-time basis to monitor their interests, advise them on how to advance their arguments, and help to persuade politicians and officials. They do help the democratic system to function but they can produce results that put particular interests at odds with the national interest and/or popular sentiment. They are often regarded as perverting the political system in exchange for payment[85] and they prefer their activities to be called public affairs or government relations. The influence of wealth and money is not confined to the United States but is an aspect of how democracy operates,[86] for example, in Britain[87] and this is not a new development.[88]

Money, Lobbying, and Perverse Policy Outcomes

Money from corporations and the wealthy funneled through the lobbying process can result in the triumph of corporate interests over that of the public. The opioid crisis provides a lucid example of how corporate America can outspend rivals interests in influencing US policy as an example. According to a report from Harvard Business School, those advocating for tighter controls on painkillers spent $4 million on lobbying, while pharmaceutical companies spent $740 million in an effort to block federal and state regulatory efforts.[89] This took place in the context where the Centers for Disease Control and Prevention report that over 702,000 people have died from drug overdoses during the period 1999 to 2017 and in 2017 alone, more than 70,000 people. Drug overdoses are now a leading cause of injury-related death in the United States. Almost 6 percent of these deaths involved a prescription or illicit opioid.[90]

Corporate Dominance of the Consultative Process

It is firms that trade not countries but trade affects everyone, therefore, trade issues and trade policy is of interest to everyone. The United States, realizing that trade concerns everyone, has established an extensive system of consultative bodies to canvas the views of the public. In practice, participation is predominantly by representatives of corporations and while there may be differences among industries, corporations coalesce into a political unity around free trade. This gives corporations dominance over US trade policy.[91] As Dreiling and Darves explain, this emanates from class cohesion, interlocking directorates, and shared membership in policy networks.[92] The various advisory bodies comprise 566 members selected by the USTR, of which 480 or 85 percent are from either corporations or industry/trade associations. The remaining 15 percent consisted of persons from academia, trade unions, civil society organizations, or government committees.[93] Selection to be a member of one of the consultative bodies is arbitrary, as the criteria for selection have never been made public and research has failed to identify any criteria.[94] The fact that representatives are drawn from different companies, industries, and sectors, common corporate policy positions are arrived at and advocated because the logic that binds and informs then is structural, not atomistic.[95]

National Versus Corporate Interests in US Trade Policy

In 1953, Charles E. Wilson, then the president of General Motors, in addressing a Congressional committee declared: "what was good for our country was good for General Motors, and vice versa." However, in reality, what is good for an individual corporation or industry is not necessarily good for the country. This is especially the situation in the US economy where the US-owned MNCs have such a prominent economic role. Indeed, this is a global issue.[96] Multinational corporations now account for about a third of world output, half to two-thirds of world trade in goods,[97] and 80 percent of the world's land cultivated for export crops.[98] Their overarching predominance is also evident in the value of foreign assets they control, the volume of foreign sales, and the size of foreign employment.[99] International production by multinational enterprises (MNEs) is expanding and rose in 2014, generating value-added of approximately $7.9 trillion. The sales and assets of MNEs' foreign affiliates grew faster than their domestic counterparts while employing about 75 million people.[100]

It is unusual for trade policy to be driven by the demands of a single corporation.[101] A notable exception was when the US government decided to save the American icon Harley-Davidson motorcycles from imports from Japanese manufacturers Honda, Kawasaki, and Yamaha. Harley-Davidson Motor Company of Milwaukee sought protection from the US government and was granted a five-year 45 percent tariff. It is normally the interests of an entire industry seeking protection from less expensive imports as has been the case with the steel and auto industries. In many instances, US trade policy is prompted by requests from industries, frequently agricultural products to force open foreign markets by having tariff and non-tariffs barriers removed or lowered.

It is firms that engage in international trade, not companies, hence a country's trade policy to open foreign markets for their firms and defend their firms or whole industries from imports. US protectionist import tariffs and subsidies were used by the US government to preserve Harley-Davidson motorcycles. The United States supported Chiquita in the dispute with the European Union over bananas. The "trade war" between the United States and the European Union over bananas is the only trade dispute which has arisen between American and European companies. The dispute over subsidies to Boeing and Airbus, the two dominant aircraft manufacturers in the world has been going since 2004.[102] The governments of the United States and the European Union have backed their companies during various rulings by the WTO. After 15 years of litigation, the WTO has confirmed in October 2019 that the United States is entitled to impose countermeasures in response to the EU's illegal subsidies.[103]

Overview

This chapter has established the importance of money in the US political process in elections and in influencing public policy including international trade policy. Because the corporate sector has far more financial resources than the other interest groups competing to influence trade policy, it is able to exercise a dominant influence. There are issues where differences exist within the corporate sector reflecting the inevitable differences among industries. One of the major differences arises from the impact of imports giving rise to two opposing demands. Calls for protectionism emanate from competing domestic producers while being lauded as liberalizing trade by those selling the finished consumer good and/or where the imported product is an essential input in the production process. The broad division between protectionists demanding measures to block or limit imports and free trade advocates lobbying for the opening of export markets cuts across US trade policy. Some authors refer to this split as internationalists versus isolationists. This bifurcation traverses foreign policy in general inclusive of trade policy.

After World War II the United States was the dominant economy in the world and was internationally competitive. Free trade was intuitively associated with the economic prosperity of the United States and indeed of the growth of the global economy. Dreiling and Darves explain that this belief became the "prima facie basis upon which to promote trade policy".[104] The platform for free trade was the assertion that free trade promotes economic growth but over time as the advantage in international competitiveness of the United States was eroded by other countries catching up and an increasing trade deficit prompted claims that foreign countries were cheating by using "disadvantaged" labor and exchange rate manipulating or government subsidies. As will be seen later in the text, Chiquita's justification for calling for US government action against the EU banana regime was based not on increasing US exports but the claim that the EU regime was discriminatory and, therefore, unfair to the interests of a

US-owned company. No bananas were grown and exported from mainland USA and no jobs in the United States were affected.

Notes

1. Judith L. Goldstein, Ides, Interests, and American Trade Policy (Ithaca: Cornell University Press, 1994).
2. Douglas A. Irwin, Clashing over Commerce: A History of US Trade Policy (Chicago: University of Chicago, 2017).
3. Douglas A. Irwin, Peddling Protectionism: Smoot-Hawley and the Great Depression (Princeton: Princeton University Press, rev. ed., 2017).
4. Simon J. Evenett and Johannes Fritz, The Tide Turns? Trade, Protectionism, and Slowing Global Growth, The 18th Global Trade Alert Report (London: Centre for Economic Policy Research, 2015).
5. Richard Gardner, Sterling-Dollar Diplomacy: the Origins and the Prospects of Our International Economic Order (New York: McGraw Hill Press, 1969), Paul Kennedy, The Rise and Fall of Great Powers. Economic Change and Military Conflict From 1500–2000 (New York: Vintage, 1989) and Niall Ferguson, Empire: The Rise and Demise of the British World Order and the Lessons for Global Power (New York: Basic Books, 2004).
6. David Harvey, A Brief History of Neoliberalism (Oxford: Oxford University Press, 2007) and Milton Freeman, Capitalism and Freedom (Chicago: University of Chicago, Press, 1962).
7. Robert A. Pastor, Congress and the Politics of U. S. Foreign Economic Policy (University of California Press, 1981).
8. J. F. Hornbeck and William H. Cooper, Trade Promotion Authority (TPA) and the Role of Congress in Trade Policy (Washington DC: Congressional Research Service, April 7, 2011).
9. United States Trade Representative. https://ustr.gov/.
10. Amy Skonieczny, Corporate Lobbying In Foreign Policy, Oxford Research Encyclopedia of Politics (New York: Oxford University Press, 2017) pages 1–29. See page 1.
11. Thomas T. Holyoke, Interest Groups and Lobbying: Pursuing Political Interests in America (Boulder: Westview Press, 2016) Chapter 9.
12. Richard Sobel, Public Opinion in U.S. Foreign Policy. The Controversy over Contra Aid (Lanham: Litchfield and Rowman, 1993).
13. Patrick O'Hefferman, Mass Media and American Foreign Policy: Insider Perspectives on Global Journalism and the Foreign Policy Process (Westport: Praeger, 1991).
14. American Apparel & Footwear Association – Wikipedia. https://en.wikipedia.org/wiki/American_Apparel_%26_Footwear_Association.

15. Bernard M. Hoekman and M. M. Kostecki, The Political Economy of the World Trading System: The WTO and Beyond (Oxford: Oxford University Press; 2nd ed., 2001) pages 149–161.
16. Jeffrey Birnbaum, The Lobbyists: How Influence Peddlers Work Their Way in Washington (New York: Three Rivers Press, reprint edition, 1993), Lionel Zetter, Lobbying: The art of political persuasion (Petersfield: Harriman House, 2014) and Frank R. Baumgartner, Jeffrey M. Berry, Marie Hojnacki, Beth L. Leech and David C. Kimball, Lobbying and Policy Change: Who Wins, Who Loses, and Why (Chicago: University of Chicago Press, 2009).
17. Hedrick Smith, The Power Game. How Washington Works (New York: Random House, 1988).
18. Mark Fagan, Lobbying: Business, Law and Public Policy, Why and How 12,000 People Spend $3+ Billion Impacting Our Government (Heathrow, FL: Vandeplas Publishing, 2015).
19. Brad Plumer, "Corporate lobbying is a very exclusive club". The Washington Post, November 8, 2011. Retrieved 10 May 2019.
20. Mark Fagan, Lobbying: Business, Law and Public Policy, Why and How 12,000 People Spend $3+ Billion Impacting Our Government (Heathrow, FL: Vandeplas Publishing, 2015).
21. Michael E. Porter, Jan W. Rivkin, Mihir A. Desai, Katherine M. Gehl, William R. Kerr with Manjari Raman, A recovery Squandered. The State of US Competitiveness in 2019 (Cambridge, Mass.: Harvard Business School. December, 2019) page 28.
22. Jeffrey Birnbaum, The Lobbyists: How Influence Peddlers Work Their Way in Washington (New York: Three Rivers Press, 1992).
23. Lee Drutman, The Business of America is Lobbying: How Corporations Became Politicized and Politics Became More Corporate (Oxford: Oxford University Press, reprint edition, 2017).
24. Lee Drutman, "How Corporate Lobbyists Conquered American Democracy", The Atlantic, April 20, 2015.
25. Thomas Medvetz, Think Tanks in America (Chicago: University of Chicago Press, 2012).
26. Laurence H. Shoup, Wall Street's Think Tank: The Council on Foreign Relations and the Empire of Neoliberal Geopolitics, 1976–2014 (New York: Monthly Review Press, 2015) and Laurence Shoup and William Minter, Imperial Brain Trust: The Council on Foreign Relations and United States Foreign Policy (Authors Choice Press, 2004).
27. Some of his books in the decade during which the banana dispute took place include Free Trade Areas and U.S. Trade Policy (Washington DC; International for International Economics, 1989), with Johanna W. Buurman, Uruguay Round: An Assessment (Washington DC:

International for International Economics, 1994), with Gary Clyde Hufbauer, Western Hemisphere Economic Integration(Washington DC: International for International Economics, 1994), The World Trading System: Challenges Ahead (Washington DC: International for International Economics, 1996), WTO 2000: Settting the Course for World Trade(Washington DC: International for International Economics, 1996), Restarting Fast-Track (Washington DC: International for International Economics, 1998) and Launching New Global Trade Talks: An Action Agenda (Washington DC: International for International Economics, 1998).

28. Gary Clyde Hufbauer, Nafta: An Assessment (Washington DC: Institute for International Economics, 1993).
29. www.citizen.org/about. About Us – Public Citizen. Accessed 8 February, 2020.
30. Lori Wallach and Michelle Sforza, The WTO: Five Years of Reasons to Resist Corporate Globalization (Seven Stories Press, 1999), Lori Wallach and Patrick Woodall, Whose Trade Organization?: The Comprehensive Guide to the WTO (The New Press; 2004) and Lori Wallach, The Rise and Fall of Fast Track Trade Authority (Washington DC: Public Citizen, Inc., 2013).
31. Chiquita's Brand of Doing Business in Honduras ((Washington DC: Council on Hemispheric Affairs, November 21, 1996).
32. Peeling Back the Truth on Guatemalan Bananas (Washington DC: Council on Hemispheric Affairs, July 28, 2010).
33. Charles Ogletree and Randall Robinson, "The banana war's missing link-campaign funding", The Christian Science Monitor, March 31, 1999.
34. Robert Z Lawrence and Susan Rosegrant, Banana Wars: Challenges to the European's Banana Regime (Cambridge: John F. Kennedy School of Government, September, 1999).
35. William Kirst, Globalization and America's Trade Agreements (Washington DC: Woodrow Wilson Center Press; Baltimore: Johns Hopkins University Press, 2013) Chapter 8.
36. Robert E. Baldwin and Christopher S. Magee, "Is Trade Policy for Sale? Congressional Voting on Recent Trade Bills", Public Choice, Vol. 105, No. 1/2 (1990) pages 79–101.
37. Union Members Summary – Bureau of Labor Statistics. www.bls.gov/news.release/union2.nr0.htm. Jan 22, 2020.
38. This process is explained in Richard L. Bernal, The Influence of Small States on Superpowers: Jamaica and U.S. Foreign Policy (Kingston: University of the West Indies Press, 2017) Chapter 4.
39. Charles Lewis, The Buying of Congress. How Special Interests Have Stolen your Right to Life, Liberty and the Pursuit of Happiness (New

York: Avon Books, 1998) page 62. For a fuller discussion see Herman von Bertrab, Negotiating NAFTA. A Mexican Envoy's Account (Westport: Praeger, 1997).

40. Charles F. Doran and Joel J. Sokolsky, Canada and Congress: Lobbying in Washington DC: (Halifax: Centre for Foreign Policy Studies, 1986), Pat Choate, Agents of Influence. How Japan's Lobbyists in the United States Manipulate America's Political and Economic System (New York: Alfred Knopf, 1990) and George W. Grayson, "Lobbying By Mexico and Canada" in Robert Pastor and Rafael Fernandez de Castro (ed.), The Controversial Pivot. The U.S. Congress and North America (Washington DC: The Brookings Institution Press, 1998) pages 70–94.
41. Edward Tivnan, The Lobby. Jewish Political Power and American Foreign Policy (New York: Touchstone Books, 1988) and John J. Mearsheimer and Stephen M. Walt, The Israel Lobby and U.S. Foreign Policy (New York: Farrar, Straus and Giroux, 2008).
42. Richard L. Bernal, The Influence of Small States on Superpowers: Jamaica and U.S. Foreign Policy (University of the West Indies Press, 2017).
43. Richard L. Bernal, The Influence of Small States on Superpowers: Jamaica and U.S. Foreign Policy (Lanham: Lexington Publishers, 2015).
44. Ramkrishna Mukherjee, The Rise and Fall of the East India Company (New York: Monthly Review Press, 1974), Antony Wild, The East India Company: Trade and Conquest from 1600 (New York: HarperCollins, 1999), Roy Tirthankar, The East India Company: The World's Most Powerful Corporation (Allan Lane, 2012) and William Dalrymple, The Anarchy: The East India Company, Corporate Violence, and the Pillage of an Empire (London: Bloomsbury Publishing, 2019).
45. Nick Robins The Corporation that Changed the World: How the East India Company Shaped the Modern Multinational (London: Pluto Press, 2006).
46. Peter Ward Fay, Opium War, 1840–1842: Barbarians in the Celestial Empire in the Early Part of the Nineteenth Century and the War (Chapel Hill: University of North Carolina, 1998 and W. Travis Hanes and Frank Sanello, The Opium Wars: The Addiction of One Empire and the Corruption of Another (Sourcebooks, 2004).
47. Military-Industrial Complex Speech, Dwight D. Eisenhower, 1961. Public Papers of the Presidents, Dwight D. Eisenhower, 1960, p. 1035–1040. http://coursesa.matrix.msu.edu/~hst306/documents/indust.html. Accessed 2 November 2014.
48. James Ledbetter, Unwarranted Influence. Dwight D. Eisenhower and the Military-Industrial Complex (New Haven: Yale University Press, 2011) page 61.

49. George L. Beckford, Persistent Poverty. Underdevelopment in Plantation Economies of the Third World (New York: Oxford University Press, 1972) and Norman Girvan, Corporate Imperialism: Conflict and Expropriation (New York: Monthly Review Press, 1978).
50. Howard J. Wiarda, American Foreign Policy: Actors, and Processes (New York: Harper Collins College Publishers, 1995) page 99.
51. G. William Domhoff, Who Rules America? The Triumph of the Corporate Rich (New York: McGraw-Hill Education, 2013).
52. Charles S. Campbell Jr., Social Business Interests and the Open Door Policy (New Haven: Connecticut College and University Press, 1951) and William Appleman Williams, "The Large Corporation and American Foreign Policy" in David Horowitz (ed.), Corporations and the Cold War (New York: Monthly Review Press, 1970) pages 71–104.
53. Lloyd C. Gardener, Economic Aspects of New Deal Diplomacy (Boston: Beacon Press, 1964).
54. Robert F. Smith, The United States and Cuba. Business and Diplomacy, 1917–1960 (New Haven: Connecticut College and University Press, 1960).
55. Michael Samuels, "Time for an Activist Export Policy," Business America, Vol. 5, No. 3 (February 8, 1982).
56. Thomas and Marjorie Melville, Guatemala. Another Vietnam (Harmondsworth: Penguin, 1971).
57. Subversion in Chile: A Case Study in US Corporate Intrigue in the Third World (London: Spokesman Books, 1972) and James Petras and Morris Morley, The United States and Chile: Imperialism and the Overthrow of the Allende Government (New York: Monthly Review Press, 1975).
58. Dennis M. Ray, "Corporations and American Foreign Relations", The Annals of the American Academy of Political and Social Science, Vol. 403 (September, 1972) pages 80–92.
59. Steve Coll, Private Empire: ExxonMobil and American Power (New York: Penguin Books, 2013).
60. David S. Painter, Private Power and Public Policy: Multinational Oil Companies and U.S. Foreign Policy, 1941–1954 (London: I.B. Taurus, 1986).
61. Nick Miroff, "Rex Tillerson got burned in Venezuela. Then he got revenge", Washington Post, January 16, 2017.
62. Dwight Eisenhower, The Military–Industrial Complex: The Farewell Address of President Eisenhower, delivered January 17, 1961. See http://www.americanrhetoric.com/speeches/dwightdeisenhowerfarewell.html. and James Ledbetter, Unwarranted Influence: Dwight D. Eisenhower and the Military-Industrial Complex (New Haven: Yale University Press, 2011).

63. William D. Hartung, Prophets of War: Lockheed Martin and the Making of the Military-Industrial Complex (Nation Books, 2010).
64. Lobbying Spending Database Defense, 2019, OpenSecrets. https://www.opensecrets.org/lobby/indus.php?id.
65. Alyssa Katz, The Influence Machine: The U.S. Chamber of Commerce and the Corporate Capture of American Life (New York: Spiegel & Grau, 2015).
66. Bill Allison, "NRA Spent Record Amount Lobbying Congress, With Little to Show", Bloomberg, February 5, 2019. https://www.bloomberg.com/news/articles/2019-02-05/nra-spent-record-amount-lobbying-congress-with-little-to-show.
67. Lee Drutman, "How Corporate Lobbyists Conquered American Democracy." The Atlantic. Atlantic Media Company, 20 April, 2015.
68. Military – Lockheed Martin. https://www.lockheedmartinjobs.com/military.
69. Carla Anderson Hills – Wikipedia. https://en.wikipedia.org/wiki/Carla_Anderson_Hills.
70. Charlene Barshefsky – Wikipedia. https://en.wikipedia.org/wiki/Charlene_Barshefsky.
71. G. William Domhoff, The Powers That Be: Processes of Ruling Class Domination in America (New York: Random House, 1978), Mark S. Mizruchi, The American Corporate Network, 1904–1974 (Beverly Hills: Sage, 1982) and G. William Domhoff, Myth of Liberal Ascendancy: Corporate Dominance from the Great Depression to the Great Recession (New York: Routledge, 2013).
72. C. Wright Mills, The Power Elite. New York: Oxford University Press, 1956).
73. G. William Domhoff, Who Rules America? (Englewood Cliffs, NJ: Prentice-Hall, 1967), G. William Domhoff, The Power Elite and the State: How Policy Is Made in America (New York: Aldine De Gruyter, 1990) and G. William Domhoff, Who Rules America: Power, Politics, and Social Change (New York: McGraw-Hill, 2006).
74. Michael Useem, The Inner Circle: Large Corporations and the Rise of Business Political Activity in the U.S. and U.K. (New York: Oxford University Press, 1984).
75. G. William Domhoff, Interlocking Directorates in the Corporate Community, August, 2013. http://whorulesamerica.net/power/corporate_community.html, William Roy, "Interlocking Directorates and the Corporate Revolution", Social Science History, Vol. 7, No. 2 (September, 1984) pages 143–164, R.C. Barnes and E. R. Ritter, "Networks of corporate interlock: 1962–1995", Critical Sociology, Vol. 27, No. 2 (2001) pages 192–220, Peter C. Dooley, "The Interlocking Directorate",

American Economic Review, Vol. 59, No.2 (June, 1969) pages 314–323 and David Bunting and Jeffrey Barbour, "Interlocking Directorates in Large Corporations, 1896–1964", Business History Review, XLV, No. 3 (Autumn, 1971) pages 317–335.

76. Michael Useem, "The Social Organization of the American Business Elite and Participation of Corporation Directors in the Governance of American Institutions", American Sociological Review, Vol. 44, No. 4 (August, 1979) pages 553–572.
77. Harland Prechel, Big Business and the State: Historical Transitions and Corporate Transformations, 1880s–1990s (Albany: State University of New York Press, 2000).
78. Val Burris, "Interlocking Directorates and Political Cohesion among Corporate Elites," American Journal of Sociology, Vol. 111, No. 1 (June, 2005) pages 249–83.
79. Adolpe A. Berle and Gardiner C. Means, The Modern Corporation and Private Property (New York: Harcourt, Brace and World, 1932).
80. David C. Korten, When Corporation Rule the World (Hartford: Kumarian Press, 2001).
81. "A large corporation can, practically speaking buy a state political organization and throughnit have powerful friends in WashingtSon". See Allen M. Potter, American Government and Politics (London: Faber & Faber, 1955).
82. John Nichols and Robert W. McChesney, Dollarocracy. How Money and the Media Election Complex is Destroying America (New York: Nation Books, 2013).
83. Charles Lewis, The Buying of Congress. How Special Interests Have Stolen your Right to Life, Liberty and the Pursuit of Happiness (New York: Avon Books, 1998) pages 46–67 and Charles Lewis, The Buying of the President (New York: Avon Books, 1996).
84. Noam Chomsky, Who rules the World? (New York: Metropolitan Books, 2016) page 64.
85. Robert G. Kaiser, So Damn Much Money: The Triumph of Lobbying and the Corrosion of American Government (New York: Vantage, 2009).
86. Greg Palast, The Best Democracy Money Can Buy (London: Pluto Press, 2002).
87. Jacob Rowbottom, Democracy Distorted: Wealth, Influence and Democratic Politics (Cambridge: Cambridge University Press, 2010).
88. Ferdinand Lundberg, The Rich and the Super-Rich: A Study in the Power of Money Today (Lyle Stuart, 1973) and G. William Domhoff, Who Rules America? The Triumph of the Corporate Rich (New York: McGraw-Hill Education; 7th ed., 2013).
89. Michael E. Porter, Jan W. Rivkin, Mihir A. Desai, Katherine M. Gehl, William R. Kerr with Manjari Raman, A recovery Squandered. The State

of US Competitiveness in 2019 (Cambridge, Mass.: Harvard Business School. December, 2019) page 29.

90. Opioid Overdose | Drug Overdose | CDC Injury Center. https://www.cdc.gov/drugoverdose. Accessed 23 December, 2019.
91. Michael C. Dreiling and Derek Y. Darves, Agents of Neoliberal Globalization: Corporate Networks, State Structures, and Trade Policy (New York: Cambridge University Press, 2016).
92. Michael Dreiling and Derek Darves, "Corporate Unity in American Trade Policy: A Network Analysis of Corporate-Dyad Political Action", American Journal of Sociology, Vol. 116, No. 5 (March 2011) pages 1514–63.
93. Christopher Ingraham and Howard Schneider, "Industry voice dominates the trade advisory system", Washington Post, February 27, 2014.
94. Michael C. Dreiling and Derek Y. Darves, Agents of Neoliberal Globalization: Corporate Networks, State Structures, and Trade Policy (New York: Cambridge University Press, 2016) pages 163–164.
95. Michael C. Dreiling and Derek Y. Darves, Agents of Neoliberal Globalization: Corporate Networks, State Structures, and Trade Policy (New York: Cambridge University Press, 2016) page 248.
96. Richard J. Barnet and Ronald Muller, Global Reach: The Power of the Multinational Corporations (New York: Simon & Schuster, 1974).
97. Raymond Vernon, In the Hurricane's Eye. The Troubled Prospects of Multinational Enterprises (Cambridge: Harvard University Press, 1998) page 10 and Multinational corporations: an overview. http://www.sharing.org/information-centre/articles/multinational-corporations-overview.
98. John Stopford and Susan Strange, Rival States, Rival Firms (Cambridge: Cambridge University Press, 1991) page 15.
99. World Investment Report, 1998: Trends and Determinants (Geneva: United Nations, 1998) page 39.
100. Information retrieved from the World Investment Report 2015 (New York and Geneva: United Nations, 2015).
101. Clyde H. Farnsworth, "U.S. Raises Tariff for Motorcycles", New York Times, April 2, 1983.
102. https://www.reuters.com/article/us-wto-aircraft-timeline/timeline-highlights-of-the-15-year-airbus-boeing-trade-war. Timeline: Highlights of the 15-year Airbus, Boeing trade war. Accessed 7 February, 2020.
103. https://ustr.gov/about-us/policy-offices/press-office/press-releases/2019/october/us-wins-75-billion-award-airbus. US Wins $7.5 Billion Award in Airbus Subsidies Case – USTR. Oct 2, 2019.
104. Michael C. Dreiling and Derek Y. Darves, Agents of Neoliberal Globalization: Corporate Networks, State Structures, and Trade Policy (New York: Cambridge University Press, 2016) page 85.

CHAPTER 3

The Importance of Bananas in the Caribbean

Introduction

Banana is the fourth most important crop in the world after rice, wheat, and corn[1] and the second largest fruit crop after watermelons and ahead of apples, grapes, and oranges.[2] There are more than 1,000 varieties of bananas produced and consumed in the world. The most widely grown is the Cavendish type banana, which accounts for around 47 percent of global production. Approximately 50 billion tonnes of Cavendish bananas are produced globally every year. The Food and Agriculture Organization (FAO) estimates that in 2017 global production amounted to 114 million tonnes having increased from 67 million tonnes in 2000. Approximately 5.6 million hectares of land are dedicated to banana production globally with productivity differing widely from country to country and from variety to variety as well as size of cultivation. Most production takes place in Asia, Latin America, and Africa. The global banana industry generates around US$8 billion per year but only 15 percent of banana production is traded. The largest producers are India, which produced 29 million tonnes and China at 11 million tonnes. Production in both countries mostly serves the domestic market. Other large producers are the Philippines with an annual average of 7.5 million tonnes between 2010 and 2017 and Ecuador and Brazil both at an average of 7 million tonnes.[3]

Bananas are a major export crop for Costa Rica, Guatemala, Honduras, Panama, Colombia, and Ecuador. It is a labor-intensive crop with labor accounting for almost 40 percent of the total cost of production. The

R. L. Bernal, *Corporate versus National Interest in US Trade Policy*, https://doi.org/10.1007/978-3-030-56950-1_3

largest banana exporter is Ecuador, which accounts for one-third of total global banana export volume followed by the Philippines (13 percent), Costa Rica (13 percent), Guatemala (12 percent), and Colombia (10 percent). The largest importers of bananas are the European Union, which accounted for an annual average of 32 percent of total global imports between 2010 and 2016, and the United States (25 percent). The world banana trade is controlled by five multinational corporations which engage in the production, purchase, transport, and marketing of bananas. These are Chiquita, Del Monte, Dole Foods, Fyffes, and Noboa (Grupo Noboa).

Much has changed since the period of the banana dispute which is the focus of this book. It is difficult to say to what extent the changes were due to the outcome of the banana dispute. Chiquita is no longer an American-owned company nor is Del Monte. In 2014, Del Monte Foods Inc. was acquired by the Filipino multinational food and beverage company Del Monte Pacific Limited for US$1.67 billion.[4] Dole Foods is now the largest producer of fruit and vegetables in the world, operating with 74,300 full-time and seasonal employees who are responsible for over 300 products in 90 countries.[5] Fyffes is still based in Dublin, Ireland but was acquired by the Japanese company Sumitomo[6] in February 2017. It is still mainly involved in trading in bananas.

The Caribbean

The Caribbean as used in this book consists of Antigua and Barbuda, Bahamas, Barbados, Belize, Dominica, the Dominican Republic, Grenada, Guyana, Jamaica, Montserrat, St. Kitts and Nevis, St. Lucia, St. Vincent and the Grenadines (St. Vincent), and Trinidad and Tobago. Of these countries, Belize, Dominica, Grenada, Jamaica, St. Kitts and Nevis, St. Lucia, and St. Vincent exported bananas. Given the focus of this study, the limitations of space, and the well-documented historical, social, economic, and political similarities between the countries of the Caribbean, it is not necessary to provide a detailed discussion of each. Basic economic data for the Caribbean banana producing countries is shown in Table 3.1.

The Caribbean can be studied as a group because of (a) the commonality of their historical experience, social characteristics, economic problems, political systems, and culture.[7] (b) The states of the region, while not having identical interests as is to be expected among any group of countries, have a substantial similarity of policy objectives. (c) The governments of the Caribbean and Suriname are committed to the coordination of their

Table 3.1 Land area, population, gross domestic product (GDP), GDP per capita of Caribbean banana exporting countries, and the United States of America (1999)

Country	*Land Area (sq. km)*	*Population*	*GDP (US$ Million)*	*GDP per Capita (US$)*
Belize	2,960	238,550	705	2,949
Dominica	750	73,000	273	3,690
Grenada	340	96,200	360	3,758
Jamaica	10,990	2,576,000	7,445	2,893
St. Lucia	620	152,000	639	3,667
St. Vincent and the Grenadines	390	113, 220	320	2,874
United States	9,363,520	270,299,008	9,256,150	33,933

Source: IMF, World Economic Outlook Database (http://www.imf.org)

foreign policies as part of their membership in the Caribbean Common Market and Community (CARICOM). (d) The United States treats these countries as a group for foreign policy purposes, logistic ease, and administrative simplicity and makes a clear distinction between the CARICOM and Cuba, Haiti, and the Dominican Republic.

This study focuses on Dominica, Grenada, Jamaica, St. Lucia, and St. Vincent. It does not cover Belize, and it should be noted that bananas from Guadeloupe and Martinique are treated as French production because they are a part of France; they were not adversely affected and are not relevant to this study.

The United States has pursued separate policies for Central America, Cuba, Haiti, the Dominican Republic, and the CARICOM countries, albeit within the leitmotif of free trade, anticommunism, and democracy. A distinctive US policy towards CARICOM emerged after the 1960s when these countries attained their political independence from Great Britain beginning with Jamaica in 1962. US engagement in CARICOM has been episodic and focused only when there is a crisis from the American perspective.[8] Engagement in its extreme form has involved military intervention resulting in regime change as occurred in 1983 in Grenada.[9]

Much of the relations of the Eastern Caribbean with the United States is taken up with responding to foreign policy initiatives of the United States, such as the Enterprise for the Americas Initiative and NAFTA. The reactions to US policies have varied from cooperation, for example, combating drug smuggling to seeking to influence (e.g., sugar), to resistance (e.g., bananas). At times, the countries of the Caribbean have operated as a very cohesive group, for example, lobbying for the CBI, and on occasions they have differed (e.g., the US invasion of Grenada). In some instances, the issue may not be of vital interest such as debt relief was important only to Guyana and Jamaica, but it was normal that all CARICOM countries would support the interests of even one state, for example, Trinidad and Tobago against anti-dumping action by the United States, Jamaica and the Caribbean acting in unison have been able in certain circumstances to influence US foreign policy.[10]

The prominent feature of the Caribbean countries is their small size which makes them vulnerable to pressure from large, developed countries. This condition is particularly evident in relations between the small states of the region and the United States where the enormous disparities in size, power, and development have led to acute dependence rather than interdependence to which the Caribbean states rightfully aspired. In their attempts to counteract the overweening power of the United States, the governments supplement bilateral diplomacy by resorting to hemispheric and multilateral forums. The banana exporting countries raised the issue at every forum in which the United States was present including the Organization of American States (OAS), the United Nations, and the Summit of the Americas.

The Caribbean economies exhibit acute macroeconomic vulnerability because they are small and highly open, that is, external transactions are large in relation to total economic activity as indicated by the high ratio of trade to GDP. The United States has a trade/GDP ratio of 15 percent. By contrast, Caribbean economies have trade GDP ratios between 40 and 204 percent. The limited range of economic activity in these small economies is reflected in the concentration on one to three exports, accompanied in most of the cases by a relatively high reliance on primary commodities. In extreme instances, one primary product export accounts for nearly all exports. For example, in 1991, bananas accounted for 92 percent of total exports in Dominica and 87 percent in St. Lucia. Export concentration is compounded by the dependence on one or two export markets (e.g., Britain absorbs 80 percent of Dominica's bananas and 90 percent of St. Lucia's exports). Economic vulnerability can be a feature of an economy of any size and level of development, but it is compounded by the CARICOM countries' small size, susceptibility to natural disasters, remoteness, and insularity. Studies of developing countries have demonstrated that there is a direct relationship between vulnerability and size, with the smallest developing countries being the most vulnerable. A World Bank/Commonwealth Secretariat study shows that of 111 developing countries, 26 of the 28 most vulnerable were small countries.[11] Canada, Brazil, Argentina, and the United States have vulnerability indexes of 0.2 or less, while Caribbean and Central American economies exceed 0.4. The smallest economies have vulnerability indexes ranging from 0.595 for Barbados to 0.843 for Antigua.[12] A multidimensional index encompassing economic and environmental factors confirmed high vulnerability of Dominica, Jamaica, Grenada, St. Lucia, and St. Vincent.[13]

Volatility in national income is a pronounced characteristic of small, developing countries that export a few primary products (particularly minerals and agricultural commodities) and experience erratic fluctuations in capital flows. This is specifically the case in small developing countries because of the severely constrained adjustment capacity that limits their ability to react. Volatility is costly because of the adverse impact on investment, resource allocation, productivity, inflation, exchange rates, and economic growth. Small economies experience higher income volatility than larger economies, estimated by the World Bank/Commonwealth Secretariat, as 25 percent higher. A study of foreign direct investment (FDI) flows in the last 20 years reveals that small developing countries are at a disadvantage in attaining FDI relative to larger developing countries because even when they have sound economic policies, small, developing countries are rated 28 percent more risky.[14]

The states of the Caribbean have sought to overcome the disadvantage of the enormous disparities in power, wealth, and size between themselves and the sole superpower, the United States, by cooperation and coordination in foreign policy through CARICOM. A.N.R. Robinson, Prime Minister of Trinidad and Tobago explains that in the region, "we are convinced that national self-determination can often be most effectively pursued within the framework of regional groupings. We are firmly of the view that it is through such associations that small nations are afforded the best opportunity to contribute to the solution of the world's problems and their own."[15] In 1967, the English-speaking countries established the Caribbean Free Trade Association and in 1973 they created CARICOM as a vehicle of regional economic integration for promoting economic development.[16] The Treaty that established the Caribbean Community (1973) speaks of "a common front in relation to the external world"[17] and Article 34.1 states as an objective "the coordination of the foreign policies of

Member States."[18] The 1981 report, "The Caribbean Community in the 1980s" admonished the governments of the region to "intensify their efforts to achieve coordination of their external trade relations." The report of the West Indian Commission, "Time For Action" called on member states to "adopt a collective approach to current and potential changes in the international community, including international political and financial institutions, and reflect this approach in common arrangements for international economic negotiations and diplomatic representation."[19]

There have been challenges in the execution of collective or joint representation because as Bryan points out, there is the issue of the willingness of these states and their leaders "to concede a little national sovereignty for the greater supra-nationality of the region."[20] In spite of the remnants of nationalism, cooperation has prevailed. The cohesion in CARICOM has been bolstered by the policy of developed countries of dealing only with small states in groups, especially when they are in the same physical region or in an integration process. Costa Rica approached the United States for a free trade agreement only to be rebuffed and much to their chagrin was told that the United States would only countenance an approach by Central America. This is the same approach taken to relations with the CARICOM by the United States and Britain. This should not have caused CARICOM any discomfort given its collaboration in external affairs for almost half a century. Yet the Ambassador of Grenada to the United States, as recently as 2007, was prompted to bemoan group "therapy" stating that: "One is not taken seriously when all the small countries are grouped in one bloc. To the extent that frontline countries like to talk to CARICOM, a country such as Grenada does not get much attention."[21] Certainly to be heard as part of a group with a common position must be better than not being seen or heard. In the struggle to change the US approach to the EU banana regime, the countries of CARICOM acted in unison. Those countries that did not export bananas were in solidarity with the banana exporting countries.

Emergence of the Banana Industry in Jamaica

The Caribbean islands were early participants in the global economy starting in the mid-seventeenth century with their livelihood coming from the export of sugar.[22] The sugar industry dominated the economic underdevelopment of the Caribbean plantation economies[23] through slavery, post-slavery, and into the contemporary period[24] eventually collapsing in Antigua, Barbados, Trinidad, and St. Kitts and contracting significantly in Jamaica. The emergence of the possibility to export bananas was a welcomed development to diversify the economy of the Caribbean islands of Jamaica and the Eastern Caribbean. The banana industry never emerged in Antigua, Barbados, and Trinidad and Tobago but was an important development in Dominica and Grenada, which depended on the export of limes and nutmeg respectively.

Jamaica was the first country in the Western Hemisphere to export bananas starting in 1868 and regular shipments began in 1870 thanks to the enterprise of Americans, George Busch and Captain Lorenzo Baker.[25] By 1890, bananas accounted for 19.1 percent of total exports and this increased to 57.3 percent in 1930,[26] a period in which the sugar industry was experiencing some difficulties. Both Jamaican[27] and American companies enriched themselves in the banana industry and it also brought prosperity to banana farmers large and small especially after the formation of the Jamaica Banana Producers Association.[28] By the mid-1930s, Jamaica was the world's largest exporter of bananas, an achievement which generated interest in both the Caribbean, the United States, and Britain. Jamaica's bananas were exported to the eastern seaboard of the United States but had not entered the British market which was supplied from the Canary Islands. In 1897, the Jamaica Fruit Importing and Trading Company tried to deliver bananas in suitable condition to the British market but failed. Clegg points out that in 1899 the Jamaican banana interest became worried that the Boston Fruit Company that had bought lands in Cuba, which were nearer to New York and Boston, might shift production from Jamaica and hence the interest in entering the British market.[29]

Boston Fruit Company whose supplies came primarily from Jamaica merged with Minor C. Keith who was supplied from Central America and, in turn, in 1899 merged with 12 smaller companies to form the UFC which dominated the banana industry. While their operations produced benefits for small farmers, because it required "no elaborate equipment and no special skills, it is peculiarly suitable to peasant cultivation".[30] A report for the Jamaica Banana Producers Association in 1935 observes: "Instances can be recalled without number to prove that whenever profits of the United Fruit Company might be improved by action (or inaction) no hesitation has been shown by those managing its affairs in doing this even if it resulted in grave hardship to the growers of banana in Jamaica."[31] The United Fruit Company systematically tried to eliminate competition.

The Jamaica Banana Producers association handled about one-third of Jamaica's banana production but as a cooperative, it was anathema to UFC. Sealy and Hart explain: "The United Fruit Co. had genuinely believed that a successful banana growers association in Jamaica would be prejudicial to their entire international banana trade, especially since Jamaica at the time was, if not the largest, certainly one of the largest banana exporters in the world. The United Fruit Co. had no objection to the growers forming a co-operative to sell their bananas to them, but they regarded a co-operative with its own shipping line and its own marketing organization abroad as a direct competitor, one likely to make serious inroads in the company's business in Jamaica and possibly throughout the world."[32]

Around 1901, Colonial Secretary Joseph Chamberlin was approached to explore the development of a market in Britain for Jamaican bananas. Various schemes were tried based on a subsidy to the shipping companies but these were not adequate to ensure commercial viability. Eventually, the service by Elder Dempster commenced in 1901 with the benefit of a subsidy of 40,000 pounds annually for ten years paid in half by the colonial government and half by Jamaica. One of the main motivations why Jamaica agreed to contribute to the subsidy was to reduce the risks of dependence on the UFC and the US market and to provide a new outlet in the British market for bananas.[33]

In 1901, Elders and Fyffes[34] was incorporated and soon ran into financial difficulties. In 1902, UFC acquired a 45 percent interest in Elders and Fyffes and guaranteed adequate supplies of bananas.[35] Since Elders and Fyffes and UFC were the main suppliers of the British market, it meant the British market was dominated by and solely dependent on an American company. While Elders and Fyffes was ostensibly a British company, the reality was that the UFC was involved in all its decision-making.[36] This was not a situation that the British authorities were comfortable with. The Jamaican banana industry was deeply concerned about the monopoly of the UFC.

Creation of the Banana Industry in the Eastern Caribbean

There were several unsuccessful attempts to introduce banana production for export in the Windward Islands from as early as 1890.[37] The banana industry in the Windward Islands did not emerge naturally from market forces but was deliberately created by the British government to provide employment and economic activity. The initiative came in the context of the damage to lime production by disease in the late 1920s.[38] Banana production was mooted by The Report on Marketing and Preparing for the Market of Foodstuffs Produced in the Overseas Territories in 1925.[39] A further impetus was the economic depression and mass social disturbances in the 1930s and was encouraged by the successful emergence of the banana export industry in Jamaica since the late nineteenth century.[40] The Great Depression caused considerable economic hardship in the Caribbean[41] and the labor disturbances across the region in the 1930s led the British government to establish the Moyne Commission which visited between November 1938 and April 1939. The Report was held back by the Colonial Office until 1945 because it might "further inflame West Indian sentiment".[42] The US government also became aware of "an explosive situation in the region".[43] The US strategic interests were oil and bauxite in the region and the commitment to protecting the shipping routes for these raw materials was evident in the destroyers-bases agreement with Britain.[44] The principal recommendations of the report which was not published fully until 1945 were aimed at salvaging the British Empire in the Caribbean by restoring stability in the Caribbean colonies.[45] This was a continuation of the British colonial policy during the interwar years.[46] There was a recognition both within and outside the Caribbean that the economic conditions needed attention and hence the Colonial Development and Welfare Act of 1940[47] and the establishment of the Anglo-American Commission in 1942 which later became the Caribbean Commission.[48]

The sugar industry, the mainstay of most Caribbean countries, declined from the halcyon days of the middle of the eighteenth century. Franklin Knight describes the situation as a "severe crisis" although "not equally acute in all the sugar-producing zones of those declining imperial outposts, impending failure hung like a heavy low cloud that blanketed the area in common."[49] Indeed, sugar had disappeared by the end of the nineteenth century in Grenada and replaced by cocoa.[50] In St. Vincent, sugar production ended shortly after 1900[51] and by the 1920s the main export industries were in decline (e.g., Sea Island Cotton) and sugar which ended shortly after 1900. Fortunately, however, a banana industry began to emerge in 1935.[52] The decline of the sugar industry continued into the contemporary period as output declined by over 50 percent between 1970 and 2000[53] making other agricultural exports more important than ever.

From the start, the banana industry in the Windward Islands required subsidies in shipping and price support to survive.[54] The preferential export arrangements were not enough to make the banana industry viable and it had to be sustained throughout its existence by financial aid from the British government.[55] This was known, and it was a deliberate policy of development aid, which had a profoundly positive effect. O'Loughlin observes that the policies "emergence in the Windward Islands has thus resulted in something of a social as well as an economic revolution."[56] Gordon Lewis describes the impact of the banana framing as a social revolution.[57] The total acreage in banana cultivation increased from 4,400 in 1946 to 38,000 in 1963 while production increased from 375,400 stems valued at $589,900 in 1950 to 12,000,000 stems in 1963 valued at $16,800,000.[58] Part of the success was attributed to the thousands of small banana farmers, the vast majority of whom farmed less than 5 hectares,[59] providing a weekly cash flow[60] and, therefore, the inflow of foreign exchange had a multiplier effect throughout the rural population and indeed, the entire economy. There also resided the vulnerability of the industry because growing bananas on a few acres of often steep hillside land provided yields that were less than a third of those on plantations of large flat tracts of land of 2,500 to 12,000 acres in Central America.[61] The preferential market access arrangement had to be kept in place by continual lobbying and diplomatic outreach especially after Britain's entry into the European Economic Community (EEC) in 1973.[62] This demarche was carried out in tandem with Geest, which was the sole purchaser of bananas from the Windward Islands, all of which was destined for the British market.

Corporate competition between US and European banana marketing companies dates back to the earliest years of the banana trade. In 1900, the British government sought to break the monopoly of UFC in the British market by subsidizing, shipping, and promoting production in the Eastern Caribbean.[63] Jamaica, where the UFC with 57.1 percent of total banana purchases in 1935[64] was the dominant producer and buyer of bananas, worried that the company would switch to supplying itself from

Central America and Cuba which was closer to US markets. Its attempts at banana cultivation in Cuba failed. This fear was brought to the attention of the British government where it received an empathetic hearing from Joseph Chamberlain ("British Empire is commerce") who decided to help through a massive subsidy to help Jamaica enter the British banana market and simultaneously develop a British banana importing and marketing company to reduce US corporate control of the British banana market. Chamberlain's ultimate move was in the maintenance of the imperial trading system as a basis for preserving the Empire. Jamaican bananas did enter the British market but the new British company, Elders & Fyffes, despite a massive subsidy, only escaped bankruptcy when UFC bought 45 percent of its shares and guaranteed supplies from Jamaica.[65]

The British government had to make special arrangements for the banana industry during World War II[66] and also induced Geest to enter the banana importing business in 1953 which it did drawing its supply of bananas from the Windward Islands.[67] Even with preferential marketing arrangements, the banana industry in the Windward Islands required British aid to sustain it.[68] The industry thrived and production expanded significantly because of the preferential trade arrangements which allowed the high-cost production of the small farmers to afford them a living.

Corporate competition between European firms had been very fierce at times (e.g., during the early 1960s). As output from the Windward Islands expanded rapidly in the 1950s, a situation of oversupply developed in the British market leading to the Windward Islands—Jamaica "banana war".[69] The corporate competition between Fyffes, the purchaser of Jamaican bananas, and Geest, the counterpart for the Windward Islands led to a post-World War II fall in prices until a market sharing agreement was brokered in which Jamaica had 52 percent of the British market and the Windwards had 48 percent.[70]

Nature of Banana Farming

In Jamaica, bananas were produced on a variety of farms ranging from a few acres through to large plantations operated by foreign and local companies. In the Eastern Caribbean, the vast majority of farmers (e.g., 86 percent in parts of St. Vincent)[71] were cultivating less than 5 hectares.[72] Bananas were grown by individual small farmers with certain aspects of the operations handled collectively by the banana growers association to which all growers belonged.[73] This was in contrast to Central America where most bananas were grown on plantations owned by MNCs with UFC having a near monopoly of all aspects of production from growing to retailing in global markets.

Downside of the Banana Industry

Although banana cultivation and export was the mainstay of the economies of the Windward Islands and was responsible for substantial economic "upliftment", there were downsides. First, the "acute vulnerability"[74] due to the near total dependence on a single export sold to a single multinational corporation, Geest and exported to a single market. Indeed, one of the little-recognized facts is that bananas were more important in the Windward Island economies than in the so-called "banana republics" of Central America.[75] Second, the banana farmers receive a very small share of the retail price for which bananas were sold and not able to exert any appreciable influence on the decisions of Geest.[76] Third, it has been suggested that banana cultivation led to the relative neglect of food production and contributed to increased reliance on imported food.[77] Fourth, Welsh points to the lack of reinvestment of the profits of the banana industry and thus "the crop has not acted as a springboard for more sophisticated forms of development."[78] Fifth, the banana farmers get a very small share of the retail price of bananas which was estimated to be 12 percent in Ecuador.[79] This is typical of small farmers when supplying agricultural products to multinational corporations because of the ability to have the value-added and profits accrue at the later stages of the value chain within the multinational corporation.[80]

Importance of the Banana Industry

As Prime Minister of St. Kitts & Nevis Dr. Denzil Douglas explained: "Bananas are the life-blood of some of our countries."[81] At the time that the United States and cohort countries took their complaint to the WTO, banana exports constituted the largest export for Dominica, St. Lucia, and St. Vincent and an important agricultural export for Belize and Jamaica. Banana exports as a share of total exports in 1993 was 50.0 percent in Dominica, 42.6 percent in St. Lucia, 40.2 percent in St. Vincent, 10.6 percent in Belize, 10.3 percent in Grenada and 3.5 percent in Jamaica.[82] The banana industry contributed 19–20 percent of GDP in Dominica during the period 1985–1993[83] and approximately 21 percent of GDP for the Windward Islands[84] as a whole. The dependency of these countries on banana exports was evident in the number of farmers and other workers employed in all aspects of the industry, for example, it was "the biggest single employer of regular full-time workers" according to Gill and Gonzales' study.[85] Oxfam estimates that the percentage of the population dependent on the banana industry was 33 percent in St. Lucia and 70 percent in St. Vincent and the Grenadines.[86]

Jamaica earned about US$29.6 million in 1999 and produced about 130,000 tonnes accounting for 2.4% of the total exports. In 1938, 320,000 tonnes were exported accounting to over 50 percent of total exports but declined to 151,000 tonnes in 1969 accounting for just under 8 percent of total exports.[87] These figures do not capture the full importance of the banana industry which was a major weekly source of cash for a large number of small and medium-sized farmers[88] who produced 60 percent of the output.[89] Some 77 percent of farmers were less than 5 acres and a further 20 percent were 5–25 acres.[90] In addition, there are farmworkers, truckers, and dock workers. In fact, the economic foundation of some towns depended on bananas, for example, Port Antonio, a port from which bananas was exported.

The banana exports of the Eastern Caribbean region in 1993 were valued at $150 million and, therefore, amounted to a small fraction of total world banana exports which in 1992 was $3122 million.[91] Wage costs differ vastly between the Eastern Caribbean and the Latin American and Central American producers: One estimate suggests that wages are twice as high in the Eastern Caribbean. Specifically, average daily wage rates were $10 in Belize, while in neighboring Guatemala it was $3.50.[92] Due to higher wage rates and lack of economies of scale, production costs in the Eastern Caribbean, estimated at 47 cents per kilo[93] were the highest among the countries exporting bananas to the European Union. Yields varied considerably between the Caribbean and Central America. The yield was 2.5 tonnes per acre in the Eastern Caribbean, 2.9 tonnes in Jamaica, 5.1 tonnes in Ecuador and 6.7 in Costa Rica.[94]

The EU market was the sole market for bananas exported from the Caribbean because these bananas received preferential market access to the EU market. The Caribbean's share of the EU market was about 8 percent and less than 3 percent of the world market.[95] Even where bananas from the Caribbean were able to compete and could have reduced dependence on the United Kingdom as their only export market, corporate control of these markets blocked these possibilities. Welch notes that at a certain time "Standard Fruit and United Fruit had such a stranglehold on the Canadian market that bananas from Jamaica could not enter although they would have been less expensive."[96]

Epilogue

The production and export of bananas was the most important economic activity in the small islands of the Eastern Caribbean measured by foreign exchange earnings, employment, number of farmers involved, and contribution to GDP. Simply put, it was the backbone of the economy and the foundation and engine of economic growth. In Jamaica, the industry due to disease, natural disasters, and droughts declined steadily since the halcyon days of the 1930s when Jamaica was the largest producer and exporter of bananas. The final deterrent to the recovery of the industry was the uncertainty about the arrangements for banana entering the UK and EU markets which started in the early 1990s. No bananas were exported from Jamaica in 2008.

Notes

1. Dan Koeppel, Banana. The Fate of the Fruit That Changed the World (New York: Hudson Street Press, 2008) page xiii.
2. Top 5 Fruit Crops | 5 Facts. https://5factsdotorg.wordpress.com/2011/08/16/top-5-fruit-crops/. Accessed 29 December, 2019.
3. EST: Banana facts – FAO. www.fao.org/economic/est/est-commodities/bananas/bananafacts/en/. Accessed 15 August 2019.
4. Michael J. de La Merced, "Del Monte Foods Sells Consumer Products Division for $1.68 Billion", The New York Times, October 11, 2013.
5. Dole Food Company – Wikipedia. https://en.wikipedia.org. Accessed 11 January 2020.
6. "Fyffes / Sumitomo: good pickings", Financial Times, December 9, 2016.
7. The meaning of the Caribbean differs depending on whether it is defined culturally, geographically or geo-politically and definitions based on culture and geo-politics have changed over time. See Norman Girvan, "Creating and Recreating the Caribbean" in Kenneth Hall and Denis Benn (eds.), Contending with Destiny. The Caribbean in the 21st Century (Kingston: Ian Randle Publishers, 2000) pages 31–36.
8. Richard L. Bernal, "The Unimportance of the English Speaking Caribbean in US Foreign Policy as told by Presidents and Secretaries of State",

Caribbean Journal of International Relations & Diplomacy, Vol.1, No.1 (February, 2013) pages 132–150.

9. Anthony Payne, Anthony, Paul K. Sutton and Tony Thorndike, Grenada: Revolution and Invasion (New York: St. Martin's Press, 1984) and Patsy Lewis, Gary Williams and Peter Clegg (eds.), Grenada: Revolution and Invasion (Kingston: University of the West Indies, 2015).
10. Richard L. Bernal, The Influence of Small States on Superpowers: Jamaica and U.S. Foreign Policy (Lanham: Lexington Publishers, June, 2015).
11. Vulnerability: Small States in the Global Society (London: Commonwealth Secretariat, 1985). A Future for Small States: Overcoming Vulnerability (London: Commonwealth Secretariat, 1997).
12. Lino Briguglio, "Small Island Developing and Their Economic Vulnerabilities", World Development, Vol. 2-3. No.9 (1995) pages 1615–1632.
13. Justin Ram, J. Jason Cotton, Raquel Frederick and Wayne Elliott, A Multidimensional Vulnerability Index for the Caribbean, CDB Working Paper No. 2019/01 (Bridgetown: Caribbean Development Bank, 2019).
14. Richard Bernal, "Globalization and Small Developing Economies. The Challenges and Opportunities," in David Peretz, Rumman Faruqi and Eliawony J. Kisanga (eds.), Small States in the Global Economy (London: Commonwealth Secretariat, 2001) pages 39–51.
15. A.N.R. Robinson, Caribbean Man. Selected Speeches from a Political Career 1960–1986 (Port of Spain: Inprint Publication, 1986) page 98.
16. The rationale for economic integration in promoting economic development in the small economies of the Eastern Caribbean is explained in Havelock Brewster and Clive Y. Thomas, The Dynamics of West Indian Economic Integration (Mona, Jamaica: Institute of Social and Economic Research, University of the West Indies, 1967) and William Demas, Essays on Caribbean Integration and Development (Mona, Jamaica: Institute of Social and Economic Research, University of the West Indies, 1976). For an assessment of the rationales for regional integration see Ian Boxill, Ideology and Caribbean Integration (Mona, Jamaica: Consortium Graduate School of Social Sciences, University of the West Indies, 1993).
17. Treaty establishing the Caribbean Community, Chaguaramas, 4th July 1973 (Georgetown: Caribbean Community Secretariat, June, 1987) page 2.
18. Treaty establishing the Caribbean Community, Chaguaramas, 4th July 1973 (Georgetown: Caribbean Community Secretariat, June, 1987) page 38.
19. Time For Action. The report of The West Indian Commission (Black Rock, Barbados: The West Indian Commission, 1992) page 457.
20. Anthony T. Bryan "The International Dynamics of the Commonwealth Caribbean: Challenges and Opportunities in the 1990's", Journal of

Interamerican Studies and world Affairs, Vol. 31, No.3 (Fall, 1989) pages 1–7. See page 7.

21. Franklin W. Knight, "Caribbean Diplomacy in Washington", The Jamaica Observer, January 24, 2007.
22. Richard S. Dunn, Sugar and Slaves: The Rise of the Planter Class in the English West Indies, 1624–1713 (Chapel Hill: University of North Carolina Press, 1972) and Richard B. Sheridan, Sugar and Slavery: An Economic History of the British West Indies, 1623–1775 (Baltimore: Johns Hopkins University Press, 1974).
23. Eric Williams, Capitalism and Slavery (Chapel Hill: University of North Carolina Press, 1994).
24. Carl Feuer, "Better Must Come: Sugar and Jamaica in the Twentieth Century", Social and Economic Studies, Vol. 33, No. 4 (December, 1984) pages and George Beckford, Persistent Poverty. Underdevelopment in Plantation Economies of the Third World (New York: Oxford University Press, 1973).
25. For the history of the emergence and early development of the banana industry in Jamaica see Ansel Hart, "The Banana in Jamaica: Export Trade", Social and Economic Studies, Vol. 3, No. 2 (September, 1954) pages 212–229. See also Peter N. Davies, Fyffes and the Banana: Musa Sapient. A Centenary History 1888–1988 (London: Athlone Press, 1990) pages 25–35.
26. Gisela Eisner, Jamaica, 1830–1930: A Study in Economic Growth (Westport: Greenwood Press, 1974) page 238.
27. Leslie Gordon Goffe, When Banana Was King: A Jamaican Banana King in Jim Crow America (Kingston: LMH Publishing Company, 2006).
28. George Beckford, "Origins, Development and Future of the Jamaican Banana Industry: A Century of Revolutionary Struggle of the Peasantry", New World Quarterly, Vol. V, No. 3 (1968) reprinted in Kari Levitt (ed.), The George Beckford Reader (Kingston: University of the West Indies Press, 200) pages 352–358 and Theodore Sealy and Herbert Hart edited by Clinton V. Black, Jamaica's Banana Industry. A history of the Banana Industry with particular reference to the part played by the Jamaica Banana Producers Association Ltd. (Kingston: The Jamaica Banana Producers Association, 1984).
29. Peter Clegg, The Caribbean Banana Trade. From Colonialism to Globalization (New York: Palgrave Macmillan, 2002) page 26.
30. Herbert Hart, Jamaica Banana Producers Association, 1935, page 3.
31. Herbert Hart, Jamaica Banana Producers Association, 1935, page 5.
32. Theodore Sealy and Herbert Hart, Jamaica's Banana Industry. A History of the Banana Industry with particular reference to the part played by The

Jamaica Banana Producers Association Ltd. (Kingston: Jamaica Banana Producers Association, 1984) page 77.
33. Peter N. Davies, Fyffes and the Banana: Musa Sapient. A Centenary History 1888–1988 (London: Athlone Press, 1990) page 105.
34. Peter N. Davies, Fyffes and the Banana: Musa Sapient. A Centenary History 1888–1988 (London: Athlone Press, 1990) pages 91–104.
35. For a more detailed account see Peter Clegg, The Caribbean Banana Trade. From Colonialism to Globalization (New York: Palgrave Macmillan, 2002) pages 24–32.
36. Peter N. Davies, Fyffes and the Banana: Musa Sapient. A Centenary History 1888–1988 (London: Athlone Press, 1990) pages 103–104.
37. Barbara Welsh, "Banana Dependency: Albatros or Liferaft for the Windwards", Social and Economic Studies, Vol.43, No.1 (March, 1994) pages 123–149. See pages 126–128.
38. James Wiley, "Dominica's Economic Diversification: Microstates in a Neoliberal Era" in Thomas Klak (ed.), Globalization and Neoliberalism: The Caribbean Context (Lanham: Rowman & Littlefield Publishers, 1997) pages 155–177.
39. Rachel Anderson, Tim Taylor and Tim Josling, "The Caribbean and the Banana Trade" in Timothy E. Josling and Timothy G. Taylor (eds.), Banana Wars. The Anatomy of a Trade Dispute (Walliford: CABI Publishing, 2003) pages 123–150. See page 125.
40. Douglas Hall, "The Early Banana Trade from Jamaica, 1868–1905. A Descriptive Account" in Douglas Hall, Ideas and Illustrations in Economic History (New York: Holt, Rinehart and Winston, 1964) pages 56–79.
41. For an overview of the Caribbean in the 1930s see Franklin W. Knight, "The Caribbean in the 1930s" in Bridget Brereton (ed.), General History of the Caribbean (Paris: UNESCO Publishing and London: Macmillan Publishers, 2004) Vol. V, pages 42–81.
42. Robert L. Tignor, W. Arthur Lewis and the Birth of Development Economics (Princeton: Princeton University Press, 2006) page 45.
43. Bernard M. Poole, The Caribbean Commission. Background of Cooperation in the West Indies (Columbia: University of South Carolina Press, 1951) page xviii.
44. Claus Fullberg-Stolberg, "The Caribbean in the Second World War" in Bridget Brereton (ed.), General History of the Caribbean (Paris: UNESCO Publishing and London: Macmillan Publishers, 2004) Vol. V, pages 82–140.
45. The Moyne Report (Kingston: Ian Randle Publishers, 2012).
46. David Meredith, "The British Government and the Colonial Economic Policy, 1919–1939", Economic History Review, Vol.28, Issue 3 (August, 1975) pages 484–499.

47. E.R. Wicker, "Colonial Development and Welfare, 1929–1957: The Evolution of a Policy", Social and Economic Studies, Vol. 7, No. 4 (December, 1958) pages 170–192.
48. Bernard M. Poole, The Caribbean Commission. Background of Cooperation in the West Indies (Columbia: University of South Carolina Press, 1951).
49. Franklin W. Knight, "The Struggle of the British Caribbean Sugar Industry, 1900–2013", The Journal of Caribbean History, Vol. 48, No. 1/2 (January 1, 2014).
50. The Decline of Sugar Production and the Rise of Cocoa Production in Grenada 1870–1917: The Changing Fortunes of a Cocoa Peasantry by Jeffrey A. Euwema Thesis submitted to the Faculty of the Virginia Polytechnic Institute and state University in partial fulfillment of Lawrence S. Grossman the requirement for the degree of Master of Science in Geography, May 19, 1993.
51. Jay Mandle, Persistent Underdevelopment: Change and Economic Modernization in the West (New York: Routledge, 2011) Table 3, Chapter 3.
52. Frederick Walker, "Economic Progress of St. Vincent, B. W. I., Since 1927", Economic Geography, Vol. 13, No. 3 (July, 1937) pages 217–234.
53. Donald Mitchell, Sugar in the Caribbean: Adjusting to Eroding Preferences, Policy Research Working Paper 3802 (Washington DC: World Bank, December, 2005) page 2.
54. Peter N. Davies, Fyffes and the Banana: Musa Sapient. A Centenary History 1888–1988 (London: Athlone Press, 1990).
55. Lawrence S. Grossman, "British Aid and Windwards Bananas: The Case of St. Vincent and the Grenadines", Social and Economic Studies, Vol. 43, No. 1 (March, 1994) pages 151–179.
56. Carleen O'Loughlin, Economic and Political Change in the Leeward and Windward Islands (New Haven: Yale University Press, 1968) page 109.
57. Gordon K. Lewis, The Growth of the Modern West Indies (Kingston: Ian Randle Publishers, 2004) page 149.
58. Carleen O'Loughlin, Economic and Political Change in the Leeward and Windward Islands (New Haven: Yale University Press, 1968) page 109.
59. Barbara M. Welch, Survival by Association. Supply Management Landscapes of the Eastern Caribbean (Montreal: McGill-Queen's University Press, 1996) Chapter 3.
60. Ramesh Ramsaran, The Commonwealth Caribbean in the World Economy (London: Macmillan Caribbean, 1989) page 71.
61. Restructuring the Loss of Preference. Labour Challenges for the Caribbean Banana Industry, page 5 and Peter Chapman, Bananas. How the United Fruit Shaped the World (New York: Cannongate, 2007) page 100.

62. Scott Barfield, "Declining diplomatic influence and the banana trade dispute" in Justin Robertson and Maurice A. East (eds.), Diplomacy and Developing Nations. Post-Cold War foreign policy making structures and processes (London: Routledge, 2005) pages xxx.
63. Barbara Welch, "Banana Dependency: Albatross or Liferaft for the Windwards," Social and Economic Studies, Vol. 43, No. 1 (March, 1994) pages 123–149. See page 127.
64. A. Hart, Jamaica Banana Producers Association, 1935, page 83.
65. This history is succinctly retold in Gordon Myers, Banana Wars. The Price of Free Trade. A Caribbean Perspective (London: Zed Books, 2004) pages 6–10.
66. Peter Clegg, The Caribbean Banana Trade. From Colonialism to Globalization (New York: Palgrave Macmillan, 2002) pages 59–63.
67. Yes, Geest will have no bananas | The Independent. https://www.independent.co.uk/News/Business. Nov 25, 1995.
68. Lawrence S. Grossman, "British Aid and Windwards Bananas, "The Case of St. Vincent and the Grenadines," Social and Economic Studies, Vol. 43, No. 1 (March, 1994) pages 151–179.
69. George L. Beckford, "Issues in the Windwards – Jamaica Banana War" in Norman Girvan and Owen Jefferson (eds.), Readings in the Political Economy of the Caribbean (Kingston: New World, 1974) pages 77–86 and Gordon Myers, Banana Wars. The Price of Free Trade (London: Zed Books, 2004) pages 22–29.
70. Peter Clegg, The Caribbean Banana Trade. From Colonialism to Globalization (New York: Palgrave Macmillan, 2002) pages 85–89.
71. Lawrence S. Grossman, the Political Ecology of Bananas. Contract Farming, Peasants, and Agrarian Change in the Eastern Caribbean (Chapel Hill: University of the North Carolina Press, 1998) page 114.
72. Barbara M. Welch, Survival by Association. Supply Management Landscapes of the Eastern Caribbean (Montreal: McGill-Queen's University Press, 1996) Chapter 3.
73. Barbara M. Welch, Survival by Association. Supply Management Landscapes of the Eastern Caribbean (Montreal: McGill-Queen's University Press, 1996) pages 24–25.
74. Richard L. Bernal, Globalization, Trade and Economic Development: A Study of the CARIFORUM-EU Economic Partnership Agreement (New York: Palgrave Macmillan, December, 2013) pages 91–92.
75. Robert Thomson, Green Gold: Bananas and Dependency in the Eastern Caribbean (London: Latin America Bureau, 1988) page 17.
76. Michel-Rolph Trouillot, Peasants and Capital: Dominica in the World Economy (Baltimore: Johns Hopkins University Press, 1988).

77. J. M. Marie, Agricultural Diversification in a Small Economy-the Case of Dominica, Occaisional Paper No. 10 (Barbados: Institute of Social and Economic Research, 1979).
78. Barbara Welch, "Banana Dependency: Albatross or Liferaft for the Windwards," Social and Economic Studies, Vol. 43, No. 1 (March, 1994) page 138.
79. "Global Communities: Coffee, Bananas", Rural Migration News, Vol. 8, No. 4 (October, 2002).
80. George L. Beckford, Persistent Poverty. Underdevelopment in Plantation Economies of the Third World (New York: Oxford University Press, 1972). Similarly for raw materials see Norman Girvan, Corporate Imperialism. Conflict and Expropriation (New York: Monthly Review Press, 1976).
81. Kenneth G. Tilley (ed.), Coming of Age. Speeches by Hon. Dr. Denzil L. Douglas (Kingston: Ian Randle Publishers, 2009) page 319.
82. Henry S. Gill and Anthony P. Gonzales, Economic Consequences of a Banana Collapse in the Caribbean, Report prepared for the CARICOM Secretariat, May, 1995, pages 15–17.
83. The Economic and Social Contribution of the Banana Industry in the OECS, Research and Information Department, Eastern Caribbean Central Bank, September, 1997.
84. Restructuring and the Loss of Preferences. Labour Challenges for the Caribbean Banana Industry (Geneva: International Labour Organization, January, 1999) page 1.
85. Henry S. Gill and Anthony P. Gonzales, Economic Consequences of a Banana Collapse in the Caribbean, Report prepared for the CARICOM Secretariat, May, 1995, page 24.
86. Restructuring and the Loss of Preferences. Labour Challenges for the Caribbean Banana Industry (Geneva: International Labour Organization, January, 1999) page 1.
87. Owen Jefferson, The Post-War Economic Development of Jamaica (Kingston: Institute of Social and Economic Research, University of the West Indies, 1972) page 100.
88. David Edwards, An Economic Study of Small Farming in Jamaica (Kingston: Institute of Social and Economic Research, University College of the West Indies, 1961).
89. Owen Jefferson, The Post-War Economic Development of Jamaica (Kingston: Institute of Social and Economic Research, University of the West Indies, 1972) page 103.
90. Owen Jefferson, The Post-War Economic Development of Jamaica (Kingston: Institute of Social and Economic Research, University of the West Indies, 1972) page 81.

91. Henry S. Gill and Anthony P. Gonzales, Economic Consequences of a Banana Collapse in the Caribbean, Report prepared for the CARICOM Secretariat, May, 1995, page 13.
92. Henry S. Gill and Anthony P. Gonzales, Economic Consequences of a Banana Collapse in the Caribbean, Report prepared for the CARICOM Secretariat, May, 1995, page 25.
93. Henry S. Gill and Anthony P. Gonzales, Economic Consequences of a Banana Collapse in the Caribbean, Report prepared for the CARICOM Secretariat, May, 1995, page 5.
94. Owen Jefferson, The Post-War Economic Development of Jamaica (Kingston: Institute of Social and Economic Research, University of the West Indies, 1972) page 104.
95. Restructuring and the Loss of Preferences. Labour Challenges for the Caribbean Banana Industry (Geneva: International Labour Organization, January, 1999).
96. Barbara M. Welch, Survival by Association. Supply Management Landscapes of the Eastern Caribbean (Montreal: McGill-Queen's University Press, 1996) page 25.

CHAPTER 4

The EU Banana Regime

Introduction

This chapter consists of three parts. The second part outlines the European Union's preferential market arrangements for bananas exported from the Caribbean. This is preceded in the first part by an overview of the rationale and operation of preferential trade arrangements for developing countries. The final part makes the point that developed countries have traditionally provided preferential trade arrangements to the small developing economies of scale in recognition that their very small size prevents them from realizing economies of scale.

Part 1

Preferential Trade Arrangements for Developing Countries

Trade preferences have, for a long time, played an important role in the stabilization and promotion of the economic growth of developing countries and, in particular, many of the small vulnerable developing economies. Indeed, trade preferences have been so important in small developing economies (SDEs) that they are described most appropriately as preference-dependent economies. Preferential trade arrangements, provided to developing countries by developed countries, have as their objective, promoting the economic development of the beneficiary countries. These arrangements are to be distinguished from preferential trade agreements[1] (PTAs)

R. L. Bernal, *Corporate versus National Interest in US Trade Policy*, https://doi.org/10.1007/978-3-030-56950-1_4

also referred to as regional trade agreements (RTAs) which exist when a group of countries agree to give to the participating members of that group, arrangements more favorable than those extended to all countries, that is, on a multilateral basis. During the period 1948–2019, some 681 such agreements have been notified to the General Agreement on Tariffs and Trade (GATT) and WTO.[2]

Rationale and Operation

Trade preferences combined with appropriate national policies can contribute to the economic growth, export promotion, and structural adjustment of SDEs. Given their structural characteristics, the importance of preferences to these economies and their minute share of world trade, SDEs should not be deprived of the support provided by trade preferences. The cost of affording this facility to these countries has been so small that it would easily be accommodated by the developed countries providing them and, by extension, the international community. The appropriate response to the issue of preference erosion as it relates to small vulnerable developing economies is not elimination of preferences. The efficacy of trade preferences could have been further improved if accompanied by policies, which address supply rigidities and enhance international competitiveness of production and exports with the support of aid and technical assistance.

Special and differential treatment (SDT) for developing countries is a foundational principle in the GATT and the WTO. The "Decision on Differential and More Favourable Treatment, Reciprocity and Fuller Participation of Developing Countries" also referred to as the Enabling Clause, which was adopted in the GATT in 1979 and carried over into the WTO agreements, enables developed members to give differential and more favorable treatment to developing countries. It does this by allowing derogations to the most favored nation (nondiscrimination) treatment in favor of developing countries. SDT provisions mandate WTO members to implement measures applicable to developing countries to (a) allow longer time periods for implementing WTO commitments, (b) increase trading opportunities for developing countries, (c) safeguard the trade interests of developing countries, (d) help developing countries develop the capacity to implement WTO obligations and deal with disputes, and (e) implement provisions related to least developed countries.[3]

Tangible benefits from SDT have never been very generous because it has proven difficult to give precise expression to the provisions. These provisions according to Page and Kleen as "a set of general principles and a legal cover for various types of preferential treatment, as well as some very general formulations on the concessions and contributions that could be expected from developing countries in trade negotiations."[4] The provisions for granting preferences have been vague because there has always been opposition to preferences by some countries limiting what measures can garner a supporting consensus. There have been four sources of opposition to preferences; first, free trade advocates and second, developed countries. In addition, preferences for a select group of developing countries were opposed by third, other developing countries that were not beneficiaries and fourth, by those who claimed that preferences did not work for the beneficiary countries. The WTO ministerial meeting in Doha in 2001 recognized the reluctance by many to implement preferences and mandated that "all special and differential treatment provisions shall be reviewed with a view to strengthening them and making them more precise, effective, and operational."[5]

The Doha Ministerial meeting established a work program on "small economies" indicating a recognition that this was a distinct genre of developing country. The case for small developing economies to receive special and differential treatment including preferential treatment has been made.[6]

Preference Erosion: The Good, The Bad, and The Ugly

There is an unresolved debate about the impact of the erosion of trade preferences on developing countries, which has both quantitative and qualitative dimensions. The calculation of the impact of the erosion of trade preference on developing countries is an issue for quantitative empirical analysis. Such an exercise must take adequate account of the preference margins (most favored nation tariff minus preferential tariff), the importance of the exports involved for the developing country and what, if any, are the compensating benefits which offset the losses. These exercises must be based on careful estimates and realistic assumptions about elasticities of substitution between domestic and foreign goods and between foreign goods from different sources.

The qualitative issues center on the question of whether preference erosion is a loss or a gain for developing countries. In this regard, there are two schools of thought on how trade preferences affect developing countries. One view is that preference erosion would be good for developing countries while the other perspective is diametrically opposed as it regards erosion of trade preferences as harmful. These contrasting views derive from the unresolved debate about the efficacy of trade preferences. The rationale for nonreciprocal trade preferences for developing countries is that these measures promote economic growth, foreign exchange earnings, investment, and employment. This is to be achieved by (a) the provision of preferential market access by discriminatory tariff regimes, (b) guaranteed volumes of export sales by quota systems, and (c) prices above world market levels. In some instances, the thinking is similar to the infant industry argument and the arrangement is viewed as a transitional mechanism allowing the "mature" export sector to graduate. Preferences may also produce secondary benefits such as fostering export-oriented attitudes and gaining familiarity with the requirements and standards for exporting to developed countries.

Critics start from the assumption that most favored nation (MFN) liberalization is a public good for the global community and hence preferences are not desirable. They allude to the potential negative effects of trade preferences, which they argue include inefficient resource allocation and a disincentive to striving for and attaining international competitive exports. Preferences have propped up some inefficient export sectors[7] and thereby depriving other more competitive industries of resources, infrastructure, and the attention of governments.[8] Page and Hewitt have suggested that some industries would collapse without preferential access to markets in developed countries.[9]

It has been argued that preferences discourage trade liberalization and even participation in negotiations aimed at trade liberalization.[10] Ozden and Reinhardt claim that countries removed from the Generalized System of Preferences (GSP) pursue more liberal trade policies than those that continue to be eligible.[11] Freeman has even proposed that "given the marginal benefit of preferential arrangements to their development, some countries may question whether the preferential approach is of use–or whether negotiating capital should be directed toward greater global liberalization for all, discarding the use of preferences."[12]

The less than full utilization of preferential market access is not an argument for the futility of preferences but directs attention to the need for the removal of contingent protection. Non-tariff barriers such as quotas, rules of origin, standards, and sanitary and phytosanitary measures undermine utilization. These barriers are estimated to disqualify half of the least developed countries (LDC) exports, which are eligible for GSP treatment: Approximately 66–69 percent textile and apparel exports from LDC and 42 percent of exports of agricultural and fishery products.[13] Complex and restrictive rules of origin can be so burdensome that they discourage the utilization of preferences by LDC.[14] Compliance with international standards is unavoidable for exports of developing countries but compliance can be expensive amounting to 2–10 percent of production costs.[15] These facts underscore the urgency of enhancing the limited capacity of preference-dependent countries to produce and export internationally competitive products and services.

Developed countries began to feel that there were a few "advanced" developing countries that did not need preference but which were benefiting from SDT for developing countries.[16] This provided support for the type of trade economics purveyed by developed countries which increasingly turned away from preferential trade arrangements and SDT.

Impact on Small Vulnerable Developing Economies

Empirical research has affirmed that the elimination of preferences would severely affect preference-dependent economies. The Commonwealth Secretariat estimated that the annual loss of income transfers from the elimination of preferences would be $1.72 billion in agriculture and $1.32 billion in textiles and apparel.[17]

Among the preference-dependent countries, the small vulnerable developing economies are those facing the most severe economic dislocation[18] as they will have to confront the reduction in export earnings consequent on the removal/reduction of preferential market access in developed countries. The adjustment would be made more difficult by the loss of fiscal revenue as these economies reduce their tariffs. This will be compounded in net food importing countries, particularly in sub-Saharan Africa and the Caribbean, as deterioration in terms of trade will follow the reduction of agricultural subsidies. Belize, Fiji, Guyana, Mauritius, St. Kitts and Nevis, and St. Lucia would suffer export declines from 7.8 percent to 11.5 percent of exports.[19] In the case of the small developing economies of the Caribbean, almost one half of US imports from the region received preferential treatment in 2003 and over 75 percent of EU imports during 1995–1999 were covered by preferences under the Lome Convention and Cotonou Agreement.[20]

It has been suggested that small vulnerable developing economies should give up the struggle to maintain preferences and invest their scarce negotiating capital in securing greater multilateral trade liberalization. This proposition assumes that opportunities flowing from multilateral MFN trade liberalization will offset or even exceed the losses resulting from preference erosion. In theory, this sounds plausible but underestimates supply-side constraints and the uncompetitive nature of small markets both of which inhibit internationally competitive economic activity that is required to take full advantage of new trade opportunities. The stimulation of increases in productivity, in even the best managed small vulnerable developing economy, will involve capacity building in the public and private sectors where all firms are microenterprises by global standards.

Causes of Preference Erosion

The erosion of trade preference derives from three sources. (1) The dismantling of preferential trade arrangements whose compatibility with the core principles of the WTO has been challenged through the dispute settlement process. (2) The extension of preferential trade arrangements to an increasing number of developing countries. (3) The imminent erosion of the value of existing nonreciprocal trade preferences as MFN trade liberalization is deepened and accelerated by the completion and implementation of the Doha Development Agenda (DDA). It should be noted that there may be circumstances in which MFN tariff reductions do not result in economic losses for the developing country beneficiary of preferential trade arrangements, for example, if the preference margin is fixed at a percentage below the MFN tariff then reduction of the tariff would not change the preference margin.[21]

Grounds for Maintaining Preferences

All three sources of preference erosion certainly have had adverse implications for preference-dependent countries. The question, therefore, is how to address the situation of the preference-dependent countries, in particular, small vulnerable developing economies. Any remedial measures taken bilaterally by developed countries and within the multilateral trading system must be guided by the following principles.

Legitimacy

The preferences accorded to developing countries are a form of SDT, which along with MFN treatment constitute the fundamental tenets of the WTO and related agreements. The legitimacy of trade preferences is not, therefore, in question nor is there any compelling economic justification for the rapid elimination of nonreciprocal preferences. Indeed, reciprocal preferences in regional trade agreements are proliferating, indicating that they are viewed as contributing to the expansion of trade.

Vulnerability

Preferences as a form of SDT reflect the recognition of the wide differences in the level of development and size among the countries and an acknowledgement that "market mechanisms tend to reproduce and sometimes exacerbate existing inequalities."[22] SDT represents a means of promoting economic growth through the expansion of the international trade of developing countries, in particular, those vulnerable because of poverty or small size. Such provisions cannot be deleted or depreciated simply because there are countries that despite benefiting from preferential trade arrangements for some time still find themselves in the position that they cannot do without preferences in the short run. In any case, economic development and structural transformation are long-term processes and hence, it would be premature to say with certainty that preferences have been tried and failed. Indeed, if per capita income, albeit a problematic indicator of economic development is employed, then it is clear that the gap between the rich and the poor has widened. Consequently, there should be caution in the disbanding of trade preferences for the LDCs and small vulnerable developing economies.

Affordability

The cost of retaining preferential trade arrangements for small vulnerable developing economies is insignificant outside of a few commodities. This is so because the share of these economies accounts for a minute share of global trade. While it is inconsequential for world trade, it is enormously important to the affected countries. The conclusion to be derived is not that preference can and should, therefore, be abolished but rather that the multilateral trading system can afford to accommodate their continuation for some time. Indeed, the fairness of the operation of the multilateral trading system must be judged not merely by the equity of the rules but by how it treats member states that are vulnerable, whether by poverty or smallness.

Imperfect Substitutability

It has been repeatedly suggested that "developing countries could benefit more from development assistance given directly rather than by receiving trade preferences".[23] However, trade preferences and development assistance have very different effects on developing economies. Therefore, aid is not a substitute for economic activity induced by preferences. Trade preferences impact on economic growth through export production, investment, employment, and tax revenue. It involves linkages to a range of sectors whereas aid can all too easily end up in government expenditure on infrastructure, social services, and safety nets. It does not generate either improved competitiveness in existing industries or stimulate new export activity. Even if governments utilize development assistance prudently to promote productive activity there is the constraint of the limit absorptive capacity of small developing countries. Birdsall, Rodrik, and Subramanian stress the deficiencies on the recipients: "Aid is only as good as the ability of a recipient's economy and government to use it prudently and productively. Thus, the fundamental dilemma: countries most in need of aid are often those least able to use it well."[24]

In the right form, properly targeted and in adequate amounts, aid is indispensable to the restructuring and diversification, which must follow the termination and/or diminution of trade preferences. Unfortunately, aid is in many instances, a political palliative and the bureaucratic nature of the disbursement process has, in the past, resulted in smaller sums being dispensed over a longer period than originally anticipated. Bearing this experience in mind, the terms of the discussion of the future of trade preference should not be prematurely shifted to calculating the size of a compensation package. Certainly, such analysis is timely but not at the expense of resolving the prior questions of; should preferences be continued, and if so, to what extent and in what form?

Retention of Preferences

The international community has not come to recognize that the problem of the ongoing and potential escalation of preference erosion and the character and magnitude of the losses, which will be suffered as a result of reduced margins of trade preferences, must be addressed. Timely and tangible solutions are necessary to ameliorate the impact on preference-dependent economies. This has elicited little empathy among the developed countries and has remained an unresolved issue in the WTO. To its credit, the European Union has provided substantial aid to assist the Caribbean to restructure and improve the competitiveness of the banana industry.

Recalibration of Preferences[25]

One of the objectives of the WTO is to improve the trade opportunities for developing countries so as to lift their growth and stimulate sustained development. The trade liberalization inherent in the WTO is likely to reduce some preferences, therefore, there must be an exploration of the recalibration of preferential trade measures by maintaining preferences where possible, improving the operation of existing preferential arrangements, and establishing new alternative preferences.

There is still some scope for the retention and even extension of trade preferences in important developed country markets. The retention needs are to exist for a period that is sufficiently long to permit preference-dependent economies to complete structural transformation. It is even possible to create compensatory preferences, for example, additional market access in specific areas of export interest to LDCs and small vulnerable developing economies. This can create opportunities for the development of alternative exports of manufactured goods and services to replace traditional food and agricultural exports on a phased basis.

The value of preferential access to the markets of developed countries has been considerably reduced by restrictive rules of origin that require prohibitively high levels of local value-added and contingent protectionist measures (e.g., antidumping, safeguards, and countervailing duties). Some estimates calculate that only half of the developing country imports, which are eligible for GSP treatment, are actually accorded such treatment because of rules of origin and tariff quotas. The threat of contingent protectionism discourages developing country exports.

The value and extent of utilization of preference could be increased if the documentation is simplified and procedures are made less bureaucratic. Required documentation entails costs equivalent to 3–5 percent of the value of the goods involved.[26]

The effectiveness of preferences could be improved by (i) binding existing preferences in the WTO for periods of 10–20 years, (ii) ameliorating the negative impact of protectionist measures such as tariff peaks and tariff escalation, (iii) expanding tariff rate quotas (TQRs) and, (iv) reducing the conditionality associated with qualifying for preferences.

Enhancement of the GSP is one possibility for providing compensation. Preferences provided to developing countries in the multilateral trading system such as the GSP should be maintained as long as needed and should give particular attention to developing countries which are vulnerable because of their poverty or small size. The Enabling Clause should be amended to allow for a focus on the LDCs and the small vulnerable developing economies where preferences should be maintained and improved where necessary.

Restructuring Preference-Dependent Economies

The stark economic reality facing preference-dependent countries, especially the small vulnerable developing economies, has to be given more attention and the specificity of the response crafted to take account of their peculiar circumstances. The extended adjustment experience of the small vulnerable developing economies of the Caribbean region in attempting to respond to the degradation of preferential export arrangements in key products such as bananas, rum, and sugar is instructive and illustrative of the challenge. The lesson is that restructuring and diversification have to be carefully planned, adequately funded, cushioned by the provision of social safety nets, and implemented over medium-term schedules.

Trade measures and aid resources are more efficacious if they are integrated into a comprehensive strategy of structural transformation and export diversification. The process for small vulnerable developing economies must be proactive, long-term strategic global repositioning aimed at the incubation of new internationally competitive export sectors. This national effort must be complemented by appropriate international measures which together can transform economies prone to income volatility, growth fragility, and acute vulnerability reflecting extreme export concentration, lack of economies of scale, and firms that are minute by global standards. This type of wholescale remake of small vulnerable developing economies goes beyond the scope, resources, and expertise of any one multilateral institution. The time has come for a consortium of the multilateral institutions, including the WTO and the World Bank, bilateral development assistance agencies, and regional development banks to provide technical and financial support to developing countries, which are engaged in the formulation and implementation of strategic global repositioning plans.[27]

The Enhanced Integrated Framework for Trade Related Assistance (EIF) for LDCs could be formalized to strengthen coordination and harmonization of donors and ensure an integrated programmatic approach. The formalization would allow the establishment of a genuine trade policy development program, which would be a hybrid of the WTO Trade Policy Review and the structural adjustment lending of the World Bank. This would ensure that trade policy is located in the mainstream of a country's economic development strategy.

It is firms and not countries that conduct international trade. Therefore, attention must be focused on improvements in the private sector of preference-dependent countries in order to enhance their international competitiveness. Small vulnerable developing economies are aggregations of "nano-firms" (i.e. firms which are minute by global standards). They are so small that there is little possibility of attaining economies of scale or scope, are not attractive for corporate alliances or joint ventures with larger foreign firms, and amalgamation/mergers do not create institutions which obviate the disadvantages of small size.

In helping small vulnerable developing economies to adjust to preference erosion, every effort must be made to design trade measures (including SDT and preferences) and financial options that specifically take account of the characteristics and circumstances of "nano-firms"

The nature, form, and extent of assistance to be extended to private sector led processes of restructuring and corporate reorganization should be instituted ahead of the adjustment. This is possible because the extent and pace of adjustment, which would result from preference erosion will be known in advance. This would help to avoid delays in project approval as programs proceed through the extended appraisal and disbursement system of donors. Administrative arrangements to be established for the mobilization and deployment of restructuring assistance must be governed by time frames, which are consistent with the capacity of the private sector to respond to evolving market conditions.

Redimensioning Development Financing

This aid is not an alternative to trade-related responses because aid has an entirely different impact on small vulnerable developing economies. Financial aid tends to be largely public sector oriented and cannot substitute for preference supported export industries, which have a significant multiplier effect through an extensive network of linkages to other sectors and generate significant tax revenue. Financial assistance must be complementary and should be provided on concessionary terms, if not, needy countries may decide not to exercise this option as it may aggravate an already heavy external debt burden.

Development financing should be guided by:

In adjusting to the reduction of preference margins or loss of preferences, small vulnerable developing economies will need both balance of payments support and medium-term development financing for restructuring and trade capacity building. The IMF and World Bank have increased the pool of resources and strengthened their activities in support of trade adjustment and trade capacity building. The response of the IMF took the form of the introduction of the Trade Integration Mechanism (TIM) in 2004. These resources are available with the usual IMF conditionality, which might make some potential borrowers hesitant to avail themselves of this facility. The World Bank has upped its engagement in technical assistance, capacity building, institutional reform, funding trade-related infrastructure, and assistance to offset adjustment costs, such as fiscal support to assist countries to make the transition from tariffs to other sources of revenue.

It is critical that development financing facilities have adequate resources to enable countries to cope with the magnitude of the adverse impact. The quantum of financing could be gauged by estimating the cost of compensation for preference erosion. This implies additional resources to existing development assistance commitments and disbursement must be within the time frame of the implementation of commitments that emerge from the WTO. In addition, preference-dependent countries will need substantial concessionary financing, if their state is to perform the catalyst in economic reform and facilitator of private sector modernization and corporate reorganization. This is especially true for the highly indebted preference-dependent countries many of whom are small vulnerable developing countries, which are among the most highly indebted countries in the world.

Compensatory financing cannot go on indefinitely and a calculation will have to be made of how much and over what period. Funding would have to be front-loaded and reduced gradually over time. Grynberg and

Silva anticipate that preference-dependent economies would require 14–20 years to adjust to the loss of $1.7 billion annually or the total net present value of losses of between $6 billion to $13.8 billion.[28] It is unlikely that the developed countries will respond to financing needs of this magnitude but a serious effort must be made to fund and sustain a multi-year program of adjustment financing. The amount necessary to compensate the small banana exporting countries would be relatively small given the little value of their banana exports. This is a point made by an IMF study as follows: "heavily concentrated in a sub-set of products and preference beneficiaries ... Accordingly, assistance to help countries cope with preference erosion can be closely targeted at the countries at risk. Many of these are small island economies that may have serious difficulties to adjust."[29]

There is now a strong case for increased assistance in the form of a judicious blend of grants and loans to finance a variety of needs ranging from technical assistance to budget support to investment lending. Such funds must be quick disbursing, concessionary, and genuinely additional to existing aid budgets. Financing should also be focused on export-oriented investments and particular attention should be paid to the specific need to reinforce the viability of enterprises in developing countries.

Where large labor-intensive traditional export sectors have to be downsized, social and economic dislocation can be considerable and adjustment can last for many years. Social safety nets to mitigate the social costs of adjustment are indispensable while resource reallocation is taking place and workers retrained for alternative employment. These mechanisms must have adequate resources to sustain their role for periods of several years depending on the circumstances.

Part II

EU Banana Regime

British trade policy in its empire was based on certain strongly held and widely accepted tenets. First and foremost, it was intended to protect the markets of its colonies for its exports of manufactured goods and to import from the colonies raw materials and agricultural products to supply its industries. In March 1932, the Import Duties Act marked Britain's retreat from a policy of free trade to protectionism[30] signaling the decline of British dominance of the world economy.[31] Second, to provide preferential market access for a limited range of agricultural products from a few colonies. This policy was continued after these colonies became politically independent.

The Caribbean economies were dominated by production and export of primary products such as sugar, coffee, and bananas with little or no processing. Industrialization of the colonies was actively discouraged.[32] The call for industrialization became more widespread and popular in the 1930s. The 1939 political program of the People's National Party advocated "the encouragement of local industries".[33] Arthur Lewis, writing in 1939, provides a rationale in "Labour in the West Indies" and states that "the Policy which seems to offer most hope of permanent success is for these islands to follow in the footsteps of other agricultural countries in industrialization."[34] The Moyne Commission Report states: "Lacking mineral resources, it is hardly to be expected that small communities, living in considerable isolation from the outside world, and with climates and traditions that are perhaps uncongenial to regular industrial life, would have developed manufacturing industries on an important scale."[35] The Moyne Commission Report also states, "Agriculture is the main basis of the economic life of the West Indies ... It must necessarily remain so."[36] It was felt in Britain that it was natural reciprocity that the colonies should provide raw materials in exchange for the expenses of the civilizing tutelage.[37]

For the small developing economies of the English-speaking Caribbean (ESC), it was recognized that they needed preferential treatment for their agricultural exports which they were not able to produce at internationally competitive prices. Britain and Canada employed preferential price arrangements for exports of sugar and bananas from the ESC. A tradition of preferential market access for sugar began with the 1925 Canada-West Indies Agreement.[38] Canada has consistently provided financial development[39] and since 1986, trade has taken place within the framework of preferential trade arrangements in the form of the Caribbean-Canada Trade Agreement (CARIBCAN)[40] which provides one-way duty-free access to the Canadian market. Sugar entering the British market was also the beneficiary of preferential arrangements. The Commonwealth Sugar Agreement was signed in 1951 and remained in operation until 1974. Its provisions ensured secure access to the British for cane sugar at guaranteed prices with a designed allocation for each supplying Commonwealth country. To further ensure the British market for cane sugar exporting countries, the Sugar Act of 1956 limited beet sugar production in the United Kingdom.

By 1899, bananas accounted for 35 percent of total exports and by the 1930s, Jamaica was the largest producer in the world. Later, the industry was hit by the Panama disease and the cessation of exports to Britain during World War II. Indeed, during the War, the British government provided financial relief to banana growers in the ESC.[41] The Great Depression of the 1930s ignited labor[42] disturbances throughout the ESC prompting the British government to establish the Moyne Commission,[43] which conducted an investigation recommending urgent action involving trade and aid. The Report supported the continued dominance of export agriculture by grants, subsidies, and preferential treatment.[44] Preferential treatment from Britain, which dates back to 1919 and 1920 for Canada, was extended in the 1930s. In 1932, the Ottawa Agreement gave a preferential price of £2.10.0 a tonne to Jamaica bananas,[45] and the British budget funded a preference of 1s. per cwt. of sugar in 1932–1933.[46] Feuer explains that during the 1940s the United Kingdom began to fix quotas and prices for Commonwealth sugar producers. This represented another form of subsidy, insulating colonial producers from international competitive pressures. The relatively stable and assured cane prices which resulted, plus the well-organized marketing arrangements which developed, were strong incentives to both the manufacturers and, in particular, to local farmers.[47]

British policy in the Caribbean was motivated by the need for the alleviation of the most pressing aspects of the increasing poverty caused by the Great Depression, with the intention of preventing or minimizing social unrest and neutralizing anti-colonial political upheavals that emerged from "unprecedented crisis"[48] which spawned the labor disturbances in the Caribbean in the late 1930s.[49] These concerns are clearly reflected in the recommendations of the Moyne Commission which urged "large expenditure on social services and development." It suggested the establishment of a West Indian Welfare Fund to disburse £1 million per annum for a 20-year period. The areas to be financed were (a) education, (b) health, (c) social welfare, (d) housing, and (e) land settlement.[50]

The Evolution of EU Banana Regime

The Import Duties Act of 1932 had imposed a 10 percent tariff on imports, with exemptions for some foodstuffs including bananas, raw materials, and some imports from the British Empire.[51] This helped Jamaica, which was supplying 87 percent of the British market by the time of World War II.[52] In 1955, the United Kingdom obtained a waiver from the GATT to allow bananas from its colonies to be treated as UK domestic products (so-called sterling bananas). This enabled the United Kingdom to (1) raise the tariff by 300 percent in 1956 to 7.50 pounds per tonne on bananas not covered by the waiver (so-called dollar bananas) and (2) imposed a quota on said bananas of 4,000 tonnes which could only be increased if sterling bananas were in insufficient supply.

The 1960s and early 1970s were years of economic difficulty, largely due to declining prices of bananas and the fierce rivalry between the Windward Islands and Jamaica. This prompted the British government to establish the Banana Advisory Committee later the Banana Trade Advisory Committee, comprised of WINBAN, JAMCO, and the three banana importing companies, Fyffes, Geest, and Jamaica Producers. These arrangements were maintained when Britain joined the European Economic Community (EEC) in 1973. The bananas from the former colonies of Europe in Africa were covered by the Yaounde Conventions of 1963 and 1969. In 1975, when the first Lome Convention replaced the Yaounde Convention, it contained a Banana Protocol, covering producers from Africa and the Caribbean. This allowed a variety of existing national arrangements to continue to operate. In spite of internal differences, a common banana regime was agreed to by 1992 when the European Common Market (ECM) came into existence. Article 115 of the Treaty of Rome, authorized EU member states to give trade preferences to African, Caribbean, and Pacific countries. Britain sourced bananas from its former colonies in the Caribbean, and France was supplied by its overseas departments of Guadeloupe and Martinique and the African countries of the Franc Zone namely Cameroon, Ivory Coast, and Madagascar. Germany and the rest of Europe were supplied by Central American and Latin American countries.

Corporate Control of the EEC Banana Market

In 1974, the EEC banana market was dominated by US companies: United Brands, formerly UFC, controlled 40 percent of the market; Dole (Castle and Cooke) and Del Monte together controlled 15 percent of the market.[53] The other 45 percent of the market was shared by European and British companies. By the late 1980s, the European Union imported 40 percent of the world's production of bananas, 75 percent of which were produced in Latin America and Central America. Banana imports into the European Union were supplied one-third by European producers

(Martinique, Guadeloupe and the Canary Islands), one-third by British colonies and ex-colonies, and one-third by Latin and Central America.[54]

Challenges to the EU Regime

Shortly after the formation of the ECM, five Latin America banana exporting countries, Colombia, Costa Rica, Guatemala, Nicaragua, and Venezuela challenged the legitimacy of the EU regime in the GATT. This action started the longest dispute in the GATT/WTO system. It took 18 years to be resolved during which GATT panels ruled that the EU regime was inconsistent with international trade rules. Continuity of the EU regime depended on getting a waiver of the rules of GATT and later the WTO because it violated the foundational principle of nondiscrimination. An agreement was negotiated in 1994 when four of the complainants agreed to their own quotas. Guatemala, where Chiquita was the largest producer, never accepted and was excluded. The waiver was granted in the GATT on December 9, 1994, as part of the Uruguay Round and remained in force until the Lome Convention IV in 2000. The Lome Convention waiver was reaffirmed in the newly established WTO in December 1995.

The EU Banana Regime of 1993

The banana regime of 1993 was a very complex combination of tariff and quantitative restrictions which combined as a tariff rate quota together with the administration of an import licensing system. The intricate details of this system need not detain the narrative, sufficient to say that it was not regarded as GATT compatible and was challenged both in the GATT and later successfully in the WTO.

The EU Position

The EU position on its banana regime was based on (1) that it was the right of the European Union to provide whatever type of preferential arrangement it chose as long as it conformed to the Treaty of Rome, enjoyed an EU supporting mandate, and was acceptable to the GATT and then the WTO as evidenced by the granting of waivers. The pride and hubris of countries that had been the so-called "great powers" with empires spanning the world cannot be underestimated because they regarded the Americans as upstarts in spite of their invaluable role in World

Wars I and II. Furthermore, conforming to rules and decisions of multilateral institutions like the WTO was an experience they were still getting accustomed to and did not relish as it represented their diminished sovereignty. (2) The former colonial powers, notably Britain and France, which still had banana exporting colonies in the Caribbean and former colonies in Africa, felt that there was a long-standing obligation to assist these developing countries. Article 1 of the Lome Convention of 1975 states: "In respect of its banana exports to the markets of the Community, no ACP state will be placed, as regards to its traditional markets and its advantages in those markets, in any less favourable situation than in the past or present." These commitments were not strongly felt by of those with limited colonial empires (e.g., Italy, Denmark, and Germany) and even less so among the new EU member states of Eastern Europe. This was believed by some desperate elements in the Caribbean to be a sacred commitment, which must always be honored in all circumstances and forever. Some with that mindset even contemplated taking the issue to the European Court to seek a decision, making permanent the commitment to a preferential regime. This type of thinking caused a loss of sympathy for the banana exporting countries because opponents portrayed them as unwilling to help in the deliberations to salvage some kind of regime which, while less favorable, could render some amount of assistance even if only for a transitional period. Critics characterized the banana exporting countries as wanting to remain permanent dependents. (3) Like all "great powers," the European Union was a consistent advocate of adhering to the rules and decisions of multilateral institutions except when those decisions differed from their perceived interest. Such was the case when the WTO ruled in favor of dismantling the banana regime. The European Union decided to accept the WTO's rules which allowed the successful petitioners to impose tariffs on the European Union for non-compliance. Some of the complainants accused the European Union of discriminating in favor of countries which were "richer" than the Latin American and Central American exporting countries. (4) The European Union refused to be publicly intimidated by the United States when it imposed tariffs on US imports from the European Union. Instead, it retaliated with an escalation of tariffs on a range of US goods. Apart from the hubris, the European Union was seeking a negotiated settlement with the United States as it had employed to secure waivers in the past. (5) The American dominance of the EU market is something the British[55] and the French were uneasy about in both the government and the business sector. Against the background of a mild anti-Americanism[56] and elements of resentment and economic nationalism,[57] the British and French wanted to have their own supply of bananas and not be totally dependent on American supplied bananas. The British position was to not be dependent totally on bananas supplied by US corporations while the French did not want to even be partially supplied by US companies. In the 1960s, half of the banana imports to Britain was supplied by Jamaica and, of this amount, more than 75 percent were imported by Elders and Fyffes a wholly owned subsidiary of United Fruit Company. Welch observes that: "Without the intervention of the British Government, Elders and Fyffes could and, almost certainly, would have destroyed the Jamaican banana industry by importing lower-priced bananas from alternative sources, ultimately in Central America."[58] (6) Britain and France used the preferential banana regime as an aid mechanism to help maintain the economic and social viability of the small farmers of these small islands with very few alternative economic activities. Without the preferential regime, these islands could not have competed in the global market. In the 1960s, bananas produced in the Eastern Caribbean cost 50 percent more than those grown in Central America.[59]

Part of the background regarding the attachment of the European Union to the preferential arrangements was how to grapple with the long-running issue of stabilization of the export earnings of ex-colony developing countries.[60] The European Union finance scheme had a positive effect on developing countries prone to fluctuating and/or deteriorating export earnings.[61] Instability of export earnings has a debilitating effect on economic growth. The banana regime was one approach to a particular commodity, but there were other attempts to address the general issue of minimizing the impact of fluctuating commodity prices and the long-term deterioration in the terms of trade between primary products and manufactured goods. The deteriorating terms of trade for primary products was an issue to which the underdevelopment of certain parts of the world was attributed to. There is substantial literature on the negative development impact of international trade subject to the deterioration in the terms of trade, for example, by the Latin American Structuralist,[62] the Dependency School[63] and by the Marxists.[64]

Part III

Tradition of Trade Preferences for the Caribbean

Developed countries have traditionally provided preferential trade arrangements to the small developing economies of scale in recognition that their very small size prevents them from realizing economies of scale. The developed countries which have a tradition of providing trade preferences to the Caribbean include the United Kingdom, Canada, the European Union, and the United States. In the case of the United Kingdom, the trade preferences date well back into the colonial period for products in general but with commodity specific preferential arrangements for rum, sugar, and bananas which carried over into protocols to the Lome conventions when Britain joined the then ECM and continues into the Cotonou Agreement of the European Union ending with transition periods accompanying the Economic Partnership Agreement between the European Union and CARIFORUM.[65]

Preferential trade arrangements were first instituted in 1898 when Canada established a 25 percent tariff preference on a range of goods including sugar. In 1900, the tariff preference on sugar was increased to 33 1/2 percent. In 1912, the tariff preferences were extended by the signing of the Canada-West Indian Reciprocal Treaty, which was subsequently revised in 1920 and became the Canada–West Indian Trade Agreement in 1925.[66] It was amended in July 1966 when duty-free treatment was accorded to sugar on the average quantity of sugar imported in the previous five years. In 1979, a Trade and Economic Cooperation Agreement was signed and in July 1986, Caribbean-Canada Trade Agreement (CARIBCAN) promulgated by parliament. It is one-way, duty-free treatment to all imports from the designated Caribbean countries. In addition, the government of Canada has consistently furnished the Caribbean with development aid.[67]

The US government since 1982 has operated a scheme of preferences for sugar from 40 countries including those in the Caribbean. The scheme allocated quotas to countries to export sugar and were paid prices that were based on those paid to domestic producers which were much higher than what prevailed in the world market then.[68] Quotas were allocated to countries based on their export shares during 1975–81 but were later modified. In an interesting sensitivity to small producers, the US Department of Agriculture's website records: "Declines in the overall quantity of the quota have reduced imports from all suppliers with the exception of the 10 small suppliers whose allocations are limited to 7,258 metric tonnes, raw value (MTRV), a quantity considered to be equal to a minimum boatload of sugar."[69] Apart from the trade preferences for Caribbean countries, the United States implicitly recognized the need for such measures for developing countries. Established by the Trade Act of 1974, the United States operated the GSP for selected "poor" countries and a designated set of products lower tariffs than it applied to imports from all other WTO member countries. Some 119 designated beneficiary countries benefited from the GSP which expired on December 31, 2017. The rationale for the GSP as explained by USTR is that the GSP is to "provide opportunities for many of the world's poorest countries to use trade to grow their economies and climb out of poverty." Moreover, it was seen to be in the national interest because moving "GSP imports from the docks to U.S. consumers, farmers, and manufacturers supports tens of thousands of jobs in the United States. GSP also boosts American competitiveness by reducing costs of imported inputs used by U.S. companies" ... "In addition to promoting economic opportunity in developing countries, the GSP program also supports progress by beneficiary countries in affording worker rights to their people, in enforcing intellectual property rights, and in supporting the rule of law."[70]

The European Union operated a trade preference program for sugar governed by the ACP-EU Sugar Protocol and was established in 1975 under the Lomé Convention. It granted preferential access to 46 countries from Africa, the Caribbean, and the Pacific (ACP). These countries were formerly colonies. The ACP-EU Sugar Protocol provided guaranteed prices for specified quantities of imports of cane sugar, raw or white, which originated in the ACP states. The Sugar Protocol was challenged in the WTO and the European Union has had to dismantle the Protocol to come into conformity with the WTO. In recognition of the serious hardships resulting to developing countries that export sugar and their cane farmers, the European Union has provided these countries with considerable amounts of development aid over many years. Over EUR 1.2 billion has been provided to the 18 countries that traditionally supplied raw sugar to the European Union for the purposes of restructuring and/or diversification.[71] These funds allowed countries to restructure up the value chain as Mauritius has done or cease sugar as was done in Trinidad and Tobago. Similar efforts were made to assist the banana industry when the EU banana regime was changed. In contrast, the United States did not provide assistance of any kind to the Caribbean banana exporting countries.

The Banana Case in the GATT/WTO

The banana case was the longest trade dispute in the multilateral trading system starting in the GATT and continuing into the WTO. It lasted from 1992 until 2020 when the EU regime finally came into full conformity with the WTO. It sparked a trade "war" between the European Union and the United States in which both sides imposed sanctions in the form of higher tariffs and embroiled countries in Africa, the Caribbean, and Latin America. The United States was determined to prevail; first, the hegemonic power in global affairs must not lose because it reduces their dominance and encourages other countries to dare to challenge its authority. Second, the hegemonic power has to ensure that the rules which enforce an increasing liberalization of international trade are observed by all participating countries in the WTO without exception. Third, the European Union resisted having to change its banana regime in an attempt to assure its right to act in a manner befitting a "great power" which many countries had conducted their international policy for several centuries. Pride, hubris, and habit all contributed to the attitude on this issue. Fourth, many in the European Union, especially those countries which had colonial empires, genuinely felt the responsibility to continue to aid their former colonies from free trade by maintaining preferential trade arrangements. A more cynical view might be that there was lingering guilt over the effects of colonialism[72] and that was a debt requiring reparations.[73] Fifth, the European Union did not want its banana market dominated by US-owned multinational corporations. This was a long-standing sentiment dating back into the early part of the twentieth century and was a motivating factor in the creation of the banana industry in the Eastern Caribbean and the establishment of preferential arrangements for their banana exports. Sixth, Chiquita had made losses due to mistakes in corporate policy and business strategy and sought to recoup these losses through capturing the share of the EU market reserved for the ACP banana exporting countries. It succeeded in driving the US government to lead the dismantling of the EU banana regime but by then the company had gone bankrupt and was sold. Sixth, the real losers who suffered serious injury were the Caribbean islands that did not even have a chance to be full participants in the WTO process. The Caribbean countries were third party and as such were restricted to making a presentation to the first meeting but did not have the right to participate in subsequent proceedings nor access to all documentation submitted by parties to the dispute. The WTO experience was disillusioning for the small developing countries of the Caribbean.[74]

The First GATT Challenge

Bananas were traditionally imported into Europe under a variety of import regimes. Bananas going to Britain came from its colonies in the Caribbean and Africa entered under a preferential import regime involving quotas and prices above those available from Central and South America. The bananas from the Caribbean and Africa did not supply the total demand in Britain and the shortfall was supplied from Central and South America. Bananas going to France were produced in the Overseas Departments of Martinique and Guadeloupe. Spain had similar arrangements for bananas from the Canary Islands and Portugal for Madeira. Imported into Germany were supplied by Central and South America. Bananas going to the rest of Europe came from Central and South America. These separate import regimes with the resulting considerably price difference only coexisted because Article 115 of the Treaty of Rome prevents the re-export of bananas within the European Union otherwise the bananas from Latin America would have taken over the market by driving out the more expensive bananas. The reason being that yields in Panama and Guatemala are almost 5 times that of the Eastern Caribbean. This is not surprising since the average farm in the Eastern Caribbean is 0.8 hectares and in Colombia, it is 86.6 hectares.[75]

The treatment of banana imports was a very contentious issue when Britain was entering the EEC. A common regime could not be agreed and the compromise was the retention of national systems.[76] With the establishment of the European Union, a single banana import regime had to be established by 1993. The EU regime for bananas had to be compatible with the Single European Act, the Banana Protocol of the Lomé Convention and the Common Agricultural Policy. The European Union was bound by Article One of the Banana Protocol which states: "As regards its exports of bananas to the markets of the Community, no ACP state will be placed, as regards access to its traditional markets, in a less favourable situation than in the past or at present."

The proposal to be put to the EU Council of Ministers in July 1993 prompted the banana exporting countries of Colombia, Costa Rica,

Guatemala, Nicaragua, and Venezuela to challenge the proposed import regime by requesting a consultation under the GATT. A three-person panel ruled in 1993 that the regimes were not compatible with the principle of nondiscrimination.[77] By that time the single EU regime was due to be established and negotiations continued.

In March 1994 the challenge was withdrawn and Colombia, Costa Rica, Nicaragua, and Venezuela agreed to the allocation of quotas under the Banana Framework Agreement (BFA). With this agreement in place, the European Union requested a waiver from Article 1 for the Banana Protocol of the Lomé Convention (1975). The waiver was granted with effect until December 2000. In late 1994 at the behest of Chiquita, the USTR instituted a Section 301 investigation of Colombia and Costa Rica to force these countries to abandon the BFA. The request was not supported by Del Monte and Dole. If not they would face the imposition of sanctions by the United States. In January 1996 these countries succumbed and exited the BFA.[78]

The Second GATT Challenge

The complexity of the tariffs, quotas, and licensing made the establishment of a single EU banana regime a difficult technical and political issue especially since Germany was opposed to quotas. The EU Commission proposed a quota of 2 million tonnes for the importation of bananas from Latin America based on the volumes in recent years and the rest of the market was reserved for African, Caribbean, and Community producers. There was opposition to quotas both within[79] and outside the European Union and "tariffication" schemes proposed. Without the quotas, the Latin America countries and the banana companies handling the marketing would shortly drive the Caribbean, African, and Community suppliers out of the EU market.

From 1992 to 1994, Chiquita accumulated $407 million in losses and its stock price plunged from $40 to $11 a share.[80] Chiquita was not satisfied with the volume of bananas which they could supply given the allocation of licenses. The other banana marketing companies were satisfied with their allocation of licenses and making profits. Chiquita decided to dismantle the EU banana regime by challenging it in the newly established WTO by enlisting the US government and as many banana exporting countries to join the United States in the challenge. The strategy to "round up" Latin American banana exporting countries into a common front by (a) getting the exporting countries without quotas to join with the United States and (b) forcing the countries in the BFA to withdraw from the agreement.

The WTO Challenge

In the early 1990s, the FAO estimated that supply capacity of bananas exceeded import demand by 1.4–2.1 million tonnes[81] hence the fierce competition for market share in Europe. Eastern European offered the only potential growth in demand. Chiquita felt that it was at a severe disadvantage in the proposed EU system with regard to the quotas, tariffs, and the allocation of licenses among the competing banana companies.

Chiquita entered the banana dispute by approaching the US government on September 2, 1994, one month before the BFA was due to take effect with a Section 301 complaint to the Office of the USTR. The Section 301 petition filed jointly by Chiquita which had been losing money and market share in the European Union and the Hawaii Banana Industry Association requested that the United States take action against the European Union and the signatory countries to the BFA. On October 7, 1994, the USTR agreed to undertake a formal investigation of the issue of whether the European Union and the BFA were harmful to Chiquita and, therefore, impaired US commerce. To ensure that the petition was successful and that this would trigger the imposition of trade sanctions on the European Union, Chiquita had to wage a campaign to get this decision from the USTR because of the tentative nature of the claim of damage given that no bananas were produced in and exported from the United States. In a preliminary determination, the USTR found on January 9, 1995, that the EU regime did cause damage. The decision was contested by submissions accompanying a letter dated February 10, 1995, from US attorneys for the Caribbean Banana Exporter Association. The letter pointed out that the action would have no effect on the European Union but would adversely affect US economic and security interests in the Caribbean because it "would grievously injure the Caribbean banana-producing states."[82] The USTR ruling was followed by unsuccessful EU-US negotiations and on April 24, 1996, the US, Ecuador, Guatemala, Honduras, and Mexico jointly request the convening of a WTO dispute settlement panel. The panel was established on May 8, 1996. Mickey Kantor, US Trade Representative explained that the United States was exasperated with the inflexibility of the European Union.[83]

In May 1997, the WTO panel tabled its report which was confirmed by the Appellate Body on September 25, 1997. It ruled that the BFA was incompatible with the principles of nondiscriminatory and most favored nation treatment. At the arbitration hearing on December 17, 1997, the European Union committed to designing a new banana regime consistent with the tenets of the WTO "in a reasonable period of time", that is, by January 1, 1999.

Chiquita claimed that it had lost $400 million to $1 billion because of the EU banana regime[84] (in 2001, Chiquita filed for Chapter 11 protection but reemerged from bankruptcy in 2002[85]) and kept pressing the White House and USTR to take some punitive action against the European Union. In January 1999, the European Union proposed a new banana system. In April 1999, the EU regime was found to be incompatible with the WTO but the United States did not wait for this decision. The Clinton administration imposed punitive tariffs of 100 percent on $250 million worth of imports from the European Union retroactive to March 3, 1999, reduced from $520 million by the WTO.[86] According to the United States, this approximates the amount of banana trade lost by American companies because of the EU banana regime.[87] US officials explained that the method to composing the list of items was to spread the pain strategically to maximize the political pressure placed on the European Union, and they did not want to target exports that would hurt American companies. Products from Denmark and the Netherlands were excused from the tariffs because those countries have sided with the United States on the banana issue. The European Commissioner for Trade and European Commissioner for External Affairs, Sir Leon Brittan retorted that the sanctions threatened jobs in the European Union that had nothing to do with bananas.[88] In reality, the increased tariffs were on luxury goods not including wine, which might only have affected those "wondering the aisles of Balducci's"[89] but it signaled a worrying concern that the WTO at the center of managing the rules of the multilateral trading system was failing in fulfilling its designated role.

Final Banana Agreement

The European Union continued to propose a regime, the United States and Latin America banana exporting countries continue to press their case and the Caribbean continued to point to the potential damage. "What is at stake for Caribbean-banana producing countries is secure access to the European market, at remunerative prices. A threat to secure market access puts at risk the livelihoods of tens of thousands of families in the Caribbean," said Director General of the Caribbean Regional Negotiating

Machinery (RNM) Ambassador Dr. Richard Bernal.[90] In December 2009, the European Union, Brazil, Colombia, Costa Rica, Ecuador, Guatemala, Honduras, Mexico, Nicaragua, Panama, Peru, and Venezuela agreed to the "Geneva Agreement On Trade in Bananas" under which it committed to a phased reduction of its import tariff on bananas from Latin America from 176 Euros (US$239) per ton to 114 Euros (US$154) during the seven-year period ending in 2016. The ACP was granted 190 million Euros (US$258 million) in compensation by the European Union.[91] Director General of the WTO welcomed the agreement: "I welcome the news that a comprehensive agreement on bananas has now been reached. This has been one of the most technically complex, politically sensitive, and commercially meaningful legal disputes ever brought to the WTO. It has also been one of the longest-running "sagas" in the history of the post-WWII multilateral trading system."[92] The United States and the European Union on December 15, 2009, signed the Geneva Agreement on Trade in Bananas (GATB).[93] Under this agreement, the European Union undertakes not to reintroduce measures that discriminate among banana distributors based on the ownership or control of the distributors or the source of the bananas, and to maintain a nondiscriminatory, tariff-only regime for the importation of bananas.[94] Subsequently, bilateral negotiations have provided to Colombia, Costa Rica, Guatemala, Honduras, El Salvador, Nicaragua and Peru a duty of 75 Euros per tonne by 2020 through a series of incremental reductions.[95]

Summary

There has been a long, well-established tradition of developed countries providing preferential trade arrangements to developing countries as a form of development aid, preferable in some respects to the provision of aid in the form of financial transfers. It is the sovereign right of these countries to provide preferential trade arrangements to developing countries that need this form of assistance because of their developing status, small amount of production, inability to produce at internationally competitive prices, and their undiversified economic structure that made them depend on a single export product. The small, undiversified developing economies of the Caribbean had, throughout their history colonial and post-colonial, been the beneficiaries of preferential trade arrangements of either a generic ambit or commodity specific scope provided by Britain, France, and Canada. The EU banana regime was one such preferential arrangement and a particularly important one since it covered the main export of some of the very small banana exporting islands.

The core principles of the WTO most favored nation and national treatment prohibit one-way nonreciprocal trade preferences to which, all countries are not eligible. The WTO permits waivers for preferential trade agreements among groups of countries. Action by a group of Latin and Central American countries and the United States led eventually to a ruling by the WTO requiring the dismantling of the EU banana regime.

It is ironic and most noteworthy that (1) the United States was not itself a banana producing country. (2) US trade policy up to that point in time was one of preferential trade provisions to the Caribbean countries in the form of the commodity specific sugar import scheme and the trade generic CBERA. (3) Both these preferential arrangements continue to exist to the present time.

The EU preferential banana regime was a mechanism of development aid and there is nothing wrong with aid if there is a need and countries are willing to respond to that need. Indeed, it is commendable. There was a need by the small island banana exporting islands of the Caribbean. Camillo Gonsalves, Minister of Foreign Affairs of St. Vincent and the Grenadines makes the point that it makes no sense to "criticize the aid recipient but not the systems and circumstances that make aid necessary."[96] As Charles Maynard who served as a Minister of Government of Dominica put it well when he said: "small countries have a right to exist, and free trade per se should not be allowed to wipe us out."[97]

Notes

1. Nuno Limão, Preferential Trade Agreements Working Paper 22138 (Washington DC: National Bureau of Economic Research, March, 2016), Jean-Pierre Chauffour and Jean-Christophe Maur, Preferential Trade Agreement Policies for Development: A Handbook (Washington DC: World Bank, 2011), World Trade Report 2011: The WTO and preferential trade agreements: From co-existence to coherence (Geneva: World Trade Organization, 2011) and Jagdish N. Bhagwati and Arvind Panagariya, The Economics of Preferential Trade Agreements (Washington DC: American Enterprise Institute, 1996).
2. WTO | Regional trade agreements and preferential trade arrangements. https://www.wto.org/english/tratop_e/region_e/rta_pta_e.htm. Accessed 1 June 2019.

3. Development—Special and differential treatment provisions—WTO. https://www.wto.org. Accessed 1 September, 2019.
4. Sheila Page and Peter Kleen, Special and Differential Treatment of Developing Countries in the World Trade Organization, Global Development Studies No. 2, EGDI Secretariat (Ministry for Foreign Affairs, Sweden, 2005) page xiii.
5. The Doha Round Texts and related documents (Geneva: World Trade Organization, 2009) paragraph 44.
6. Richard L. Bernal, "Special and Differential Treatment for Small Developing Economies" in Roman Grynberg (ed.), WTO at the Margins. Small States and the Multilateral Trading System (Cambridge: Cambridge University Press, 2006) pages 309–355, Richard L. Bernal, Integration of Small Economies in the Free Trade Area of the Americas, CSIS, Policy Paper on the Americas, Vol. IX, Study No.1. (Washington, DC: Center for Strategic and International Studies, February 2, 1998) and Richard L. Bernal, "Small Developing Economies in the World Trade Organization" in Merlinda D. Ingco (ed.), Agriculture, Trade, and the WTO (Washington DC: World Bank, 2003) pages 108–122.
7. Bernard Hoekman and Susan Prowse, Economic Policy Responses to Preference Erosion: From Trade as Aid to Aid for Trade World Bank Research Policy Paper 2721 Washington DC: World Bank, August, 2003) pages 4–31.
8. Caribbean sugar producers that export under preferential trade arrangements with the United States and the European Union have production costs which in some cases are twice and triple that of the world's leading free market exporters. See A Time to Choose. Caribbean Development in the 21st Century (Washington DC: World Bank, April 2005) page 83.
9. Sheila Page and A. Hewitt, "The New European Trade Preferences: Does 'Everything But Arms' (EBA) Help the Poor", Development Policy Review, Vol. 20, No.1 (2002) pages 91–102.
10. Anna Krueger, Trade Policies for Developing Countries (Washington DC: Brookings Institution, 1995), Caglar Ozden and Eric Reinhardt, The Perversity of Preferences: Generalized System of Preferences and Developing Country Policies, 1976–2000, World Bank Policy Research Working Paper No. 2955 (Washington DC: World Bank, January 2003) and Arvind Panagariya, "EU Preferential Trade Arrangements and Developing Countries", World Economy, Vol. 25, No. 10 (2002) pages 1415–32.
11. Caglar Ozden and Eric Reinhardt, The Perversity of Preferences: Generalized System of Preferences and Developing Country Policies, 1976–2000, World Bank Policy Research Working Paper No. 2955 (Washington DC: World Bank, January 2003).

12. Helen Freeman, "Special Trade Arrangements to Improve Market Access" in Merlinda D. Ingco and John D. Nash (eds.), Agriculture and the WTO. Creating a Trading System for Development (Washington DC: World Bank, 2004) page 312.
13. Escaping the Poverty Trap. The Least Developed Countries Report 2002 (Geneva: United Nations Conference on Trade and Development, 2002).
14. Stefano Inama, Trade Preferences for LDCs: An Early Assessment of Benefits and Possible Improvements (Geneva; UNCTAD, 2003) and Helen Freeman, "Special Trade Arrangements to Improve Market Access" in Merlinda D. Ingco and John D. Nash (eds.), Agriculture and the WTO. Creating a Trading System for Development (Washington DC: World Bank, 2004) page 310.
15. Barbara Kotschwar, Gary Hufbauer and Wilson, Trade Policy, Standards and Development in Central America, World Bank Research Paper 2576 (Washington DC: World Bank, 2001).
16. Constantine Michaelopoulos, Th Role of Special and Differential Treatment for Developing Countries in the GATT and World Trade Organization, World Bank Policy Research Working Paper No. 2388 (Washington, DC: World Bank.2003) pages 9–10.
17. Roman Grynberg and Sacha Silva, Preference-Dependent Economies and Multilateral Liberalization: Impacts and Options (London: Commonwealth Secretariat, October, 2004).
18. Luca Monge-Roffarello, Michael Swidinsky and David Vanzetti, "Small Island Developing States and Agricultural Trade Liberalization: in Lino Briguglio and Gordn Cordina (eds.), Competitiveness Strategies for Small States (Islands and Small States Institute of the University of Malta and the Commonwealth Secretariat, 2004) pages 307–337.
19. Katerina Alexandraki and Hans Peter Lankes, The Impact of Preference Erosion on Middle-Income Developing Countries, IMF Working Paper WP/04/169 (Washington DC: International Monetary Fund, September, 2004).
20. A Time to Choose. Caribbean Development in the 21st Century (Washington DC: World Bank, April, 2005) page 78.
21. See section 8 of Stefan Tangermann, The Future of Preferential Trade Arrangements for Developing Countries and the Current Round of WTO Negotiations on Agriculture (Rome: Food and Agriculture Organization of the United Nations, 2002).
22. Jose Antonio Ocampo and Juan Martin (eds.), Globalization and Development. A Latin American and Caribbean Perspective (Palo Alto: Stanford University Press/Washington DC: World Bank, 2003) page 112.

23. Preferential Trade and Developing Countries. Bad Aid, Bad Trade. Prepared for the Cairns Group Farm Leaders meeting, Uruguay, 2001, page x.
24. Nancy Birdsall, Dani Rodrik and Arvind Subramanian, "How to Help the Poor Countries', Foreign Affairs, Vol. 85, No. 4 (July/August, 2005) page 143.
25. Richard L. Bernal, "Special and Differential Treatment for Small Developing Economies" in Roman Grynberg (ed.), WTO at the Margins. Small States and the Multilateral Trading System (Cambridge: Cambridge University Press, 2006) pages 309–355.
26. This range is derived from estimates by Paul Brenton and Miriam Manchin, "Making EU Trade Agreements Work: The Role of Rules of Origin", The World Economy, Vol. 26, Issue 5 (May, 2003) pages 755–769 and Paul Brenton and T. Ikezuki, "The Impact of Agricultural Trade Preferences with Particular Attention to Least Developed Countries" in Atamon Aksoy and John Beghin (eds.), Global Agricultural Trade and the Developing Countries (Washington DC: World Bank, 2004) pages 55–74.
27. Richard L. Bernal, "Globalization and Small Developing Countries: The Imperative for Repositioning" in Denis Benn and Kenneth Hall (eds.), Globalization: A Calculus of Inequality (Kingston: Ian Randle Publishers, 2000) pages 88–128.
28. Roman Grynberg and Sacha Silva, Preference-Dependent Economies and Multilateral Liberalization: Impacts and Options (London: Commonwealth Secretariat, October, 2004).
29. Katerina Alexandraki and Hans Peter Lankes, The Impact of Preference Erosion on Middle-Income Developing Countries, IMF Working Paper WP/04/169 (Washington DC: International Monetary Fund, September, 2004) page 27.
30. Tim Rooth, British protectionism and the international economy: overseas commercial policy in the 1930s Cambridge: Cambridge University Press, 1992) Chapter 3.
31. Robert J. Skidelsky, "Retreat from leadership: the evolution of British foreign economic policy, 1870–1939" in Benjamin M. Rowland (ed.), Balance of Power or Hegemony? The Interwar Monetary System (New York: New York University Press, 1976).
32. Richard L. Bernal, "The Great Depression, Colonial Policy and Industrialization in Jamaica," Social and Economic Studies, Vol. 37, Nos. 1 and 2 (March–June, 1988) pages 33–64.
33. Stacey H., Widdicombe Jr., The Performance of Industrial Development Corporations: The Case of Jamaica (New York: Praeger, 1972) page 38.
34. W. Arthur Lewis. "The Industrial Development of Puerto Rico", Caribbean Economic Review, Vol. 1 Nos. 1 & 2 (1949) in Patrick A. M. Emmanuel

(ed.), Sir William Arthur Lewis, collected Papers 1941–1988, Vol I, pages 793–823.
35. The Report of the West India Royal Commission. The Moyne Report (Kingston: Ian Randle Publishers, 2012) page 14.
36. The Report of the West India Royal Commission. The Moyne Report (Kingston: Ian Randle Publishers, 2012) page 17.
37. David Meredith, "The British Government and Colonial Economic Policy, 1919–39", The Economic History Review, Vol. 28, Issue 3 (August, 1975) pages 484–499. See page 485.
38. K. Levitt and A. McIntyre, Canada-West Indies Economic Relations (Montreal: Centre for Developing Area Studies, McGill University, 1967).
39. Richard L. Bernal and Winsome Leslie, "Canadian Economic Assistance to CARICOM Countries: Assessment and Future Prospects" in Jerry Haar and Anthony Bryan (eds.) Canadian-Caribbean Relations in Transition: Trade, Sustainable Development and Security (London: Macmillan and New York: St. Martin's Press, 1999) pages 190–209.
40. Sahadeo Basdeo, "CARIBCAN: a continuum in Canada-Caricom economic relations", Caribbean Studies, Vol. 25, Nos. 3–4 (1992) pages 189–219 and Basdeo Sahadeo, "CARIBCAN: A Continuum in Canada-Commonwealth Caribbean Economic Relations", Canadian Foreign Policy, Vol.1, No. 2 (1993) pages 55–79.
41. Gordon Myers, Banana Wars. The Price of Free Trade. A Caribbean Perspective (London: Zed Books, 2004) page 16.
42. These labour disturbances had profound political repercussions see Richard Hart, Towards Decolonisation. Political, labour and economic development in Jamaica, 193–1945 (Kingston: Canoe Press University of the West Indies, 1999), O Nigel Bolland, On the March: Labour Rebellions in the British Caribbean 1934–39 (Kingston: Ian Randle Publishers, 1995), Colin A. Palmer, Freedom's Children: The 1938 Labor Rebellion and the Birth of Modern Jamaica (Chapel Hill: University of North Carolina Press, 2014) and Adrian Fraser, The 1935 Riots in St. Vincent: From Riots to Adult Suffrage (Kingston: University of the West Indies Press, 2016).
43. The Report of the West India Royal Commission. The Moyne Report (Kingston: Ian Randle Publishers, 2012).
44. Report of the Sugar Industry Commission 1944–1945 (Kingston: Jamaica Sugar Industry Commissions, 1945) page 9.
45. Ken Post, Arise Ye Starvelings (Hague: Martinus Nijhoff, 1978) page 87.
46. Ken Post, Arise Ye Starvelings (Hague: Martinus Nijhoff, 1978) page 89.
47. Carl Feuer, "Better Must Come: Sugar and Jamaica in the 20th Century", Social and Economic Studies, Vol. 33, No. 4 (December, 1984) page 8.
48. Franklin Knight, "The Caribbean of the 1930s" pages 42–81 in Bridget Brereton (ed.), General History of the Caribbean. Vol. 5.The Caribbean in

the Twentieth Century (Paris: UNESCO Publishing and London: Macmillan Publishers, 2004) page 69.

49. W. Arthur Lewis, Labour in the West Indies—The Birth of a Workers' Movement (London: New Beacon, 1977; original edition Fabian Society, 1939), Ken Post, Arise Ye Starvelings (Hague: Martinus Nijhoff, 1978), O. Nigel Bolland, On the March: Labour Rebellions in the British Caribbean 1934–39 (Kingston, Ian Randle Publishers, 1995) Richard Hart, Labour Rebellions of the 1930s in the British Caribbean Region Colonies (Socialist History Society, 2002) and Adrian Fraser, The 1935 Riots in St Vincent From Riots to Adult Suffrage (Kingston: University of the West Indies Press, 2016).
50. E.R. Wicker "Colonial Development and Welfare, 1929–1957: The Evolution of a Policy", Social and Economic Studies, Vol. 7, No. 4 (December, 1958) pages 180–81.
51. Tatsumi Inoue, "The British Import Duties Act of 1932 and the Ottawa Preferential Agreements", The Journal of Political Economy and Economic History, Vol. 53, Issue 1 (2010) pages 16–29.
52. Gordon Myers, Banana Wars. The Price of Free Trade. A Caribbean Perspective (London: Zed Books, 2004) page 15.
53. Peter Clegg, The Caribbean Banana Trade. From Colonialism to Globalization (New York: Palgrave Macmillan, 2002) page 111.
54. Jaime de Melo, Bananas, the GATT, the WTO and US and EU Domestic Politics Fondation pour les Etudes et Recherches sur le Development International, Working Paper No. 45 (December, 2012) page 4.
55. Peter Davies, Fyffes and the Banana: Musa Sapientum-A Century of History 1888–1988 (London: Athlone Press, 1990).
56. Andrei S. Markovits, Uncouth Nation: Why Europe Dislikes America (Princeton: Princeton University Press, 2007).
57. Jean-Jacques Servan-Schreiber, The American Challenge (Harmondsworth: Penguin, 1969) and Herbert J. Spiro, "Anti-Americanism: Origins and Context", The Annals of the American Academy of Political and Social Science, Vol. 497, (May, 1988) pages 120–132.
58. Barbara M. Welch, Survival by Association. Supply Management Landscapes of the Eastern Caribbean (Montreal: McGill-Queen's University Press, 1996) page 25.
59. Barbara M. Welch, Survival by Association. Supply Management Landscapes of the Eastern Caribbean (Montreal: McGill-Queen's University Press, 1996) page 23.
60. Bishnodat Persaud, "Export Earnings Stabilization in the ACP/EEC Convention" in Frank Long (ed.), The Political Economy of EEC Relations with African, Caribbean and Pacific States. Contributions to the

Understanding of the Lome Convention on North-South Relations (Oxford: Pergamon Press, 1980) pages 91–106.

61. Francesco Aiello, "The stabilisation of LDCs' export earnings. The impact of the EU STABEX programme", International Review of Applied Economics, Vol.13, No. 1, (1999) pages 1–14.
62. Raul Prebisch, The Economic Development of Latin America and Its Principal Problems (New York: United Nations Economic Commission for Latin America, 1950); "Commercial Policy in the Underdeveloped Countries," American Economic Review 49, no. 2 (May 1959): 251–273 and Celso Furtado, Development and Underdevelopment (Berkeley: University of California, 1974).
63. Fernando Henrique Cardoso and Enzo Faletto, Dependence and Development in Latin America (Berkley: University of California, 1979), F. H. Cardoso, "Dependency and development in Latin America", New-Left Review, No. 74 (July-August, 1972) pages 83–90, T. Dos Santos, "The Structure of Dependence", American Economic Review, vol. 60, No. 2 (1970) pages 231–36 Osvaldo Sunkel, "The Centre-Periphery Model", Social and Economic Studies, Vol. 22, No. 1 (March, 1973) pages 132–176 and Osvaldo Sunkel, "National development policy and external dependence in Latin America", Journal of development Studies, Vol. 6, Issue 1 (1969) pages 23–48.
64. Arghiri Emmanuel, Unequal Exchange. A Study of the Imperialism of Trade (New York: Monthly Review Press, 1972), Samir Amin, Accumulation on a world scale (New York: Monthly Review Press, 1973) and Samir Amin, Imperialism and Unequal development (New York: Monthly Review Press, 1996).
65. Richard L. Bernal, Globalization, Trade and Economic Development. A Study of the CARIFORUM-EU Economic Partnership Agreement (New York: Palgrave Macmillan, 2013).
66 H. R. Brewster and C.Y. Thomas, "Trade Between the West Indies and Canada: The Development, Structure and Terms of West Indian Trade with Canada" in Kari Levitt and Alister McIntyre, Canada-West Indian Economic Relations (Montreal: Centre for Developing Area Studies, McGill University, 1967) pages 14–61.
67. Richard L. Bernal and Winsome Leslie, "Canadian Economic Assistance to CARICOM Countries: Assessment and Future Prospects" in Jerry Haar and Anthony Bryan (eds.) Canadian-Caribbean Relations in Transition: Trade, Sustainable Development and Security (London: Macmillan and New York: St. Martin's Press, 1999) pages 190–209.
68. Donald Mitchell, Sugar in the Caribbean: Adjusting to Eroding Preferences, Policy Research Working Paper 3802, (Washington DC: World Bank, December 2005) page 5.

69. https://www.fas.usda.gov/programs/sugar-import-program. Sugar Import Program | USDA Foreign Agricultural Service. Accessed 6 February 2020.
70. Generalized System of Preferences (GSP) | United States. https://ustr.gov/issue-areas/trade-development/preference-programs/generalized-system-preference-gsp. Accessed 14 February 2020.
71. ec.europa.eu › sites › agriculture › files › sugar › doc › sugar-faq_en. Frequently Asked Questions "The abolition of EU sugar ... Oct 1, 2016". Accessed 7 February 2020.
72. Walter Rodney, How Europe Underdeveloped Africa, Eric Williams, Capitalism and Slavery (Chapel Hill: University of North Carolina Press, 2014).
73. Hilar McD Beckles, Britain's Black Debt: Reparations for Caribbean Slavery and Native Genocide (Kingston: University of the West Indies Press, 2013).
74. Dr. Richard Bernal ambassador of Jamaica to the U.S. remarked: "Support for continued membership by Caribbean countries in the World Trade Organization is eroding because of the WTO ruling....Caribbean countries generally have been favourably disposed toward multilateral institutions...They saw these institutions as a protective shield....but nowadays sentiment is changing following the WTO ruling". Michelle Williams, "Caribbean Shiprider Agreements Sunk by Banana Trade War", University of Miami Inter-American Law Review, Vol. 31, No.1 (Spring, 2000) pages 163–195. See footnote 16, page 166.
75. FAO, World Banana Economy, 1970–84 (Rome: Food and Agriculture Organization, 1985).
76. The politics of the process is discussed in discussed in detail in Peter Clegg, The Caribbean Banana Trade. From Colonialism to Globalization (London: Palgrave Macmillan, 2002) pages 100–118.
77. For more detail see Gordon Myers, Banana Wars. The Price of Free Trade. A Caribbean Perspective (London: Zed Books, 2004) pages 66–67.
78. "U.S. Will Not Impose Sanctions On Costa Rican, Colombian Bananas", Latin America Data Base, News and Educational Services, 25 January, 1996, page 1.
79. In internal E.U. politics is well discussed in Gordon Myers, Banana Wars. The Price of Free Trade. A Caribbean Perspective (London: Zed Books, 2004).
80. Main Causes of the Banana War. www.soc.duke.edu. Accessed 27 March 2020.
81. Intergovernmental Group on Bananas CCP; BA 1991/7 (Rome: Food and Agriculture Organization, 1991).

82. Letter to Irving A. Williamson, Deputy General Counsel, USTR from Raymond S. Calamarro, C. Christopher Parlin and David S. Christy of Wintrop, Stimson, Putnam & Roberts, February 10, 1995.
83. "Banana Dispute Heats Up", Latin America Data Base, News and Educational Services, November 2, 1995, page 2.
84. "World Trade Organization sides with Chiquita Brands International versus European Union trade preferences", U.S. News and World Report, May 12, 1997 and Thomas K. Grose, "Two Sides of the Banana Split. Fyffes: Looking for Stability", USA Today, March 3, 1999 page 3B.
85. Marcelo Bucheli, "Banana War Maneuvers", Harvard Business Review, Vol. 83, No. 11 (November, 2005) pages 22–24.
86. Robert Evans, "WTO approves US sanctions", Journal of Commerce, April 20, 1999, page 3A.
87. Edmund Andrews, "What Bananas? Tariff Fight Baffles Europe." New York Times, March 5, 1999.
88. David E. Sanger, "U.S.-Europe Trade War Looms Over Bananas", New York Times, December 22, 1998.
89. David E. Sanger, "U.S.-Europe Trade War Looms Over Bananas", New York Times, December 22, 1998.
90. WTO Banana Ruling Devastating Blow To Vulnerable Caribbean Economies, Caribbean Community (CARICOM) Press Release Ref #: 12/200504 August 2005.
91. Lamy hails accord ending long running banana dispute. Press/591 15 December 2009. WTO: 2009 Press Releases.
92. Lamy hails accord ending long running banana dispute. Press/591 15 December 2009. WTO: 2009 Press Releases.
93. The Geneva Agreement on Trade in Bananas (GATB) is reproduced in and explained in Eckart Guth, "The End of the Bananas Saga", Journal of World Trade, Vol. 46, No. 1 (2012) pages 1–32.
94. U.S., EU Sign Agreement Designed to Settle Bananas Dispute …geneva. usmission.gov › 2010/06/08 › u s eu-sign-agreement-bananas. Jun 8, 2010.
95. "Bananas: Geneva Agreement Signed; Bilaterals Cut Tariffs Further", Bridges, Vol. 14, No. 20, 2 June, 2010.
96. Camillo M. Gonsalves, Globalized. Climatised. Stigmatised (Kingstown: Strategy Forum Inc., 2019) page 44.
97. "Dominica: Much ado about bananas", The Courier, N°140 (July–Aug 1993).

CHAPTER 5

Chiquita and Its Influence on US Trade Policy

Introduction

Chiquita was the final stage in the long corporate evolution of a company dating back to the 1980s and reaching its zenith as the United Fruit Company (UFC). In collaboration with the US government, UFC exercised near omnipotence in Central America in the first half of the twentieth century. Chiquita, in the period of the dispute with the European Union over its banana regime, acquired political influence largely through its substantial financial contributions to both the Republican and Democratic Parties. Chiquita was relentless in the execution of its strategy and prevailed in getting the EU banana regime dismantled but this was not enough to salvage the company from losses due to faulty marketing and production strategies.

Evolution

In 1877 an American, Minor C. Keith, began planting bananas as a cheap source of food for workers engaged in the construction of a railroad in Costa Rica. In 1882, the government defaulted on its debt and settled by granting a 99-year lease of the railroad and ceded 800,000 acres of land. Over time, Keith achieved dominance in the banana trade in Central America and along the Caribbean coast of Colombia. In 1870, Captain Lorenzo Baker established Boston Fruit Company sourcing bananas from Jamaica. In 1899, Keith's Tropical Trading and Transport Company

R. L. Bernal, *Corporate versus National Interest in US Trade Policy*, https://doi.org/10.1007/978-3-030-56950-1_5

merged with Baker's Boston Fruit Company to establish United Fruit Company.

In 1968, Eli M. Black bought a controlling interest in UFC, and later in 1970 Black merged the UFC with his company, AMK creating the United Brands Company. The financial health of UFC turned out to be less robust than anticipated by the new owner. This situation was compounded by some poor management decisions which led to an unsustainable build-up of debt. Hurricane Fifi damaged production in Central America in 1974, and this together with difficulties in Morrell Meat Co., an associated meatpacking business,[1] made a bad situation worse. Tragedy occurred on February 3, 1975, when Black committed suicide by jumping out of his office on the 44th floor of the Pan Am Building in New York City.[2] Subsequently, in 1975 the Securities and Exchange Commission discovered that United Brands had paid a bribe of $1.25 million to President Oswaldo López Arellano of Honduras to secure a reduction of taxes on banana exports. Chiquita International was formed in 1984 when United Brands was bought by the American Financial Group owned by Carl Lindner, Jr. United Brands was renamed Chiquita International and its headquarters was transferred to Cincinnati in 1985.

State-Corporate Nexus

Without engaging in a semantic discussion of whether it was colonialism, neocolonialism, informal empire, or imperialism, the fact is that US policy in Central America in the first half of the twentieth century was one of domination. This policy had two main characteristics, first, the willingness of the United States to use their military and naval forces to subdue and compel compliance by the governments in the region[3] and the close nexus between the US government and US companies. The American entrepreneurs in addition to the active involvement of the US armed forces employed mercenaries and soldiers of fortune. Langley and Schoonover explain the connection this way: "In Central America the United States fashioned an informal empire, using its considerable military power directly and, at times, relying indirectly on the growing influence of entrepreneurs and mercenaries … Zemurray, Christmas, and other banana men were essential to this process."[4] For executives of UFC, the economic mission of the state and their company were one and the same. An executive of UFC saw US foreign policy towards Latin America in the New Deal era as "We (U.S.) have a larger reservoir of unemployed capital and every dictate of self-interest, national policy and good neighborliness indicates this sphere (Latin America) in which to put idle dollars to work."[5]

Chiquita and its corporate forebears have long practiced the art of influencing the US government to act in their corporate interests as well as wielding its own considerable influence. Writing in 1935, Kepner and Soothill had this to say. "Whether mutual assistance is rendered by the United States and the United Fruit Company to each other in attaining their respective political and economic ends is of minor importance in comparison to the great fruit company's to attain its own economic ends through its own economic and political strength."[6]

Monopolizing the Banana Business

United Fruit Company attained an 80–90 percent share of the US banana market and 77 percent of the world market in the first decade of the twentieth century[7] through takeovers achieved by purchasing a majority interest in other companies in the banana business, of which there were as many as 114 banana trading companies in the last quarter of the nineteenth century.[8] The dominance of UFC was such that the US government called for it to reduce its market share, which it did by selling a subsidiary company in Guatemala to West Indies Fruit Company, a wholly owned subsidiary of Del Monte.[9] United Fruit Company's business strategy of seeking dominance approaching monopoly was not confined to the marketing end of the banana business but was applied to the production side of the business. The company held enormous amounts of land not only to increase supply but to deprive other actual and potential producers[10] and limited farming so as to ensure adequate supplies of labor. At one time, the UFC owned 1.6 million acres of land.[11] At times, as much as 50 percent of the lands were not in banana cultivation. It was the unused lands in Guatemala that Arbenz sort to redistribute for land reform by the 1952 promulgation of Decree 100. Almost a quarter million acres was transferred to 100,000 families.[12]

The UFC began aggressively and ruthlessly, some would say with economic justification, to acquire land for banana growing, and by 1930 it is estimated to have controlled 3.5 million acres of land in Central America and the Caribbean. The company has a long and thoroughly disgraceful history of oppression of workers and political interference while introducing infrastructure and some modernization. According to numerous sources, the conduct ranged from shooting workers, to bribing political leaders, to engineering coups.[13] The conduct in the first half of the twentieth century has been described as "corporate colonialism".[14] By the mid-twentieth century, local political conditions began to change in ways that required UFC to change its previously unchecked conduct.[15] The corporate conduct of its successor Chiquita seemed to have continued aspects of its traditions into the period of the banana dispute. In 1998, after a year-long investigation, the Cincinnati Enquirer concluded that "Chiquita Brands International Inc., the world's largest banana company, is engaged in a range of questionable business practices."[16]

United Fruit Company was ruthless in eliminating competition by companies and producing countries and was particularly vicious to governments that interfered in any way with the freedom to operate. Some of the business practices were not peculiar to Central America and Colombia but were the practices of that era. How the UFC operated was also a consequence of the political environment in which it operated as certain kinds of conduct which were unconstrained in Central America would not have been tolerated by the British government in its colonies. The difference was demonstrated by the experience in Jamaica, which was a more developed democracy and still a British colony. Differences between the workers and UFC were settled by negotiations between Zemurray and Norman Manley, a leading attorney and political leader.[17] This was a remarkable event because Zemurray's repertoire of business techniques did not include negotiations.[18] Described by his biographer Rich Cohen as emblematic of the "Ugly American" and "corporate pirate" who "could change the course of history with a phone call."[19]

Corrupt Practices

United Brands (formerly United Fruit Company), the immediate corporate forerunner of Chiquita was engaged in corrupt practices, specifically bribing government officials in Honduras. This incident is cited here because Chiquita was accused of bribing government officials in an exposé in the Cincinnati Enquirer. In 1974, Colombia, Costa Rica, Ecuador, Guatemala, Honduras, Nicaragua, and Panama established the Union of Banana Exporting Countries (UBEC),[20] a cartel of banana-exporting countries. The objective of the UBEC was to influence the returns from banana exports to the United States. At the time, the US market was controlled by three American companies, United Brands, Standard Fruit, and Del Monte. The UBEC proposed a tax of one US dollar per box. The

Government of Honduras in 1974 passed a law to increase the tax on banana exports from 25 cents per 40-pound box to 50 cents. In response to threats from the companies, Ecuador declined to impose the tax and Costa Rica withdrew its proposed tax increase. In response, United Brands paid Oswaldo López Arellano, President of Honduras a bribe of US$2.5 million and the tax increase was rescinded.[21]

The Securities and Exchange Commission (SEC) investigated and found evidence of the bribe[22] and that United Brands had also bribed Italian officials. The discovery was followed by the suicide of the president of United Brands, the collapse of the UBEC, removal of the president of Honduras by a military coup, and the passage of the Foreign Corrupt Practices Act of 1977. United Brands through their law firm tried to unsuccessfully convince the State Department to prevent disclosure of the bribe on the basis that such information if made public would harm the company and relations between the United States and Honduras.[23]

Playing Hardball with Critics

Illustrative of the type of conduct, Lindner and Chiquita were capable of and were prepared to execute was how it responded to an eighteen-page exposé of Chiquita's operations in the Cincinnati Enquirer on May 3, 1998, entitled "Chiquita Secrets Revealed", which was written by Michael Gallagher and Cameron McWhirter after a year-long investigation. The report boldly made allegations that Chiquita prevented workers from being unionized,[24] that its ships had been found with drugs on board,[25] that it bribed foreign government officials,[26] exposed workers to dangerous pesticides banned in the United States,[27] and that it had paid protection money to terrorist groups in contravention of US laws among other unethical practices. It also accused Lindner of using his political contributions to "buy" influence in trade policy.[28]

Chiquita denied all the allegations and sued after it was revealed that Gallagher had repeatedly hacked into Chiquita's voice-mail system. A Wikipedia item on Chiquita reports the following. "On 28 June 1998, the Enquirer retracted the entire series of stories and published a front-page apology saying it had" become convinced that [the published] accusations and conclusions are untrue and created a false and misleading impression of Chiquita's business practices. "The Enquirer also agreed to pay a multi-million-dollar settlement. The exact amount was not disclosed, but Chiquita's annual report mentions" a cash settlement in excess of $10 million". Gallagher was fired and prosecuted and the paper's editor, Lawrence K. Beaupre, was transferred to the Gannett's headquarters amid allegations that he ignored the paper's usual procedures on fact-checking.[29] According to Koeppel, the Enquirer agreed "to never write about Lindner or any of his businesses again."[30] It is most important to note that the authenticity of the information was not proved or disproved but the Enquirer had to back down because of how the information was acquired. Furthermore, the veracity of the allegations about paying terrorist groups was proven by the Department of Justice in March 2007 which revealed that Chiquita had paid US$1.7 million to the United Self-Defence Forces in Colombia.[31]

Lindner's Political Influence

The owner of Chiquita, Carl Lindner was a large financial contributor to the Republican Party but the presidency was held by Bill Clinton, a Democrat who was campaigning for a second term. In this context, Lindner started to increase contributions to the Democratic Party once the administration decided to challenge the EU banana regime in the WTO. It is reported that the donations were made in a disguised disaggregated manner. Funds were not given to the Democratic National Committee but a series of state-level campaigns. Michael Weisskopf explains that: "he gave the Democratic National Committee only $15,000 in the final 15 months of the campaign. Instead, D.N.C. officials instructed Lindner to give directly to state-party coffers, which are subject to far less public scrutiny than federal-election accounts. On April 12, 1996, the day after Kantor asked the WTO to examine Chiquita's grievance, Lindner and his top executives began funneling more than $500,000 to about two dozen states from Florida to California, campaign officials."[32] As many as 53 members of Congress benefited from financial contributions to their campaigns from Lindner.[33] According to a report by Cox News Service, "Lindner and at least nine other members of his family exceeded the legal limit on contributions to congressional candidates."[34] Several sources have linked the donation of $500,000 directly to meetings with the Clinton administration.[35]

Chiquita did not rely only on financial donations, Lindner was personally involved in the lobbying campaign. He was frequently in the presence of Senate majority leader Bob Dole, President Clinton, and Mickey Kantor. He had coffee with Vice President Gore, he attended events at the

White House, and even spent a night in the Lincoln bedroom.[36] An editorial in the respected Washington Post was incredulous that: "As a favour to this generous man (Lindner), Mr. Lott (Senate majority leader) is now weighing whether to give his firm a veto over the position the administration can take in its banana dispute with Europe. It would in effect put Mr. Lindner, a private citizen, on an equal-footing with the president."[37]

Congressional Tactics

Those in Congress who supported Chiquita's claim that the European Union was not making a genuine effort and that by delaying the reform to its banana regime to bring it into conformity with the ruling of the WTO sought to introduce legislation to keep in place US duties on EU goods until the European Union complied with the WTO requirements. Led by Newt Gingrich, Senator Lott, and Congressmen Archer and Crane attempted to introduce legislation in October 1998 that would mandate US sanctions on the European Union until the United States was satisfied that the European Union had complied. The legislation was introduced in the evening of Thursday, October 8, 1998 at a time when most representatives had left Washington DC for their districts. If this was successful, it would have hastened the dismantling of the EU banana regime before it expired in 2002 to the detriment of the Caribbean. If passed, it would have deprived the Caribbean of the time to adjust to a new regime. Strong resistance came from Maxine Waters and Sheila Jackson Lee. Congresswoman Waters condemned "this punitive attack" which "would devastate the economies of the Caribbean and cause the kind of economic damage and hopelessness that leads to massive migration and the growth of the drug trade." The action was despicable because "this is not primarily a debate between the US and the EU. This is an ongoing campaign by Republican contributor Carl Lindner, the owner of Chiquita, and many small, family banana farmers that Lindner wants to wipe out."[38] The Bill was withdrawn, perhaps reflecting the wide differences in the House on the banana dispute. At one extreme, Congressman Dreier spoke of hoping that "the European Union recognizes the self-destructive folly of their unfair trading regimes."[39] At the other extreme was Congressman Moakley who wondered aloud: "I do not know why we are debating this bill dealing with the World Trade Organization's treatment of bananas which this country does not even grow."[40]

On October 9, Newt Gingrich and Trent Lott sent a letter to President Clinton advising that: "If the Administration will not take action to protect trade agreements, Congress will have no choice but to take action on its own."[41] On October 10, 1998, in response to a letter from Newt Gingrich, Richard Gephardt, Trent Lott, and Tom Daschle, White House Chief of Staff, Erskine Bowles wrote: "I firmly believe that legislation limiting my discretion, and directing the specific details of how the Trade Representative pursues this three-track approach, will have the unintended effect of undermining our ability to achieve a meaningful solution for U.S. interests rather than strengthening our hand in these cases."[42]

Conflating Corporate and National Interest

There has been a long well-established tradition of companies fusing national and corporate issues and the US government intervening diplomatically and by military force to defend and advance the interests of American companies. This was certainly the case in Central America, in particular in the banana industry and trade. This was no surprise because by the 1920s, UFC was worth over $100 million, employed 67,000 (mainly outside the United States) and owned 1.6 million acres of land in thirty-two countries.[43] The United States intervened in two ways, first, using its armed forces (e.g., in 1903, 1907, 1911, 1912, 1919, 1924 and 1925 in Honduras and 1918 in Colombia, Guatemala, and Panama) and second, having local army and police take actions to support the objectives and needs of the UFC.[44] These became monocrop economies in which the banana companies were a foreign-owned enclave.[45] In later years, the defense of the property and interests of the UFC in Central America was made synonymous with the fight against the possible spread of communism by an orchestrated public relations campaign paid for by the UFC.[46] The US government was particularly receptive given the nationalization of US oil companies by the Mossadegh government in Iran.[47] What followed was corporate instigated US regime change of the Arbenz government in Guatemala.[48]

The key strategy of Lindner and Chiquita was to conflate the corporate interest of Chiquita with the national interest of the United States playing to the old dictum of what is good for General Motors is good for America. This had some validity in the era of national companies but was certainly not a truism in the era of multinational corporations. Chiquita from its inception as UFC was operating as a multinational corporation; indeed, its business was by nature, transnational. By fusing corporate and national interests in the minds of the public and policymakers it aroused their sense of nationalism and made them feel that in their advocacy for Chiquita, they were doing their patriotic duty for their nation. No doubt the contributions to the political campaigns may have engendered some feelings of obligation. The "crusade" was successful because to secure Chiquita's objective, the US government engaged in a trade war with the European Union initiating the imposition of tariffs on a raft of European goods even before the final WTO ruling. This so-called "banana war" was very costly to a wide cross-section of industries, US exports, and American consumers. National pride and hubris were involved but basically, it showed how far the United States could be driven at the behest of a single firm if it could mobilize the necessary political influence.

Dole did not join in the complaint to the WTO. Indeed, Chiquita executives were part of the official US delegations to certain international conferences. At the UN's Food and Agriculture (FAO) banana conference in Rome, May 1998, the US delegation consisted of three US trade diplomats and four other people listed as 'advisers'. The advisers were Michael O'Brien, President of European offices of Chiquita; Manuel Rodriguez, Chiquita's assistant general counsel from Cincinnati; Ms Gleason, US lobbyist for Chiquita, and Robert Moore, the head of a banana trade group that represents the entire industry. No one from Del Monte or Dole was represented on the US delegation.[49] A spokesman for Dole said: "We are puzzled as to why the USTR did not consult with half of the industry."[50]

When the European Union responded to the WTO ruling which required changing the banana regime, the USTR without consulting Dole rejected the latest proposals by the European Union. This is indicative that Chiquita was pushing the US government and Dole was not an active complainant.

No Common Industry Position

At no time was the banana policy of the US government an industry position, it was always a Chiquita position. This remained so during the entire course of the banana dispute. There was never a united industry position because the two largest American fruit trading multinational corporations, Chiquita and Dole were never in agreement on a US banana policy. Dole was not a complainant in Section 301. Indeed, Dole had complained that the USTR had consistently acquiesced to Chiquita's demands without taking Dole's positions sufficiently into consideration. In fact, Dole was not consulted. This difference between the positions of the two corporations was evident when the European Union announced that it was contemplating a first come, first served (FCFS) system for banana imports. On Monday, October 9, 2000, the European Union member states (EU Foreign Ministers meeting) gave their backing to the European Commission's proposals for the adoption of a first come, first served method with a transitional period of 6 years leading to a tariff-only regime. The USTR had earlier rejected the EU's proposal for a FCFS system but their position was not consonant with that of Dole's preferences as a major importer. Dole accused the USTR of favoring the position held by Chiquita which supports a licensing system based on pre-1993 historical performance. Dole has expressed its support for a FCFS system and claims that the USTR did not consult with them in reaching their decision to reject the EU's proposals.[51] Throughout the process, Dole and Chiquita have differed, so the US government could never claim to be pursuing the interest of an "industry" when there was never an industry position, only a Chiquita position. One of the factors at play was that Dole remained profitable and did not experience the plight which Chiquita suffered because of errors in its corporate strategy. Even when the EU banana regime was changed Chiquita did not return to profitability and resorted to suing the European Union to attempt to recover its losses.

Differences in Corporate Strategy

Five multinational corporations, Chiquita, Dole, Del Monte, Noboa, and Fyffes controlled 80 percent of the international banana trade. Chiquita was the dominant company but it is difficult to know to what extent because: "Chiquita secretly controls dozens of supposedly independent banana companies".[52] Chiquita was experiencing some financial strain and seemingly was convinced that it could gain an increased share of the EU market by eliminating the small Caribbean producers that supplied about 8 percent of that market. Apparently, the company was also looking at the predicted increase in per capita banana consumption in the new members of the European Union. It was long felt that the fastest possible growth of demand for bananas would have been in the Soviet Union and Eastern Europe where banana consumption was as low as 0.1 lb per capita compared to 17–19 lbs per capita in the United States. This was common knowledge from as early as the late 1960s.[53]

Departure from Traditional US Trade Policy

US trade has been dominated by a dialectic between (1) efforts to increase exports by forcing foreign countries to open their markets by reducing or eliminating tariffs and non-tariff barriers (e.g. agricultural products) and (2) protecting domestic producers from imports.[54] The Chiquita case was one in which no US produced exports were disadvantaged and no domestic production was being protected such as steel,[55] automobiles, and Harley-Davidson motorcycles. In arguing its case, Chiquita was playing to an audience of sympathetic nationalist politicians who were reared on a steady diatribe of US companies being put at a disadvantage by foreign companies and foreign countries using unfair trade practices. This explains the persistence of protectionist policies in overall US trade policies. Where several major trading countries are involved, a competitive, retaliatory escalation of tariffs and other trade barriers, known in economics by the arcane term of "beggar thy neighbor policies" it can cause a spiral of declining international trade. The upsurge of protectionism symbolized by the Smoot-Harley Act[56] in the United States, at least in part, is attributed to causing or contributing significantly or exacerbating the Great Depression of the late 1920s and 1930s.[57]

Chiquita was portrayed as a case of an American corporation in need of relief from unfair trade practices by foreigners. This would have resonated with the American public and lawmakers who would have regarded the action of the Reagan administration in shielding Harley-Davidson, the sole surviving American manufacturer from imports of Japanese motorcycles as a success. The Clinton administration in 1999 declared: "The Harley-Davidson experience is an example that US trade policy can work."[58] Research has subsequently revealed that the import restrictions had little to do with the resuscitation of the company's fortunes.[59]

Banana War

Chiquita's influence was such that the then US government was prepared to engage in a trade war with the European Union, its North Atlantic Treaty Organization (NATO) ally and one of its most important trading partners in order to secure the corporate interests of Chiquita. This dispute between the European Union and the United States, two of the largest trading countries in the world, involved over $500 million and put at risk the newly established WTO.[60] Even before the final panel ruling, the

United States imposed tariff on a raft of European products. The United States claimed with some justification that the European Union was delaying reform with procedural steps.[61] At the same time, the European Union had a more time consuming consultative process and certainly did not want to appear to be acquiescing to American bullying tactics. The United States imposed tariffs on a range of EU products from Scottish cashmere to French cheese which threatened an estimated $520 million of EU exports per year.[62] So pervasive was the influence of Lindner that it was frequently said it prompted Randall Robinson, head of Trans-Africa to opine that Lindner "bought American policy".[63] Staffers at USTR were not clear as to why the United States was pursuing the case. Indeed, it is reported that "they were baffled by their boss' (Kantor) gusto for the banana case" ... and assumed that he engaged in some political horse-trading."[64]

The Europeans were also displeased because some felt that the WTO case was triggered by Chiquita. This sentiment was expressed by the Guardian: "what grates on the Europeans is that Chiquita in particular has made political donations."[65] Furthermore, "The Clinton administration took the" banana wars "to the WTO within 24 hours of Chiquita Brands, a powerful, previously Republican-supporting banana multinational, making a $500,000 donation to the Democratic Party."[66] The British and French were offended at the absence of any empathy for the small Caribbean producers by the United States. As British Minister of Agriculture declared in the House of Commons as far back as 1992: "We have not only a legal responsibility but a fundamental moral responsibility. These are societies that depend on bananas to an extent which is incomprehensible."[67]

No Special Relationship

Relations between two countries usually embrace dimensions and the result is an amalgam of the various elements and interests. The banana dispute was primarily between the United States on one side and Britain and France on the other. Emboldened by the United States was a group of Latin American and Central American countries and more than twenty European countries acting in consort as the European Union. At times, one aspect of the several interests will dominate the relations between countries and in the case of bananas, the economic considerations took precedence over diplomatic, political, and security concerns. This was a surprise because the Cold War had only recently ended and NATO was still the most important security arrangement. Britain, Europe, with the exception of, Germany had been allies with the United States during both World Wars. Indeed, Britain regarded its relations with the United States as "The Special Relationship" a term coined in 1946 by Winston Churchill. In addition to the diplomatic, security, and diplomatic dimensions there were cultural, historic, and ethnic ties. The relationship was more in the mind of the British[68] than the Americans for whom the relationship was not particularly special as demonstrated on many occasions. Guy Arnold explains that with growing American imperium "the Americans often derided or scorned the British insistence on a special relationship, belittled Britain in the process, they still invoked it when it was useful in support of their policies."[69] With Europe, there was always discomfort with American suzerainty[70] and this grew as the regional project consolidated and expanded. Indeed, it was the action of the French which precipitated the United States ending the convertibility of the US dollar into gold.

Chiquita's Bankruptcy and Demise

US trade policy in support of Chiquita Corporation was unique as already explained because it had nothing to do with any goods produced in the United States. Chiquita claimed that before the EU regime it controlled 40 percent of the EU banana market but the establishment of the EU banana regime cause it to lose market share, loss of $1 billion in profits and 4,000 jobs in the United States.[71] These figures were never independently verified. At the time, Chiquita had claimed that its profitability and indeed its very viability depended on capturing the additional 7–8 percent of the EU market which was supplied by the exports from the Caribbean and Africa. Chiquita, by manipulating US trade policy, succeeded in capturing this additional market share but because of mistakes in corporate strategy, went into bankruptcy, collapsed, was sold and ceased to exist. The lesson is that in some cases protectionism to shield a company from international competition does not work. What makes the Chiquita case so egregious is the enormous cost in the form of economic damage to the small neighbouring Caribbean countries and the loss of goodwill for the United States in the Caribbean region and the European Union.

Dole and other global corporations in the banana trade continued to exist and operate profitably. Dole Fruit Company, founded in 1851, is today the largest fruit and vegetable company in the world with 74,300 employees handling over 300 products in 90 countries.[72] Jamaica Producers, a company which is based in Jamaica and Jamaican-owned, reorganized its product mix by reducing its involvement in the cultivation of bananas and continues as a profitable enterprise to this day. The smallest Caribbean islands continue to struggle with limited economic options and now depend primarily on tourism.

Notes

1. Peter Kihss, "44-Story Plunge Kills Head of United Brands", New York Times, February 4, 1975.
2. Robert J. Cole, "Direct Bribe Bid is Laid To Black". The New York Times, May 17, 1975.
3. Lester D. Langley, The Banana Wars: United States Intervention in the Caribbean, 1898–1934 (Lanham: Rowman & Littlefield Publishers, 2nd ed. 2001).
4. Lester D. Langley and Thomas David Schoonover, The Banana Men: American Mercenaries and Entrepreneurs in Central America, 1880–1930 (Lexington: University Press of Kentucky, 1995) page 167.
5. Lloyd C. Gardner, Economic Aspects of New Deal Diplomacy (Boston: Beacon Press, 1971) page128.
6. Charles Davis Kepner, Jr. and Jay Henry Soothill, The Banana Empire. A Case Study of Economic Imperialism (New York: Russell & Russell, 1967, originally published 1935) page 341.
7. Tim Taylor, "Evolution of the Banana Multinationals" in Timothy E. Josling and Timothy G. Taylor (eds.), Banana Wars. The Anatomy of a Trade Dispute (Walliford: CAPI Publishing, 2003) pages 67–95.
8. Robert Read, "The growth and structure of multinationals in the banana export trade" in Mark Casson (ed.), The Growth of International Business (London: George Allen and Unwin, 1983) pages 180–213.
9. Tim Taylor, "Evolution of the Banana Multinationals" in Timothy E. Josling and Timothy G. Taylor (eds.), Banana Wars. The Anatomy of a Trade Dispute (Walliford: CAPI Publishing, 2003) pages 78–79.
10. Peter Chapman, Bananas. How the United Fruit Company Shaped the World (New York: Cannongate, 2007) page 49.
11. Dan Koeppel, Banana. The Fate of the Fruit That Changed the World (London: Hudson Street Press, 2008) page 78.
12. Dan Koeppel, Banana. The Fate of the Fruit That Changed the World (London: Hudson Street Press, 2008) page 126.
13. Thomas and Marjorie Melville, Guatemala-Another Vietnam (Harmondsworth: Penguin Books, 1971), Stephen Schlesinger and

Stephen Kinzer, Stephen, Bitter Fruit: The Untold Story of the American Coup in Guatemala (New York: Doubleday, 1982), Allison Acker, Honduras: The Making of a Banana Republic (Boston: South End Press 1989), Charles J. Shields, Honduras Becomes the "Banana Republic" (Broomall, PA: Mason Crest Publishers, 2003), Marcelo Bucheli, Bananas and Business: The United Fruit Company in Colombia, 1899–2000 New York: New York University Press, 2005), Jason M. Colby, The Business of Empire: United Fruit, Race, and U.S. Expansion in Central America (Ithaca: Cornell University Press, 2011), Marcelo Bucheli, Multinational Corporations, Totalitarian Regimes and Economic Nationalism: United Fruit Company in Central America, 1899–1975", Business History, Vol. 50, Issue 4 (July, 2008) pages 433–454, Steve Striffler, In the Shadows of State and Capital: The United Fruit Company, Popular Struggle, and Agrarian Restructuring in Ecuador, 1900–1995. (Durham: Duke University Press, 2018) and James W. Martin, Banana Cowboys: The United Fruit Company and the Culture of Corporate Colonialism (Albuquerque: University of New Mexico Press, 2018).

14. Jason M. Colby, The Business of Empire: United Fruit, Race, and U.S. Expansion in Central America (Ithaca: Cornell University Press, 2011) pages 79–117.
15. Marcello Bucheli, "United Fruit Company in Latin America" in Steve Striffler and Mark Moberg (eds.), Banana Wars (Durham: Duke University Press, 2003) pages 80–100.
16. Mike Gallagher and Cameron McWhirter, "Chiquita: An empire built on controversy", Cincinnati Enquirer, May 3, 1998, page 1.
17. Arnold Bertram, N. W. Manley. The Making of Modern Jamaica (Kingston: Arawak Publications, 2016) pages135–136.
18. Rich Cohen, The Fish That Ate the Whale: The Life and Times of America's Banana King (London and New York: Picador, 2013).
19. Rich Cohen, The Fish That Ate the Whale: The Life and Times of America's Banana King (London and New York: Picador, 2013) page xi.
20. Walter Lafeber, Inevitable Revolutions: The United States in Central America (New York: W. W. Norton & Company, 2nd ed., 1993) pages 207–208 and James Wiley, The Banana. Empires, Trade Wars and Globalization (Lincoln: University of Nebraska, 2008) pages 59–61.
21. David Pauly and Rich Thomas "The Great Banana Bribe". Newsweek, 21 April 1975, page 76 and "United Brands Bribe Is Laid to Honduran", The New York Times, May 16, 1975.
22. At the time bribes were not illegal but it was illegal not to make disclosure to shareholders.
23. David Pauly and Rich Thomas "The Great Banana Bribe". Newsweek, 21 April 1975, page 76.

24. Mike Gallagher and Cameron McWhirter, "Village destroyed. Armed soldiers evict residents in Chiquita plan to eliminate union", Cincinnati Enquirer, May 3, 1998, page C5.
25. Mike Gallagher and Cameron McWhirter, "Drugs found on Chiquita ships". Cincinnati Enquirer, May 3, 1998, page C8.
26. Mike Gallagher and Cameron McWhirter, "Bribe scheme covered up". Cincinnati Enquirer, May 3, 1998, page C8.
27. Mike Gallagher and Cameron McWhirter, "Death on Farm shows danger". Cincinnati Enquirer, May 3, 1998, page C14, Mike Gallagher and Cameron McWhirter, "Some pesticides highly toxic". Cincinnati Enquirer, May 3, 1998, page C12 and Mike Gallagher and Cameron McWhirter, "Unregistered toxins despite claims", Cincinnati Enquirer, May 3, 1998, page C12.
28. Mike Gallagher and Cameron McWhirter, "Contributions buy influence", Cincinnati Enquirer, May 3, 1998, page C15.
29. Chiquita Brands International—Wikipedia, https://en.wikipedia.org/wiki/Chiquita_Brands_International, Accessed 16 July 2019.
30. Dan Koeppel, Banana. The Fate of the Fruit That Changed the World (London: Hudson Street Press, 2008) page 222.
31. Dan Koeppel, Banana. The Fate of the Fruit That Changed the World (London: Hudson Street Press, 2008) page 225.
32. Michael Weisskopf, Going Bananas: Chiquita's Slippery Influence. The Busy Back-Door Men. All Politics—Going Bananas: Chiquita's Slippery Influence—Mar.31,1997,www.cnn.com/ALLPOLITICS/1997/03/24/time/banana.money.html, March 31, 1997.
33. Paul Barton, "Lindners gave widely in politics", The Enquirer, February 20, 1998.
34. Andrew Mollison, "Lindner family was too giving", The Cincinnati Enquirer, November 6, 1997.
35. Dan Koeppel, Banana. The Fate of the Fruit That Changed the World (London: Hudson Street Press, 2008) page 221.
36. James Cox, "Chiquita: Controversial CEO", USA Today, March 3, 1999.
37. "Banana Republic", The Washington Post, October 26, 2000.
38. Congressional Black Caucus Fights Sneak Attack on Caribbean Banana Trade and Small Banana Farmers. Republican Initiative On Behalf of Chiquita Blocked, Press Release, Congressional Black Caucus, October 10, 1998.
39. Congressional Record-House, October 10, 1998, H10365.
40. Congressional Record-House, October 10, 1998, H10366.
41. Letter to President William J. Clinton from Newt Gingrich, Speaker and Trent Lott. Majority Leader, 7 October, 1998. Source: Inside US Trade, Vol. 16, No. 40.

42. Letter from Erskine Bowles to Newt Gingrich, Richard Gephardt, Trent Lott and Tom Daschle, 10 October, 1998, The White House.
43. Dan Koeppel, Banana. The Fate of the Fruit That Changed the World (London: Hudson Street Press, 2008) page 75.
44. Dan Koeppel, Banana. The Fate of the Fruit That Changed the World (London: Hudson Street Press, 2008) page 64.
45. Walter LaFeber, Inevitable Revolutions. The United States In Central America (New York: W. W. Norton & Company, 2nd ed., 1993).
46. Dan Koeppel, Banana. The Fate of the Fruit That Changed the World (London: Hudson Street Press, 2008) pages 125–131.
47. Stephen Kinzer, All the Shah's Men: An American Coup and the Roots of Middle East Terror (New York: Wiley, 2nd. ed., 2008).
48. Stephen Schlesinger and Stephen Kinzer, Bitter Fruit: The Story of the American Coup in Guatemala, Revised and Expanded (David Rockefeller Center for Latin American Studies, 2006).
49. Cameron McWhirther and Mike Gallagher, "Influence: This is just money politics", Cincinnati Enquirer, May 3, 1998, page C16.
50. Geoff Winestock, "U.S. Starts a Fight with Dole Food Co. In the Banana war", Wall Street Journal, October 9, 2000.
51. "Importers go bananas over sanctions on EU trade", Journal of Commerce, March 5, 1999 and Geoff Winestock, "U.S. Starts a Fight with Dole Food Co. In the Banana War," The Wall Street Journal, Monday, October 9, 2000.
52. Mike Gallagher and Cameron McWhirter, "Chiquita: An empire built on controversy", Cincinnati Enquirer, May 3, 1998, page 1. For full expose see Mike Gallagher and Cameron McWhirter, Power, money & control. Chiquita secrets revealed. Hidden control crucial to overseas empire", Cincinnati Enquirer, May 3, 1998, pages C1–C2 and Mike Gallagher and Cameron McWhirter, "Locals front for Chiquita", Cincinnati Enquirer, May 3, 1998, pages C-3.
53. Jean-Paul Valles, The World Market for Bananas, 1964–1972 (New York: Praeger Publishers, 1968) pages 90–91.
54. Douglas Irwin, Clashing Over Commerce (Chicago: University of Chicago Press, 2017).
55. Michael O. Moore, "The Rise and Fall of Big Steel's Influence on U.S. Trade Policy" in Anne O. Krueger (ed.), The Political Economy of Trade Protection (Chicago: University of Chicago Press, 1996) pages 15–34.
56. Douglas A. Irwin, Peddling Protectionism: Smoot-Hawley and the Great Depression (Princeton: Princeton University Press, 2011). For the argument that the Smoot-Harley Act had limited contractionary effect see Peter Temin, "The Great Recession & the Great Depression", Daedalus.

Journal of the American Academy of Arts and Sciences, Vol. 139, No. 4 (2010) pages 115–124.
57. A.G. Kenwood and A.L. Lougheed, The growth of the international economy 1820–2000 (New York: Routledge, 1999) pages 228–229.
58. James Pethokoukis, "Remember when protectionism 'saved' Harley-Davidson motorcycles in the 1980s?" AEIdeas June 12, 2018.
59. Douglas Irwin, Clashing Over Commerce (Chicago: University of Chicago Press, 2017) and 33 Years Ago, Tariffs Saved Harley-Davidson Inc.—or Did They ..., https://www.fool.com/investing/general/2016/04/05/33-years-ago-today-tariffs-saved-harley-davidson.aspx#:~:text=Image%20source%3A%20Harley%2DDavidson.,import%20tariffs%20on%20Japanese%20motorcycles.
60. Going bananas", The Economist, March 6, 1999, page 20.
61. Guy de Jonquieres, "US and EU in fresh battle over bananas", Financial Times, December 15, 1998.
62. Patrick Barkham, "The banana wars explained", The Guardian, International Edition, 5 March, 1999.
63. James Cox, "Chiquita: Controversial CEO", USA Today, March 3, 1999.
64. James Cox, "Chiquita: Controversial CEO", USA Today, March 3, 1999.
65. Stephen Bates, "Billion dollar banana split", The Guardian, 6 March, 1999.
66. Patrick Barkham, "The banana wars explained", The Guardian, International Edition, 5 March, 1999.
67. Gordon Myers, Banana Wars. The Price of Free Trade. A Caribbean Perspective (London: Zed Books, 2004) page 35.
68. John Baylis, "The 'special Relationship' A Diverting British Myth?" in Cyril Buffet and Beatrice Heuser (eds.), Haunted by History: Myths in International Relations (Oxford: Berghahn Books, 1998), Chapter 10.
69. Guy Arnold, America and Britain. Was There Ever a Special Relationship? (London: Hurst & Company, 2014) pages 192–193.
70. Jean Jacques Servan-Schreiber, The American Challenge (Harmondsworth: Penguin, 1968).
71. James Cox, "Chiquita: Controversial CEO", USA Today, March 3, 1999.
72. Dole Fruit Company, https://en.wikipedia.org/wiki/Dole_Food_Company, Accessed 16 July 2019.

CHAPTER 6

Chiquita Overwhelms the Small Caribbean States

Introduction

This chapter discusses how Chiquita overwhelmed the small island banana exporting economies and their supporters. The narrative concentrates on the political struggle in the United States although it was a worldwide dispute involving governments, companies, and civil society organizations and was fought in arenas and forums across the world in an interconnected process.

The Start

On October 17, 1994, the USTR initiated an investigation under Section 301 of the Trade Act of 1974 to determine whether the EU banana import regime was "unreasonable" and "burdens or restricts US commerce". The petitioner, Chiquita Brands International Inc. (CBI), claimed that the EU regime discriminated against US companies and consequently harmed Chiquita by reducing its market share. On March 21, 1995, Prime Minister Manuel Esquivel of Belize, then Chairman of CARICOM, wrote to Mickey Kantor, US Trade Representative, making the point that "action under Section 301 would harm US economic and security interest" and "would devastate the economies and undermine the established democracies of longstanding allies." It was argued that "there is no appreciable banana production in the United States and relatively few US jobs depend on banana. Moreover, our producers pose no threat to US corporate

R. L. Bernal, *Corporate versus National Interest in US Trade Policy*, https://doi.org/10.1007/978-3-030-56950-1_6

interest." The Prime Minister also reminded the United States that "for many of us, bananas are the largest and, in some cases, the only cash crop: Europe is the only market. Without the EU banana import regime, we could not sell our bananas. The loss of our traditional European banana markets would be catastrophic." The letter in its entirety is shown in Appendix 1.

When the challenge to the EU banana regime was announced in early 1995, the banana exporting countries of the Caribbean acting through their private sector banana organization, Windward Island Banana Growers Association (WINBAN) and Jamaica Producers in Jamaica, immediately retained trade lawyers, Ray S. Calamaro and C. Christopher Parlin of the well-known law firm of Winthrop, Stimpson, Putman, and Roberts. On their advice, a public relations firm was retained to disseminate information to the media in an attempt to raise public awareness. This outfit was the Frateli group, whose account executives were Francis O'Brien and Page S. Gardner. The budget was US$50,000, a large sum, indeed an unprecedented expenditure by the CBEA. In collaboration with the Caribbean embassies in Washington, DC, particularly the trade and legal staff of the Embassy of Jamaica, a package of information was distributed to Congress and the media under the auspices of the Caribbean coalition. The gist of the message was that the loss of preferential access to the EU market for Caribbean bananas would "devastate the economic stability of their longstanding democracies and destabilize the entire Caribbean region" with serious security implications for the United States. The missive called on the US government not to pursue any action under Section 301.[1]

Dialogue Suddenly Terminated

The Clinton administration promised on several occasions to engage in meaningful dialogue with the governments of the banana exporting countries of the Caribbean. In August 1993, at a meeting at the White House between President Bill Clinton and the heads of government of Barbados, Guyana, Jamaica, and Trinidad and Tobago, the first issue to be discussed was bananas. Prime Minister P. J. Patterson of Jamaica made the analogy that bananas were to the Caribbean what cars were to Detroit.[2] The Caribbean leaders accepted the assurances that their concern would be addressed. At the Summit of the Americas in December 1994, President Clinton instructed Secretary of State Warren Christopher to meet with

Caribbean ministers. Prime Minister Patterson recalls: "The Secretary of State accepted the justice of our case. President Clinton accepted the outcome of our negotiation with his secretary of state and assured us that the United States would not act in the matter—but within two weeks of the Summit, the United States proceeded against the EU banana import regime in the WTO."[3]

Half way through a meeting of all countries involved in the banana dispute held in Coral Gables, Miami, on April 9, 1996, Ecuador on behalf of the United States, Latin America, and Central America stated that the decision had been taken to refer the issue to the WTO. The United States was party to this action but had not agreed to the manner in which the decision was announced.[4] The immediate reaction was summed up by the Ambassador of Jamaica as "premature to go to a WTO panel before we have fully explored the process of a dialogue. One day's dialogue in Miami is not sufficient to accomplish that goal."[5] "We were given assurances by Kantor that the United States wanted to resolve this. It was a breach of faith with the Caribbean."[6]

In shock[7] and frustration, the Washington based ambassadors of the Caribbean countries abandoned the normal diplomatic courtesies and wrote a joint letter to Kantor after the abrupt announcement of the referral of the dispute to the WTO in preference to a negotiated solution. The ambassadors felt that the meeting was a charade, they stated "this was not consistent with the understanding reached at the last meeting where you gave us the assurance that while a dialogue was continuing in a constructive way, the matter would not be referred to the WTO panel. This kind of conduct does not constitute a good faith commitment to a constructive dialogue."[8]

The Banana Industry in the Caribbean

Jamaica was the first country in the Western Hemisphere to export bananas. The export of bananas started in Jamaica in 1868. Bananas accounted for 19.1 percent of total exports in 1890 and increased to 57.3 percent in 1930,[9] a period in which the sugar industry was experiencing some difficulties. Both Jamaican[10] and American companies enriched themselves in the banana industry and it also brought prosperity to banana farmers large and small, especially after the formation of the Jamaica Banana Producers Association.[11] By the mid-1930s, Jamaica was the world's largest exporter of bananas, an achievement which generated interest in both the Caribbean and Britain. The industry suffered from Panama Disease in the 1930s and World War II. Shipments of Jamaican bananas to Britain started in December 1945.[12]

The banana industry in the Windward Islands did not emerge naturally from market forces but was deliberately created by the British government to provide employment and economic activity. The initiative came in the context of the mass social disturbances in the 1930s and was prompted by the successful market driven emergence of the banana export industry in Jamaica since the late nineteenth century.[13] From the start, the banana industry in the Windward Islands required subsidies in shipping and price support to survive.[14]

Corporate competition between US and European banana marketing companies dates back to the earliest years of the banana trade. In 1900, the British government sought to break the monopoly of the UFC in the British market by subsidizing, shipping, and promoting production in the Caribbean.[15] Corporate competition between European firms was very fierce at times, for example, during the early 1960s. As output from the Windward Islands expanded rapidly in the 1950s, a situation of oversupply developed in the British market leading to the Windwards—Jamaica "banana war."[16] The corporate competition between Fyffes, the purchaser of Jamaican bananas, and Geest, the counterpart for the Windwards, led to a post-War fall in prices until a market sharing agreement in 1986. Even with preferential marketing arrangements, the banana industry in the Windwards required British aid to sustain it.[17]

Prime Minister of St. Kitts & Nevis Dr. Denzil Douglas described bananas as the "lifeblood" of some of the banana exporting countries.[18] At the time of the complaint to the WTO, banana exports were the largest export for Dominica, St. Lucia, and St. Vincent and a very significant export for Belize and Jamaica. As a share of total exports in 1993 bananas accounted for 50.0 percent in Dominica, 42.6 percent in St. Lucia, 40.2 percent in St. Vincent, 10.6 percent in Belize, 10.3 percent in Grenada. The figure was only 3.5 percent in Jamaica.[19] The banana industry contributed 19–20 percent of gross domestic product (GDP) in Dominica during the period 1985–1993[20] and approximately 21 percent of GDP for the Windward Islands.[21] An even more meaningful measure of the vital role of the banana industry is its importance as a source of employment (i.e. the number of farmers and workers employed in all aspects of the industry). Indeed the banana industry was "the biggest single employer of regular full-time workers".[22] The percentage of the population dependent on the banana industry was estimated by Oxfam as 33 percent in St. Lucia and 70 percent in St. Vincent.[23]

In 1993, the banana exports of the Caribbean amounted to $150 million and, therefore, represented a minute fraction of total world banana exports which in 1992 was $3122 million.[24] In the Windward Islands, average yields per acre are estimated to be 5–7 tonnes.[25] Wage costs differ vastly between the Caribbean and the Latin American and Central American producers and, for example, one estimate suggests that wages are twice as high in the Caribbean. Specifically, average daily wage rates are $10 in Belize, while in neighboring Guatemala it was $3.50.[26] Due to higher wage rates and lack of economies of scale, production costs in the Caribbean, estimated at 47 cents per kilo,[27] are the highest among the countries exporting bananas to the European Union.

The EU market was the sole export market for bananas exported from the Caribbean because these bananas received preferential market access. The Caribbean's share of the EU market was about 8 percent and less than 3 percent of the world market whereas Latin America and Central America accounted for 80 percent. Between 1985 and 1996 both volume and value of banana exports increased but between 1997 and 2000 volume continued to increase but value declined.[28]

Chiquita: Descendent of United Fruit Company

Chiquita Brands International Inc., an American-owned corporation, was in the1990s, the world's largest producer and distributor of bananas under its "flagship" brand, Chiquita. Chiquita, whose majority ownership was held by Carl H. Lindner, Jr. is the successor to the infamous UFC. The company was formed in 1899 when two banana trading companies merged. One was the Boston Fruit Company that had been established by Lorenzo Dow Baker, a sailor, who in 1870 had bought the first shipment of bananas from Jamaica. United Fruit Company dominated the United States (estimated to be 80 percent),[29] and at times the European banana market, despite competition from the Standard Fruit Company which had become Dole Food Company by the 1990s. From the 1930s, UFC came to dominate the economic life of the small Central American countries through its ownership and millions, its business practices, and the support of the US government.[30] Its economic dominance gave it control of the governments of these monocrop dependent economies; hence, they came to be known as "Banana Republics".[31] The UFC's style of management was intimately linked to the support of the US government described as "corporate colonialism".[32] Perhaps the most notorious incident was a clash between a government attempting land reform and the UFC in Guatemala[33] which ended with its removal by a coup[34] aided and abetted by the Central Intelligence Agency (CIA). The new president was to be "the saviour of the landowning class and the protector of the United Fruit Company's interests."[35] In contrast, the UFC, which also operated in Jamaica and which was a colony of Britain, settled its problems and differences through negotiations between Samuel Zemurray and Norman Manley.[36]

United Fruit Company, later United Brands, later Chiquita, in all its incarnations has achieved its market dominance by increasing, by taking over, or driving rivals out of business and by ruthless control of workers, communities, and governments. The company has been headed by strong leader, Carl Lindner, whose style was according to Koeppel: "aggression". "It wasn't the all-encompassing muscle the company wielded through most of the twentieth century, but at times it resembled it."[37] Relentless expansion of market remained the overarching leitmotif of the corporate strategy. Consistent with this approach was taking the market share supplied by the Caribbean and simultaneously increasing market share in the European Union. The EU market after the expansion of its membership was larger than the US market. Importantly, the European Union was thought to have significant growth potential, certainly more so than the saturated US market. The growth in the EU market was forecasted to come from the increase in banana consumption per capita from the Eastern European consumers who would now have more available and more affordable bananas. World consumption per capita of bananas and plantains was stagnant during the15 year period 1970–1984.[38]

Chiquita's Spurious Claim

Chiquita's claims of losses due to the EU regime are not credible. Chiquita's volume may have decreased, for, since its pre-regime peak in 1992 Chiquita lost \$52.5 million on sales in Europe. Under the EU regime, Chiquita is again trading profitability in Europe—Chiquita reported a \$78.7 million profit in 1993. This belief claims that the EU regime has cost Chiquita and others "hundreds of millions of dollars". When the European countries officially became the European Union, Chiquita apparently expected them to abandon their Lomé commitments, thereby allowing competition from Chiquita and other multinationals to eliminate the higher-cost Caribbean and other ACP bananas from the European markets. With the seeming expectation of eliminating ACP bananas, Chiquita invested in expanding production in Latin America and shipping. However, Chiquita erred, instead of abandoning its Lomé commitments the European Union upheld them. As a result, Chiquita's speculative overproduction flooded world markets (except ironically, the regulated EU market). Thus, the complaint of the Hawaii Banana Industry Association is properly directed at Chiquita. Chiquita's bad business judgments are the cause of any alleged harm, not the EU regime.[39]

Chiquita's argument that the EU regime was discriminatory resonated with many officials and members of Congress who felt this was a hangover of the mercantilist trade arrangements of European empires which hampered American goods from the markets in Europe. This attitude persisted in the United States from the post-World War II period when "there was a strong feeling that the protectionist empire and the sterling block were major barriers to the creation of open free markets throughout the world, to which the US government was committed."[40] Gone were the days when Britain controlled a quarter of the world's land area and a quarter of the world's population, from rule Britannia to Pax Americana.[41]

Dynamics of Us Banana Policy

The formulation of US banana policy and the subsequent struggle to change or reverse that policy was an extremely complex process involving the Executive, the Congress, bureaucracy, media, US business interests, think tanks, and a vigorous lobbying campaign by the governments of the Caribbean. The banana policy of the Clinton administration is beyond doubt a clear case of a policy bought and paid for by a US corporation through large and well-timed contributions of money to the Democratic Party. Chiquita also spent large sums to keep a constant diatribe in the media, particularly the leading national newspapers, to persuade the public, the Congress, and the bureaucracy that US banana policy devised by Kantor was the right course of action. The array of forces opposing Chiquita and the Clinton White House included the Caribbean governments, their lobbyist, the Caribbean community in the United States and elements in the Congress and civil society. They were "outgunned" by vastly superior financial resources. The entities involved in the banana

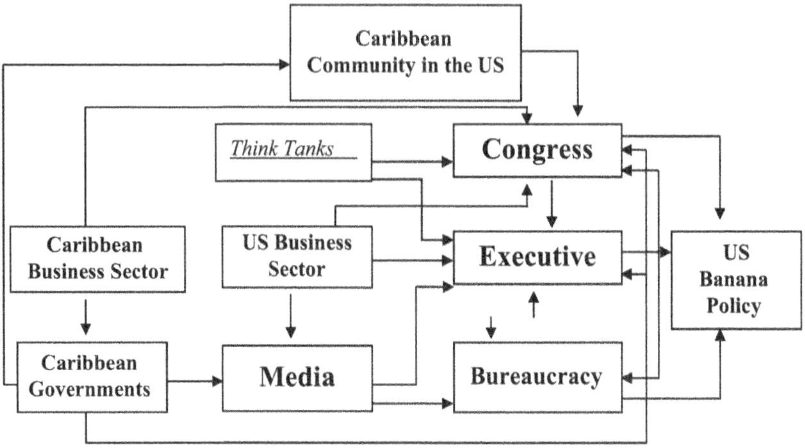

Fig. 6.1 Actors influencing US banana policy

dispute and their interactions and interrelations in trying to influence US policy on bananas are shown in Fig. 6.1.

Bureaucracy

The US bureaucracy was split on US policy on the banana issue as the State Department appreciated the broader implications, and the USTR strictly defined the banana issue as a trade dispute in which the United States was the injured party. The State Department exhibited a sympathetic approach and an appreciation of the wider economic, social, and political implications for the Caribbean of dismantling the EU banana regime. Indeed, the State Department took its cue from the repeated assurances by President Clinton that the United States understood the economic importance of the industry and would seek a solution, which did not harm the small countries of the Caribbean. Many senior diplomats took the President's statements literally and articulated them with conviction, and in some cases, genuine empathy. The banana issue never appeared to engage the attention of Secretary of State Warren Christopher.[42] However, in spite of its best efforts, the State Department was not able to exercise a salutary effect on the USTR. An anonymous senior State Department official voiced the concerns of the Department when stating that "You do not want to hurt the banana trade or the tourism industry.

It destabilizes governments, it kills jobs, it promotes the drug trade, it increases migration—it's a world class headache for the United States."[43]

Prime Ministers Owen Arthur of Barbados (which does not export bananas) and Dr. Keith Mitchell of Grenada led a delegation including the Minister of Trade of Belize to Washington DC and held discussions with Secretary of State Madeleine Albright and Governor Bob MacKay, presidential advisor. There was no discernible change in the positions of either side as was the case with the technical level meetings at the USTR. The next opportunity to engage the Secretary was not until within the margins of the United Nations General Assembly in September.

The Caribbean tried to heighten the awareness of the National Security Council to the security implications of the elimination of the EU banana regime when a Caribbean delegation led by Edison James, Prime Minister of Dominica met with them in October 1998.

The USTR freely disregarded the pleas of the State Department with a self-assured arrogance, based on their jurisdictional control of the issue that this was a trade issue and, therefore, technical and free of social and political considerations. The USTR's position was set by Mickey Kantor whose considerations were in part political based on the fact that Carl Lindner was exerting pressure on the White House on US policy relating to this issue. Kantor facilitated the trade specialist who saw, in this case, an opportunity for a sure win in the Dispute Settlement Mechanism of the WTO, having won on this issue on previous occasions. Such a victory was badly needed because the United States had lost the first couple of cases in the WTO. That offended many members of Congress who regarded the WTO as encroaching on the sovereign powers of the United States to take bilateral action under Section 301. The staff of the Office of the USTR also needed the victory to restore their reputation and as a morale booster. Furthermore, a win in the banana case would yield important breakthroughs in the area of services, which was important to the United States because of its wider applicability. A memo to Kantor by two USTR staff members on October 13, 1994, acknowledges that the banana case "would break new ground, as this would be the first time that the USTR had ever used Section 301 in connection with a product not exported from the United States but from elsewhere but we have been persuaded by Chiquita that the practices here do have a significant effect on US commerce."[44] The relationship between the US government and Chiquita involved Chiquita participating in official US government negotiations. Chiquita played a uniquely influential role in formulating US banana policy. The Cincinnati Enquirer documented that at "the UN's Food and Agriculture (FAO) banana conference in Rome, May 1998, the US delegation consisted of three US trade diplomats and four other people listed as 'advisers'. The advisers were Michael O'Brien, President of European offices of Chiquita; Manuel Rodriguez, Chiquita's assistant general counsel from Cincinnati; Ms. Gleason, U.S. lobbyist for Chiquita; and Robert Moore, the head of a banana trade group that represents the entire industry."[45] It is important to note that Del Monte or Dole was not represented on the US delegation.

The USTR's attitude even after Kantor was replaced by Charlene Barshefsky, who brought new qualities to the leadership of the USTR, namely a knowledge of trade, negotiating skills, and diplomacy, was to pursue a new arrangement to facilitate the interest of Chiquita. Those in charge of the issue in the USTR felt that "the real discussions" were those between the European Union and the United States and that the Caribbean was unwilling to adjust to free trade and, therefore, the technical solutions proposed by the Caribbean were "unrealistic" because they sought to facilitate the continuation of preferential arrangements. There was a weariness of meeting with politicians and diplomats but a willingness to engage with "technical experts" from the banana industry in the Caribbean countries. This disposition of being impatient to debate led to an unwillingness to engage in dialogue with the Caribbean, and it became increasingly difficult for the Caribbean to engage the USTR at the most senior levels. For example, Prime Minister Edison James of Dominica representing CARICOM had to settle for a meeting with Ralph Ives, a senior level bureaucrat in the USTR, on a visit to Washington which was specifically intended to meet with the USTR or at the very least the Deputy USTR. On another occasion, a meeting between the USTR and the Washington-based ambassadors of the Caribbean countries on March 1, 1996, was only forced by the intervention of representatives of Charles Rangel and Maxine Waters and Randall Robinson of TransAfrica, who insisted on a trilateral discussion, both as a way of demonstrating their support but also to ensure that the USTR would meet with the Caribbean spokespersons.

One of the mistakes which the USTR made in its anxiety to appear effective in forcing the European Union to adhere to the WTO ruling was to impose sanctions hastily and prematurely without allowing the WTO appeal process to be completed. This set off a storm of criticisms including from conservative institutions such as the Heritage Foundation[46] and the Financial Times. The latter's article, "The U.S. and EU go Bananas" in

November 1998 states that "the U.S. imposition of sanctions on the EU was 'reprehensible'. To impose unilateral sanctions that would almost certainly breach WTO rules would surely undermine the very body whose authority Washington purports to defend."[47] The Clinton administration, in particular Mickey Kantor and the USTR, was criticized for overreacting to the banana issue and risking or inciting a trade war with the European Union over a commodity that was not exported from the United States. Congressman Charles Rangel (D) abhorred the imminent trade war between the United States and European Union: "Unless either the E.U. or U.S. change their current positions, the two biggest trading entities in the world will begin a trade war over a commodity that, for the most part, is produced by neither one of them ... I find it difficult to believe this issue is beyond negotiation ... the U.S. and EU must resolve this dispute without escalating to trade war and without ignoring the important interests of small Caribbean farmers working hard to make a decent living."[48] The pillorying by the United States and foreign press appears to have had little or no effect on the maneuvering of the Kantor-Lindner tryst. The Financial Times in an editorial warned that "Unless the U.S. and EU come quickly to their senses, they risk doing immense damage to multilateral trade when stability is vital to global economic recovery."[49] The Heritage Foundation criticized the administration for its precipitate action in imposing sanctions pointing to the damage in relations with the European Union and the Caribbean.[50] There were very few who supported the specious posture by the Clinton administration that they were defending US economic interest and that the EU's banana policy was 'the line in the sand.'[51]

The USTR persisted in pursuing the banana issue at the WTO. Not satisfied with only obtaining a ruling in their favor at the WTO, they insisted on trying to coerce the European Union into proposing an alternative which met the requirements of the United States. When this was not done to the satisfaction of the United States, they went ahead on March 3, 1999, to impose sanctions even before the appellant process was completed in the WTO. They had to wait until April 19, to get approval from the WTO to impose sanctions for a reduced sum, $191.4 million. In a face-saving maneuver, the United States announced that retroactively, from March 3, sanctions in the form of 100 percent tariffs on a range of EU exports would be enforced. The administration sought to justify this churlish behavior, not as punitive tactics but as a way of getting the Europeans to put in place on the WTO prescribed schedule, a regime acceptable to the United States. Rita Hayes, US Ambassador to the WTO explained that “retaliation is a last resort. We want the EU to sit down now and discuss a regime that will take into account the interest of all banana producers and comply with WTO rules.”[52] The prime ministers of the banana exporting countries of the Caribbean publicly stated that they were “appalled” and that the action was “incomprehensible” that “the United States appears determined to pursue a course of trade confrontation to the detriment of the Caribbean.”[53] Sir Leon Brittan, European Vice President in charge of External Trade Relations described it as politically unwise, unilaterally contrary to WTO obligations, and damaging to EU/US relations.[54]

US Business Community

The dominant factor in US policy on bananas was the campaign contribution of Carl Lindner who made large contributions to both the Democratic and Republican parties (see Table 6.1). Time magazine reports that Lindner heads “a corporate agglomeration that includes American Financial Group, Inc., an insurance business (annual revenue: $4 billion); Chiquita Brands International, Inc., the fruit-and-vegetable giant ($2.7 billion); and an array of other businesses, including Provident Financial Group, Inc., a bank holding company (assets: $8 billion); and American Heritage Homes, one of Florida’s largest builders.”[55]

Table 6.1 Lindner’s campaign contributions (1991–99)

Year	*Republicans*	*Democrats*	*Total*
1991	$37,000	$4,000	$41,000
1992	$56,000	$11,500	$67,500
1993	$220,000	$264,000	$484,000
1994	$446,000	$254,000	$700,000
1995	$519,500	$132,000	$651,500
1996	$736,000	$114,500	$850,500
1997	$459,000	$116,000	$575,000
1998	$1,132,500	$217,000	$1,349,500
1999	$555,000	$260,000	$825,000
1991–1999	$4,161,000	$1,373,000	$5,534,000

Source: Donald L. Bartlett and James B. Steele, “Big Money & Politics. Who Gets Hurt?”, Time, February 7, 2000

Newsweek reported that when it comes to spreading political cash around, Carl Lindner has few equals. Between 1993 and 1996 when the USTR was preparing and arguing his case, Chiquita chairman, Carl Lindner donated more than $1 million to the Democratic Party. The secretive, Cincinnati-based tycoon has been pumping money into campaign coffers for decades. After giving the Democrats nothing in the 1992 election, he handed them $250,000 in December 1993—and $75,000 more a year later. Then in the 1996 campaign, Lindner continued making large financial contributions to both political parties: he gave $712,000 to the Republicans and more than $800,000 to the Democrats.[56] Among the beneficiaries were several prominent senators and congressmen including Senator Bob Dole, who frequently traveled on jets belonging to Chiquita's Carl Lindner[57] and was active in support in Congress[58] and arranged meetings between Mickey Kantor and Carl Lindner. The impact of Lindner's money was spread widely in the Democratic Party. On the advice of the National Democratic Committee (NDC), the funds were distributed to several state-level campaigns and the funds were registered at the state level making it harder to aggregate the total.[59] Funds were distributed to campaigns in Ohio, Georgia, Oregon, New Jersey, New Hampshire, and California.[60] According to Paul Barton: "The campaign contributions of Cincinnati businessman Carl Lindner, his family, and executives of his major companies touch 53 current members of Congress including 12 committee chairmen and several top party leaders."[61] Whether members of the House and Senate believed in the validity of Chiquita's claim that free trade rules were breached causing the company to lose nearly $400 million is a question but many whose campaigns received money actively supported Chiquita's cause.[62] It is unlikely that support following financial contributions was merely a coincidence. Joseph Hagin, Vice President for Corporate Affairs of Chiquita, dismissed any connection by claiming that "The charge that Carl's contribution was linked to policy changes simply do not reflect reality."[63] The reality is that beneficiaries Senator Mike DeWine (Ohio), and Representatives Rob Portman and Steve Chabot both of Ohio were described by the conservative Washington Times to have "led congressional advocacy for Chiquita".[64]

On March 1, 1996, Congresswoman Maxine Waters and Randall Robinson arranged a tri-lateral meeting between Mickey Kantor, African American leaders, and Caribbean ambassadors.[65] During the meeting, Randall Robinson enquired whether Chiquita's donations to the Democratic Party for the Clinton presidential campaign had any influence on the administration's decision to refer the banana dispute to the WTO. Mickey Kantor categorically denied this, stating that "Carl Lindner's activities and actions had no impact on American trade policy."[66] In response to questions from the influential journalist William Safire, Kantor, who was Clinton's campaign manager in 1992, states "I had no earthly idea of his (Lindner) contributions" and claims that his advice to the White House staff was not to meet Lindner. These answers were, of course, complete fabrications, since he had met with Lindner on several occasions, a fact which led to the whole sordid connection being dubbed as "Bananagate".[67]

Another instance of Kantor's dishonesty was in a meeting between himself and representatives of Caribbean governments, including Prime Minister John Compton of St. Lucia, the day before the first Summit of the Americas in Miami. During this meeting, Kantor committed to engaging in a dialogue with the Caribbean instead of taking action under Section 301 or taking the issue to the WTO. This promise was elicited to ensure that the Caribbean governments did not carry out their threat of not being signatories to the Summit of the Americas document.

Lindner's campaign contributions grew steadily during the period 1991—1999 from $41,000 in 1991 to $1.3 million in 1998, with a total of over $5.5 million for the nine-year period. The contributions, particularly to the Democrats, reflected losses by Chiquita of $407 million from 1992–1994, accompanied by a dramatic collapse in the value of its shares from $51 per share in 1991 to $11 in 1994. In 1993, Lindner wrote a letter to US representative, Mickey Kantor and, not surprisingly, his contribution to the Democrats in that year jumped to $264,000, compared to $11,500 in 1992. The contributions to the Republicans yielded the desired return as Senator Bob Dole and other prominent Republicans began to vigorously pressure the Clinton administration. In 1995, Lindner's campaign of ingratiation with the Clinton administration moved to another level as Lindner, now one of the top ten donors to the Democrats attended State dinners and slept over in the White House. In 1996, Kantor instructs the United States to join a group of Latin American and Central American countries in filing a formal complaint to the WTO. In 1998, the United States decides to impose sanctions on the European Union in the form of a punitive 100 percent tariff on a selected group of products.

One section of the US business community whose concerns received scant attention from the Administration and bureaucracy were the small businesses hit by tariff increases on European imports. Their plight was reported in a special on CNN and in the print media (e.g., Time magazine).[68] The agony of small businesses placed in jeopardy by the increased prices of imports from Europe penalized by the sanctions never became a groundswell of sufficient proportions to be a political irritant or counterweight to Chiquita's campaign.[69]

In contrast to Chiquita which was losing money because of errors in its corporate strategy, Dole remained profitable. Dole was never a complainant in Section 301 nor a party to the US government's actions in the WTO. At no time during the course of the banana dispute did the US Congress and Executive have the benefit of a united industry position because the two largest fruit trading multinational corporations, Chiquita and Dole, never agreed on what should constitute a US banana policy. Dole complained that the USTR had consistently acquiesced to Chiquita's demands without taking Dole's positions sufficiently into consideration. The difference between the two corporations was graphically revealed when the European Union announced that it was contemplating a first come, first served (FCFS) system for banana imports. On Monday, October 9, 2000, the European Union member states (EU foreign ministers meeting) gave their backing to the European Commission's proposals for the adoption of a first come, first served method with a transitional period of 6 years leading to a tariff-only regime. The USTR had earlier rejected the EU's proposal for a FCFS system. Their position ignored Dole's preference and prompted Dole to accuse the USTR of favoring the position held by Chiquita which supported a licensing system based on pre-1993 historical performance. Dole expressed its support for a first come first served system and complained that the USTR had not consulted with them in reaching their decision to reject the EU's proposals.[70] Throughout the process, Dole and Chiquita have differed, so that the US government could never claim to be pursuing the interest of an "industry," there was never an industry position, only a Chiquita position.

The Washington Times reported on how money galvanizes policy when it pointed out that in September 1996, "a month after Mr. Lindner gave the DNC another $100,000 through his insurance and investment holding company, American Financial Corporation—Mr. Kantor, joined by Guatemala, Honduras, and Mexico, commenced a U.S. challenge to EU trade policies."[71] Further evidence that Chiquita had bought and paid for US policy on bananas was the fact that Kantor and the USTR always followed the wishes of Chiquita. Dole, the other US multinational corporation involved in the international banana trade was never a party to taking the banana issue to the WTO and indeed were conducting their corporate affairs profitably under the extant EU banana regime. After the WTO decision to dismantle the EU system, Dole became active in order to ensure that their views would be taken into account in any US proposal or any EU-US negotiated solutions.

The US business community beyond those firms directly involved in the banana trade was not concerned or involved in the contentious banana issue until the United States imposed sanctions on imports from the European Union. The major concerns were first, how the increase in the price of European goods would harm those who sold these products; secondly, the response of the European Union was to threaten retaliatory actions against the United States; and thirdly, the escalation of the banana and beef hormone dispute into a full scale "trade war" between the European Union and the United States. Barshefsky blamed the Europeans stating that she was "extremely dismayed that the EU would jeopardize the operation of the WTO."[72] Japan, South Korea, India, Indonesia, and six central European nations moved to back the European Union in arguing that the United States cannot request sanctions without a WTO ruling on compliance. This view was clearly shared by many other WTO members that did not necessarily endorse the EU's banana import regime.[73]

Media

Mobilization of public opinion through the media can be an important means of influencing politicians in Congress and the White House. However, it has to be an issue that Americans, in sufficient numbers, feel directly affects their lives in an adverse way (e.g., immigration). One of the best examples was how media coverage affected the views of the Vietnam War. For this reason, the media was prohibited from showing the coffins of soldiers killed in Iraq and Afghanistan. Getting the story out to the wider public is very important when those interested are small in number and lack the financial resources to mount campaigns with lobbyists and public relations agencies. Unfortunately, at the time of the banana dispute, social media was not as developed as it is today, making access to the media even more important. Media items can appeal to two groups, those with particular interest in a topic or familiar with the subject and the public in general. Trade issues can often be technical and not intuitively appealing to the layman. Such was the dilemma of the banana issue. A debate was waged in the print media but never aroused any general issue because bananas were cheap and always available, so consumers were not motivated, and the fruit was not produced in the United States. Hence, no farming community was affected. Most Americans knew nothing about where bananas came from. They knew only that bananas are part of a healthy diet as a natural source of potassium. Even when bananas were the cover story of Newsweek it did not penetrate the awareness of many. Indeed, raising the issue of bananas often was a cause of amusement.

The major print media became interested in the story of the US banana policy because it raised the issue of the buying of influence in the American political process. Since this was so commonplace in US politics, the print media had to be induced to become interested in the issue by an intensive campaign by Hazel Ross-Robinson, the Caribbean's lobbyist on bananas. Newsweek devoted its cover to the banana dispute on April 28, 1997, and one of its lead articles exposed the link between US policy and Lindner's donations.[74] A front-page feature in USA Today warned that "The costs of giving in to Chiquita's avarice were high. The rewards for the U.S. were very low."[75] The European press highlighted the Chiquita money trail and the irony that no bananas were exported from the United States.[76] Allusions to corporate greed, unfair trade practices, and underpaid labor did not incite outrage or the famous American sense of fair play among the American public.

Any publicity favorable to the Caribbean side of the issue or even balanced reporting was soon countered by Chiquita's money which was used to portray the issue as US companies losing business and jobs because of the unwillingness of the European Union to play fair in international trade. The Cincinnati Enquirer devoted a special section and most of its front page on Sunday, May 3, 1998, to exposing the business practices of Chiquita.[77] The special eighteen-page supplement traces Chiquita's subversion of laws in Guatemala and Honduras related to ownership, the safety and rights of workers, and environmental pollution. The supplement also claimed that Chiquita tried to cover up a bribery scheme in Colombia. The article caused a furor in which Chiquita sued the newspaper on the basis that the information had been improperly acquired and claimed that the reports were based on stolen voice mail messages. The publisher, Harry M. Whipple and editor, Lawrence K. Beaupre of the newspaper apologized by running three front-page apologies,[78] paid more than $10 million to Chiquita and were further muzzled by a Confidentiality Agreement with Chiquita which prevented them from providing access to voice mail messages and Chiquita's records. But, as the New York Times pointed out, "some of the allegations cannot be dismissed so easily, despite the questions raised about the reporting method ... no-one has disputed the authenticity of the voice mail and internal Chiquita records that form the basis" of the articles.[79] The information disclosed prompted the Securities and Exchange Commission to begin an investigation of Chiquita and the Federal Bureau of Investigations to continue their criminal investigation.

The Caribbean governments and their embassies in Washington DC had to be vigilant in monitoring and responding to propaganda disseminated in the media by Chiquita sources. On a number of occasions, the Caribbean had to respond through letters to the Editor (e.g., Bernal's letter on "Bananas and Drugs" in the Washington Post, October 1999).[80] Unfortunately, many of the responses and corrections were not published (e.g., Hazel Ross-Robinson's letter to Don Logan, Chairman and CEO of Time Magazine in February 1999), which sought to correct inaccurate statements such as "Chiquita denied access to the European market."[81] Time Magazine acknowledged the "candid criticism" and information provided but regretted that they were unable to publish the comments but circulated the letter to their editors.[82] Several sympathetic articles were decrying US policy as destabilizing the region, pointing out that the decline of banana production had led to increased production of marijuana.[83] Prime Minister James F. Mitchell of St. Vincent and the Grenadines put it frankly that he regarded the United States as a friend in anti-drug cooperation but a foe of that effort because of its stance on bananas.[84]

Part of the Chiquita strategy was to link bananas with other EU-US trade disputes such as beef hormones and to portray the European Union as the villain. This tactic resonated with a wide cross-section of members of Congress and many ill-informed sections of the public. An integral part of the strategy was to convince government officials and the public at large that in addition to damaging US corporate interests, the European Union was actually taking advantage of the powerless and/or unsophisticated governments and farmers in the Caribbean region. At the request of Chiquita's lawyers in Washington, a meeting took place with the Caribbean ambassadors at the Embassy of Jamaica in which these lawyers made an absurd and patronizing attempt to convince the ambassadors that Chiquita was prepared to agree to a long-term contract to buy all the bananas fit for export over an extended period. This attempt was summarily dismissed.

The counter arguments and the Caribbean's case for the retention of the existing EU banana regime or a new arrangement which preserved the region's market access were also aired in the media. TransAfrica organized an investigative mission to the Caribbean to see the banana industry first hand.[85] Robinson and TransAfrica dumped 2,000 pounds of bananas on the steps at the entrance to the USTR. That April 15, 1997 demonstration was shown by CNN nationally and worldwide. Other television networks carried the incident in every major market except Chicago. Newsweek and the Washington Times[86] covered it, but not the Washington Post.[87] Surprisingly, the radical, liberal, and minority press that should naturally have been sympathetic voices, paid little attention to the issue or in some cases displayed indifference (e.g., Afro-American press).[88] In the print media, there was coverage of the dispute, especially after the United States escalated the hostility by imposing sanctions on the European Union. There were also opinion editorials (e.g., Ambassador Bernal's opinion editorials in the Journal of Commerce on April 4, 1997, and February 3, 1999).

The outrageous maneuvering of elected officials on behalf of Chiquita prompted even the normally restrained and conventional Washington Post to condemn these actions in an editorial entitled "Banana Republic". The Post pointed out the enormous political donations of Lindner and his family and stated that "As a favor to this generous man, Mr. Lott is now said to be weighing whether to give his firm a veto over the position that the administration can take in its banana dispute with Europe. It would in effect put Mr. Lindner, a private citizen, on a near-equal footing with the President."[89]

Part of the strategy to ameliorate the position of the USTR was to mobilize support including from the public at large for the banana situation to be recognized as causing a major threat to US national security by increased drug trafficking, money laundering, illegal migration, and political instability. Ambassador Bernal told Newsweek, "This is not a simple issue of economics but of survival ... this is not just about trade, but security."[90] This theme was a leitmotif of media coverage (e.g., Newsweek devoted its April 28, 1997 cover and lead story to bananas stating that the "island economies were the new victims of free trade" and one of the repercussions could be increased drug trafficking as "some banana farmers are already diversifying into pot)." The report also highlights the concern that "the steppingstone islands of the Eastern Caribbean are the fastest growing trafficking zones."[91]

Another theme which the press articulated was the deterioration in US Caribbean relations as a result of US banana policy. The CARICOM leaders issued a communiqué on March 5, 1999, which states that "the countries of the Caribbean community have agreed to immediately review the Bridgetown Accord to determine the basis for continued cooperation."[92] The Miami Herald, in an editorial, chided the United States and warned that "While the US remains blithely indifferent, some of its island neighbors see the resentment over a long list of grievances." They pointed specifically to the issue of bananas stating that "The United States has angered the Caribbean by challenging the preferential treatment that European nations have given to bananas from their former Caribbean colonies … continued U.S. indifference towards its neighbors in this region could cause problems larger than most Americans realize—problems that have nothing to do with Castro or the Cold War."[93] Interviewed by the Miami Herald, Ambassador Bernal described Caribbean-US relations as a "long-standing friendship that is strained."[94] The Caribbean while being very angry had to be careful not to suggest or threaten that it would "review" its cooperation on narcotics trafficking as was reported at one point in the Washington Times. A calmer disposition was put on this as the same paper reported: "Jamaican Ambassador Richard Bernal, at the forefront of pleading the case of the small islands cautioned that, 'There has been no treaty abrogation or singling out of drug interdiction for retaliation.'"[95]

The small Caribbean countries were seen as the victims of a bullying super power and a powerful multinational corporation whose resources dwarfed those of the governments and the small banana farmers.[96] The total exports of the banana exporting countries of the Caribbean accounted for less than 3 percent of the world market and 9 percent of the European market compared to Chiquita's share of 26 percent of the world market and 19 percent of the European market.[97] The enormous disparity between Chiquita and the combined Caribbean region elicited sympathy across the board in US society and the body politic. An anonymous high-ranking State Department official told the New York Times that damaging the banana trade destabilizes governments, reduces jobs, promotes drug trafficking, and increases migration—this creates a world class headache for the United States.[98]

The Caribbean was faced with several commentaries in the media by persons who may either have been in the pay of Chiquita or angling for work with the multinational firm. Many opportunists were able to do this under the guise of defending US economic interests and/or as savants of free trade. It was good publicity for those in the trade lobbying and advisory business, as their comments appear as opinion editorials in prominent newspapers. For example, Clayton Yeutter, former US Trade Representative in the Reagan administration took up the cause of Chiquita in an article in the conservative Washington Times in mid-1995.[99] This like other articles of this propagandist genre overlooked facts and implications. The reply on behalf of the CBI pointed out that "Clayton Yeutter ignores a central aspect of the banana trade dispute between the United States and the European Union—the continued US national interest in the viability and health of Caribbean economies. The United States—at the encouragement of Chiquita Brands International—is working to eliminate the banana-import regime. Such a move would undermine the US-Caribbean economic relationship, upsetting a region whose stability is critical to US national security. In advocating the short-term fix to dismantle the European Union banana-import regime, Mr. Yeutter may indeed advance the interests of one or two US-based companies. But in the long run, this policy would undermine the positions of many other US firms that depend on a sound US-Caribbean trading relationship."[100]

The ability of Caribbean journalists was important, especially if their articles and commentaries were carried in international media. Highly regarded Jamaican journalist Canute James who was a correspondent for both the Financial Times of London and the Economist magazine was very helpful in articulating the issue from an empathetic Caribbean perspective.[101]

Think Tanks

The most influential think tanks did not become involved in the debate over US banana policy, largely because institutions like the IIE and The Brookings Institution regarded this as a question of free trade versus preferential trade by the European Union to developing countries. There were no major publications by institutions with a research or policy interest in the Caribbean, except The North South Center.[102] This was unfortunate because the Caribbean struggled to counter technical reports by the World Bank (e.g., the infamous "Bananarama" report), which argued that the EU's banana regime should be replaced by direct aid because this would be better and cheaper. Borrell also claimed that protectionist schemes are an "exceptionally inefficient method of transferring resources" citing the EU banana regime as costing European consumers $1.6 billion to transfer

$300 million to eleven beneficiary economies.[103] A study by the University of Exeter makes the critical point that a "perfectly competitive model is inappropriate for the banana market. Account must be taken of the oligopolistic elements in that market. Once that is done, it ceases to follow that full liberalization maximizes consumer welfare ... it is not, therefore, a correct formulation of the problem to say it is solely about how much consumers would lose in order to favor some producers and suppliers. It is in the interest of EC consumers to maintain genuine access to the banana market by a wide range of suppliers, (i.e., to ensure real competition in the market place) ... there are technically several ways of doing this ... some combination of effective tariffs and quotas is desirable. In our judgment then, however, the EC must move to more explicit regulation of the market."[104]

The Council on Hemispheric Affairs did a very revealing exposé of Chiquita's operations in Honduras, documenting the disreputable business practices of Chiquita and condemning the "buying of access in Washington".[105] The principal findings of this report were summarized in the Washington Post bringing them to the attention of a wider audience.[106]

To counter the technical studies arguing that the dismantlement of the EU banana regime not only conformed to the principles of free trade but would actually be good for the Caribbean as they would shift into products in which they enjoy a comparative advantage, the CBEA commissioned its own study. The study entitled "The Economic Consequences of a Banana Collapse in the Caribbean" was produced by two well-known Caribbean academic/trade policy analysts, Henry S. Gill and Dr. Anthony P. Gonzales. They conclude that "were the foundations of the present EU banana regime to be modified in such a way as to reduce the provisions in favor of Caribbean exporters, a disastrous economic situation would ensue in the Caribbean and economic collapse would be inevitable for the smaller banana producing territories."[107] There were severe constraints involved in diversification out of banana production, a finding with which Welch concurs.[108]

The Executive

President Clinton repeatedly assured his counterparts in the Caribbean that the United States intended no harm to the Caribbean and that in any future arrangement it would endeavor to ensure that the Caribbean banana exporters would have continued access to the EU market. Several prime ministers of CARICOM wrote to President Clinton in the first half of 1995 urging him to honor an earlier promise that the region's banana industry would not be harmed by the US challenge to the EU's import regime. In response, President Clinton, in June 1995, assured them that "I am very sensitive to the importance of bananas to the Caribbean economies" and stated that "Our objectives are to encourage the EU to adopt a regime that allows Caribbean nations to continue to supply the EU market, retaining preferences for Caribbean bananas, but not discriminating against U.S. marketing companies."[109] Despite these assurances, US policy remained unchanged prompting the CARICOM Heads of Governments in July 1995 reiterate its call "for the need for the termination of the 301 action".[110] Prime Minister Edison James lamented that the "message to President Clinton is that you cannot undermine our ability to develop while saying that you are our friend."[111]

Clinton extended these assurances to Prime Minister P.J. Patterson when they met in Washington in 1995 and to the meeting between himself and leaders of the CARICOM countries in Bridgetown, Barbados in May 1997. These sentiments were included in the Bridgetown Accord. President Clinton and his key advisors heard first hand from Caribbean leaders the uncertainty and potential fallout of a continuation of the US campaign to dismantle the EU banana regime. Dr. Vaughan Lewis, Prime Minister of St. Lucia, speaking at the Clinton-CARICOM Summit in May 1997 pointed to a "doomsday scenario" of the economic and social consequences of the collapse of the banana industry.[112] The Caribbean became disillusioned by the difference between statements from the president and other senior officials and the actual policy pursued by the USTR. The disillusionment was formalized when CARICOM met in Suriname March 7–9, 1999, when it was decided to undertake an immediate review of the Bridgetown Accord with a view to conveying the disappointment of the region to US Secretary of State Madeleine Albright at the annual meeting between the Secretary of State and the foreign ministers of CARICOM. This was done to little avail when this meeting took place in New Orleans in early 2000. Meanwhile, throughout the Caribbean, there was a strong new undercurrent of resentment toward the United States resulting in the suggestion that CARICOM would reconsider their counter narcotics cooperation with the United States if it imposed sanctions against the European Union.[113]

The Clinton administration could not possibly have ignored steadily increasing contributions from Lindner as $500,000 in donations during

1993 and 1994 made him one of the top donors to the Democratic Party. These contributions could not be unconnected with his regular attendance at White House functions and the several meetings he held with Mickey Kantor. When asked by Time Magazine about the connection between Lindner's contribution and the US policy on bananas, the consistently disingenuous Kantor stated categorically and unequivocally "It made no difference to us whatsoever. We didn't hear a word from the White House."[114] The assurances and pronouncements from the Clinton administration were greeted with increasing skepticism. Randall Robinson in a public lecture in Jamaica accused President Clinton of lying and admitted that initially he and others had been deceived by the assurances from US Trade Representative Mickey Kantor.[115]

The banana policy of the Clinton administration was deprived of any semblance of legitimacy by the fact that it was widely known that this was a policy bought and paid for by Lindner's campaign donations to the Democratic Party. The dubious policy was harshly condemned by some members of Congress as risking a full scale and damaging trade war with the European Union to benefit a single company whose product did not originate in the United States. Representatives Waters, Bonior, Kaptur, Meek, Maloney, and DeFazio in a 'Dear Colleague' letter, state, "There is only one company—Chiquita Brands—that claims to have been harmed by the banana regime. However, the bananas that Chiquita sells in the European Union are not produced in the United States … There is simply no reason to begin a trade war with our European trading partners or threaten the stability of our Caribbean neighbors in order to promote the narrow interests of one company."[116] Congresswoman Maxine Waters of the Democratic Party introduced a draft Bill on March 22, 1999, to bar the imposition of increased tariffs or other retaliatory measures against the products of the European Union in response to the banana regime of the European Union. This unprecedented initiative, however, never became legislation.

President Clinton was personally engaged on this issue, for example, he discussed the banana issue at the White House with Sir Leon Brittan[117] and with EU Commission President Jacques Santer.[118] Clinton was unmoved by criticism and entreaties from a wide range of interests in the United States and allowed the country to endure disparaging remarks about its conduct towards the small Caribbean countries that have been longstanding allies with a shared commitment to democracy and private sector-led, market economic strategies. Meanwhile, leading officials in the administration continued to regurgitate platitudes, for example, Barshefsky who informed Congressman Rangel in writing that at "the Bridgetown Summit, the President reiterated his personal commitment to resolving the WTO banana case in a manner which allows WTO consistent tariff preferences for traditional Caribbean bananas."[119] The President made no discernible changes in US policy despite sustained pressure from a cross-section of Republicans and Democrats, for example, receiving a letter signed by 40 members of Congress on July 31, 1997. This letter made the modest suggestion that his administration "allow the present system to remain in place until its date of expiration, with all parties in consultations to arrive at a workable option, which will not result in the destruction of the Caribbean banana industry."[120]

Congress

There is a clear correlation between campaign donations and members of the House and Senate who were supportive of the Chiquita-inspired US stance on bananas. These include Senator and Republican presidential candidate, Bob Dole who received over $121,000 during the period 1994–1996. Other fervent advocates of Chiquita interests include Senator Mike DeWine (R) of Ohio, Senator John Glenn (D) of Ohio, Representative Bob Portman (R) of Ohio, and Representative Steve Chabot (R) of Ohio, all of whom received campaign contributions from Lindner. Another important supporter was Senator Trent Lott (R) who undoubtedly was aware of $4 million plus worth of contributions to the Republican Party. The influence of Lindner's money was evident in the actions of many senior Republicans. Examples include Newt Gingrich, who received over $55,000 and Trent Lott who consistently tried to pressure the Clinton administration. For example, they wrote to President Clinton on October 7, 1998, calling on the President to "publicly spell out a specific timetable the Administration will take to ensure compliance with the WTO's ruling" and went as far as threatening "If the Administration will not take action to protect trade agreements, Congress will have no choice but to take action on its own."[121] Senator Bob Dole was Chiquita's special emissary and lobbyist, using every device to pressure a morally flexible Kantor to make US policy and Chiquita's demands one and the same. At one of a series of meetings, which Kantor attended in Dole's Capitol Hill office to work on how to secure passage of the Uruguay Round trade pact, Kantor was surprised to discover that "the subject was bananas—specifically, bananas shipped from Latin America by Chiquita Brands International, owned by Carl Lindner, who was sitting in Mr. Dole's office."[122]

The Caribbean, with the guidance of lobbyist Hazel Ross-Robinson, mounted a concerted effort to lobby Congress (e.g., at the behest of Ross-Robinson, the Caribbean Banana Exporters Association met in Washington DC, June 11–12, 1997, to facilitate meetings with Congress). The representatives on that occasion met with the following members: Congressmen Bill Lipinski, Dale Kildee, Duncan Hunter, James Clyburn, Jerry Costello, Thomas Foglietta, Jack Kingston, Richard Gephardt, Todd Tiahrt, Peter DeFazio, Congresswomen Lynn Rivers, Patsy Mink, and Senator Charles Hagel.

American political parties do not adhere to strict party doctrine or principles and objectives. The divide between the Democratic Party and the Republican Party is a very broad and loose philosophical one and at the margins allowing local economic concerns, and members may differ little from the opposing party. Party discipline is flexible and generous. Thus, varying philosophies of trade influenced the stance taken on trade. Trade policies are also affected by the general prevailing disposition towards international trade, reflected nationalism, protectionism, and liberalization.[123] There were supportive representatives, both Republicans and Democrats who took up the cause of the Caribbean for a variety of motivations. On July 31 1997, 40 members of Congress including many from the Congressional Black Caucus, as well as Nancy Kaptur, Joseph P. Kennedy II, Republican J.C. Watts, David Bonior, Carolyn C. Kirkpatrick, and Peter DeFazio, called on the President to "decline to implement the WTO ruling on the European Banana Regime" and "allow the present system to remain in place until its date of expiration." This, they suggested, would allow the Caribbean states "sufficient time to achieve increased efficiency and diversification of its economic base."[124]

The ever devious congressional operatives of Chiquita, led by Senator Trent Lott, were able to slip into the CBI Enhancement component of the Africa Trade Bill, a provision known as the "Carousel Provision", which allows the USTR to rotate the list of European products on which prohibitive 100 percent tariffs are imposed. The objective of this provision is to spread the pain around and to threaten all imports, thereby involving more industries in Europe in the repercussions of the EU's banana policy.[125]

The Clinton administration had "serious concerns" about legislation proposed by Senate Majority Leader Trent Lott that would make it harder to remove $308.2 million in US retaliation against the European Union in beef and banana disputes. Lott, a Mississippi Republican, tried to attach his amendment to one of the few remaining bills that Congress was expected to approve before it adjourned for the November 2000 elections. "The administration has serious concerns about this proposal and strongly opposes it," said Brendan Daly, spokesman for the USTR's office. According to a draft version, the Lott amendment would have required US sanctions to remain in place until the WTO rules that the EU has changed its policies to conform to international trade rules or the affected US industry in each case agrees retaliation is no longer necessary. The Clinton administration was concerned that the second provision would subordinate US government interests by effectively giving cattle producers or Chiquita Brands International, a banana marketing giant, veto power over any deal the United States might make with the European Union. Maxine Waters and other members of the Congressional Black Caucus were able to mobilize over 170 members to oppose the bill.

Congressional Black Caucus

Members of the Congressional Black Caucus were on the whole supportive, particularly Maxine Waters and Charles Rangel. Another outspoken critic of Chiquita and ally of the Caribbean was Marcy Kaptur of Ohio. Support took the form of writing letters to the President (e.g., letter from Waters, Dellums, Kaptur, Hunter and Bartlett in June 1997), which called on him to allow the present system to remain in place; decline to implement the WTO ruling; exercise a salutary influence on other complaining parties; and allow the Caribbean states sufficient time for economic diversification.[126] Members of Congress were also instrumental in providing media access, for example, interviews with Ambassador Bernal on the radio talk show of Congresswoman Marcy Kaptur and the radio and television shows of Congressman Ed Towns. Some members of Congress responded to the briefings by spokespersons and ambassadors of the Caribbean, for example, Senator Paul D. Coverdell and Representative Saxby Chambliss wrote to Ambassador Barshefsky in September 1998 requesting that "the U.S. refrain from disrupting further the EU banana regime since the U.S. does not export bananas nor are any U.S. jobs threatened. Furthermore, the contraction or collapse of the banana industry in the Caribbean region could lead to a social and economic disaster and make it vulnerable to drug traffickers as well as an immigration problem for our nation."[127]

Senator Dole's Lobbying For Chiquita

Carl Lindner owner of Chiquita had personal wealth estimated at $830 million and that of his family at well over $1 billion.[128] It is reported by numerous sources that during 1993 and 1994 Carl Lindner donated almost $1 million shared between the Republican and the Democrats thereby becoming one of the largest donors.[129] Twelve senators and 50 representatives wrote letters supporting Chiquita's request for Section 301 investigation of damages to Chiquita from the EU banana regime.[130] Supporters in Congress included Senators Trent Lott and John Glenn and Congressmen Newt Gingrich who received financial contributions from Lindner[131] and Dick Gephardt.[132] The support in the House of Representatives is not surprising given that Lindner made financial contributions at the state level as well as at the national level.[133] Chiquita made financial contributions to Senator Bob Dole's campaigns and allowed him the use of the company plane during his presidential campaign, 12 flights alone according to the Federal Electoral Commission.[134] Senator Dole arranging meetings between himself, Lindner and Mickey Kantor, US Trade Representative.[135] As the New York Times described it: "Dole at Forefront of Trade Battle To Aid Donor's Banana Empire".[136] The problem was that the technical staff of the USTR could not find a real or devised justification for Section 301 or taking the case to the WTO.[137]

Dole led the campaign at the request of Carl Lindner to pressure the Latin American banana exporting countries to resile from the BFA by trying to persuade the US government to put pressure on them.[138] The reason for this was they would more susceptible to pressure than the Europeans and Chiquita was producing bananas in countries that did not have fixed quotas under the BFA, namely, Guatemala, Honduras, and Panama. Debora Spar recounts that: "Among the measures Dole sought legal provisions that would strip Colombia of the aid it received under U.S. programs designed to reduce the international flow of illicit drugs and a bill that would have required Colombia and Costa Rica undo the Framework Agreement or lose preferential access to the U.S. market."[139] Del Monte Foods and the Dole Food Company did not support Chiquita's request.

Lobbyists

During the first six months of the banana issue when the focus was on preventing the United States from taking action under Section 301, the Caribbean governments retained the services of lawyers Ray Calamaro and Christopher Parlin of Winthrop, Stimson, Putnam, and Roberts and the Fratelli Group, public relations consultants. This proved very expensive; in fact, the cost was unsustainable and the banana exporting countries decided to retain the services of Ross-Robinson and Associates.

Hazel Ross-Robinson was born and grew up in St. Kitts and was president of Ross-Robinson & Associates (RRA) in Washington, DC, which specialized in US foreign policy monitoring, analysis, and advocacy. Prior to establishing Ross-Robinson & Associates, Ms. Ross-Robinson held a number of senior staff positions within the United States Congress: 1993–1995, Foreign Policy Advisor to the Chairman of the House Armed Services/National Security Committee; 1991–1993, Deputy Staff Director, House Subcommittee on Insular and International Affairs; 1985–1991, Foreign Policy Advisor to Congressman Bill Gray in his sequential capacities as Chairman of the House Budget Committee, Chairman of the House Democratic Caucus, and House Majority Whip; and served as Associate Staff Director, House Appropriations Subcommittee on Foreign Operations. Prior to her congressional career, Ms. Ross-Robinson was the Legislative Assistant for Caribbean and Economic Affairs at TransAfrica in Washington, DC from 1982–1985. Ms. Ross-Robinson holds a B.A. (Economics, Loyola University, Montreal 1975) and an MBA (Concordia University, Montreal 1977). She is married to Randall Robinson of TransAfrica Forum.

Ross-Robinson was responsible for several of the initiatives, which the Caribbean representatives executed in their attempts to sway the US government, in particular, the Congress. Ross-Robinson played a significant part in generating press coverage of the banana issue and the view of the banana exporting countries of the Caribbean. For example, a press briefing arranged by RRA allowed the ambassadors of Belize, Grenada, Jamaica, St. Lucia and St. Vincent to address journalists from CNN, Washington Times, Journal of Commerce, USA Today, Associated Press, Business Week, National Journal, and Reuters. This resulted in valuable coverage by Business Week, Associated Press, and Reuters. She was able to have the support of TransAfrica headed by Randall Robinson. He was a vital link to the African American community and Congressional Black Caucus and a highly respected activist who had done much to end apartheid in South Africa. He called for reparations for African Americans.[140] Robinson was able to widely publicize the banana issue by dumping boxes of bananas on the front steps of the USTR.[141]

Caribbean Community in the United States

The Caribbean community in the United States was fully mobilized to lobby elected officials and the federal government to change US policy on bananas. The Ambassador of Jamaica to the United States wrote to a list of Jamaican organizations throughout the United States regularly providing them with information, which they would find useful in their lobbying efforts.[142] Community organizations wrote letters to government officials, elected representatives at state and federal levels and to the press. Citizens of Caribbean origin expressed their consternation and disgust at every available opportunity. As a result, elected officials were made aware of the importance of this issue particularly in cities where there are large concentrations of Caribbean Americans. However, given the size of the Caribbean population in the United States and the fact that contrary views were being expressed by the Central American community, the banana dispute never became a 'do or die' issue for any elected official. The black caucus members responded by expressing their concern to the executive and forestalling the escalation of punitive measures against the European Union. For example, an attempt to pass a resolution on beef hormones and bananas (late in the evening near the close of a session of Congress) was thwarted in no small measure by the resolute opposition of Sheila Jackson-Lee (D) of Houston and of Jamaican descent. The National Coalition on Caribbean Affairs (NCOCA), at the instigation of Ambassador Bernal and lobbyist, Hazel Ross-Robinson, met with the State Department and the National Security Council articulating concerns about the precipitate action of the United States and calling for a resolution which would not jeopardize the viability of the export of bananas from the Caribbean to its sole market, the European Union. They called for a transition period to allow the small banana producing countries to become more competitive because four out of five families in the Eastern Caribbean depended on banana production. In the calculation of NCOCA, "whatever gains the United States might enjoy from the elimination of preferences for Caribbean bananas, they would be more than offset by the cost of drug interdiction and political and social instability."[143] The meetings which took place in April 1998 involved Professor Ransford Palmer, Dr. Alston Meade, Leopold Edwards, and Curtis Ward Esq.

At the instigation of the Embassy of Jamaica and other Caribbean missions, the Caribbean community was encouraged to lobby all political representatives from the White House to locally elected officials. Professor Donald Morgan, President of the Jamaica Volunteers Association wrote to the Washington Post and to President Clinton.[144] In one instance, the Ambassador of Jamaica wrote to all the governors attending the National Governors' Association encouraging support for the FTAA, the CBI, and the EU/US banana issue. Although most of the replies were perfunctory[145] and noncommittal, this initiative served to put Caribbean issues on the agenda of the governors. Caribbean professionals in Washington formed the Committee to Save Caribbean Banana Farmers and engaged in several activities including picketing outside the White House.

African American Community

The domestic constituency that showed the greatest sympathy for the dilemma faced by the Caribbean was the African American community. Most of this support was galvanized and guided by the Randall Robinson-led TransAfrica Forum. Robinson, a graduate of Harvard Law School, who has a distinguished reputation for integrity and fearless advocacy against apartheid and US opposition to the Aristide government, became very involved in the struggle to reverse the direction of the US banana policy. Prominent African Americans including Bill Cosby, Earl Graves, Bob Johnson, Joseph Lowery, Ed Lewis, Jesse Jackson, Danny Glover, Susan Taylor, and Roger Wilkins wrote to President Clinton on November 6, 1996. They strongly urged the administration to take seriously "predictions of economic destabilization, social dislocation, heightened vulnerability to drug trans-shipments headed to the United States, and an outflow of displaced workers to the United States and elsewhere if the U.S. does not modify its position."[146]

Robinson was instrumental in organizing and participated in a mission, which examined the banana issue by visiting the Caribbean. The mission included Randall Robinson, Congresswoman Maxine Waters (D), Congresswoman Carrie Meek (D), Professor Charles Ogletree of Harvard Law School, Willie L. Baker Jr., International Vice President of the United Food and Commercial Workers Union, and Professor Ibrahim J. Gassama, University of Oregon Law School. The participants were not confined to

African Americans as the group included Kenneth A. Cook of the Environmental Working Group, Katherine Ozer of the National Family Farm Coalition, and Lori Wallach, Director of Public Citizens Global Trade Watch (which was founded by Ralph Nader) who later masterminded the demonstrations at the WTO Ministerial Meeting in Seattle.[147] The mission visited Jamaica, Dominica, and St. Lucia and met with ministers, government officials, trade unionists, and banana farmers and visited banana farms. Their report found that (a) no other legal crop could immediately play the role of the banana industry; (b) a collapse of the banana industry would lead to massive job losses, social disorder, increased illegal immigration to the United States and increased drug trafficking; (c) US banana policy "can be explained only as a result of political pressure from a single multinational company: Chiquita"; and (d) the United States should refrain from interfering with the current marketing arrangements for Caribbean bananas. The recommendations were (a) the United States should immediately resume "serious discussions at the highest possible level" with the Caribbean nations, "without the threat of unilateral sanctions;" (b) withdraw its complaint from the WTO and end its threat of sanctions; (c) if the WTO panel rules before the United States withdraws its complaint and if the ruling favors the United States, it should not enforce the ruling; and (d) the United States should use its influence with the other complaining parties to encourage and negotiate its solution.[148]

When the United States was preparing to impose sanctions, the USTR was obliged to invite comments from the public by way of a public hearing announced in the Federal Register on November 10, 1998. This provided an opportunity for African American supporters of the Caribbean cause to submit statements.[149] The leading members of the African American community took their advocacy to a wider audience through the media such as an opinion editorial in the Christian Science Monitor by Professor Ogletree of Harvard University Law School and Randall Robinson of TransAfrica.[150] This paralleled similar concerns expressed in other leading newspapers such as the exposé on Lindner's campaign contributions in The Washington Times,'[151] Newsweek, Time, and the Cincinnati Enquirer.

In order to widen the political support for the Caribbean position on the banana issue, Ambassador Bernal sought to engage the National Council of Black Republicans (NCBR)[152] because the Republican Party with few exceptions had ignored the banana issue. The NCBR responded by outlining a number of ways in which the organization could be helpful to CARICOM states on the banana issue.

Caribbean Business Community

The senior managers and technicians of Caribbean private sector firms in all aspects of farming, shipping, and overseas marketing were involved on a continuous basis in trying to dissuade the United States from its banana policy. The business community representatives participated in joint missions with the Caribbean governments in technical discussions. Their views, concerns, and suggestions were solicited regularly and found an essential component of the campaign. One of the important players was Dr. Marshall Hall, Chief Operating Officer of Jamaica Producers, a Jamaican multinational corporation with offices in Kingston and London. A former professor in the School of Management at the University of the West Indies at Mona, he was a forceful and pragmatic advocate who combined an intimate knowledge of the industry and market with a sound knowledge of economics. He was chairman of the CBEA during most of the duration of the banana dispute. The CBEA evolved from what was the Commonwealth Banana Exporters Association which was originally established in 1972. The CBEA consisted of representatives from the banana growers and exporting companies from all the Caribbean countries involved in the banana trade namely Belize, Dominica, the Dominican Republic, Grenada, Jamaica, St. Lucia, St. Vincent and the Grenadines and Suriname. There was very close cooperation and continuous dialogue between the private sectors of the banana exporting countries of the Caribbean. The CBEA along with the individual companies invested substantial resources to finance travel, research, and lobbying. The CBEA even held some of its meetings in the United States including one in Washington DC to facilitate lobbying Congress, government officials, and the press.

Us Business Community

The banana issue was not one which galvanized wide support in the US business community because there was not a united or common industry position, which meant it was a complaint by Chiquita. Moreover, the product was not produced in the United States and no jobs in the United States were directly in danger. An exception was the American Farm Bureau Federation which in a statement to the USTR in December 1998 called for "the immediate and unconditional implementation of the EU banana and beef hormone rulings."[153]

EU Business Community

The European companies that have for many years imported bananas from the Caribbean countries were allies with the private sector and governments of the Caribbean as their interests in preserving the extant EU regime coincided. These companies, which include Fyffes,[154] contributed their skills, provided financial support, shared their European contacts, and lobbied vigorously in Britain and the European Union. Fyffes PLC in December 1994 made written submission to the USTR during the adjudication of Section 301. Their submission made the case of why Caribbean produce could not compete with bananas from Latin and Central America and hence the need for preferential treatment by the EU.[155] Company Secretary Philip Halpenny and the company's legal advisor Philip Lee were constantly involved and supportive of the Caribbean governments. They, along with Gordon Myers, a London representative of CBEA travelled to Washington to lobby the US government. The trio met with Congressional staff members during February 15–16, 1996, and senior officials of the USTR, and the Departments of Commerce and State.[156]

It was often not appreciated that the US and European governments saw the banana dispute as a corporate battle for market share of the global banana market. The respective governments were consciously supporting their companies. Indeed, one of the motivations for the British government establishing a preferential banana import arrangement for the Caribbean was to avoid dependence on supplies of bananas by American corporations and to deny them control of the British retail market.[157] This happily was complementary to an aid mechanism for the Caribbean some of which had little else. This aid mechanism had many advantages, among which were support for national companies, the consumers noticed no discernable cost in terms of the price of bananas and the payments for bananas went directly to the farmers on a weekly basis without the sometimes problematic filtering through governments.

Caribbean Governments

The governments of the banana exporting countries in unison with the other CARICOM governments waged a multidimensional campaign against US banana policy. The campaign was operationalized in three arenas: The United States, the European Union, and in South and Central America. Every opportunity was utilized to air the concerns and recommendations of the Caribbean in both bilateral meetings and multilateral forums (e.g., the OAS,[158] U.N., World Bank), even if bananas were not explicitly on the agenda. At one stage, the Caribbean governments appealed to Canada to intervene in finding a resolution to the banana crisis.[159] Prime ministers and ministers of trade, foreign affairs, and agriculture met with and wrote letters to their counterparts. Meetings and exchanges of correspondence took place with the White House, Congress, the USTR, and the State Department. Members of the political directorate also were readily available to radio, television, and the newspapers. The ambassadors of the Caribbean to the United States played a pivotal role on a day-to-day basis interacting with all branches of the US government, society, and the media. They were tireless and relentless in their lobbying.[160]

In August 1994, five CARICOM heads of government (Jamaica, Barbados, St. Lucia, Trinidad and Tobago, and Guyana) discussed Caribbean-US relations including bananas over lunch with President Clinton at the White House. Prime Minister Patterson articulated the region's concerns about bananas and outlined the Caribbean's preferred solution during his meeting with President Clinton in Washington D.C. in 1995. Bananas were a central issue in the May 1997 Caribbean US Summit in Bridgetown, Barbados. On this occasion, Dr. Vaughn Lewis, Prime Minister of St. Lucia, the designated spokesperson for CARICOM, explained to President Clinton and Secretary of State Albright that bananas are as important to the Caribbean as motorcars are to Detroit. On October 14, 1998, Prime Minister Edison James of Dominica led a CARICOM mission, which met with Ambassador Charlene Barshefsky. The CARICOM delegation included Daniel Silva, Minister of Agriculture of Belize, Anthony Hylton, Minister of State, Ministry of Foreign Affairs and Foreign Trade of Jamaica, Byron Blake of the CARICOM Secretariat and the ambassadors of Belize, Grenada, Jamaica, and St. Lucia to the United States. Also included were representatives of the banana industry: Dr. Marshall Hall, Jamaica Banana Producers and Bernard Cornibert, WIDECO. The discussions were inconclusive as there was no softening of the US position.

Ministers and officials met with Mickey Kantor the day before the Summit of the Americas meeting in Miami, in 1994 and in May 1997, CARICOM trade ministers met with Ambassador Barshefsky in Bel Horizonte, Brazil during the FTAA ministerial meeting. The foreign ministers of CARICOM and Secretary of State Albright discussed bananas during consultations at the UN General Assembly in New York in 1997, 1998, 1999 and 2000. Bananas were high on the agenda at the meetings of foreign ministers that the Secretary of State established to follow up the implementation of the Bridgetown Accord, which took place in Port-of-Spain in April 1998 and New Orleans in April 2000.

On September 13, 1995, P.J. Patterson, Prime Minister of Jamaica met with President Bill Clinton at the White House and the issue of bananas was discussed[161] but there was no resolution and the concerns expressed were noted but no assurances were given as to how and when there would be a resolution. This was a clear indication that the US administration was not rethinking or changing its approach.

The technicians and experts from the United States and CARICOM met on numerous occasions in both formal meetings and informal exchanges of views. The official consultative process took the form of the CARICOM/US technical working group, which was established in 1994. This body met in St. Lucia on March 2–3, 1995 and again in January 1997. On May 11, 1997, there was a US-CARICOM Summit which signed the Barbados Accord. The issue of bananas proved to be divisive and contentious. The wording on bananas was not settled until the evening before although the text had been negotiated in several meetings over the course of months.[162] "Although they signed a polite joint statement to continue negotiations over bananas, the Caribbean leaders indicated that they would continue resisting a United States effort to eliminate a trade preference that Caribbean bananas have in Europe."[163]

Free Trade Advocates

Chiquita calculated that its case which was argued on the basis of free trade would appeal to those who advocate free trade and by extension globalization. Chiquita argued that the EU banana regime was discriminatory and was unfair causing damage to their company. As such, it was in contradiction to the principles on which the WTO is established and the law of comparative advantage. Reality differs from theory and this is acknowledged in the rules of the WTO which provides special and differential treatment for developing countries. The WTO also permits preferential trade arrangements by granting waivers. There has been a long-running debate about whether free trade delivers the professed benefits for all countries, in particular developing economies. If fact, there are those who argue that international trade has resulted in a disproportionate share of the gains accruing to the more developed countries.[164]

The Financial Times newspaper was a highly regarded print media which carried articles supporting the dismantling of the EU banana regime because it was unfair and discriminatory. Martin Wolf, who writes for the Financial Times, is a well-known proponent of globalization.[165] The gravamen of his column of March 25, 1999, was: "Far from helping poor producers, the EU banana regime is discriminatory and makes no sense". He correctly pointed out that most of the difference between the prices paid by EU consumers and the world market price accrues to the companies that have import licenses and a smaller amount goes to the banana exporting countries.[166] For him, this is a very inefficient subsidy system. This concurs with the earlier work of Brent Borrell who estimates that in 1994 over one half of the cost to EU consumers accrues to banana companies and only a small amount to the beneficiary countries.[167] In spite of these inequities, the benefit to the small banana exporting countries was vitally important.

Whether advocacy articles were deliberately not published is not clear, but they appeared periodically and had to be responded to. In these, the Journal of Commerce was even-handed. For example, an editorial on April 11, 1997, noted that the preliminary ruling in the WTO in favor of the United States was a victory for trade liberalization.[168] Richard Bernal, the Jamaican ambassador to the United States, was allowed to respond pointing out that the ruling amounted to "friendly fire" harmful to the Caribbean allies of the United States and that this was not in the interest of the United States.[169]

The advocacy of free trade and further trade liberalization in the WTO was that this has become too intrusive interfering with and constraining policy space even in the countries that were the most vigorous advocates of free trade. Governments committed to progressive trade liberalization were desirous of accommodating some national goals not compatible with "pure" free trade. One of the issues then was genetically modified food and specifically beef hormones. As the Economist put it: "It is a battle about how far countries are willing to accept constraints on domestic policy in sensitive areas."[170]

World Trade Organization

The World Trade Organization is the largest intergovernmental organization whose purpose is to regulate multilateral trade between its member states. Based in Geneva, Switzerland it officially commenced on January 1, 1995, under the Marrakesh Agreement, signed by 123 nations.[171] It replaced the General Agreement on Tariffs and Trade (GATT), which commenced in 1948. The WTO is based on nondiscrimination which is founded on two principles (1) the most favored nation (MFN) and (2) the national treatment policy. Both are based on the main WTO rules on goods, services, and intellectual property. The MFN rule requires that a WTO member must apply the same terms and conditions on all trade with other WTO members.[172] National treatment requires that imported goods should be treated no less favorably than domestically produced goods.[173]

The WTO has three functions: (1) Negotiating the rules which govern the conduct of multilateral trade and the reduction in tariffs and barriers to international trade. (2) Assisting member states, in particular, developing countries, least-developed countries, and small vulnerable developing economies to implement the provisions of the WTO agreement. (3) Adjudicating disputes over the application and interpretation of existing rules. The WTO is not currently succeeding at negotiating new trade rules, but it continues to have a valid role in the implementation of the provisions of the WTO agreement and dispute settlement. The WTO has been extensively and intensively criticized as being dominated by the powerful developed countries and, in turn, corporations molded the international trade policy of their home countries. It is natural that in a capitalist economy trade policy would be shaped by the corporations, after all, it is firms that trade not countries. This being so, it is reasonable to deduce that the decisions of the WTO reflect the interests of the corporations of the powerful developed countries.[174] In this perspective, the WTO is a vehicle through which "nations are effectively used by corporations to challenge regulations in other countries".[175] This conclusion is not shared by many authors[176] but what is beyond dispute is that the developed countries have dominated the WTO. Given the disproportionate influence of developed countries, the WTO has not worked to the advantage of economic growth and export promotion of developing countries. Small developing countries are particularly at a disadvantage in the decision-making arrangements in the WTO.[177] In many respects, the small states could be said to be at the "margins" of the WTO.[178]

The WTO dispute settlement system (DSS) operates under the WTO Understanding on Rules and Procedures Governing the Settlement of Disputes. Participation requires specialized knowledge of national and international trade law and the WTO agreements. Sometimes governments of developing countries do not have the requisite legal skills and persons with the relevant experience. This could mean that the governments have to pay for legal services or get help from other governments or international organizations or allow the private parties involved to stand the expense of the legal services. Many small countries have foregone filing because of the expense involved and the fact that the process could take several years to be resolved. Most of the cases brought to the DSS are referred by the larger developing countries.[179] Developing countries, particularly small states, tend to be at a disadvantage in the dispute settlement system.[180] The WTO does recognize this problem and there are some concessionary provisions aimed at partially offsetting the disadvantages faced by developing countries.[181] An Advisory Centre on WTO Law was established in 2001.

In the case of the banana exporting countries of the Caribbean, their interests and those of Geest coincided. This confluence of interest resulted in the affected WTO Members Dispute Settlement Understanding (DSU) engagement also being supported by the legal efforts of their commercial partners' lawyers. Under the DSU, a number of interested Caribbean states secured third party status to the dispute. As third party members, the Caribbean states could provide a written submission, take part in all the proceedings, and make oral statements during the many iterations of the dispute.

Transatlantic Nexus

The attempts to influence US policy on bananas were conducted in tandem with a concerted effort at all political levels in Europe. The objectives in the European arena were, first, to bolster the resolve of the EU member states that supported the continuation of some type of preferential market access for bananas from the Caribbean and ACP countries (i.e., Great Britain, France, and Spain). Second, discourage or at least restrain the pressure mainly from Germany to have a completely unregulated market for bananas. The sustained diplomatic offense was executed on a day-to-day basis by embassies, particularly at the EU bodies in Brussels, at the

World Trade Organization in Geneva, and in London where most Caribbean countries had diplomatic missions.

The Caribbean sought every opportunity to keep the banana issue on the agenda of European governments by visiting missions from the banana exporting countries usually led by a prime minister or minister of foreign affairs and/or trade. Sir James Mitchell, Prime Minister of St. Vincent and the Grenadines led a delegation to Brussels during April 27–29, 1999. He met with Commissioners Neil Kinnock, Sir Leon Britain, and Frischler on the 27th and with parliamentarians John Come, Lord Plum, and Hans Swoboda on the 29th. Sir James went on to London and on May 4, held discussions with Brian Wilson, Minister of Trade of the United Kingdom. He was accompanied by Minister of Trade of Belize, Ralph Fonseca and Anthony Hylton, Minister of State in the Ministry of Foreign Affairs and Foreign Trade of Jamaica. Also, in May 1999 Prime Minister Edison C. James of Dominica met with Ministers and top officials in Spain, Belgium, and Finland and in June 1999, Prime Minister P.J. Patterson of Jamaica met with Prime Minister Blair of the United Kingdom and in Finland with President Maarti and Prime Minister Paavo Lipponen. Finland was due to accede to the presidency of the European Union on July 1, 1999. Prime Minister Patterson indicated that the Caribbean banana producing countries were "in a process of diversifying and enhancing the competitiveness of the banana industry, but undoubtedly would require a stable market for a reasonable period of time."[182] The Caribbean efforts were vigorously and tirelessly supported in the European Parliament by Mrs. Glenys Kinnock.[183]

The sale of Jamaica's banana exports to the United Kingdom has been handled since 1971 by the Jamaica Marketing Company Limited (JAMCO) based in London. JAMCO, as it was popularly known, was an external trade agency of the Government of Jamaica that served as the export marketing agent of the Banana Export Company of Jamaica (BECO). However, JAMCO was also involved in the diplomatic and technical initiatives. During much of the period of the 1990s when the banana dispute was raging on both sides of the Atlantic, JAMCO was headed by Courtenay Rattray and later by Junior Lodge. As an active trader in the European banana market, JAMCO, in tandem with WINBAN (now WIBDECO), was able to serve as an effective counterpart to Caribbean diplomats lobbying in Geneva, Brussels, and Washington, DC. Its commercial knowledge of the banana trade was useful in underpinning the policy positions that were being developed and advocated. JAMCO also provided lobbying support to Caribbean diplomats among whom the leaders were Derek Heaven, the High Commissioner of Jamaica to the United Kingdom and Ambassador Edwin Laurent of St. Lucia who was accredited in Brussels and Geneva. The CARICOM Secretariat provided technical support to the missions to the European Union. In nearly all such missions, the officer assigned was Byron Blake, Assistant Secretary General for Regional Trade and Economic Integration.

A major concern on both sides of the Atlantic was the damage, which the banana dispute caused to EU/US relations, particularly trade relations and the adverse impact on the multilateral trading system including the newly established WTO. The Financial Times warned that the banana dispute "not only threatens to inflict economic damage either side of the Atlantic, it could fatally weaken the system."[184] Eliza Paterson in an article published by the American Society for International Law opined: "In the end, the major impact of the dispute between the US and the EU over the latter's banana regime likely will be, not on that regime, but rather on the rules and laws for resolving international trade disputes. The case has raised serious questions about the process by which the US decides which trade disputes to pursue in the WTO: specifically, whether the system provides too much discretion to the Administration and thereby favors the politically connected."[185]

Strategy

The governments of the Caribbean, their lobbyists, and representatives of the banana industry tried to hold the bureaucracy, specifically the USTR to the promises and statements made by President Clinton and reiterated by other spokespersons. The strategy to change the banana policy of the United States was to make known that while it might benefit a single corporate entity, Chiquita, it would be seriously detrimental to US economic and political national interests. Material distributed to all members of Congress by the lobbyists for the Caribbean banana exporting countries stated, "Across a host of sectors, significant numbers of jobs will be lost if the United States proceeds with this misguided attempt to fortify the offshore activities of a U.S.—based multinational" and "elimination of Caribbean bananas from the EU market would deal a possibly fatal blow to the economic viability and stability of the long standing democracies of the region. The economic devastation would create social and political instability and undermine otherwise stable democracies."[186] This thrust focused on the State Department, the White House, the National Security Council, and the Congress through direct lobbying and the public through the media. These efforts were simultaneously accompanied by a dialogue with the USTR to find a technical solution to retain the existing EU banana regime or postpone its termination.

The spokespersons for the Windward Islands (including those based in Europe) advanced one position; the regime must not be changed. This was partly for tactical reasons and from an unwillingness to contemplate the possible disaster and to avoid political suicide. It was known to the banana farmers and the public that they had even conceded the possibility.[187] They and other representatives of the Caribbean and supporters of the Caribbean cause pointed to the catastrophic economic fallout, likely political instability, and the damage to countries that were friends and allies over a long time. This was the argument articulated by Prime Minister Edison James in October 1998, when he headed a Caribbean delegation of Washington based ambassadors and officials from the region to meet Ambassador Barchefsky and Ambassador Sheer (responsible for agricultural issues) of the USTR. These ministrations were politely acknowledged but completely ignored because the USTR regarded itself as a purely technical organization and such concerns were, strictly speaking, outside of their purview and should properly be directed to the State Department which should not "interfere" in trade matters. Prime Minister James presented the same points to senior staffers of the National Security Council and the National Economic Council where there was more receptivity and some empathy.[188]

The technical discussions involved technicians from the industry in the region with Dr. Marshall Hall of Jamaica Producers playing a lead role and there was valuable support from Bernard Cornibert, the London based representative of the Windward Islands Banana Development Company, who was always able to provide the latest thinking in European circles. The technical discussions were very constructive but were subsumed by the political negotiation, as all the participants were aware. Even though there was a sense of futility surrounding the technical exchanges, the Caribbean was obliged to participate in order to signal their seriousness in finding a solution rather than being branded by the United States as unwilling to change. Finding a technical solution was a euphemism by which the United States really meant to agree to a new regime, which would allow the United States to have what it wanted. Proposals from the

Caribbean, which did not accord with US views, were characterized as not being constructive.

President Clinton's letters to Congresswoman Maxine Waters and Congressman DeFazio illustrate this disingenuous tactic when he said, "we have made numerous offers to meet with them to discuss the WTO ruling against the EU banana regime and possible alternatives to this regime." At the United Nations General Assembly, Secretary of State Albright suggested to the Caribbean foreign ministers that a joint "brainstorming" session be held. We have reiterated this invitation through our embassies. I hope our Caribbean neighbors will engage with us in a common search for a solution".[189] This ploy was echoed by US officials in the media prompting a categorical denunciation by a wide cross-section of Caribbean officials citing the limited use of the meetings which had taken place and that the invitations were forthcoming only after the United States had won a favorable ruling from the WTO.[190] It is noteworthy that in a follow-up letter to President Clinton after the Bridgetown Summit, Prime Minister Patterson found it necessary to state: "We noted your commitment to raise this matter with the heads of state and government of the European Union (EU) during your recent visit. While we urgently await the outcome of these discussions, we must remind you of our desire to be involved in the discussions before any agreement is finally struck."[191]

At the instigation of Ambassador Bernal, a decision was taken by the CARICOM ambassadors in Washington and the banana lobbyists to give more attention to portraying the banana issue as one which posed a serious threat to the national security of the United States because a contraction or collapse of the banana industry would cause increased production and transshipment of drugs, money laundering, and illegal migration to the United States. In an interview with Newsweek, Ambassador Bernal pointed out that, "This is not a simple issue of economics but of survival. This is not just about trade, but security."[192] The strategy commenced with a press conference at the National Press Club on December 16, 1997, at which ambassadors from all the CARICOM countries spoke. The Ambassador for Guyana, Dr. Odeen Ishmael, put it baldly when he said, "If bananas decrease drugs will increase." This concern was soon picked up in the press and was understood by members of Congress, the State Department, the Drug Enforcement Agency (DEA) and agencies concerned with national security. US Gen. John Sheehan, commander of the US Atlantic Command responsible for drug interdiction efforts in the Caribbean, told a Washington, DC policy forum that the Caribbean banana industry must be maintained for US interests. "If you start deteriorating the economic infrastructure in the region, it is going to become my problem," he told the group.[193] The concerns about increased drug trafficking were based on empirical evidence, according to the US Drug Enforcement Administration, 40 percent of the cocaine and heroin in the United States comes through the Caribbean—and the steppingstone islands of the Eastern Caribbean are the fastest-growing trafficking zones.[194] The reduction in banana production and exports, which accompanied the uncertainty about the future of the EU banana regime was compounded by the adverse impact of NAFTA on apparel exports. According to the Caribbean Textiles and Apparel Institute, more than 150 apparel plants closed in the Caribbean between 1995 and 1996, resulting in the loss of about 123,000 jobs, mostly in Jamaica and the Dominican Republic.[195]

The CARICOM countries threatened to review their agreements with the United States, such as those related to counter narcotics cooperation and the Bridgetown Accord. This was a signal that the CARICOM countries were prepared to consider some kind of retaliation against the United States. While this played well to Caribbean audiences, it almost backfired and had to be delicately handled in the United States, where the immediate reaction was to accuse the Caribbean of breaking treaties with the United States. Quizzed by the Washington Times, Jamaican Ambassador Richard Bernal explained that "at this point, this is a review, there has been no treaty abrogation or the singling out of drug interdiction for retaliation."[196] This threat to not participate in agreements or forums important to the United States was first resorted to at the first Summit of the Americas in Miami but averted by certain assurances given by Kantor to the prime ministers and ministers of the Caribbean in a meeting held the evening before the start of the Summit. These assurances subsequently turned out to be a pack of lies.[197] What was significant about this proposed action was the solidarity of all the governments of the Caribbean speaking and acting as one unit, namely CARICOM. The support of states within CARICOM, which did not export bananas for those countries, which exported bananas, was constant in all arenas and forums in which the issue was discussed. The banana question was raised by any government that had an opportunity to do so, even at meetings and in institutions where the banana issue was not a part of the agenda (e.g., at the Organization of the American States and the International Monetary Fund).

One of the proposals which the Caribbean repeatedly recited was the need for an extended period of adjustment about 5 years, during which the industry would improve productivity, reduce costs of production, if possible, and diversify by transferring the farmers who could not compete into other agricultural pursuits. In July 1997, 40 members of Congress urged the President to recognize that Caribbean states must be allowed sufficient time to achieve increased efficiency and diversification.[198] The Congressional Black Caucus wrote to President Clinton in October 1997, pointing out that a 15 month adjustment period permitted by a recent WTO ruling on bananas was not reasonable and warned that the "failure" of US negotiators to be cognizant of this would "plunge these small, proud, stable, democracies into a state of pitiable dependency."[199] The need for an adjustment period was so necessary and reasonable that the United States could not find a way to refuse while maintaining a posture of concern, which it had professed on numerous occasions. The United States was totally noncommittal when there was a suggestion that a pool of financial resources, to which it would be a contributor, should be established to assist in the adjustment process in the affected countries on the Caribbean. The other approach taken by the United States to the proposal for financial aid was to suggest that the European Union should fund any such scheme from tariff revenue from non-ACP bananas.

Epilogue

At the end of 2000 when Clinton demitted office as president, the banana dispute remained unresolved as the EU-US Summit of Heads of Government of December 18, 2000, failed to make a breakthrough on bananas.[200] President Clinton's administration went to extraordinary lengths, risked a major trade war with the European Union, and was willing to bear the cost of EU sanctions to pull down the EU banana regime. Meanwhile, there was a refusal to concede the devastation which would result in the Caribbean. The United States offered no aid but suggested that it was the responsibility of the European Union to provide aid for the banana industry. The fact that the United States was prepared to pursue this course of potential costly action was indicative of the influence being brought to bear on the administration. As the "Banana War" went on, the British and French became increasingly willing to settle. In fairness, they had displayed strong resolve over many years and many rulings against the regime in the WTO. Based on reports from their counterparts in Europe, the feeling among Caribbean diplomats in Washington DC on July 20, 1999, was: "There is a strong desire in Europe to conclude this banana war with the United States as soon as possible. There seems to be a reluctance in Europe to discuss bananas with the Caribbean. Europe, therefore, not only wants a regime, which will end the fight now but one which will not be open to challenges in the future. The traditional strong supporters of St. Lucia and the Caribbean—France and Britain seem to be weakening. The British are wavering on the nature of a new regime and have not made a definite commitment to one which favours the Caribbean. The French Government has not been actively supporting Caribbean interests and is more concerned with protecting their own suppliers."[201]

At the beginning of January 2001, the EU agriculture ministers approved a new banana regime, a "first come, first served" system for all parties until 2006, while allowing a tariff preference in favor of ACP producers. This system afforded little comfort to the Caribbean exporters and did not satisfy Chiquita or the Clinton administration.

Having been a major donor to the Republican party over many years and with former Chiquita vice president Joseph Hagin safely ensconced as deputy chief of staff in the White House, Chiquita switched strategy. First, it claimed that despite being the largest producer of bananas in the world, it would likely have to go into bankruptcy court due to the unresolved banana dispute between the European Union and the United States. According to the company, European quotas against bananas grown in Latin America, Chiquita's main supplier, have cost the company $200 million a year since 1992, thus resulting in their financial hardships. Other reports have attributed the company's woes to faulty planning and bad business. Chiquita admitted on January 16, 2001, that it could not meet payments on its publicly traded debt of $862 million and that it would default on debt payments due March 28, 2001. It proposed to restructure its debt by converting a significant proportion of the debt into common stock. This would dilute existing shareholdings contributing a 48 percent plunge in market value ofits share.[202] Second, Chiquita Brands International filed suit in the European Court of Justice suing the European Commission for E564 million ($528 million) in damages. It claimed that its damages arose from the EU banana regime's restrictions in the two previous years.[203] Its company also claimed that it had lost more than $1.3 billion since 1992 because of EU banana quotas.[204]

In April 2001, the United States and the European Union arrived at an agreement,[205] which settled the long-running and bitter dispute over the

EU banana regime. Initially, Ecuador the world's largest producer and exporter of bananas balked at the settlement but agreed shortly after a change in position widely believed to be the result of the salutary effect of US suasion. Dole Food Co. seemed to have been caught off guard because at the time the settlement was announced, executives of the company were preparing to meet, at their request, the embassies of banana exporting countries of the Caribbean. The reaction of Dole was one of shock and indignation. Indeed, one spokesman was quoted in the Wall Street Journal as saying that they were "sold up the river" and accused the USTR of being concerned "to get a system that would take care of Chiquita."[206] It was clear that "money walks and talks in Washington DC" and Chiquita outspent Dole in buying political influence. According to the Wall Street Journal, Lindner and his American Financial gave $1.03 million to the Republicans and $676,750 to the Democrats, for a total of $1.7 million in donations. Dole, by comparison, contributed $134,190 to Republicans and $25,560 to Democrats for a paltry total of $159,750.[207] In addition, Chiquita spent heavily on lobbyists and public relations, having in its employment, Tony Podesta, brother of President Clinton's Chief of Staff John Podesta.[208]

Despite the settlement favoring Chiquita, the company indicated that it intended to pursue a lawsuit against the European Union in an effort to recover damages it claims resulted from the operation of the EU banana regime. Meanwhile, a plea by Congressman Charles Rangel for the US government to alleviate the impending damage to the banana exporting countries of the Caribbean, by spearheading an aid package including multilateral financial institutions to finance adjustment and diversification,[209] fell on deaf ears in the White House. The lingering impression was that the role of Chiquita in the US-EU banana dispute gave credence to the words of President Rutherford B. Hayes: "it is a government of the people, by the people and for the people no longer. It is a government of corporations, by corporations, and for corporations."[210]

Notes

1. "Caribbean Nations Ask U.S. to Abandon Harmful Trade Proceeding", The Caribbean Coalition, Washington D.C., March 22, 1995.
2. P. J. Patterson, My Political Journey. Jamaica's Sixth Prime Minister (Kingston: University of the West Indies Press, 2018) page 316.

3. P. J. Patterson, My Political Journey. Jamaica's Sixth Prime Minister (Kingston: University of the West Indies Press, 2018) page 316.
4. Embassy of Jamaica, Report of the Western Hemisphere Banana Meeting, Coral Gables, Miami, April 9, 1996, page 19.
5. "Latins to seek WTO panel on EU banana regime this month", Inside U.S. Trade, April 12, 1996, page 5.
6. Mike Gallagher and Cameron McWhirter, "Contributions buy influence", Cincinnati Enquirer, May 3, 1998 page C 15.
7. See comments of Ambassador Bernal in Canute James, "US banana move shocks Caribbean", Financial Times, April 30, 1996.
8. Letter to The Hon. Michael Kantor, Secretary of Commerce from the Ambassadors of the Caribbean banana exporting countries, April 16, 1996.
9. Gisela Eisner, Jamaica, 1830–1930: A Study in Economic Growth (Westport: Greenwood Press, 1974) page 238.
10. Leslie Gordon Goffe, When Banana Was King: A Jamaican Banana King in Jim Crow America (Kingston: LMH Publishing Company, 2006).
11. George Beckford, "Origins, Development and Future of the Jamaican Banana Industry: A Century of Revolutionary Struggle of the Peasantry", New World Quarterly, Vol. V, No. 3 (1968) reprinted in Kari Levitt (ed.), The George Beckford Reader (Kingston: University of the West Indies Press, 200) pages 352–358.
12. Joe Moran, "Defining moment: the banana returns to Britain, December 30, 1945", Financial Times, July 31, 2009.
13. Douglas Hall, "The Early Banana Trade from Jamaica, 1868–1905. A Descriptive Account" in Douglas Hall, Ideas and Illustrations in Economic History (New York: Holt, Rinehart and Winston, 1964) pages 56–79.
14. Peter N. Davies, Fyffes and the Banana: Musa Sapientum. A Centenary History 1888–1988 (London Athlone Press, 1990).
15. Barbara Welch, "Banana Dependency: Albatross or Life raft for the Windwards," Social and Economic Studies, Vol. 43, No. 1 (March, 1994) pages 123–149. See page 127.
16. George L. Beckford, "Issues in the Windwards – Jamaica Banana War" in Norman Girvan and Owen Jefferson (eds.), Readings in the Political Economy of the Caribbean (Kingston: New World, 1974) pages 77–86.
17. Lawrence S. Grossman, "British Aid and Windwards Bananas, "The Case of St. Vincent and the Grenadines," Social and Economic Studies, Vol. 43, No. 1 (March, 1994) pages 151–179.
18. Kenneth G. Tilley (ed.), Coming of Age. Speeches by Hon. Dr. Denzil L. Douglas (Kingston: Ian Randle Publishers, 2009) page 319.

19. Henry S. Gill and Anthony P. Gonzales, Economic Consequences of a Banana Collapse in the Caribbean, Report prepared for the CARICOM Secretariat, May, 1995, pages 15–17.
20. The Economic and Social Contribution of the Banana Industry in the OECS, Research and Information Department, Eastern Caribbean Central Bank, September, 1997.
21. Restructuring and the Loss of Preferences. Labour Challenges for the Caribbean Banana Industry (Geneva: International Labour Organization, January, 1999) page 1.
22. Henry S. Gill and Anthony P. Gonzales, Economic Consequences of a Banana Collapse in the Caribbean, Report prepared for the CARICOM Secretariat, May, 1995, page 24.
23. Restructuring and the Loss of Preferences. Labour Challenges for the Caribbean Banana Industry (Geneva: International Labour Organization, January, 1999) page 1.
24. Henry S. Gill and Anthony P. Gonzales, Economic Consequences of a Banana Collapse in the Caribbean, Report prepared for the CARICOM Secretariat, May, 1995, page 13.
25. Henry S. Gill and Anthony P. Gonzales, Economic Consequences of a Banana Collapse in the Caribbean, Report prepared for the CARICOM Secretariat, May, 1995 page 25.
26. Henry S. Gill and Anthony P. Gonzales, Economic Consequences of a Banana Collapse in the Caribbean, Report prepared for the CARICOM Secretariat, May, 1995, page 25.
27. Henry S. Gill and Anthony P. Gonzales, Economic Consequences of a Banana Collapse in the Caribbean, Report prepared for the CARICOM Secretariat, May, 1995, page 5.
28. Pedro Arias, Cora Dankers, Pascal Liu and Paul Pilkauskas, The World Banana Economy 1985–2000 (Rome: Food and Agriculture Organization, 2003).
29. United Fruit Company https://en.wikipedia.org/wiki/United_Fruit Company.
30. Nick Cullather, Secret History: The CIA s Classified Account of Its Operations in Guatemala 1952–1954 (Stanford: Stanford University Press; 2 ed., 2006).
31. Grace Livingstone, America's Backyard: The United States and Latin America from the Monroe Doctrine to the War on Terror (London: Zed Books, 2013, Stephen Schlesinger and Stephen Kinzer, Bitter Fruit: The Story of the American Coup in Guatemala (New York: David Rockefeller Center for Latin American Studies; 2 ed. 2005) and Alison Acker, Honduras: The Making of a Banana Republic (Boston: South End Press 1989).

32. James W. Martin, Banana Cowboys: The United Fruit Company and the Culture of Corporate Colonialism (Albuquerque: University of New Mexico Press, 2018) and Jason M. Colby, The Business of Empire: United Fruit, Race, and U.S. Expansion in Central America (Ithaca: Cornell University Press, 2011).
33. For a detailed discussion of the attempt land reform and the reaction of United Fruit Company see Thomas and Marjorie Melville, Guatemala-Another Vietnam (Harmondsworth: Penguin Books, 1971) pages 57–98.
34. Stephen Schlesinger and Stephen Kinzer Bitter Fruit: The Story of the American Coup in Guatemala (New York: David Rockefeller Center for Latin American Studies, 2nd ed., 2005).
35. Thomas and Marjorie Melville, Guatemala-Another Vietnam (Harmondsworth: Penguin Books, 1971) page 98.
36. Arnold Bertram, N. W. Manley, The Making of Modern Jamaica (Kingston: Arawak Publishers, 2016) pages 135–136.
37. Dan Koeppel, Banana. The Fate of the Fruit That Changed the World (New York: Hudson Street Press, Penguin Group, 2008) page 219.
38. The World Banana Economy, 1985–2002 - FAO www.fao.org/3/y5102e/y5102e04.htm.
39. Caribbean Banana Exporters Association, U.S.-E.U. Dispute Targets Fragile Economies of the Caribbean, The Caribbean Coalition.
40. Lawrence James, the Rise and Fall of the British Empire (New York: St. Martin's Press, 1994) page 512.
41. Peter Clarke, The Last Thousand Days of the British Empire. Churchill, Roosevelt, and the Birth of Pax Americana (New York: Bloomsbury Press, 2008).
42. Secretary Christopher seemed concern in the Caribbean were exclusively with Haiti and Cuba e.g. in testimony to Congress on U.S. foreign policy he mentioned both countries but made no reference to the CARIBBEAN despite the banana dispute and the pending Congressional action on CBI legislation. See verbal and written statements by Secretary Christopher in Review of United States Foreign Policy, Hearing before the Committee on International Relations, House of Representatives, One Hundred Fourth Congress, Second session, July 31, 1996 (Washington, DC: Government Printing Office, 1997) pages 2–8 and 41–53.
43. Bob Herbert, "In America: Banana Bully", New York Times, May 13, 1996, page A15.
44. Donald L. Bartlett and James B. Steele, "How to become a top banana", Time, February 7, 2000, page 49.
45. Cameron McWhirther and Mike Gallagher, "Influence: 'This is just money politics'", Cincinnati Enquirer, May 3, 1998, page C16.

46. John P. Sweeney, "The High Cost of Clinton's Trade War with the European Union", The Heritage Foundation Executive Memorandum, No. 584, March 26, 1999.
47. "The U.S. and EU go bananas", Financial Times, November 11, 1998.
48. Charles Rangel, "Will dispute squash banana growers?", Washington Times, February 16, 1999, page A14.
49. "The US and EU go bananas", Editorial, Financial Times, November 11, 1998. See also "Banana split", Editorial, Financial Times, December 18, 1998 and Guy de Jonquieres and Nancy Dunne, "A partnership in peril", The Financial Times, March 8, 1999.
50. John P. Sweeney, "The High Cost of Clinton's Trade War with the European Union", Executive Memorandum, No. 584, Washington D.C., The Heritage Foundation, March 26, 1999.
51. Lester C. Thurow, "When trade partners go bananas, don't ease up; get tough", USA Today, March 31, 1999, page 15D.
52. Roy Evans, "WTO approves US sanctions", Journal of Commerce, April 20, 1999.
53. Press Statement of Prime Ministers of the Windward Islands, Panama and Belize, November 11, 1998.
54. The US/EU Banana Dispute, European Union News, No. 96/98, November 10, 1998.
55. "How To Become a Top Banana", Time, February 7, 2000, page 43.
56. Michael Isikoff and Brook Larmer, "And Now, Bananagate?" Newsweek, April 28, 1997, pages 13–14.
57. Alexander Cockburn and Ken Silverstein, Washington Babylon (London: Verso, 1996) page 64.
58. George Archibald, "Banana baron peeled off half a mil, White House paid back in WTO fight", Washington Post, August 25, 1997, page A 7.
59. Michael Weisskopf, "The Busy Back Door Men", Time Magazine, March 31, 1997, page 40 and George Archibald, "Banana baron peeled off half a mil, White House paid back in WTO fight", Washington Post, August 25, 1997, page A 7.
60. George Archibald, "Banana baron peeled off half a mil. White House paid back in WTO fight", Washington Times, August 25, 1997.
61. Paul Barton, "Lindners gave widely in politics", The Enquirer, November 12, 1997.
62. George Archibald, "Banana baron peeled off half a mil. White House paid back in WTO fight", Washington Times, August 25, 1997.
63. Michael Isikoff and Brook Larmer, "And Now, Bananagate?", Newsweek Magazine, April 28, 1997, page 14.

64. George Archibald, "Did Democrats trade WTO help for 500k skins from banana king?", The Washington Times, August 25, 1997.
65. Randall Robinson, Defending the Spirit. A Black Life in America (New York: Dutton, 1998) page 248.
66. Randall Robinson, Defending the Spirit. A Black Life in America (New York: Dutton, 1998) page 251.
67. William Safire, "Bananagate", The New York Times, March 26, 1997.
68. Timothy Dove, Action Battery, "Hit by a $200,000 Bill from the Blue", Time, February, February 7, 2000, page 54 and Arthur Kaplan, Galaxy of Graphics, "Goodbye, Art", Time, February 7, 2000, page 56.
69. "Importers go bananas over sanctions on EU trade", Journal of Commerce, March 5, 1999.
70. Geoff Winestock, "U.S. Starts a Fight With Dole Food Co. In the Banana War," The Wall Street Journal, Monday, October 9, 2000.
71. George Archibald, "Banana baron peeled off half a mil. White House paid back in WTO fight", Washington Times, August 25, 1997.
72. Naomi Koppel, "Banana dispute deadlocks US, EU," Washington Times, January 26, 1999. See also Elizabeth Olson "Banana Talks With Europe Turn Nasty," The New York Times, January 26, 1999.
73. Frances Williams, "Island growers spike US sanctions move," Financial Times, January 26, 1999.
74. Michael Isikoff and Brook Larmer, "And Now, Bananagate?", Newsweek, April 28, 1997, page 14.
75. DeWayne Wickham, "Banana wars: Give Caribbean a break", USA Today, May 15, 1995.
76. James Adams and Jaimie Seaton, "Washington goes bananas over Britain's colonial fruit run", London Sunday Times, April 9, 1995.
77. Mike Gallagher and Cameron McWhirther, "Chiquita: An empire built on controversy", The Cincinnati Enquirer, May 3, 1998, page A1& A12; and Section C pages 1–18.
78. John Fox and Nancy Fuior, "bananasplit," Mother Jones, November/December, 1988, page 62.
79. Douglas Frantz, "Chiquita Still Under A Cloud After Newspaper's Retreat", The New York Times, July 17, 1998.
80. Letter to the Editor by Richard Bernal, "Bananas and Drugs", The Washington Post, October 23, 1999.
81. Karl Taro Greenfield, "Banana Wars", Time Magazine, February 8, 1999.
82. Letter to Mr. Don Logan, Chairman, CEO Time Magazine by Hazel Ross-Robinson, February 10, 1999; And Letter to Hazel Ross-Robinson by Amy Musher, Time Magazine, February 18, 1999.

83. David Beard, "In Jamaica, they'll have no bananas," Sun Sentinel, March 29, 1998 and Christina Lamb, "US action on bananas a nightmare for islands," Washington Times, March 16, 1999.
84. Mireya Navarro, "Outpost in Bananas and Marijuana Wars," New York Times, March 4, 1999.
85. Randall Robinson, Defending the Spirit. A Black Life in America (New York: Dutton, 1998) pages 120–121.
86. "Caribbean growers' lobby goes bananas" The Washington Times, April 16, 1997. See also Susan Taylor Martin "Banana war squeezes tiny Dominica," The Washington Times, April 15, 1997.
87. Randall Robinson, Defending the Spirit. A Black Life in America (New York: Dutton, 1998) pages 251–259.
88. Richard Bernal, "WTO Banana Case, Friendly Fire Hits Caribbean," The Journal of Commerce, April 24, 1997 and Richard L. Bernal, "Banana trade vital to Caribbean," The Journal of Commerce, February 3, 1999.
89. "Banana Republic", Washington Post, October 26, 2000.
90. Brook Larmer, "The Banana Wars", Newsweek, April 28, 1997, page 15.
91. Brook Lamer, "The Banana Wars", Newsweek, April 28, 1997, page 15.
92. "Caribbean Nations warn US on Drug Cooperation after Banana Retaliation," Inside US Trade, Vol. 17 No. 11, March 12, 1999.
93. "Caribbean disturbance," Editorial, The Miami Herald, August 10, 1998, page A10.
94. Don Bohning, "U.S. relations with Caribbean under strain", Miami Herald, October 27, 1998.
95. Gus Constantine, "Caribbean nations hurt by banana dispute threaten to retaliate", The Washington Times, March 9, 1999, page A13.
96. Bob Herbert, "In America: Banana Bully", New York Times, May 13, 1996, page A15.
97. Estimates provided by Ross-Robinson & Associates.
98. Bob Herbert, "In America: Banana Bully", New York Times, May 13, 1996, page A15.
99. Clayton Yeutter, "The Banana Battlements," Washington Times, August 7, 1995).
100. Richard L. Bernal, "Fighting a banana battle now will mean US will lose lots of trade later", Washington, Times, August 24, 1995.
101. Canute James, Caribbean leaders want bananas on the plate", Journal of Commerce, May 7, 1997, Canute James and James Wilson, "The big place of the banana in a small part of The world", Financial Times, March 19, 1999.
102. Anthony Bryan, "U.S. – Caribbean Relations Strained Over U.S.-European Banana Dispute", North South Center Update, October 3, 1999.

103. Brent Borrell, "EU Bananarama III", Washington D.C., World Bank, Policy Research Working Paper, No.1388, 1994. See also Brent Borrell and Yang Maw-Cheng, "EC Bananarama 1992", Washington D.C., World Bank, Working Paper No. 523, 1990 and Brent Borrell and Yang Maw-Cheng, "EC Bananarama 1992: The Sequel", Washington D.C., World Bank, Working Paper, No. 958, 1992).
104. David Hallam and Steve McCorriston, "Fair Trade in Bananas?", Agricultural Economics Unit, University of Exeter, December, 1992, pages 50–51.
105. "Chiquita's Brand of Doing Business in Honduras", COHA Occasional Paper, Vol. 1, No. 3, November 1996.
106. Cliff Peale, "Report blasts Chiquita's Honduran links" Washington Post, November 21, 1996.
107. Henry S. Gill and Anthony P. Gonzales, "Economic Consequences of a Banana Collapse in the Caribbean", Report prepared for the CARICOM Secretariat, May 1995 (62 pages).
108. Barbara Welch, "Banana Dependency: Albatross or life raft for the Windwards", Social and Economic Studies, Vol. 43, No. 1, 1994, pages 123–149. For a more extensive treatment of the peculiarities of banana cultivation in these islands which makes efficiency and transformation very difficult and limited see Barbara M. Welch, Survival by Association. Supply Management Landscapes of the Eastern Caribbean (Montreal: McGill-Queen's University Press, 1996).
109. Canute James, "Clinton Backs Preferences For Caribbean Bananas", Journal of Commerce, June 20, 1995.
110. COMMUNIQUÉ ISSUED AT THE CONCLUSION OF ... – Caricomcaricom.org › Communiques July 7, 1995 – The Sixteenth Meeting of the Conference of Heads of Government of the ... Community was held in Georgetown, Guyana on 4 – 7 July, 1995. Accessed 6 March, 2020.
111. Canute James, "Caribbean lose patience with US over banana row", Financial Times, July 13, 1995.
112. Report of the CARICOM Secretariat, Caribbean/United States Summit, REP. 97/1/61 CAR/US, Bridgetown, Barbados, November 4, 1997, page 13.
113. Canute James and George Parker, "U.S. faces Caribbean threat to quit drugs treaty" Financial Times, March 8, 1999.
114. Donald Bartlett and James P. Steele, "How to Become a Top Banana," Time, February 7, 2000, page 49.
115. "Clinton lied", The Daily Gleaner, March 19, 1999.

116. 'Dear Colleague' Letter, "A Trade War? Over Bananas?" from Representatives Maxine Waters, David Bonior, Marcy Kaptur, Carrie Meek, Carolyn Maloney and Peter Defazio, March 18, 1999 and Letter to Charlene Barshefsky, USTR from Congresswoman Maxine Waters, March 5, 1999.
117. David E. Sanger, "U.S.-Europe Trade War Looms Over Bananas", The New York Times, December 22, 1998.
118. Peter Clegg, The Caribbean Banana Trade. From Colonialism to Globalization (London: Palgrave Macmillan, 2002) pages 160–161.
119. Letter to Congressman Charles Rangel from Charlene Barshefsky, USTR, June 23, 1997.
120. Letter to President Clinton, from 40 Members of Congress - See Appendix 3, July 31, 1997.
121. Letter to President William Clinton from Newt Gingrich and Trent Lott, October 9, 1998, Inside U.S. Trade, Vol. 16, No. 40, October 9, 1998.
122. John Maggs, "In Banana Dispute, Discretion Gives Way to Politics", Journal of Commerce, May 2, 1995.
123. For political and philosophical changes in U.S. policy see Janes Shoch, Trading Blows: Party Competition and U.S. Trade Policy in a Globalizing Era (Chapel Hill: University of North Carolina Press, 2000), Martha Liebler Gibson, Conflict Amid Consensus in American Trade Policy (American Governance and Public Policy (Washington DC: Georgetown University Press, 2000), A. Lovett, Alfred E. Eckles Jr. and Richard L. Brinkman U.S. Trade Policy. History, Theory, and WTO (New York: M. E. Sharpe, 1999) pages 51–105, I.M. Destler, American Trade Politics (Washington DC: Institute for International Economics, 3rd ed., 1995) and Judith L. Goldstein Ideas, Interests, and American Trade Policy (Ithaca: Cornell University Press, 1994).
124. Letter to President William J. Clinton from Maxine Waters et al, July 31, 1997.
125. Edward Alden, "US carousel sanctions are ready to spin", Financial Times, July 13, 2000.
126. Letter to President William Clinton by Maxine Waters, Ronald Dellums, Marcy Kaptur, Duncan Hunter, Roscoe Bartlett, June 9, 1997.
127. Letter to Ambassador Charlene Barshefsky from Senator Paul D. Coverdell and Representative Saxby Chambliss, September 9, 1998.
128. Ben Laurance, "The Big Banana", The Guardian, 7 March 1999.
129. Brook Larmer and Michael Isikoff, "Brawl over bananas", Newsweek, 28 April, 1997, Susan Rosegrant, Banana Wars: Challenges to the European Union's Banana Regime, Kennedy School of Government, Case Study

1534 (Cambridge, Maas.: Harvard University, 1999) pages 9–11 and John Maggs, In Banana Dispute, Discretion Gives Way to Politics", Journal of Commerce, May 2, 1995, page 1A–3A.
130. John G. Stovall and Dale E. Hathaway, "US Interests in the Banana Trade Controversy" in Timothy E. Josling and Timothy G. Taylor, (eds.), Banana Wars. The Anatomy of a Trade Dispute (Walliford: CABI Publishing, 2003) pages 151–167 See page 153.
131. James Adams and Jalnie Seaton, "Washington goes bananas over Britain's colonial fruit run", Financial Times, 9 April, 1995, page 1.
132. Ben Laurance, "The Big Banana", The Guardian, 7 March 1999.
133. Michael Weisskopf and Viveca Novak, The Busy Back-Door Men", Time, March 31, 1997, page 40.
134. David E. Sanger, "Dole at Forefront of Trade Battle To Aid Donor's Banana Empire", New York Times, December 5, 1995 and Carl Lindner-Frontline PBS. www.pbs.org › wgbh › pages › frontline › president › players › lindner. Accessed 24 March, 2020.
135. John Maggs, In Banana Dispute, Discretion Gives Way to Politics", Journal of Commerce, May 2, 1995, page 1A–3A.
136. David E. Sanger, "Dole at Forefront of Trade Battle To Aid Donor's Banana Empire", New York Times, December 5, 1995.
137. John Maggs, In Banana Dispute, Discretion Gives Way to Politics", Journal of Commerce, May 2, 1995, page 1A–3A.
138. Debra L. Spar, Managing International Trade and Investment: Casebook (London: Imperial College Press, 2003) page 103.
139. Debra L. Spar, Managing International Trade and Investment: Casebook (London: Imperial College Press, 2003) page 103 and "Banana Republican", The Economist, 18 November, 1995.
140. Randall Robinson, The Debt: What America Owes to Blacks (New York: Plume, 2001).
141. Randall Robinson dumps a case of bananas in front of the US Trade … https://www.gettyimages.com/…/randall-robinson-dumps-a-case-of-bananas-in-front. April 15, 1997.
142. For example, letter to Ms. Rose Lanam, President, Jamaica Awareness Association in Los Angeles from Ambassador Richard Bernal, March 15, 1990.
143. The National Coalition on Caribbean affairs (NCOCA), Statement on Banana Preferences, April 29, 1998.
144. Letter to the Editor of the Washington Post from Donald G. Morgan, President of the Jamaica Volunteers Association, December 3, 1998 and letter to President William Clinton from Donald G. Morgan, President of the Jamaica Volunteers Association, November 13, 1998.

145. The Governor of Guam assured the Ambassador that "in my interaction at the National Governors' Association, I will be sensitized to the unique needs of the Caribbean." Letter to Ambassador Richard Bernal from Carl T. C. Guitierrez, Governor of Guam, March 11, 1999.
146. Letter to President Clinton, November 6, 1996, from Bill Cosby, Earl Graves, Bob Johnson, Ed Lewis, Jesse Jackson, Joseph Lowery, Susan Taylor and Danny Glover.
147. "Lori's War": The FP Interview, Foreign Policy, No. 118 (Spring, 2000) pages 29–55.
148. "Report on The Impact of the United States Challenge to the European Union Banana Regime on Political, Economic and Social Order in the Caribbean, and the Consequences for U.S. National Interests", Eminent Persons Group, Mission to Jamaica, Dominica and St. Lucia, January 1997.
149. Statements were submitted by Professor Charles Ogletree of Harvard University Law School and Randall Robinson of TransAfrica.
150. Charles Ogletree and Randall Robinson, "The banana war's missing link – campaign funding", The Christian Science Monitor, March 31, 1999.
151. George Archibald, "Did Democrats trade WTO help for 500k skins from banana king?", The Washington Times, August 25, 1997.
152. Letter to Mr. Aaron T. Manaigo, Chairman, National Council of Black Republicans, March 11, 1999.
153. Statement of the American Farm Bureau Federation to the Office of the U.S. Trade Representative Regarding Uruguay Round Agreement Compliance Act of 1998. December 9, 1998.
154. Peter N. Davies, Fyffes and the Banana: Musa Sapientum. A Centenary History 1888–1988, (London: Athalone Press, 1990).
155. Response of Fyffes PLC to section301 Petition of Chiquita Brands International, Inc. and the Hawaii Banana Industry Association, Docket No. 301–94, December1, 1994.
156. Meetings were held with Congressional committee staff Mary Jane Wignot, Meridith Broadbent, Donna Swanson, Gil Kapen, Eric Autor and Kathleen McAuliffe. Meetings were held with Peter Allgeier, USTR, Walter Bastian, Department of Commerce and John Hamilton of the State Department.
157. Peter N. Davies, Fyffes and the Banana: Musa Sapientum. A Centenary History 1888–1988 (London Athlone Press, 1990).
158. Tony Best, "The Caribbean, Bananas And the OAS," New York, Carib News, Week ending June 24, 1997.
159. Canute James, "Caribbean leaders ask Canada for assistance in banana dispute", Journal of Commerce, 11 March, 1996.

160. The Caribbean diplomatic corp during much of the banana campaign during Dr. Richard Bernal, Jamaica (1991–2001), Kingsley Layne, St. Vincent ( ), Dr. Joseph Edmunds, St. Lucia and Sonia Johnny, St. Lucia, Dr. Courtney Blackman, Barbados, Denis Antoine, Grenada, Timothy Donaldson, The Bahamas, Dr. Ismael, Guyana,
161. Recollection of Ambassador Richard L. Bernal who was present.
162. Recollection of Dr. Richard L. Bernal. Ambassador of Jamaica to the United States who led the negotiations of the economic aspects. The negotiations of the security aspects was led by David Simmons, the Attorney General of Barbados.
163. James Bennett, "Clinton In Caribbean: No Bananas Today", The New York Times, May 11, 1997.
164. This debate is summarized in Richard L. Bernal, Globalization, Trade and Economic Development: A Study of the CARIFORUM-EU Economic Partnership Agreement (New York: Palgrave Macmillan, 2013) pages XXX.
165. Martin Wolf, Why Globalization works (New Haven: Yale University Press, 2005).
166. Martin Wolf, "Going Bananas", Financial Times, March 25, 1999.
167. Brent Borrell, EU bananarama 1993: the story gets worse (Canberra and Sydney: Centre for International Economics, June, 1996).
168. "Ending banana insanity", Journal of Commerce, April 11, 1997.
169. Richard L. Bernal, "Friendly Fire hits Caribbean", Journal of Commerce, April 24, 1997.
170. "At daggers drawn", The Economist, May 8. 1999, page 17.
171. The WTO Agreements: The Marrakesh Agreement Establishing the World Trade Organization and its Annexes (Geneva: World Trade Organization, 2017).
172. Mitsuo Matsushita, Thomas J. Schoenbaum, Petros C. Mavroids and Michael Hahn, The World Trade Organization. Law, Practice, and Policy (Oxford: Oxford University Press, 3rd ed., 2015) pages 155–178 and 179–213.
173. Mitsuo Matsushita, Thomas J. Schoenbaum, Petros C. Mavroids and Michael Hahn, The World Trade Organization. Law, Practice, and Policy (Oxford: Oxford University Press, 3rd ed., 2015) pages 179–213.
174. Lori Wallach and Patrick Woodall, Whose Trade Organization? The Comprehensive Guide to the WTO (New York: The New Press, 2004) and Mi Park, The IMF and WTO. How does Geopolitics influence Global Finance and International Trade? (Coal Harbour Publishing, 2018). For an attempted rebuttal see Kent Jones, Who's Afraid of the WTO? (Oxford: Oxford University Press, 2004).

175. Lori Wallach and Michelle, Whose Trade Organization? (Washington DC: Public Citizen, 1999) page 6.
176. Bernard M. Hoekman and Petros C. Mavroidis, World Trade Organization (WTO): Law, Economics, and Politics (New York: Routledge, 2nd ed., 2015).
177. Richard L. Bernal, ""Improving the Participation of Small Developing Countries in the Governance of the Multilateral Trading System" in Carolyn Deere Birkbeck (ed.), Making Global Trade Governance Work for Development. Perspectives and Priorities from Developing Countries (Cambridge: Cambridge University Press, 2011) pages 231–258 and Richard L. Bernal, "Participation of Small Developing Economies in the Governance of the Multilateral Trading System", Working Paper No. 44, Centre for International Governance Innovation (December, 2009).
178. Roman Grynberg (ed.), WTO at the Margins: Small States and the Multilateral Trading System (Cambridge: Cambridge University Press, 2012.
179. For a discussion of the problems faced by developing countries in using the DSS see Fatoumata Jawara and Aileen KWA, Behind the Scenes at the WTO: The Real World of International Trade Negotiations (London: Zed Books, 2004) and Kent Jones, The Doha Blues. Institutional Crisis and Reform in the WTO (Oxford: Oxford University Press, 2010) pages 119–139.
180. Richard L. Bernal, "The WTO Dispute Mechanism: A Developing Country Perspective" International Lawyer, Vol. 32, No. 3 (Fall, 1998) pages 871–873.
181. Peter Gallagher, Guide to the WTO and Developing Countries The Hague: Kluwer Law International, 2000) pages 187–188.
182. Letter to CARICOM Heads of Government from Prime Minister P.J. Patterson of Jamaica: EU Banana Import Regime, 15 June, 1999.
183. "EU MP backs Caribbean in banana trade dispute", The Jamaica Gleaner, April 16, 1999.
184. Guy de Jonquiéres and Nancy Dunne "A partnership in peril," Financial Times, March 8, 1999.
185. Eliza Patterson. "The US-EU Banana Dispute", American society for International, Insights, Vol. 6, Issue 4, February 27, 2001.
186. Caribbean Banana Exporters Association U.S.-EU Dispute Targets Fragile Economies of the Caribbean (Washington DC: The Caribbean Coalition, June 1, 1995.
187. Prime Minister Sir James F. Mitchell spoke of the need "to hammer home the message to our people that banana protection in the market place will in a few years' time come to an end". See James F. Mitchell, Guiding

Change in the Islands (Waitsfield, Vermont: Concepts Publishing, 1996) page196.

188. Meeting between Prime Minister Edison James and Ambassador James Dobbins and Holly Hammond of the National Security Council and Lael Brainard of the National Economic Council on October 14, 1998.
189. Letter from President William Clinton to Congresswoman Maxine Waters, December 12, 1997 and Letter from President William Clinton to Congressman Peter A. DeFazio, December 12, 1997.
190. Canute James, "Caribbean, US blame each other in banana split", Journal of Commerce, December 15, 1997.
191. Letter from Prime Minister P.J. Patterson to President William J. Clinton, June 2, 1997.
192. Brook Larmer, "The Banana Wars," Newsweek, April 28, 1997, page 15.
193. Cameron McWhirther and Mike Gallagher, "Influence: 'this is just money politics", Cincinnati Enquirer, May 3, 1998, page C16 and Christopher Marquis, "Bananas or drugs, Caribbean tells US," Miami Herald, June 13, 1996.
194. Brook Larmer, "The Banana Wars," Newsweek, April 28, 1997, page 14.
195. Brook Larmer, "The Banana Wars," Newsweek, April 28, 1997, page 14.
196. Gus Constantine, "Caribbean nations hurt by banana dispute threaten to retaliate", The Washington Times, March 9, 1999, page A1.
197. Notes of Ambassador Dr. Richard L. Bernal.
198. Letter to President William Clinton from forty Members of Congress including Maxine Waters, Charles Rangel, Marcy Kaptur, J.C. Watts, Sheila Jackson Lee, David Bonior, Ed Towns, John Lewis and Joseph P. Kennedy II.
199. Letter from the Congressional Black Caucus to President Clinton, October 22, 1997.
200. 200. Edward Alden, "US ad EU still split on beef and bananas", Financial Times, December 19, 2000.
201. Update on Developments Relating to the Modification of the European Banana Marketing Regime, 20 July, 1999.
202. "Chiquita shares halve on debt woe," Financial Times, January 17, 2001.
203. Edward Alden and Christopher Bowe, "Chiquita sues Brussels over losses caused by banana import curbs," Financial Times, January 26, 2001.
204. Anthony De Palma, "Citing European Banana Quotas, Chiquita Says Bankruptcy Looms," New York Times, January 17, 2001.
205. Anthony DePlama, "U.S. and Europeans Agree on Deal to End Banana Trade War", New York Times, April 12, 2001.
206. Helene Cooper, "Dole Fails to Find Much Appeal in Accord to End to Banana War", Wall Street Journal, April 13, 2001.

207. Helene Cooper, "Dole Fails to Find Much Appeal in Accord to End to Banana War", Wall Street Journal, April 12, 2001.
208. Helene Cooper, "Dole Fails to Find Much Appeal in Accord to End to Banana War", Wall Street Journal, April 12, 2001.
209. The Banana Agreement: Opportunity and Challenge for the Caribbean, Press Release, Congressman Charles Rangel, U.S. House of Representatives, Washington DC, April 13, 2001.
210. David C. Korten, When Corporations Rule the World (West Hartford: Kumarian Press, 1995) page 58.

CHAPTER 7

Impact of US Banana Policy on the Caribbean

Introduction

The success of the United States in dismantling the EU banana regime had a serious adverse impact on the Caribbean, in particular the banana exporting countries. The harm was both immediate and long-term and encompassed all aspects of relations between the United States and the Caribbean countries and was, therefore, detrimental to US national interest in the region. The process of getting to the ruling in the WTO was acrimonious, involving the imposition of tariffs by both the United States and the European Union.[1] The consistent refusal to work out an accommodation that would allow the Caribbean to retain the sliver of the European Union and world market was both profoundly disappointing and disillusioning. It seriously damaged relations with the Caribbean inclusive of those countries that did not export bananas. The notion that the United States was a benevolent partner, empathetic to the small and vulnerable as the Americans have always said was their creed, was not evident in the US approach to the banana issue. It was widely claimed that America was for the underdog as was the Caribbean in the banana dispute. Support for the underdog is evoked when their struggle is heroic if they are "opposed by forces which are significantly mightier than themselves and are likely to retaliate against them when they pursue their noble causes".[2] Rocky Balboa and small businesses are part of the American Dream. The desire to preserve small business from large corporations and monopolists is the underlying rationale for antitrust legislation (e.g.,

R. L. Bernal, *Corporate versus National Interest in US Trade Policy*, https://doi.org/10.1007/978-3-030-56950-1_7

Sherman Antitrust Act of 1890). Loss of small businesses and the family-owned farm is frequently bemoaned phenomena in the United States.[3] The Caribbean governments felt that the plight of the small banana exporting islands would illicit sympathy which would be reflected in US foreign and trade policy. This is expressed in Prime Minister Patterson of Jamaica's rhetorical question at the Inter-American Press Association: "What has prompted the United States administration to take such a hostile a position to countries as small as we are and as vulnerable as we are?"[4]

Erosion of Confidence, Build-Up of Resentment

Newsweek Magazine observes that "throughout the Caribbean, there was a strong new undercurrent of resentment towards the United States."[5] As Randall Robinson, executive director of Trans Africa explained: "These countries have done everything right. They are neighbors and staunch allies of the United States. They are stable both politically and economically. Their literacy rates are in the 90th percentile and political prisoners are unheard of."[6] The trust in the United States has never fully recovered and a feeling of relative neglect has lingered in the region,[7] as Dr. Kenny Anthony, Prime Minister of St. Lucia puts it: "There is now a serious credibility problem. I think distrust is a more appropriate word."[8]

The most affected banana exporting countries felt further neglected and aggrieved because their hope of receiving financial aid from the United States to assist them in adjusting to the collapse of the main export industry never materialized. Second, in the medium- and long-term, the US action led to the severe decline of the industry, the dominant economic activity of these small islands. The banana industry was vital to the small exporting countries of the Caribbean. In the late 1980s, the industry in Dominica accounted for 32 percent of GDP and 50 percent of employment, in St. Lucia 37 percent of GDP and 46 percent of employment, and in St. Vincent 25 percent of GDP and 46 percent of employment.[9]

The erosion of confidence in the goodwill of the US government deteriorated until it turned to resentment and "fueled anti-US feeling". Anticipating the destruction of the banana industry, the head of the St. Lucia Banana Growers Association accused the United States of "conducting the worst kind of economic warfare against a defenseless people."[10] A mood of wanting to, if possible, retaliate against the United States emerged.[11] Dame Billie Miller, Minister of Foreign Affairs of Barbados intimated that CARICOM should "not renew Shiprider agreements without them being tied to a resolution of the banana issue."[12] Subsequently, the Caribbean which had traditionally been willing to pursue nonalignment in foreign policy[13] became less willing to comply with US foreign policy goals.

This is evident looking at CARICOM's positions on Cuba, Venezuela, and China. CARICOM voted against the United States in lifting exclusion of Cuba from the OAS, several countries sided with Venezuela in the Bolivarian Alliance for the Peoples of Our America in preference to the Summit of the Americas, and in maintaining relations with the People's Republic of China.

Genesis of Economic Crisis

The dismantling of the EU banana regime was a significant contributing factor to the genesis of the prolonged economic crisis of the English-speaking Caribbean (ESC), but it was not the only factor. The small middle-income developing economies of the Caribbean depended on the export of bananas as its principal economic activity and largest source of foreign exchange earnings. Jamaica was less dependent on banana exports which had declined from the halcyon days of the pre-1930s when the industry was hit by the disease. Nevertheless, the industry remained an important earner of foreign exchange and an employer of labor. An often-overlooked advantage of export arrangements with Britain and the European Union was the fact that it served to stabilize export earnings when primary products from what was then called the West Indies had traditionally experienced instability. McFarlane explains that: "The possibility of change in the present structure of the international market. The history of primary exports from the West Indies is a record of advances and declines brought about by developments in consuming countries in Europe and the North American Continent, and by agreements to which the West Indies were seldom signatories but which nevertheless influenced the level and direction of exports for particular commodities."[14]

The banana industry existed only because of preferential exporting arrangements. Production could not compete in an open world market because yields are four times higher in Central America than in the Caribbean.[15] Caribbean farmers' cost of production is twice that of Central America and Latin America.[16] The smaller banana exporting islands were, in reality, monocrop economies in which the economic alternatives are very limited and the reallocation of resources is difficult, especially labor.

Shifting to processed products such as banana chips, condiments, flavoring, and puree has to contend with the problems and lack of economies of scale of micro-scale manufacturing. The opportunities for niche markets for specialty bananas and "fair trade" exports are not as easy as they are appealingly intuitive.[17] This difficulty in resource allocation through the market is not fully appreciated by the paradigm of conventional economics, the prescriptions of which are best known by the moniker of the "Washington Consensus".[18] An understanding of the impact of the dismantling of the EU banana regime must fully appreciate the extremely limited alternatives to bananas[19] and the difficulty of the relocation of labor out of banana farming into other employment to the extent that such employment existed.[20] The scale of this reallocation of labor is a major task because direct and indirect employment could involve 45–55 percent of the workforce.[21] There has been some success, notably Sainsbury, the largest British supermarket chain that purchased 80 percent of Dominica's banana exports as "fair trade" bananas.[22]

In Dominica, the banana industry provided work for 6,000 farmers and another 700 employed at boxing plants. In St. Lucia, it provided employment for about 10,000 workers and about 5,000 banana farmers in St. Vincent and the Grenadines.[23]The vast majority of farmers were very small; in Dominica 70 percent of the farms were under an acre, 69 percent in St. Lucia and 61 percent in St. Vincent.[24] The banana industry in Dominica directly employs 10,225 persons, 23,653 persons in St. Vincent, 20,000 persons in St. Lucia, and indirectly an estimated 60,000 persons.[25] The contribution of bananas to the GDP of St. Vincent was 25.5 percent, 20.9 percent in Dominica, and 22.2 percent in St. Lucia.[26] Banana exports as a percentage of total domestic exports was 57.6 in Dominica, 56.2 in St. Vincent, and 52.6 in St. Lucia.[27] Sandiford estimates that before the dismantling of the EU regime, direct and indirect employment from the banana industry amounted to 143,184, or 32.85 percent of the population of the Windward Islands.[28] Direct employment was 35,796 and is estimated to have declined to 8,949 after adjustment to the EU banana regime.[29] Banana export was the major contributor to these economies and it increased in the 1980s but suffered a significant decline following the changes in the EU banana regime from 1993. Banana export in 2006 had declined to 6.0 percent of total exports in St. Lucia, 4.8 percent in St. Vincent, and 5.7 percent in Dominica. Contribution to GDP dropped to 2.9 percent in St. Lucia, 2.0 percent in St. Vincent, and 2.4 percent in Dominica.[30]

The IMF research paper estimates that the EU preferential trade arrangements for banana exports provided the Windward Islands with implicit assistance which peaked at about 13 percent of GDP in the late 1980s but declined to about 1 percent of GDP by 2008. "In tandem with dramatic declines in official development assistance, over the last two decades, most of the Windward Islands have experienced the loss of annual external assistance flows equivalent to about 10 percent of GDP."[31]

Jamaica was the world's largest producer and exporter of bananas in the 1930s and the largest supplier to the British market from the 1950s. In an industry that is susceptible to diseases,[32] hurricanes, and drought, production declined from the 1950s to the 1980s and then increased significantly only to start declining with the uncertainties of the early 1990s[33] and consequently, bananas exports ceased in 2008.[34] In 2018, exports of bananas were 675.5 tonnes valued at $563,000 down from 204,700 tonnes in 1966.[35] While the changes in the EU banana import regime following the WTO ruling was not the only factor leading to the demise of the banana export industry, it was the main cause. A study by the Eastern Caribbean Central Bank also observed that the banana industry in the Eastern Caribbean began to decline in the early 1990s after expansion in the last decade. Exports for the group dropped from 277,460 tonnes in 1990 to 168,318 tonnes in 1994 with a concomitant decline in earnings of almost 40 percent.[36]

Three companies dominated the British market, United Brands through Fyffes (Chiquita) had 40 percent, Geest had 36 percent and Jamaica Producers had 4 percent.[37] While selling bananas to a single marketing company has the disadvantage of having to deal with a monopolist it did provide stability and predictability. Tate and Lyle had a similar role in the export of Caribbean produced sugar to the British market.

Decline in Economic Growth

The small developing economies of the Eastern Caribbean experienced robust economic growth in their GDP during the 1970s and 1980s. Indeed, they achieved the status of middle-income developing countries. The engine of growth during this period was the increase in earnings from the export of bananas[38] reflecting both increased prices and a 270 percent increase in the volume of banana exports from between 1977 and 1990.[39] Since 1990, growth rates of GDP have been low, despite high levels of foreign direct investment, earnings from tourism, and remittances. The

World Bank notes that: "Successive changes in the European Union trade preference regime, starting in 1993, eroded OECS countries' preferential access to European markets, especially for bananas."[40] While this was a critical factor it is not being suggested that this was the only factor, as the Caribbean as a whole was affected by the global financial crisis[41] of 2007–2008 and natural disasters but what was absent was the stabilizing influence of banana exports with its network of inter-sectoral linkages. Inder Ruprah of the Inter-American Development Bank observes that there has been a widening gap in economic growth and GDP per capita between the Caribbean and other small economies.[42] Again, the World Bank points out that the "loss of trade preferences for OECS banana exports to Europe disrupted progress in poverty reduction, most notably in Grenada, St. Lucia, and St. Vincent and the Grenadines. Tourist arrivals fell sharply during the global financial crisis."[43]

Clear and Present Danger of Economic Fallout

There is no question that the US government could have been unaware of the likely damage to the ESC by the dismantling of the EU banana regime. Warnings to this effect had been expressed for decades from academics,[44] international organizations, nongovernmental organizations, and the governments in the ESC.

In 1955 the West India Committee, a group of UK and Caribbean businesses encouraged the widespread engagement of farmers in banana production and the local private enterprise system as a bulwark against communism.[45]

In 1990, Borrell and Young estimate that free trade in bananas in the EU market would result in a drop in the ACP countries' share of the market of 30–50 percent.[46] Such an impact would be devastating because: "These small islands were dependent on their banana exports more than any other state in the world".[47]

In 1993, the Prime Minister of Dominica, Eugenia Charles said that the issue was "the survival of our country. The Latins are talking about losing some million dollars. We might not just be losing dollars we might be losing a country too."[48]

In 1994, Eugenia Charles, the pro-US Prime Minister of Dominica who stood beside President Ronald Reagan to announce the US invasion of Grenada on October 25, 1983, was perhaps the most strident of critics of the US action on bananas often accusing the United States of "killing" the banana industry, the lifeblood of Dominica. During a meeting with US Trade Representative Ambassador Carla Hills in her offices in Washington DC, Prime Minister Eugenia Charles startled everyone by saying "if you kill my bananas I will kill you."[49] She declared: "If we lost the industry, we would lose the country. It would be the beginning of despair."[50]

In 1995, the European Union in a press release[51] warned of the fallout: "In 1995, a total of 2,653,441 tonnes were imported under the tariff quota, almost exclusively from Latin America, that is, 453,441 tonnes more than the EU's bound commitment, and 678,311 tonnes were imported under the traditional ACP arrangements, 179,389 tonnes less than the potential volume available to these countries." Nevertheless, the United States, which does not itself export bananas, has found this situation so unsatisfactory that it is pursuing a complaint against the European Union at the WTO in a bid to dismantle the trade preferences which exist to help Caribbean exporters.

In 1996, a group of eminent persons visited the banana exporting countries of Jamaica, Dominica, and St. Lucia. The group consisted of Leah Allen (Chief of Staff of Congresswoman Maxine Waters), Willie l. Baker, Jr. (International Vice President of the United Food and Commercial Workers International Union), Jack A. Blum (partner Lobel, Novins & Lamont), Kenneth A. Cook (President, Environmental Working Group), Ibrahim J. Gassama (University of Oregon Law School), Jason C. Hill (News Anchor, Black Entertainment Television), Congresswoman Carrie P. Meek (Democrat, Florida), Charles J. Ogletree, Jr. (Professor, Harvard Law School), Kathrine Ozer (Executive Director, National Family Farm Coalition), Lori Wallach (Director, Public Citizen's Global Trade Watch) and Congresswoman Maxie Waters (Chair, Congressional Black Caucus). The report of the group noted that the European Union banana regime is "crucial" to the survival of the banana industry and cannot be replaced by a direct aid program. The demise of the industry would lead to social disorder, unstable governments, increased illegal migration, and more drug trafficking. The complaint instigated at the behest of a single multinational corporation, Chiquita, is contrary to US interest while providing neither trade nor employment benefits to the United States.[52]

In 1997, the Economist magazine, noted for its unapologetic advocacy of globalization and free trade, summed up the likely impact of pulling down the EU banana regime on banana farmers in the Caribbean as "Expelled from Eden".[53]

In 1998, a paper from Oxfam warned "livelihoods of over 60,000 people (one-third of the population) depend on the banana industry in Saint Lucia. In St. Vincent, the proportion is almost 70 per cent. The islands' export earnings are roughly 50 per cent dependent on bananas. The banana trade brings US$2–3 million per week to the Windward Islands alone, and it is the major source of foreign exchange, which underpins their whole economies. Clearly, the European banana market is essential to the islands' economic survival."[54] Also in May 1998, part of a year-long investigation by the Cincinnati Enquirer involved interviews with banana farmers in Dominica who were all in trepidation of what they regarded as the certain demise of the banana industry with no plausible prospect of an alternative legal crop.[55]

In 1999, research from the International Labour Organization (ILO) reports: "Fears exist that the demise of this crucial export sector will impact negatively, not only on the many individual banana producers and their families but equally affect other vital economic sectors and provoke a general downturn of economic prospects for the region at large."[56]

Region-Wide Impact

While the economic fallout was most serious in the smallest banana exporting countries, it was felt throughout the ESC because of the integration of these economies consequent on both their location and their intra-regional trade within the Caribbean Community (CARICOM), which is a group of 20 countries, 15 member states, and 5 associate members. Members include Antigua and Barbuda, The Bahamas, Barbados, Belize, Dominica, Grenada, Guyana, Haiti, Jamaica, Montserrat, Saint Kitts and Nevis, Saint Lucia, Saint Vincent and the Grenadines, Suriname, and Trinidad and Tobago. CARICOM came into being on July 4, 1973, with the signing of the Treaty of Chaguaramas and the revised treaty of 2002 which established the goal of creating the Single Market and Economy (CSME) bounded by a Common External Tariff (CET). The eight smallest countries which include the banana exporting countries are engaged in a deeper level of integration including a single currency and central bank. This subregion integration arrangement is known as the Organization of Eastern Caribbean States (OECS). The OECS was created in 1981 when the Treaty of Basseterre was signed. An indication of CARICOM integration is that intra-regional domestic exports accounted for 19.1 percent of total exports in 2000.[57]

World Bank data reveals that the Caribbean small states during the period 2000–2018 experienced a rate of growth in GDP of less than 2 percent average per annum in 2010 constant US$ which is less than small states in the Pacific, small states in general, low-income countries, lower middle-income countries, and upper middle-income countries.[58] Without the security of the foreign exchange earnings from the banana exports which had stabilized the banana exporting islands, these small islands would have been even more vulnerable to adverse external events. The governments all turned to strengthening the tourist industry but this could not be done quickly and easily because it is a much more complex industry requiring expensive international market campaigns, a higher level of human skills, and the installation and upgrading of modern international standard infrastructure, in particular international airports and cruise ship docking facilities.

Structural Adjustment

There was a view (e.g., in the World Bank) that the EU banana regime could be easily replaced by direct aid and indeed, that this would be better for the Caribbean than the export of bananas and less expensive for the European Union.[59] The capacity to ignore the obvious adverse implications was derived from the assumption that a structural adjustment could be accomplished relatively quickly and easily because of the GDP per capita and the level of education of the population. In reality, the transition out of bananas was extremely difficult as those engaged in banana growing had very few skills that were transferable to other economic activities. The options in some countries were extremely limited, Dominica being a prime example of these limitations.[60] When these countries voiced concerns about the limited options and the difficulties to be overcome, these were dismissed as protestations borne out of an unwillingness to change or even to contemplate change. Nothing could have been further from the truth. The CBEA commissioned a study on the consequences of the dismantling of the EU banana regime and the possible alternatives such as tourism, services, manufacturing, and export agriculture. The report by Gill and Gonzales concluded that "economic restructuring cannot be considered as an alternative to banana cultivation, but rather as a supplement to it. Restructuring must develop alongside the banana industry. In view of the importance of this industry and the fact that "the chances for successful restructuring are themselves dependent on the continuation of banana cultivation and trade."[61]

Alternative Crops Not Feasible

The Caribbean banana exporting countries had for a long time worried about their dependence on bananas and recognized the need for diversification and so, a lot of work had been devoted to this issue. However, shifting from bananas to other crops was difficult because alternative crops faced the same circumstances that made banana production so high cost (i.e., small landholdings, steep hillsides, lack of economies of scale).[62] In addition, bananas bear every week whereas other crops tend to be seasonal except for vegetables which are not as lucrative as bananas. The transition to other crops while intuitively logical was easier said than done. Besides the loss of regular income to farmers and foreign exchange earnings to the economy, there were effects peculiar to the small islands. One such difficulty as pointed out by the Banana Exporters Association (BEA) was that banana exports provided the externality of generating "the volume to justify economically the regular shipping service vital for all exports and essential imports and can provide the necessary physical and economic infrastructure."[63]

US Palliative

The banana case in the WTO was set in motion by powerful American multinational companies petitioning under Section 301 of the US Trade Act. This unleashed the full force of the legal and administrative resources of the United States against the struggling democracies of seven small Caribbean countries whose combined wealth is less than 0.4 percent of that of the United States. The thrust of the United States's view was that the Caribbean states and the European Union were deliberately misrepresenting the US's position on this issue, whilst in reality, the United States was fully supportive of the Caribbean and had no wish or intention of harming Caribbean economies, inhibiting development, or restricting trade opportunities for Caribbean produce, including bananas. These laudable sentiments were not, however, borne out by the facts. In reality, the reverse was true and since October 1994, the US authorities pursued a strategy which would lead directly to the destruction of the Caribbean banana industry and would consequently provoke severe economic hardship and political instability in a region already struggling against considerable difficulty and deprivation.

President Bill Clinton held the first-ever meeting between the United States and heads of government of all the countries of the Caribbean (except Cuba) in May 1997 in Barbados. On the eve of signing the Partnership for Prosperity and Security, he told the Caribbean leaders that: "This is not a meeting between Caribbean nations and the United States; it is a meeting among Caribbean nations, including the United States."[64] The feeling in the ESC was one of US neglect and in the case of its policy on bananas a sense of being aggrieved by US policy which was regarded as inimical to the ESC. Dr. Denzil Douglas, prime minister of St. Kitts and Nevis, speaking about the United States's position on the EU preferential banana regime, said that Washington must not "see everything within the crucible of narcotics. There are other social problems that exist in the Caribbean, and a lot of these social problems, to some extent, the United States can help and has not helped."[65]

Lack of US Aid Compounded the Crisis

The United States did not feel the necessity to provide financial aid to help the affected countries cope with the decline of the banana industry and make a transition to other activities. In fact, in the years before the dismantling of the EU banana regime, US aid to the Caribbean declined. One estimate is that US aid declined from US$225 million in 1986 to US$26 million in 1996, approximately 90 percent.[66] At the same time, the United States terminated Section 936 tax credit which generated a pool of corporate investment for the Caribbean.[67] The US approach was in contrast to that of the European Union, which provided financial aid to the countries hit by the dismantling of the banana regime. Compensation of €190m for the decline of banana farming in the Caribbean and African countries was provided in the form of budget support to governments. The imminent decline of the banana industry was preceded by the deleterious impact of NAFTA on the apparel industry in the countries eligible under CBERA popularly known as the Caribbean Basin Initiative.[68]

One aspect of keeping US aid flowing to the region was adhering to US foreign policy goals. Compliance with US foreign policy positions does not necessarily bring a reward as compliance is expected. Lewis explains that: "this meant adopting an anticommunist posture, particularly for the

Eastern Caribbean ... it also meant supporting the United States in international forums. This policy was not particularly successful, as this support was not necessarily rewarded by increased U.S. aid."[69]

Even if there had been plenty of financial aid this could not substitute for the system of aid operated by the EU banana regime. As the CBEA explained in a submission to the UK parliament, the best-intentioned financial aid (a) could not "provide adequate protection against determined attempts to drive the Caribbean out of their markets", (b) would "remove the incentive to improve quality and productivity", (c) "would be vulnerable to increasing pressures on donor governments to reduce aid expenditure and would therefore not provide an adequate basis on which to invest in the industry", and (d) "conventional development aid does not filter down to farm level as effectively as income earned by growers themselves from the weekly sales of their bananas".[70] The banana exporting Caribbean countries were a case where they needed what Jeffrey Sachs refers to as "trade plus aid".[71]

Increased Drug Trafficking

Crime and the violence associated with it has steadily increased during the 1990s,[72] it is pervasive and has continued unabated to the present. A central underlying factor in the surge in crime has been the increase in drug trafficking bringing with it transnational criminal connections related to the location between the country with the biggest demand for cocaine and marijuana, the United States and the main supply source of cocaine, Colombia. The decline in the banana industry and the expansion in drug production and distribution are correlated. This was evident by 2000 when: "Many believe, the future of the drug trade in the Caribbean is intimately related to the future of the banana trade".[73]

During the 14 years ending in 2001, CARICOM governments received full certification from the United States for their cooperation in the fight against drug trafficking. Once the EU banana regime was dismantled there was an increase in economic hardship and a concomitant increase in drug trafficking. The real possibility was that small banana farmers would easily and quickly shift into marijuana growing[74] especially since the banana farms were very small plots in hilly terrain inadequately monitored by governments without sufficient resources to mount effective counter-narcotics campaigns. The weak capacity of individual states was compounded by the less adequate regional cooperation efforts.[75] The Eastern Caribbean became a major "transit point for drug traffickers going to the United States and Europe". The numerous small islands constitute several trans-shipment points for narcotics from Colombia and Venezuela in addition to locally produced marijuana. There was an increase in the seizure of marijuana, and cocaine increased in all the banana exporting islands during the years 1994–2001.[76] In 2013, an estimated 16 percent of cocaine imported into the United States came through the Caribbean islands up from 4 percent in 2011.[77] The escalation in drug trafficking brought with it money laundering and transnational crime.[78] Drug trafficking drives crime in a variety of ways including undermining institutions by corruption[79] and this was not difficult because in these small societies a little money can have a major influence. This gives rise to what Griffith has called "political penetrability".[80]

It may very well have been felt that the dismantling of the banana regime/made the former banana exporting countries more susceptible to drug trafficking. Prime Minister Eugenia Charles in demanding that the European Union resolutely resist US pressure declared: "The Europeans have a choice. They either continue to import bananas, or their children may well buy cocaine that comes through these islands."[81] This perspective was articulated by Haiti's Minister of Foreign Affairs. He remonstrated that drug trafficking was a problem of external origin to the region, which was "foisted" upon the Caribbean and that it was a reflection of the fact that the Caribbean is located between the United States, the country with the largest demand and South America, the region with the most supply capacity.[82] He did have a valid point because cocaine use in the Caribbean was two-thirds less than in North America.[83] In addition to the importation of cocaine, the decline of bananas stimulated the domestic production of marijuana, particularly in St. Vincent where it was sold internally and exported and for distribution to St. Lucia.[84] The production and distribution of marijuana increased crime, violence, and smuggling.

One of the problems is that the Clinton administration was treating the banana issue as a trade dispute with the European Union in which Chiquita, an American company repeatedly claimed to be losing millions of dollars and not fully appreciating the wider implications. The truth is that Chiquita was sustained before the regime came into effect in mid-1993 and made a profit in Europe of US$78.7 million in 1993 and US$73.7 million in 1994.[85] It may have been a case of "willful ignorance" because Caribbean spokespersons at all level and on every possible occasion had been pointing out the likely damage to the banana exporting islands.

Jamaica's ambassador to the United States Dr. Richard Bernal explained in the widely-read Newsweek magazine that: "This is not a simple issue of economics but of survival. This is not just about trade, but security."[86] More important than a Caribbean ambassador pointing out implications for US security was a letter to President Clinton from Representatives Maxine Waters, Nancy Kaptur, Ronald V. Dellums, Duncan Hunter, and Roscoe G. Bartlett. They stated emphatically that: "This ruling will inadvertently make an economically destabilized Caribbean more vulnerable to the aggressive overtures of international drug cartels."[87]

Transnational Organized Crime

Drug trafficking, once a significant factor contributing to the emergence of transnational crime in the Caribbean region has become hemispheric in its scope.[88] Transnational organized crime is crime organized and executed across national borders by involving organized groups or networks of criminals. Transnational organized crime involves every conceivable type of crime conducted by every means possible. The activities involved cause major losses to legitimate economic activities, deprives governments of revenue, and significantly increase the cost of combatting crime. Beyond the negative economic impact, transnational crime undermines, and in some situations, overwhelms national security, destroys fundamental aspects of democracy, and cripples the law and order function to the State. All countries have to contend with transnational organized crime and cope in varying degrees, but small island developing states such as those in the Caribbean are particularly vulnerable because of their small size, limited institutional capacity and openness both economically and topographically.

The extent to which transnational organized crime has been metastasized and entrenched in some Caribbean countries was clearly evident in the 2010 extradition of Christopher "Dudus" Coke from Jamaica to the United States.[89] Building on his father's crime organization, Dudus extended his drug trafficking network the "Shower Posse" beyond Brooklyn and New York City. His extradition took five weeks and involved gun battles between the Jamaican police, army, technical support from the United States, and gang members based in Tivoli Gardens. During the armed conflict between the police supported by the Jamaica Defense Force and gang members in support of Dudus, 76 people were killed.

Violence

On a per capita basis, the Caribbean is one of the most violent places in the world. While violence emanates from a raft of old and new vulnerabilities,[90] narcotics trafficking has also been accompanied by an inflow of firearms[91] and a concomitant escalation in violence. Violence increased very significantly as many homicides are as a result of "turf wars" for control of drug distribution. By 2000, the Caribbean was one of the most violent regions in the world.[92] By 2007, the World Bank was reporting: "Murder rates in the Caribbean—at 30 per 100,000 population annually—are higher than for any other region of the world and have risen in recent years for many of the region's countries."[93] Between 1982 and 1997, the rate of homicides more than doubled.[94] In St. Lucia, the murder rate more than doubled from 9 to 20 per 100,000, during the 1999–2003 period.[95] If Jamaica was able to reduce its murder rate to that of Costa Rica, it would have boosted per capita growth by 5.4 percent per annum. Such is the magnitude of the economic cost.[96]The vital tourist arrivals in Jamaica and some other Caribbean destinations are negatively affected by crime.[97]

9/11 and Tourism

Since the Moyne Commission Report of the mid-1940s, tourism has been cited as the next engine of economic growth but it evolved slowly in the Eastern Caribbean lacking behind Barbados and Jamaica, which had long been established as cruise ship destinations. The smaller islands lacked adequate seaports, airports, hotels, infrastructure, and professional staff. This would have taken time to develop requiring investment, marketing, and training. Just as this process was beginning to develop momentum, the events of September 11, 2001 were a setback to tourism across the entire region but the less developed tourist sector of smaller islands was less resilient. During September to December 2001, tourist arrivals in the Caribbean dropped by 16.7 percent.[98] On October 11–12, the heads of governments of CARICOM met in Nassau, Bahamas, and made a number of decisions to address the fallout in the tourism sector.[99] The package of policy measures included enhancement of aviation and maritime security and approaching the European Union and the Inter-American Development Bank for emergency financing.

Debt Debacle

The small middle-income developing economies of the Caribbean had been experiencing a prolonged economic crisis. The most profound characteristic of the crisis of the Caribbean is the extraordinary level of debt. An empirical study by the Inter-American Development Bank has shown that this debt problem was exacerbated by the fact that the Caribbean was the region that has suffered the most adverse impact from the global economic crisis.[100] Debt is not unique to the Caribbean countries it is a perennial one across a wide range of countries over recorded history.[101] Writing in 1986, Norman Girvan was already calling attention to the fact that in Jamaica, "the debt constitutes a major impediment to growth and development."[102] The economies of the Caribbean are now highly indebted measured by a variety of criteria. The build-up of debt preceded the global financial crisis of 2008. Between 1997 and 2004, the average debt/GDP of the Caribbean countries increased from 54 percent to 84 percent[103] with the most indebted having levels of over 100 percent. Debt payments, which in the case of Jamaica, exceeded 50 percent of fiscal revenue severely constrained expenditure on education, health, and infrastructure prompting King to opine: "almost every element of the physical, economic infrastructure failed to expand at a rate commensurate with the needs of a modern economy."[104]

The Caribbean comprises the economies that were most adversely affected by the shocks emanating from the post 2008 global financial cum economic crisis. The fact that the Caribbean suffered a comparatively more deleterious effect than anywhere else including other small developing economies has been documented by the Inter-American Development Bank.[105] Robinson shows that 8 of the 12 most indebted middle income countries are from the Caribbean, and the region holds 4 of the top 5 places: a dubious distinction indeed.[106] Undoubtedly, the debt situation has not only reached crisis proportions but this has been so over a prolonged period. Don Harris[107] has warned that a strategy of "'debt financed growth' must of necessity be short-term because beyond certain limits it creates a barrier to growth. Countries could end up borrowing to repay, a situation that in the 1980s I labelled a 'vicious circle of foreign indebtedness'."[108]

A variety of approaches to debt restructuring was employed by Caribbean governments. The governments involved have been Belize, Grenada, Jamaica, and St. Kitts. These debt restructuring exercises provided some relief but had limited impact on debt to GDP or on the debt service burden.[109] The Caribbean is still left striving for sustainable economic growth restrained by the "ball and chain" of a substantial debt stock. This is evidenced by the high debt/GDP ratio and deprived of a large share of fiscal expenditure which could be devoted to stimulating or supporting economic activity. The debt exchanges carried out by Belize in 2006–2007 and 2012–2013, provided temporary liquidity but did not adequately address the sustainability of the debt in the long-term.[110]

Defaults have occurred in Antigua in 2010, Belize in 2012, Dominica in 2004, Grenada in 2005 and 2013, Seychelles in 2009, and Jamaica in 2010 and 2013. Debt restructuring in circumstances of extreme fiscal stress often leads to relief which is motivated by liquidity concerns rather than substantial relief.

The debt problem is a major aspect of the economic crisis of the Caribbean. The high levels of debt stifle economic growth via several channels including distorting fiscal policy, depriving the economy of public investment in infrastructure, and the provision of public goods and services particularly, health, and education. A substantial reduction of the debt burden will be a critical component of achieving sustainable economic development in the Caribbean. For these reasons, all concerned with the future of the small island developing states need to be informed on the debt-development dilemma. The debt is not only constraining the present welfare of the people of the Caribbean and mortgaging the future because of the inter-generational transfer of debt[111] but places the repayment of debt on future generations.

The outlook for debt in the Caribbean is worrying. First, the Inter-American Development Bank reports that the debt-to-GDP ratios in the Caribbean in 2016 were higher than they were in 2013 except for two countries, Guyana and Jamaica. Suriname experienced the largest increase of 168 percent between 2013 and 2016.[112] Second, the debt could continue to rise. The IMF's April 2017 World Economic Outlook projects that debt-to-GDP ratios in 2020 will remain at current levels for most countries with a possible rise in the Bahamas and Barbados.[113]

Resort To Unorthodoxy

In a calculated strategy of expediency, some governments (not confined to banana exporting countries) resort to Citizenship by Investment Programs. Citizenship by Investment in Dominica[114] is available through two options.

First by making a financial donation to the country under the government's investor visa program. This starts at $100,000 for a single person plus fees or $200,000 for a family of four. Second, since January 2015, by investing in real estate. Applicants making such a contribution are granted full citizenship for themselves and their family allowing visa-free travel to over 137 countries including the UK and the EU Schengen zone. Citizenship is granted for life and there is no requirement to reside in Dominica. Applicants from any country are eligible and the processing time is 60–90 days. The State Department 2017 report International Narcotics Control Strategy Report on Money Laundering and Financial Crimes, Vol. II. Regarded the Citizenship by Investment Program as "susceptible" to abuse by criminal actors.[115]

In St. Lucia, the minimum donations are $100,000 for a single applicant, $165,000 for a couple and $190,000 for a family of four. For real estate investment, the minimum is $300,000. In Grenada, applicants can be from any country. Processing is done within four months without an interview. No physical residency requirements. The benefits include visa-free travel to over 125 countries, including Europe's Schengen zone and there is no tax on worldwide income.

Established in 1984, The St Kitts-Nevis Citizenship Investment Program offered visa-free travel to 135 countries.[116] There are two investment options. First, the Sugar Industry Diversification Foundation (SIDF) a charity established in 2006 to raise funds for the displaced sugar industry workers. The minimum non refundable contribution was $250,000 per person and entitles the donor to citizenship and a passport. Second, investment in a pre-approved real estate project at a minimum cost of $400,000 to be maintained for a period of not less than 5 years. Questions persist about the transparency and fiduciary status of the Citizen Investment Program. Canada has withdrawn visa-free entry from St. Kitts. A Chinese national wanted by Interpol was extradited to the People's Republic of China after a prolonged process. Applicants for the St Kitts-Nevis Citizenship Investment Program must: be at least 18 years old, of good character, have no criminal record, pass a detailed background check, provide proof of source of funds and be healthy. There is no way to know how stringent the scrutiny is especially since there is no requirement to visit St Kitts and Nevis before, during, or after application and no interview. The US Financial Crimes Enforcement Network in an advisory in May 2017, described the program as: "maintains lax controls as to who may be granted citizenship," and as a result, "illicit actors, including individuals intending to use the secondary citizenship to evade sanctions, can obtain a SKN passport with relative ease."[117] The government immediately took some remedial measures. Antigua and Barbuda has also had a case of a Chinese person carrying their passport who was wanted by Chinese authorities.[118] This can happen in even a well-run program. The prime minister of Dominica has vigorously promoted the Citizenship by Investment Program while visiting the People's Republic of China.[119]

Summary

Today, the Caribbean, in particular the former banana exporting countries, remains a region which has relatively high per capita incomes but one suffering from a complex of economic and security vulnerabilities. Economic growth rates have been low and driven by a single sector, in most cases tourism. Meanwhile, on a per capita basis, the Caribbean has one of the highest rates of violence in the world. While this cannot be attributed solely to the collapse of the EU banana regime, it is certainly true that it was an important contributory factor. Moreover, it need not have happened. The episode harmed the relationship between the United States and the Caribbean, and this was reflected in the inability of the United States to dissuade the Caribbean countries from close relations with China and Venezuela.

Notes

1. Described as "embittered" see Gordon Myers, Banana Wars. The Price of Free Trade (London: Zed Books, 2004) page 167.
2. Nadav Goldschmied, Yair Galily and Kenneth Keith, "Evidence for Cross-Cultural Support for the Underdog: Is the Affiliation Driven by Fairness and Competence Assessments?", Frontiers in Psychology (2018).
3. Derek Thompson, "America's Monopoly Problem. How big business jammed the wheels of innovation", The Atlantic, October, 2016 and Sarah Eames, "Number of family farms continues to decline", The Daily Star, April 14, 2019.
4. Dan Perry, "Jamaica Criticizes US on Banana War", Associated Press, March 21, 1999.
5. Brook Larmer, "The Banana Wars", Newsweek Magazine, April 28, 1997, page 12.
6. Bob Herbert, "In America; Banana Bully", New York Times, May 13, 1996.

7. Richard L. Bernal, The Unimportance of the English Speaking Caribbean in US Foreign Policy as told by Presidents and Secretaries of State", Caribbean Journal of International Relations & Diplomacy, Vol.1, No.1 (February, 2013) pages 132–150.
8. Don Bohning, "Banana Wars Snag Caribbean Island Nations", Miami Herald, December 23, 1998, page C 1.
9. Sir Roland Sanders, Crumbled Small. The Commonwealth Caribbean in World Politics (London; Hansib Publications, 2005) page 15.
10. Brook Larmer, "The Banana Wars", Newsweek Magazine, April 28, 1997, page 12.
11. Michelle Williams, "Caribbean Shiprider Agreements: Sunk by Banana Trade War?", Inter-American Law Review, Vol.31, No.1(Spring, 2000) pages 163–195. See page 165.
12. Michelle Williams, "Caribbean Shiprider Agreements: Sunk by Banana Trade War?", Inter-American Law Review, Vol.31, No.1(Spring, 2000) pages 163–195. See page 165, Footnote 10.
13. The Influence of Small States on Superpowers: Jamaica and U.S. Foreign Policy (Lanham: Lexington Publishers, 2015).
14. Dennis McFarlene, "The Future of The Banana Industry in The West Indies: An Assessment of Supply Prospects for 1965 and 1975", Social and Economic Studies, Vol. 13, No. 1 (March, 1964) pages 38–93. See page 81.
15. George L. Beckford, "The West Indian Banana Industry: The Scope for Rationalization and Regional Collaboration", Social and Economic Studies, Vol. 2, No.3 (1967) Supplement.
16. Mark Moberg, Slipping Away: Banana Politics and Fair Trade in the Eastern Caribbean (New York: Berghahn Books, 2008).
17. Mark Moberg, Slipping Away: Banana Politics and Fair Trade in the Eastern Caribbean (New York: Berghahn Books, 2008).
18. John Williamson, "What Washington Means by Policy Reform", in John Williamson (ed.), Latin American Readjustment: How Much has Happened (Washington DC: Peterson Institute for International Economics 1989) and Pedro-Pablo Kuczynski and John Williamson, After the Washington Consensus: Restarting Growth and Reform in Latin America (Washington DC: Peterson Institute for International Economics, 2003).
19. Eudine Barriteau, "The Economic Philosophy of Eugenia Charles and Dominica's Development, 1980–1995" in Eudine Barriteau and Alan Cobley (ed.), Enjoying Power: Eugenia Charles and Political Leadership in the Commonwealth Caribbean (Kingston: University of the West Indies Press, 206) pages 183–213.

20. The Impact of Banana Supply and Demand Changes on income, employment and food security (Rome: Food and Agriculture Organization, 1999) page 3.
21. Keith Nurse and Wayne Sandiford, Windward Islands Bananas: Challenges and Options Under the Single European Market (: Kingston: Friedrick Ebert Stiftung, 1995) page 11.
22. Wendy-Ann Isaac, Michael Joseph, Wayne Ganpat, Marisa Wilson and Richard Brathwaite, "The Caribbean's Windward Islands Banana Industry: A Heritage of Dependency". Journal of Rural and Community Development, Vol. 7, No. 2 pages 98–117. See page 114.
23. Banana production in the Caribbean – Wikipedia. https://en.wikipedia.org/wiki/Banana_production_in_the_Caribbean.
24. The World Banana Economy, 1970–84, FAO Social and Economic Development Paper No. 57 (Rome: Food and Agriculture Organization, 1986).
25. Data cited in Keith Nurse and Wayne Sandiford, Windward Inlands Bananas: Challenges and Options Under the Single European Market (Kingston: Friedrich Ebert Stiftung, 1995) page 3.
26. Keith Nurse and Wayne Sandiford, Windward Inlands Bananas: Challenges and Options Under the Single European Market: (Kingston: Friedrich Ebert Stiftung, 1995) page 3.
27. Keith Nurse and Wayne Sandiford, Windward Inlands Bananas (Kingston: Friedrich Ebert Stiftung, 1995) page 3.
28. Wayne Sandiford, On the Brink of Decline. Bananas in the Windward Islands (St. George's: Fedon Books, 2000) page 117.
29. Wayne Sandiford, On the Brink of Decline. Bananas in the Windward Islands (St. George's: Fedon Books, 2000) page 121.
30. The EU Banana Regime: Evolution and Implications of its Recent changes (Brussels: Directorate-General for External Policies of the Union, Policy Department, 2010) page 48.
31. Montfort Mlachila, Paul Cashin and Cleary Haines, Caribbean Bananas: The Macroeconomic Impact of Trade Preference Erosion, IMF Working Paper WP/10/59 (Washington DC: International Monetary Fund, March 2010) page 27.
32. There several varieties of the banana plant and they have suffered from periodic ravaging diseases which have destroyed the most popularly grown and traded varieties. Panama disease caused the Gros Michel to be replaced by the Cavendish variety. Today the banana is facing yet another crisis of a potentially devastating disease. See Dan Koeppel, Banana. The Fate of the Fruit That Changed the World (New York: Hudson Street Press, 2008) pages xi–xix. See also What We Can Learn From the Near-Death of the Banana, TIME, 18 Nov 2019.

33. Pedro Arias, Cora Dankers, Pascal Liu and Paul Pilkauskas, The World Banana Economy, 1985–2002 (Rome: Food and Agriculture Organization, 2003) page 32.
34. The EU Banana Regime: Evolution and Implications of its Recent Changes (European Parliament, Directorate-General for External Policies, Policy department, 2010) page 34.
35. Economic and Social survey (Kingston: National Planning Agency, 1967) and Economic & Social Survey Jamaica 2018 (Kingston: Planning Institute of Jamaica, 2019) page 160.
36. The Economic and Social Contribution of the Banana Industry in the OECS, Research and Information Department, Eastern Caribbean Central Bank, September, 1997.
37. The World Banana Economy, 1970–84, FAO Social and Economic Development Paper No. 57 (Rome: Food and Agriculture Organization, 1986) page 82.
38. Organisation of Eastern Caribbean States Systematic Regional Diagnostic, Report Number 127046-LAC (Washington DC: World Bank, June 27, 2018) page 3.
39. Paul Cashin, Mlachila Montfort and Cleary Haines, Caribbean Bananas: The Macroeconomic Impact of Trade Preference Erosion, IMF Working Papers 10/59 (Washington DC: International Monetary Fund, 2010).
40. Organisation of Eastern Caribbean States Systematic Regional Diagnostic, Report Number: 127046-LAC (Washington DC: World Bank, June 27, 2018) page 4.
41. Inder Jit Ruprah, Does Size Matter? Yes, If You are Caribbean!, Country Department Caribbean Group Policy Brief No. IDB-PB-201 September 2013 (Washington DC: Inter-American Development Bank 2013).
42. Inder Ruprah, Karl Melgarejo and Ricardo Sierra, Is There a Caribbean Sclerosis? (Washington DC: Inter-American Development Bank, 2014).
43. Organisation of Eastern Caribbean States Systematic Regional Diagnostic, Report Number: 127046-LAC (Washington DC: World Bank, June 27, 2018) page 5.
44. Carleen O'Loughlin, Economic and Political Change in the Leeward and Windward Islands (New Haven: Yale University Press, 1968) page 111.
45. Green Gold. Bananas and Dependency in the Eastern Caribbean (London: Latin American Bureau, 1987) pages 4–5.
46. Brent Borrell and Maw-Cheng Yang, EC Bananarama 1992, Policy Research Working Paper Series 523, (Washington DC: World Bank, 1990).
47. Gordon Myers, Banana Wars. The Price of Free Trade (London: Zed Books, 2004) page 34.
48. "Interview with Edison James, Leader of the Opposition", The Courier N°140 (July–Aug), 1993.

49. Dame Mary Eugenia Charles A personal reflection on her legacy. https://searchlight.vc/searchlight/features/2008/10/03/dame-mary-eugenia-charles-a-personal-reflection-on-her-legacy/. Oct 3, 2008.
50. Lucretia Stewart, "Bananas are their only fruit: The trade which sustains the Windward Islands", The Independent, 4 September, 1994.
51. EC fact sheet on Caribbean bananas and the WTO, Memo/97/28 (Brussels: European Commission, 18 March, 1997.
52. Report of Eminent Persons Group mission to Jamaica, Dominica and St. Lucia, The Impact of the United States Challenge to the European Union Banana Regime on Political, Economic and social Order in the Caribbean and the consequences for U.S. National Interests (January, 1997).
53. "Expelled from Eden", The Economist, December 20th, 1997, pages 35–38.
54. Claire Godfrey, A Future for Caribbean Bananas-the Importance of Europe's Banana Market to the Caribbean (Policy Department, Oxfam, UK, March, 1998).
55. Cameron McWhirter and Mike Gallagher, "Island economies on the line", Cincinnati Enquirer, May 3, 1998, page C 17.
56. David Nii Addy, Restructuring and the loss of preferences: labour challenges for the Caribbean banana industry, Working Papers 993341213402676 (Geneva: International Labour Organization, 1999) page 4.
57. CARICOM's Intra-Regional Trade, Vol. 1 1990–2000 (Georgetown: CARICOM Secretariat, 2992) page 6.
58. World Development Indicators (Washington DC: World Bank, 2019).
59. "EU's Banarama-slipping", World Bank, Development Brief, No. 50 (March, 1995).
60. Eudine Barriteau, "The Economic Philosophy of Eugenia Charles and Dominica's Development, 1980–1995"in Eudine Barriteau and Alan Cobley (eds.), Enjoying Power. Eugenia Charles and Political Leadership in the Commonwealth Caribbean (Kingston: University of the West Indies Press, 2006) pages 183–213.
61. Henry S. Gill and Anthony P. Gonzales, Economic Consequences of a Banana Collapse in the Caribbean. Prepared for the Caribbean Banana Exporters Association, May 1995, pages 40–41.
62. J. M. Marie, Agricultural Diversification In A Small Economy: The Case For Dominica, Occasional Paper No.10 (Cave Hill: Institute of Social and Economic Research, University of the West Indies, 1979).
63. Memorandum from the Caribbean Banana Exporters Association Select Committee on International Development Minutes of Evidence. www.parliament.uk/. Accessed 7 March 2020.

64. Richard L. Bernal, "The Unimportance of the English Speaking Caribbean in US Foreign Policy as told by Presidents and Secretaries of State", Caribbean Journal of International Relations & Diplomacy, Vol.1, No.1 (February, 2013) pages 132–150. See page 133.
65. Don Bohning "US Relations with the Caribbean Under Strain." Miami Herald, Oct. 27, 1998.
66. Sir Roland Sanders, Crumbled Small. The Commonwealth Caribbean in World Politics (London: Hansib Publications, 2005) page 170.
67. Richard L. Bernal and Steve Lamar, Caribbean Basin Economic Development and the Section 936 Tax Credit. North-South Agenda Paper, No.22 (Miami: North-South Center, University of Miami, December 1996).
68. Richard L. Bernal, "NAFTA at Three: The Case for NAFTA Parity," Statement submitted to the House on Ways and Means Trade Subcommittee, House of Representative One Hundred Fifth Congress, First Session, September 11, 1997 (Washington, DC: Government Printing Office, 1998) pages 261–263.
69. Patsy Lewis, Surviving Small Size. Regional Integration in Caribbean Ministates (Kingston: University of the West Indies Press, 2002) page 63.
70. Memorandum from the Caribbean Banana Exporters Association Select Committee on International Development Minutes of Evidence. www.parliament.uk/. Accessed 7 March, 2020.
71. Jeffrey D. Sachs, The End of Poverty. Economic Possibilities for our Time (New York: Penguin Press, 2005) page 281.
72. Crime, Violence and Development. Trends, costs, and policy in the Caribbean (Washington DC: World Bank, March, 2007).
73. Michelle Williams, "Caribbean Shiprider Agreements: Sunk By Banana Trade War?", Inter-American Law Review, Vol.31, No.1(Spring, 2000) pages 163–195.
74. Nora Boustany, "Yes We Have No Banana Pact", Washington Post, 20 November, 1998, page A 50.
75. Suzette A. Haughton, Drugged Out. Globalisation and Jamaica's Resilience to Drug Trafficking (Lanham: University Press of America, 2011) pages 151–152.
76. Caribbean Drug Trends 2001–2002 (Bridgetown: Caribbean Regional, United Nations Office on Drugs and Crime, February, 2003).
77. "Full Circle. Drugs trafficking in the Caribbean", The Economist, 24 May 2014.
78. Anthony P. Maingot, "The Decentralization Imperative and Caribbean Criminal Enterprises" in Tom Farer (ed.), Transnational Crime in the Americas (New York: Routledge, 1999) pages 144–170.

79. Crime, Violence and Development: Trends, Costs and Options in the Caribbean (Washington DC: World Bank, 2007).
80. Ivelaw Griffith, "Security and Sovereignty in the contemporary Caribbean: Probing /elements of the Local-Global Nexus" in Cynthia Barrow and Don Marshall (eds.), Living at the Borderlines: Issues in Caribbean Sovereignty and Development (Kingston: Ian Randle Publishers, 2003) pages 209–225. See page 218.
81. Rachel Anderson, Tim Taylor and Tim Josling, "The Caribbean and the Banana Trade" in Timothy E. Josling and Timothy G. Taylor (eds.), Banana Wars. The Anatomy of a Trade War (Walliford: CABI Publishing, 2003) pages 123–150. See page 147.
82. "Drug trafficking is a global problem foisted upon the Caribbean countries", Jamaica Observer, 18 June, 2019, page 14.
83. Global Overview of Drug Demand and Supply. Latest Trends, Cross-Cutting Issues (Vienna: United Nations, 2018).
84. Dave Ramsaran, "Understanding the Socio-cultural Dynamics of Globalisation: The Case of St. Lucia and St. Vincent and the Grenadines" in Cynthia Barrow and Don Marshall (eds.), Living at the Borderlines: Issues in Caribbean Sovereignty and Development (Kingston: Ian Randle Publishers, 2003) pages 95–117.
85. Gordon Myers, Banana Wars. The Price of Free Trade (London: Zed Books, 2004) page 78.
86. Brook Larmer, "The Banana Wars", Newsweek Magazine, April 28, 1997, page 15.
87. Letter to President Clinton from Representatives Maxine Waters, Nancy Kaptur, Ronald V. Dellums, Duncan Hunter and Roscoe G. Bartlett, June 9, 1997.
88. R. Evan Ellis, Transnational Organized Crime in Latin America and the Caribbean. From Evolving Threats and Responses to Integrated, Adaptive Solutions (New York: Lexington Books, 2018).
89. Paul Ashley, Dudus. The Extradition of Jamaica's #1 Drug Don (Kingston: Paul Ashley, 2018).
90. W. Andy Knight, "The nexus between vulnerabilities and violence in the Caribbean", Third World Quarterly, Vol. 40, No.2 (March, 2019) pages 1–22.
91. Randy Sandiford, "Crime, Violence and Public Safety" in M. Raymond Izarali (ed.), Crime, Violence and Security in the Caribbean (New York: Routledge, 2017) pages 19–51.
92. Caribbean Human Development Report, Human Development and the Shift to Better Citizen Security 2012 (New York: United Nations, 2012) page 19.

93. Crime, Violence and Development: Trends, Costs and Options in the Caribbean (Washington DC: World Bank, 2007) page iii.
94. Crime, Violence and Development: Trends, Costs and Options in the Caribbean (Washington DC: World Bank, 2007) page 8.
95. Crime, Violence and Development: Trends, Costs and Options in the Caribbean (Washington DC: World Bank, 2007) page 9.
96. Crime, Violence and Development: Trends, Costs and Options in the Caribbean (Washington DC: World Bank, 2007) page 59.
97. Dillon Alleyne and Ian Boxill, "The impact of crime on tourist arrivals in Jamaica", International Journal of Tourism Research, Vol. 5, Issue 5 (September/October, 2003) pages 381–391.
98. Caribbean tourism overview – Caribbean Tourism Organization. https://www.onecaribbean.org/content/files/TourismOverview.pdf.
99. Odeen Ishmael. The Impact of the September 11 Terrorist Attack Against the United States on the Caribbean Political Economy. www.guyana.org/Speeches/ishmael_112801.html. Nov 29, 2001.
100. Inder Jit Ruprah, Does Size Matter? Yes, If You are Caribbean! Inter-American Development Bank Country Department Caribbean Group Policy Brief No. IDB-PB-201(September, 2013).
101. David Graeber, Debt. The First 5000 Years (New York: Melville House Publishing, 2011) and Carmen M. Reinhart and Kenneth Rogoff, This Time Is Different: Eight Centuries of Financial Folly (Princeton: Princeton University Press, 2011).
102. Norman Girvan, "Notes on Jamaica's External Debt" in Omar Davis (ed.), The Debt Problem in Jamaica, Monograph No. 1, Economics Department (Mona, Jamaica: University of the West Indies, 1986) page 72.
103. Charles Amo-Yartey and Therese Turner-Jones, "Fiscal Consolidation and Debt Reduction in the Caribbean: An Overview" in Charles Amo-Yartey and Therese Turner-Jones (ed.), Caribbean Renewal. Tackling Fiscal and Debt Challenges (Washington DC: International Monetary Fund, 2014) page 1.
104. Damien King and Anika Kiddoe, Achieving Fiscal Sustainability in Jamaica: The JDX and Beyond (Kingston: Caribbean Policy Research Institute, 2010).
105. Inder Ruprah, Karl Melgarejo and Ricardo Sierra, Is There a Caribbean Sclerosis? (Washington DC: Inter-American Development Bank, 2014).
106. Michele Robinson, "Does Debt Restructuring Work? An Assessment of Remedial Actions" in Damien King and David Tennant (eds.), Debt and Development in Small Island Developing States (New York: Palgrave Macmillan, 2014) pages 207–218.

107. Donald J. Harris, Jamaica's Debt-Propelled Economy: A Failed Economic Strategy and Its Aftermath, SALISES Working Paper Series No.1, University of the West Indies, 2010.
108. Richard L. Bernal, "The Vicious Circle of Foreign Indebtedness: The Case of Jamaica," in Antonio Jorge, Jorge Salazar-Carrillo and Frank Diaz-Pou (eds.), External Debt and Development Strategy in Latin America (New York: Pergamon Press, 1985) pages 111–128.
109. Michele Robinson, "Does Debt Restructuring Work? An Assessment of Remedial Actions" in Damien King and David Tennant (eds.), Debt and Development in Small Island Developing States (New York: Palgrave Macmillan, 2014) page 214.
110. Tamon Asonuma, Gerardo Peraza, Kristine Vitola, and Takahiro Tsuda, Sovereign Debt Restructurings in Belize: Achievements and Challenges Ahead, IMF Working Paper WP/14/132 (Washington DC: International Monetart Fund, May, 2014.
111. Andrew L. Yarrow, Forgive Us Our Debts: The Intergenerational Dangers of Fiscal Irresponsibility (New Haven: Yale University Press, 2008).
112. Inter-American Development Bank, Caribbean Region Quarterly Bulletin, Revising Fiscal Challenges, Vol. 6, Issue 3 (September, 2017) page 7.
113. World Economic Outlook April 2017 (Washington DC: International Monetary Fund, 2017).
114. Apply for citizenship – Dominica Citizenship by Investment. https://cbiu.gov.dm/dominica-citizenship/how-to-apply/.
115. 2017 International Narcotics Control Strategy Report on Money Laundering and Financial Crimes Vol. II (Washington DC: Department of State, 2018).
116. All information on the Citizenship – Investment Programme taken from St Kitts & Nevis Citizenship – Investment Programme – aaa-ii.com Ad. www.aaa-ii.com/.
117. US: St. Kitts citizenship program is being abused | Daily Mail Online, May 22, 2014.
118. "Chinese Mother and Daughter with Antigua & Barbuda CIP Passports wanted by Chinese Gov", Times Caribbean, January 26, 2016.
119. Dominica offers citizenship to Chinese investors for $200,000. https://dominicanewsonline.com/news/homepage/news/business/dominica-offers-citizenship-to-chinese-investors-for-200000/. Apr 1, 2015.

CHAPTER 8

Implications for US National Interest in the Caribbean

The National Interest

The "national interest" is defined to be what is good for the nation or nation state, and this, in turn, is easily translated to mean what increases the well-being of the majority of people of a country/nation state. What constitutes the well-being of a people can be multidimensional inclusive of the attainment of economic, political, social, cultural, security, and diplomatic objectives or more realistically a combination of some or all of these. Euphemisms include the "public interest" and the "national good". Apart from the definitional imprecision, there is the issue of who defines the national interest. Usually, this is the government but practically it is what is construed to be the national interest by those who are in government. Therefore, the possibility that what the government has defined as the national interest may differ from what the public or part thereof believe to be in their interest. It is a fact that not everyone agrees with the government's notion of the national interest. In reality, the national interest is some amalgamation of a multiplicity of competing interests and societal variety of goals and perspectives. Not surprisingly, some have spoken of the concept of national interest as ambiguous and indeed, it has been an issue in international relations theory.[1]

This chapter outlines the multifaceted US national interests in the Caribbean.

R. L. Bernal, *Corporate versus National Interest in US Trade Policy*, https://doi.org/10.1007/978-3-030-56950-1_8

US National Interest in the Caribbean

A 2019 report to Congress captures US national security interest as "increased drug interdictions, improved regional law enforcement, and enhanced countering of violent extremists." The evaluation highlights the state of the Caribbean as "having some of the highest murder rates in the world. Rising crime and endemic corruption threaten governments' ability to provide security and good governance. Small but significant numbers of extremists from the region have joined the ISIS. These factors drive illicit trafficking and irregular migration to the United States while threatening the millions of Americans that visit the region annually."[2] The Caribbean is, therefore, seen by the United States as a region which has increasingly developed new security issues while long-standing persistent problems remain. The region is one in which the United States has always sought allies among the ESC islands[3] in order to stabilize the wider Caribbean in which the United States has not achieved a comfort level with Cuba and Venezuela and in more recent years the growing influence of China.

US foreign policy towards the ESC, which consists of Antigua and Barbuda, Bahamas, Barbados, Belize, Dominica, Grenada, Guyana, Jamaica, Montserrat, St. Kitts and Nevis, St. Lucia, St. Vincent and the Grenadines, Trinidad and Tobago, was driven by a range of interests from economic to national security. Specifically, US national interests in the Caribbean were and continue to be:

Political:	Neighboring countries that are electoral democracies.
Diplomatic:	Countries that are allies and are favorable to US interests and policies.
Economic:	Prosperous economies providing export markets and investment opportunities and that are not constantly dependent on bilateral development aid.
Social:	Countries that are not a source of illegal non-Caucasian migrants.
Security:	Cooperate on countering the trafficking of narcotics entering the US and not a source of terrorism.

Political

The United States has an abiding interest in having neighbors that are electoral democracies. The English-speaking Caribbean has, since adult suffrage in 1944, practiced electoral democracy. The culture, practice, and institutions of democracy were instituted under the tutelage of the British during the long colonial period. Constitutions modeled on the British system have endured. The United States has generally been comfortable with elections in the region, which a 2005 report to Congress describes as "regular, free, and fair".[4] Democracy has operated uninterruptedly with very few exceptions, notably the Grenada Revolution terminated by an invasion by US armed forces in 1983 and two attempted coups in Trinidad and Tobago. In addition, there have been some controversial elections in Guyana and a military intervention in 1955 to dislodge a Marxist party. Democracy has prevailed despite increased drug trafficking, crime, and violence in the Caribbean. The democratic tradition in the ESC is very different from the experience of Cuba, the Dominican Republic, and Haiti.

Diplomatic

The Caribbean has, for a long time, not received the attention from the United States that it liked or felt that it should have been given. There was some dissonance over the amount and type of aid which it believed was required and not asking too much of the United States. The United States's instigated dismembering of the EU banana regime should not by itself be responsible for the attitude of the Caribbean, but it certainly contributed to a deterioration in the relationship. Furthermore, it should be noted that foreign policy disagreements with the United States preceded the banana issue, for example, Eric William's repatriation of the American base in Chaguaramas in Trinidad, the non-alignment of Michael Manley in Jamaica, and the stance on Cuba by Barbados, Guyana, Jamaica, and Trinidad and Tobago. As Brook Larmer observes in Newsweek Magazine: "Washington's assault on export barriers has shocked the sleepy island economies of the Caribbean and is ushering in a new era of ill feelings."[5]

The United States emphasized security aid when the Caribbean believed that the deterrent to crime and drug trafficking was economic development and that US financial aid could make a valid contribution. US aid to the ESC declined steadily since the mid-1980s. The US rationale for its approach to providing aid to the region was that these are middle-income developing economies which should be "graduated" from the most concessionary aid facilities including from multilateral development finance lending institutions such as the World Bank and the Inter-American Development Bank. The United States seemed to have forgotten the old dictum of the use of foreign aid as an instrument of foreign policy. As President Kennedy explained it: "Foreign aid is a method by which the United States maintains a position of influence and control around the world, and sustains a good many countries which would definitely collapse or pass into the Communist bloc."[6]

The result is that other donors have become particularly important in the region and along with that relationship has come to an increasing willingness to not align with US foreign policy positions. Several governments in the Caribbean maintain positions diametrically opposed to those of Washington DC. The most notable examples are on relations with Cuba, Venezuela, and China. It has reached a point where the United States has resorted to threats to cut off aid to prevent the Caribbean from voting against its position in the United Nations.[7]

Cuba

The United States has, since the Cuban Revolution, sought the support of Caribbean countries for its policy towards Cuba. US policy is one of seeking to engineer regime change in the self-confessed communist state. This policy was part of a wider Cold War anti-Communist strategy which reached a potentially catastrophic crisis in the now famous incident known as the Cuban Missile Crisis.[8] A prolonged campaign at the core of which has been an array of sanctions. How vigorously the sanctions have been applied has varied with some administrative easement during the administrations of Bill Clinton and Barrack Obama. The leadership in Cuba, particularly after Fidel Castro, relinquished the presidency, relaxed the extent of state control of the economy giving more latitude to private enterprise, and continued to open the tourism industry to foreign direct investment (FDI). Cuba has held fast to its own brand of socialism and resiled from rhetoric about the spread of revolution in the developing world. In the United States, well into the current century, there was concern that poor countries in Central America and the Caribbean would find Cuba an attractive model. This anxiety was palpable in the late 1970s and 1980s with Michael Manley's Democratic Socialism in Jamaica,[9] Forbes Burnham's Co-operative Socialism in Guyana, The Sandinistas in Nicaragua, and Maurice Bishop's New Jewel Movement in Grenada.

Reagan in his diaries referred to the Caribbean as a "becoming a Red lake".[10]

Cuba's relationship with the Caribbean has been close, consolidated by a belief in Cuba's right to self-determination and Cuba's exceptional generosity in providing medical doctors and nurses to work in the public health system in the region. Furthermore, though not explicitly articulated, there has been admiration for Cuba's unwillingness to conform to US pressure, no doubt born of the ever-present limitation of the sovereignty of a small island state. The Caribbean governments maintain embassies in Havana and students study in Cuba free of cost.

Actions by President Trump have reaffirmed the blockade policy based on the Helms-Burton Act which was never repealed or even challenged. None of the measures taken by the Obama administration displaced the Helms-Burton Act, which can only be repealed or replaced by Congress. The Caribbean did not oppose the liberalization by Obama, which could have led to a surge in Cuba's tourism earning[11] and could have adversely affected tourism elsewhere in the Caribbean. This is certainly the case for the countries that are located closest to Cuba and most likely to be affected: the Dominican Republic, the Bahamas, and Jamaica. Since 1953, Cuba's share of tourist going to the Caribbean declined from over 50 percent to 3 percent[12] but studies of the potential impact of the competition from Cuba reveal that there will not be a serious disruption.[13]

The leadership of the Caribbean and CARICOM have openly, publicly, and repeatedly criticized US sanctions on Cuba and much to the annoyance of the United States repeatedly called for a repeal of this policy. The Caribbean countries were active in the decision to restore Cuba's eligibility for membership in the OAS by lifting the 47-year-old suspension.[14] This stance is definitely not what the United States regards as in its national interest.

Venezuela

Venezuela, from the 1960s, has had an interest in the Caribbean and has felt that it was an arena where it should wield influence. Of the Caribbean countries, Trinidad and Tobago, given its physical location, has had the closest and most complex relationship with Venezuela. The movement of people has always been fluid with many Venezuelans opting to reside in Trinidad or in both countries. There are many bilingual Trinidadians of Venezuelan origin with family in both places. Fishermen from both countries frequently strayed into the other country's territorial waters and were apprehended and returned. There has been conflict over maritime demarcation in the Gulf of Paria.[15] Some have been suspicious of Venezuela's motives, notably Eric Williams who characterized its interest and objectives as "imperialism".[16] At the other end of the political spectrum was the warm relationship between Michael Manley and Carlos Andres Perez.[17]

In recent years, in the midst of the throes of the crisis engendered by high oil prices, President Hugo Chavez (1999–2013) offered to supply oil to Cuba in a scheme where part of the payment would be delayed. It is said that Fidel Castro persuaded him to extend it to the oil-importing Caribbean countries and hence Petro Caribe[18] was launched on June 29, 2005. It has proven to be invaluable to the economic survival of the Caribbean beneficiary countries. It allowed for the purchase of oil at prevailing market prices with immediate part payment and the balance payable after a grace period of 1 to 2 years. When the price of oil was below $40 per barrel, 5–25 percent could be paid through a financing arrangement over a period of 17 years at 2 percent interest. If the price of oil were sold over $40 per barrel, 30–75 percent could be paid over 25 years at 1 percent. To make more use of Petro Caribe, the Government of Jamaica established The Petro Caribe Development Fund in December 2006. Through this fund, the Government of Venezuela agreed to convert a portion of each payment due for petroleum products supplied to PetroJam Ltd., the state-owned refinery, into a long-term concessionary loan.

Chavez established the Bolivarian Alliance for the Peoples of Our America (ALBA) or *Alianza Bolivariana para los Pueblos de Nuestra Américas* as an alternative to the US inspired and birthed, Summit of the Americas. As a consequence, the Summit of the Americas no longer had membership of all countries in the Western Hemisphere except Cuba. ALBA's membership is Antigua and Barbuda, Bolivia, Cuba, Dominica, Ecuador, Nicaragua, Saint Lucia, Saint Vincent and the Grenadines, and Venezuela. It is not surprising that among those who were prepared to show their gratitude to Venezuela and to incur the displeasure of the United States were the former banana exporting countries of Dominica, St. Lucia, and St. Vincent.

In the case of whether to recognize the re-election of Nicholas Maduro or the self-declared Juan Guaido, the Caribbean as a whole did not align with the US position and did not support the resolution in the OAS in favor of intervention in Venezuela. The Bahamas, the Dominican Republic, Guyana, Haiti, Jamaica, and Saint Lucia supported the January 2019 resolution at the OAS and refused to recognize the legitimacy of the Maduro presidency. Dominica, St. Vincent and the Grenadines, and Suriname opposed intervention and recognized Maduro's presidency. The other Caribbean states, Antigua and Barbuda, Barbados, Belize, St. Kitts, and Trinidad and Tobago have maintained their neutrality. This spread has remained in spite of US diplomatic entreaties.[19] On the issue of the re-election of the US favored Luis Almagro who was elected Secretary General of the OAS on March 18, 2015; his approach to the recognition of Maduro's re-election proved controversial and member states were split on how the OAS should proceed. The United States strongly supported Almagro's re-election but the Caribbean was divided and resisted the attempts of the United States to persuade them to support Almagro and his proposal to recognize Juan Guaido as the legitimate government of Venezuela.

The differences over policy towards Venezuela have so divided the Caribbean that when President Trump and Secretary of State Mike Pompeo met the political leaders of the Caribbean not all countries were invited as is the tradition. In January 2020, the Prime Minister of Barbados, Chair of CARICOM, Mia Mottley and the Prime Minister of Trinidad and Tobago declined to attend a meeting with Pompeo in Jamaica over the non-inclusion of all CARICOM member states.[20] The United States has put pressure on the Caribbean countries to support its approach to the Maduro government and made it clear that any country doing business with Venezuela will be subject to US sanctions.[21] Trinidad and Tobago canceled an agreement with Venezuela for the joint development of a natural gas field because of US sanctions on Venezuela's state energy company PDVSA.[22]

China

Yet another example of the Caribbean being prepared to hew their own path in international affairs disregarding US opposition has been the increasing engagement of some countries with the People's Republic of China.[23] The annoyance of President Trump can only be imagined when Gaston Browne, Prime Minister of Antigua, all 108 sq. miles and 80,161 population responded to Secretary of State Pompeo warning against Chinese aid by saying: "Those who are opposed to China's deepening influence in the hemisphere need to talk less and perhaps they need to put some diplomatic dollars or development assistance on the table. Perhaps they may wish to consider spending less on artillery. Spend less on useless wars and interventions in the affairs of other states and to utilize the savings to help underprivileged countries here in the Caribbean and elsewhere."[24]

Secretary of State Mike Pompeo recently warned Latin America and the Caribbean against what he described as China's "predatory economic practices". He warned Panama that Chinese investment is "not transparent, not market driven and is designed to benefit the Chinese government."[25] While this may have been part of the escalating economic and diplomatic joisting between Beijing and Washington DC, the comments were directed at countries in what the United States has traditionally regarded as an American sphere of influence. During the last decade, the presence of the People's Republic of China has increased in the Caribbean, a region which the United States regards as its Third Border.

Why would China be interested in a region comprised of small developing countries facing challenging economic circumstances, without energy resources and with minute potential for trade and FDI? A motive peculiar to the Caribbean and Central America is the rivalry for diplomatic recognition between the People's Republic of China (China) and the Democratic Republic of China (Taiwan), a traditional ally of the United States. In recent years, a growing number of governments have switched diplomatic recognition from Taiwan to China. The countries of Central America were committed to the diplomatic recognition of Taiwan for 60 years. China's presence in Central America has increased significantly in scope and intensity in the last few years. The leadership in these countries are acutely aware of the enormous potential to benefit from Chinese aid, loans, and FDI. The first domino was Costa Rica.[26]

On June 1, 2007, Costa Rica became the first country in Central America to switch diplomatic relations from Taiwan to China. Imports of manufactured goods from China is increasing in all the countries of Central America and the Caribbean although unevenly. Imports have far exceeded exports resulting in an expanding trade deficit. China's development aid is concentrated in those countries with which it has diplomatic relations. Costa Rica has sought to expand trade with China with the conclusion of a free trade agreement (FTA), which was entered into force on August 1, 2011. When phased implementation was completed, approximately 90 percent of goods traded at zero tariff and liberalized some services sectors. The FTA also included intellectual property rights, trade remedies, customs procedures, technical barriers to trade and rules of origin. Now a decade later, exports have increased by over 100 percent consisting mainly of food such as bananas and beef and agricultural products (e.g. leather). There has been substantial development financing from China for construction and infrastructure. The two countries have agreed to strengthen relations through the Joint Action Plan on China–Costa Rica Cooperation 2016–2020.

The Dominican Republic and China in May 2018 signed an agreement to establish diplomatic ties, ending an almost 77-year relationship with Taiwan. The motivation of the Dominican Republic was three-fold: first to increase exports to China, especially given the large and growing trade deficit with China; second, the prospect of significant inflows of FDI and third, the opportunity to benefit from projects financed by loans from China almost invariably executed by Chinese companies of the order of $800 million.

Panama, which since 1949, has had relations with Taiwan has now shifted its diplomatic allegiance to China. The switch to a "One China" policy will expand trade and investment and shipping through the Panama Canal. This reduces the number of countries keeping up the farce of recognizing Taiwan to eleven in the Caribbean and Central America and to twenty across the world. The changes made by Panama and China is the discarding of long-term political positions in favor of economic possibilities. The latest country to establish diplomatic relations with China is El Salvador in August. This did not attract much attention in Washington DC, because of its limited economic and strategic importance. Not so with Panama which, with the expanded Canal, is a security concern and holds potential to be a regional hub for trade, investment, and finance rivaling Miami's commercial pre-eminence.

Diplomatic recognition is split in the Caribbean but weighted in favor of China. Antigua, The Bahamas, Barbados, Dominica, Grenada, Guyana, Jamaica, Suriname, and Trinidad and Tobago adhere to a "One China" policy. It may not be long before Belize and Haiti make the switch as China seeks to reduce the number of countries recognizing Taiwan which clines to support from a few very small countries: St. Kitts, St. Lucia, and St. Vincent. Part of China's success is the diplomatic attention they are prepared to devote to relations with small island states[27] something the ESC feels it does not get from the United States.

China has gained considerable goodwill in the Caribbean through development assistance in the form of grants and loans for construction and infrastructure projects to fiscally constrained governments[28] and from some FDI.[29] Loans from China became available just when Caribbean economies, the worst affected in the world according to the

Inter-American Development Bank, were struggling after the global economic crisis of 2008. As middle-income economies, they are not eligible for the most concessionary development financing facilities in the context of a steady decline in financial aid from the United States. Compounding all of this has been the disastrous effects of earthquakes in Haiti and hurricanes in Dominica and Antigua and Barbuda.

Gaston Browne, Prime Minister of Antigua responded to Secretary Pompeo's statement, by asserting that China had contributed significantly to socio-economic development in the Caribbean and that the United States should worry less about Chinese influence and think of more development assistance for the struggling region. Speaking about influence, former prime minister of Jamaica, Bruce Golding stated, "China had not sought to exercise influence on Jamaica in spite of providing considerable aid to Jamaica."[30] Prime Minister Skerrit of Dominica has explained that China has not made "any undue demands on Dominica. China has not sought to, as some others have done, impose its will on Dominica" and "that there is really nothing that Dominica has to give to China besides its friendship."[31]

Increased Chinese presence could be viewed as the natural, even inevitable spread of China's presence as it assumes an enhanced international outreach of the global power it has become. Another perspective would view China's activities as a part of a global challenge by China as an aspect of the diminution of US suzerainty, which has been unchallenged in this region. Since engagement can be a prelude to influence, it would be timely for the United States to initiate a new region-wide strategy to assist in the promotion of economic development. Such an initiative should encompass debt restructuring, long-term development loans, and private sector investment. This would boost trade and job creation in both the United States and Central America and the Caribbean. The urgency is demonstrated by the march of Hondurans towards the United States.

Economic

At the economic level, the United States's interest in the Caribbean emanates from seeing these small developing economies as markets for American goods and services, sources of raw materials, outlets for direct foreign investment, and an appreciation that economic development enhances the prospects for democracy, peace, and less drug trafficking.

Export Markets

The markets of the Caribbean countries other than Haiti and the Dominican Republic are extremely small but they are very secure with much of the trade passing through the ports of Miami, New York, New Jersey, and Baltimore. The markets have grown in part reflecting demand generated by the growing tourist industry. Locational proximity is sufficient to give the United States a considerable advantage in cost including shipping. The United States faces strong competition in electronics from Korea and increasingly from China in manufactured goods. Japan dominates the importation of automobiles. There is no strong overall challenge to the United States as a supplier to the Caribbean, and the small size of the markets together ensures that the retention of the markets of the small developing economies of the Caribbean has never been vital to US national interests.

Source of Raw Materials

The Caribbean is not particularly well endowed with raw materials which are vitally important, rare, or not easily and more inexpensively available from other suppliers. Three exceptions are: first, bauxite in the 1950s in Jamaica which was so close to Baton Rouge that the shipment could be given continuous air protection by land-based aircraft;[32] second, the refined products based on natural gas in Trinidad and Tobago; and third, the recently discovered oil deposits offshore Guyana. Guyana and Suriname supplied 82 percent of US imports of bauxite and alumina at the end of World War II[33] and Jamaica became a leading supplier by the 1960s.[34] Secure access to critical raw materials has been an enduring factor in US foreign policy not only because policymakers perceive it to be in the national interest but also because of the political power wielded by US multinational corporations.[35]

Foreign Direct Investment (FDI)

The governments in the region have always encouraged direct foreign investments and these investments have played an important role in capital formation. Like all developing countries, those in the Caribbean have tried to accelerate economic growth by raising the level of investment. One way of doing so has been encouraging and garnering inflows of FDI. Foreign direct investment can have positive effects on economic growth such as transfer of technology, increasing competitiveness, increasing economies of scale and expanding productive capacity, and creating new exports. This is in addition to generating employment, taxation, and foreign exchange. Throughout its history, the Caribbean has received FDI from a variety of countries in all sectors of the economy. As private-sector led, market-driven economies, FDI has had an established and important role in investment.

Foreign direct investment can make a significant contribution to the growth targets of developing economies through increased productive capacity, raised exports and foreign exchange, higher taxes, and employment. It can also create positive spillover where it generates learning and feeds best practice with regards to management techniques, business innovation, and integration into global value chains.[36] The extent to which spillover occurs, depends on the development of backward and forward linkages[37] and the domestic factor of productivity, in particular human capital.[38] FDI can alleviate investment, foreign exchange and trade constraints,[39] and can, therefore, be mobilized in an effort to raise the level of gross investment above that financed from national savings. FDI has costs and benefits for the host country,[40] especially when that country is a developing economy.

The generally accepted conclusion from this debate is that FDI can make a positive economic contribution under the appropriate conditions. The small developing countries like Jamaica, while welcoming FDI, remain wary of its implications, particularly where multinationals and large corporations enter the domestic market with revenues above national GDP levels. Upmost among concerns is the impact on market share, where overseas actors secure significant ownership and control of specific sectors and attendant assets such as land. Equally, overseas ownership can feed narratives of asset-stripping where profits are removed from the national economy, harming longer-term development aims. The appropriate conditions vary from country to country and will depend on the local laws, regulations, guidelines, institutions, and policy framework within which FDI is expected to operate. The issue for the host country is to ensure that the benefits of FDI are maximized and exceed any costs.[41]

The United States has always encouraged FDI even after Cuba expropriated US property. From the end of World War II until the end of the twentieth century, the United States was the most important source of FDI especially after British firms like Barclays in banking and Tate and Lyle in sugar production started to withdraw. Canadian investment in the banking sector has been long-standing. In the last 20 years as the tourist industry expanded, diversity of investors have entered the region from Mexico, Spain, and China.

The relationship has been relatively free of investment disputes with the exception of the nationalization of a bauxite mining operation in Guyana and negotiations between US mining multinational corporations and the government of Jamaica that increased tax rates on bauxite and alumina exports but at no stage involved the treat of expropriations.[42] Jamaica's economic policy has always been based on receptivity to and encouragement of FDI.[43]

Peace and Democracy

The belief that the best guarantee of democracy is prosperity is a tenet of US foreign policy. Emblematic of this is a recent statement from the Centre for Strategic and International Studies: "Reducing corruption and improving governance in developing countries opens up markets for U.S. products and levels the playing field for U.S. companies operating abroad. Economic growth in developing countries reduces unemployment, increases stability, and supports U.S. national security interests in the process."[44] The problem has been that the United States no longer see the need for the economic foundation for democracy as involving foreign aid which can bolster economic growth as well as strengthen governance and human rights.[45] The result is to be satisfied that holding elections are synonymous with democracy[46] and hence as a former State Department official explains, there are only "recurring bouts of interest in the promotion of democracy."[47]

National Security

Both the United States and the Caribbean agree that economic development is an important bulwark for national security. This is more strongly felt in the Caribbean than in the United States where aid related to security is seen as more immediate and likely to produce tangible results. The Bridgetown Accord of 1997 states explicitly that in the Caribbean there are "inextricable links between trade, economic development, security and prosperity in societies." Economic slowdown which set in after the dismantling of the EU banana regime made the banana export countries more vulnerable to drug trafficking and the crime and violence associated with it. These countries were less viable as trade partners not that these were a major factor for the United States. The impact of the decline in the banana industry was compounded by the effect of the terrorist attack of

9–11 on tourism and then the 2008 global financial crisis. One of the manifestations of this was the debt crisis of these countries dealt with in Chapter 7. Public sector weakens the capacity of the state to deliver social services and poverty relief and that, in turn, can weaken democracy.[48]

Trade Policy

An integral aspect of US economic policy towards the Caribbean has been its trade policy, which has traditionally been based on preferential arrangements in recognition of the need for such an approach to small developing countries.

Sugar

Starting in 1982, the US government has operated a scheme of preferential pricing for imports of sugar from 40 countries including some in the Caribbean. The scheme allocated quotas to countries for the export of sugar up to the amount of their designated quota. The prices paid were based on those paid to domestic producers which were much higher than prevailing world market prices.[49] Quotas were assigned to countries based on their export volume during 1975–1981 but were subsequently adjusted. As an indication of sensitivity to small producers, the US Department of Agriculture's website records: "Declines in the overall quantity of the quota have reduced imports from all suppliers with the exception of the 10 small suppliers whose allocations are limited to 7,258 metric tonnes, raw value (MTRV), a quantity considered to be equal to a minimum boatload of sugar."[50]

Generalized System of Preferences (GSP)

Apart from the trade preferences for Caribbean countries, the United States implicitly recognized the need for such measures for developing countries. Established by the Trade Act of 1974, the United States operated the generalized system of preferences (GSP) for selected "poor" countries. For a designated set of products, lower tariffs were applied than for imports from all other WTO member countries. Some 119 designated beneficiary countries benefited from the GSP which expired on December 31, 2017. The rationale for the GSP as explained by USTR is that the GSP is to "provide opportunities for many of the world's poorest countries to use trade to grow their economies and climb out of poverty." Moreover, it was seen to be in the national interest because moving "GSP imports from the docks to US consumers, farmers, and manufacturers support tens of thousands of jobs in the United States. GSP also boosts American competitiveness by reducing costs of imported inputs used by US companies" … "In addition to promoting economic opportunity in developing countries, the GSP program also supports progress by beneficiary countries in affording worker rights to their people, in enforcing intellectual property rights, and in supporting the rule of law."[51]

Caribbean Basin Initiative (CBI)

The CBI[52] was announced in 1983 and its trade component was given effect by the Caribbean Basin Economic Recovery Act. Implemented on January 1, 1984, the CBERA has no expiration date. The benefits were expanded in 2000 by the US-Caribbean Basin Trade Partnership Act (CBTPA) of 2000 and subsequently by the Trade Act of 2002. The CBTPA is scheduled to expire on September 30, 2020.

The USTR explains the purpose of the CBI as: "The trade programs known collectively as the Caribbean Basin Initiative (CBI) remain important elements of U.S. economic relations with our neighbors in the Caribbean. The CBI is intended to facilitate the development of stable Caribbean Basin economies by providing beneficiary countries with duty-free access to the U.S. market for most goods."[53]

Dominican Republic-Central America Free Trade Agreement

Further confirmation of the US approach to trade policy towards the Caribbean was one based on special and differential treatment. The United States, recognizing their small size, encouraged the Central American countries and the Dominican Republic to negotiate the Dominican Republic-Central American Free Trade Agreement.[54] This agreement involving the United States, Costa Rica, El Salvador, Guatemala, Honduras, Nicaragua, and the Dominican Republic is based on reciprocity and these countries are no longer eligible for the CBERA. The agreement was signed by President George W. Bush effective August 2005 and ratified by all members by January 2009. The US-Caribbean trade remained under the CBERA and subsequent legislation. Panama and the United States signed the Panama–US Trade Promotion Agreement in October 2012.

Social

Although the United States of America is populated by migrants, the prospect of a steady flow of migrants that are not Caucasian arouses very strong anxiety and hostility. Like other regions, but to a lesser extent than Mexico, the Caribbean region is seen as a source of migrants. While the largest source countries are Cuba, Haiti, and the Dominican Republic, there is concern about even the smallest islands. David Simcox, executive director of the Center for Immigration Studies in Washington DC, opines: "Tiny states like St. Kitts and Nevis, Grenada, and Belize are sending 1 to 2 percent of their citizens to the United States every year, meaning they are basically exporting all of their population growth to us."[55] The apprehensiveness was heightened although the numbers were small because of the reputation of Jamaicans in the drug trade in the United States. The Jamaican "posses"[56] achieve considerable notoriety in the media and from US law enforcement agencies.

Another concern of the United States is that the region with its hundreds of islands does not become a major conduit for human trafficking. Apart from the prospect of large numbers of Haitians and Cubans traversing the Bahamas, the United States is concerned that non-Caribbean people, in particular Chinese, are using the Caribbean. Even if the numbers are not large, the flow could overwhelm the limited capacity of governments in the region. Reviewing the situation in 2018, US authorities conclude that although the governments of the Caribbean were making efforts to control human trafficking, it was not adequate.[57] As the 2005 International Organization for Migration report warns: "The potential for its growth makes a proactive approach in addressing the issue of trafficking in persons important for the Caribbean region."[58]

National Security

National security is a multidimensional concept encompassing military, political, and economic aspects. In military terms, the United States in the 1990s would still feel that it was necessary to launch a military and naval invasion on the tiny state of Grenada to prevent what Washington regarded as the drift of the Maurice Bishop government towards communism aided and abetted by Cuba. The pretext was to protect the lives of American students at the privately-owned American St. Georges Medical University. Apart from the abiding apprehension about leftist regimes and the influence of communist governments, there was by the mid-1990s, the concern over crime-related drug trafficking. The anxiety over terrorism came much later especially after the events of September 11, 2001. National security also has an economic component of protecting US property and ensuring the safe passage of trade through the sea lanes of the Caribbean. The Caribbean would have had some interest for the United States because of natural gas based industries in Trinidad, and bauxite deposits in Jamaica and Guyana. Of more vital concern would be oil from Venezuela, trade to South America, and the volume of shipping passing through the Panama Canal. The United States has a general interest in the economic well-being of the countries of the region as drug trafficking can distort the economic system especially where domestic security capability is weakened by economic factors such as public sector debt.[59] Politically, the region was to be kept safe from communism and to maintain governments supportive or at least friendly towards the United States and its foreign policy objectives.

The overriding concern in the security arena is the impact of drug trafficking on propagating transnational crime, gun smuggling, and violent organized crime.[60] While it is not possible to plot direct causality, the reduced employment and foreign exchange in a section of the farming community with virtually no viable alternative would make the resident more susceptible to involvement in crime. The pronouncements of politicians, the police, policymakers, politicians, and the farmers themselves are too numerous to be dismissed as purely anecdotal. One indication of the adverse effect is the increase in marijuana production and cocaine transshipment judged by seizures and by the number of arrests in Jamaica where the impact would have been less than in the smaller islands of the Eastern Caribbean. Between 1990 and 1999, seizures of cannabis increase from 29.0 metric tonnes to 56.2, seizures of cocaine increased from 0.76 to 2.46 tonnes, and arrests increased from 5,432 to 6,718.[61] US Narcotics Control Report 2019 describes Jamaica as the largest Caribbean source country of marijuana and a significant transit point for cocaine trafficked from South America to North America and other international markets.[62]

In St. Vincent, marijuana production increased to $40 million in the year 2000 more than earnings from bananas[63] cultivated by young men displaced from banana farming.[64] St. Vincent exported the product to the United States, Canada, the United Kingdom, and Europe. Dominica has been a producer of marijuana; its hilly terrain makes interdiction difficult and by 2010 the country was involved in the transshipment of cocaine from Latin America.[65] There is drug trafficking and arms dealing in St. Lucia involving Colombians and Venezuela. The United States has continued to complain about inadequate efforts to control human trafficking.[66]

In the years after the contraction of banana, drug trafficking increased, and this was accompanied by crime-related violence involving guns smuggled from the United States. The murder rate per 100,000 of the population has risen steadily over the last 20 years. By 2017, the rate was 34 in St. Lucia, 40 in Belize, and 56 in Jamaica–all former banana exporting countries.[67] Most of these murders are by guns illegally imported from the United States[68]or neighboring countries often as a part of drug trafficking. In 2014, guns seized and traced to the United States accounted for 46 percent in Trinidad and Tobago, St. Kitts, 57 percent, and in Jamaica 83 percent.[69] The Centre for American Progress reports that during 2014 to 2016, across 15 countries in North America, Central America, and the Caribbean, 50,133 guns that originated in the United States were recovered as part of criminal investigations. Put another way, during this span, US-sourced guns were used to commit crimes in nearby countries approximately once every 31 minutes.[70] The battle to stem the flow of illicit guns has been a major area of concern for the Caribbean where the murder rate and other violent crimes have reached astonishing levels. The traffic in illegal weapons emanating mainly from the United States has played a significant role in increased violence and criminal activity in the region. The Caribbean states including Jamaica have joined the United States in signing the Inter-American Convention against the Illicit Manufacturing of and Trafficking in Firearms, Ammunition, Explosives and Other Related Materials and are committed to efforts to stem the flow of guns to the region. The Caribbean has repeatedly asked the United States to do more to prevent illicit arms flowing into the region.

The small states of the Caribbean in recent years have been threatened by transnational crime, related primarily to narcotics trafficking and have benefited from US cooperation in the form of assistance under the Caribbean Basin Security Initiative (CBSI). Priorities the CBSI seeks to address include: (1) maritime and aerial security cooperation, (2) law enforcement capacity enhancement, (3) border/port security, (4) firearms interdiction, (5) justice sector, and (6) citizen security and at-risk youth.[71] This is praiseworthy but the lynchpin of foreign policy of the Caribbean countries is economic for both development and security.

To the Detriment of US National Interests

The acute vulnerability of the small states of the ESC has made them very sensitive to policy changes in the United States. Prime Minister L. Erskine Sandiford of Barbados explains, "we are aware of the fragility and vulnerability of our microstates. Our vulnerability is manifold. Physically, we are subject to hurricanes and earthquakes; economically, to market decisions taken elsewhere; and now politically to the machinations of terrorists, mercenaries, and criminals."[72] In an economic sense, dependency was at an extreme in the small banana exporting countries, for example, in Dominica, nearly all the economic activity is related to the export of a single primary product, bananas, to a single external market through a single multinational corporation. A situation aptly described by Prime Minister Kenny Anthony of St. Lucia as "the dependency of monocultural imperialism".[73]

The overall impact on US national interests in the Caribbean of the dismantling of the EU banana regime was adverse, see Table 8.1. The preceding comparative analysis of the US national interest during the operation of the EU preferential banana regime and after it was dismantled at the behest of Chiquita, revealed that the ESC was more economically vulnerable with an escalation in debt and a concomitant need for financial aid. This was accompanied by an escalation in crime, violence, and narcotics trafficking, which in turn impelled governments in the region to explore relations with China, Venezuela and a raft of non-traditional partners in a quest for economic assistance.

The United States is the main economic partner of the countries in the Caribbean. These small developing countries are long-standing friends and consistent allies. In spite of transnational crime and narcotics transiting the air and sea space, they have maintained an enviable record of democracy. Their economic growth and sustainability is strongly influenced by the state of the US economy and the impact of US policies both domestic and foreign. The removal of the EU banana regime had a deleterious impact which is still affecting the former banana exporting islands. The US Department of State in its March 2017 International Narcotics Control Strategy Report names 14 of the 15 CARICOM states as major money laundering countries.[74] The concerns of the region center on the distinct possibility that it will cause increasing unwillingness of international banks to conduct correspondent banking services for countries in the region (Table 8.1).

Table 8.1 Status of US National interests during and after the EU banana regime

Type of interest	*National interest*	*During the EU banana regime*	*After the EU banana regime*
Political	Peace	Moderate crime	Increased crime and violence
	Democracy	Functioning	Functioning with stress
Diplomatic	Harmony with allies	Cooperation	Disaffection by EU and ESC
Economic	Exports	Largest supplier to region	Still largest supplier to region
	Imports	Not significant	Not significant
	Investment	Not significant	Not significant
	Aid	Declining	Increased demand
Social	Migrants	Not significant members	More unployment but limited numbers
Security	Narcotics	Cooperation	Increased trafficking and need for US help
	Terrorism	Not a source country	Made more vulnerable to external elements

The dismantling of the EU banana regime at the behest of Chiquita was detrimental to the Caribbean and, in turn, was harmful to US national interests in the Caribbean. The major impact was the economic damage in a small undiversified developing country almost entirely dependent on the banana industry. The economic fallout made these countries more vulnerable to drug trafficking, transnational crime, and corruption. These combined to undermine democracy. However, it should be noted that the implosion of the banana industry was not the only factor which caused economic difficulties in the region, but it was compounded by other events such as 9/11 and the global financial crisis of 2008. It was felt by the Caribbean governments that the United States did little to assist the region during its escalating economic problems starting with not providing financial aid to help the countries adjust to the collapse of the banana industry. US economic aid continued to be reduced in successive years although nearly all the countries in the region struggled to recover from high oil prices, a stifling debt crisis, hurricane damage, and rising crime.

Notwithstanding these difficulties, democracy continued as evidenced by fair elections and the United States remained the main trade partner of the region and millions of Americans were tourists in all parts of the region. In political terms, the United States did not suffer from any diminution in democracy in the region and there has been no attempt at regime change since Grenada in 1983. On the economic front, trade may have grown more robustly but was not large enough to be a vitally important market. The region has remained open to US foreign direct investment although flows have not been significant except for the energy sector. US national interests were seriously damaged in the fields of national security and diplomatic relations.

The Caribbean region produces drugs (i.e., marijuana), most of which is destined for the United States and a major conduit for cocaine from Colombia also headed for the United States. Associated with the escalation of the transnational narcotics trade is increased crime including very high murder rates employing firearms made in the United States and money laundering. While these developments cannot be attributed entirely to the collapse of the banana industry, it served to create a socio-economic environment fertile for the expansion of drug trafficking and once it gained an expanded foothold in some parts of the region it spread like a cancer throughout the region.

In diplomatic relations, the United States has suffered possibly irreversible impairment as the region has increasingly felt neglected in its need for economic aid and taken for granted in the assumption that it will comply with what it regards as US dictates. The region is not hostile to the United States but feels no compunction to comply with US policy. There is goodwill but the harsh realities of economic survival have led to a diversification of international relations for oil from Venezuela, infrastructure financing from China, and health care from Cuba. These are not going to change easily and the United States has now resorted to publicly expressed threats of cutting off aid, revocation of visas, and other sanctions to secure Caribbean cooperation much easier won by economic aid and debt relief.

Given what has been presented in this book, it is an entirely reasonable inference that the US dismantling of the EU banana regime set in motion effects which have been harmful to US national interests in the Caribbean. The damage is evident in the fact that in Congress it has been recognized that the situation requires a major initiative to repair the damage. The US-Caribbean Strategic Engagement Act (H.R. 4939) was passed in December 2016. Representative Eliot Engel (D-NY) explains: "With constant crises around the globe that demand U.S. attention, we must not lose sight of our long-term interests close to home. At a time when our friends in the Caribbean need us more than ever, this bill will prioritize our partnership with the sub-region for many years to come. It is long past time to have a multi-year strategy that will allow us to increase engagement with the Caribbean."[75]

The Phyrric Victory of Chiquita

During the process in which Chiquita, successor to United Fruit Company was able to influence the US government to dismantle the EU banana regime, it was controlled by majority owner American businessman, Carl Lindner. The dismantling of the EU banana regime allowed the company to attempt to capture the part of the EU market formerly supplied in part by the small countries of the Caribbean. This opportunity did not prevent Chiquita from entering Chapter 11. Lindner and his family own about 37 percent of Chiquita through Lindner's American Financial Group.[76]

In January 2001, Chiquita warned of pending its bankruptcy claiming that European quotas limiting bananas from Latin America, which is where Chiquita sourced its bananas, had cost the company $200 million a year since 1992.[77] In November 2001, Chiquita filed a prearranged bankruptcy plan. The Chapter 11 of the US Bankruptcy Code filing in US Bankruptcy Court for the Southern District of Ohio allowed the company to restructure roughly $900 million in debt and reduced accrued interest by $700 million thereby brought annual interest payments to approximately $60 million. At the time of taking this action, the company was counting on getting a boost from the dismantling of the EU banana regime. President and Chief Executive Officer of Chiquita, Steven Warshaw said that the WTO ruling "had brightened business prospects".[78]

Lindner's majority ownership of the company ended when Chiquita Brands International completed Chapter 11 bankruptcy proceedings on March 19, 2002. On October 24, 2014, the shareholders of Chiquita accepted the $611 million offer of acquisition by Brazilian companies Cutrale and Safra Group. The decision followed after months of negotiations of a proposed merger with Fyffes, the Irish banana company.[79]

The claim by Chiquita Brands International that not having the small share of the EU market reserved for the African and Caribbean producers, which amounted to 7–8 percent of the European Union, the equivalent of 3 percent of the world market was credible. This was borne out by its subsequent bankruptcy. Further proof of the spurious nature of its claim is that the other American banana companies Dole and Del Monte, which are smaller than Chiquita, did not experience any financial difficulties and it should be recalled that they were not complainants about the EU banana regime. The answer must be found in the differences in corporate strategies and the competence of management. An article in Fortune magazine points out that it "is a chronicle not simply of unfair quotas and bad luck, but of poor management--of an executive corps that placed risky bets, made poor decisions, and alienated customers and supporters on Wall Street. The company's dispute with Europe did not cause these problems."[80] The company dominated the global banana trade and at one time owned more than 1.7 million acres of land and employed more than 60,000 workers, in Colombia, Costa Rica, Ecuador, Guatemala, Honduras, and Panama that collectively produce 60 percent of world banana exports. The company also operated the world's largest private shipping fleet and 1100 miles of railroads.[81] Chiquita was a globally recognized brand name for one of the world's most popular fruits.

Notes

1. Scott Burchill, The National Interest in International Relations Theory (New York: Palgrave Macmillan, 2005).
2. Report to Congress on Progress of Public Law (PL) 114–291: Efforts to Implement the Strategy for U.S. engagement in the Caribbean Region (Washington DC: U.S. Department of State, 2019) page 1.
3. The U.S. distinguishes two types of allies, regional allies who support the U.S. in their region and allies that support the U.S. in their region as well as in international affairs. See at Our Own Peril: DoD Risk Assessment in a Post-Primary (Washington DC: Strategic Studies Institute and U.S. Army War College Press, 2017) page 100.
4. Mark P. Sullivan, Caribbean Issues in U.S. Relations (Washington DC: Congressional Research Service, 25 May, 2005).
5. Brook Larmer, "The Banana Wars", Newsweek Magazine, April 28, 1997, page 12.
6. Jerome Levinson, and Juan De Onis, The Alliance that Lost Its Way. A critical report on the Alliance for Progress (Chicago: Quadrangle Books, 1970) page 7.
7. "US threatens to end aid to Caribbean", Jamaica Observer, December 21, 2017.
8. Robert F. Kennedy, Thirteen Days: A Memoir of the Cuban Missile Crisis (New York: W. W. Norton & Company, 2011).

9. Richard l. Bernal, The Influence of Small States on Superpower. Jamaica and U.S. Foreign Policy (Lanham: Lexington Publishers, 2015).
10. Ronald Reagan, The Reagan Diaries Edited by David Brinkley (New York: Harper Perennial, 2007) page 1.
11. Richard Feinberg, Tourism in Cuba. Riding the Wave Toward Sustainable Prosperity (Washington DC: Brookings Institution, December, 2016).
12. Sebastian Acevedo, Trevor Alleyne, and Rafael Romeu, Revisiting the Potential Impact to the Rest of the Caribbean from Opening US-Cuba Tourism, IMF Working Paper WP/17/100 (Washington Dc: International Monetary Fund, March, 2017) page 2.
13. Rafael Romeu, "Vacation Over: Implications for the Caribbean of Opening U.S.-Cuba Tourism," IMF Working Paper WP/08/162, (Washington, DC: International Monetary Fund, July, 2008), Rafael Romeu, "The Vacation Is Over: Implications for the Caribbean of Opening U.S. Cuba Tourism," Economía, Vol. 14, No.2) pages 1–24 and Sebastian Acevedo Mejia, Lu Han, Marie S Kim and Nicole Laframboise "Flying to Paradise: The Role of Airlift in the Caribbean Tourism Industry," IMF Working Paper WP/16/33, (Washington, DC: International Monetary Fund, 2016).
14. Ginger Thompson, "Imposing Conditions, O.A.S. Lifts Its Suspension of Cuba", The New York Times, June 3, 2009.
15. Henry Gill, "Conflict in Trinidad and Tobago relations with Venezuela" in Leslie F. Manigat (ed.), The Caribbean Yearbook of International Relations 1975 (St. Augustine: Institute for International relations, 1976) pages 466–485.
16. Eric Williams, "The Threat to the Caribbean Community" in Leslie F. Manigat (ed.), The Caribbean Yearbook of International Relations 1975 (St. Augustine: Institute for International relations, 1976) pages 600–601.
17. The author was in attendance at some of these meetings.
18. Partnering for Development—Petro Caribe Development Fund .... www.petrocaribejm.org/, Accessed 11 July 2017.
19. Enticed by US Carrots, Some Caribbean Countries Break with Venezuela's Maduro, https://www.worldpoliticsreview.com/.../enticed-by-u-s-carrots-some-caribbean-countr, March 26, 2019.
20. Kenya Evelyn, "Caribbean leaders boycott Pompeo talks as row grows over US relations", The Guardian, 21 January 2020.
21. Renuka Singh, "US probes T&T fuel shipment linked to Venezuela", Trinidad & Tobago Guardian, Sunday, May 10, 2020, page 1.
22. Linda Hutchinson-Jafar and Luc Cohen, "Trinidad cancels gas deal over U.S. sanctions on state-run Venezuelan company". www.reuters.com/article/us-trinidadtobago-venezuela, February 3, 2020.

23. Richard L. Bernal, Dragon in the Caribbean: The Global Re-Dimensioning of China. Opportunities and Challenges for the Caribbean (Kingston: Ian Randle Publishers, revised, updated and expanded second edition, October, 2016) and Richard Bernal, "U.S. shouldn't ignore China's influence in the Caribbean", Miami Herald, August 16, 2018.
24. "Antigua PM Says US Should Invest in Developing Countries and Not Focus on China's Influence", The Gleaner, October 22, 2018.
25. Edward Wong, "Mike Pompeo Warns Panama Against Doing Business with China", New York Times, October 19, 2018.
26. Richard L. Bernal, "Central America and the Caribbean: Relations with China and the United States: Contrasting Experiences! Converging Prospects?" in David Denoon (eds.), China, the U.S. and the Future of Latin America (New York: New York University Press, September, 2017) pages 232–267.
27. Richard L. Bernal, "China and Small Island Developing States", Africa-East Asian Affairs, The China Monitor, Issue 1 (August, 2012) pages 3–30.
28. Richard l. Bernal, "The Growing Economic Presence of China in the Caribbean", The World Economy, Vol. 38, Issue 9 (September, 2015) pages 1409–1437, "China's Rising Investment Profile in the Caribbean", Economics Brief, Inter-American Dialogue, October, 2013 and "Dragon in the Caribbean: China-CARICOM Economic Relations", Round Table, Vol. 99, Issue. 408 (June, 2010) pages 281–302.
29. Richard L. Bernal, Chinese Foreign Direct Investment in the Caribbean. Potential and Prospects, Inter-American Development Bank, Technical Notes IDB-TN-1113, November, 2016.
30. Bruce Golding, "Exploring the opportunities in deepening economic relations with China", Sunday Observer, October 14, 2018, page 29.
31. Dominica: Prime Minister defends relationship with China, https://www.stlucianewsonline.com/dominica-prime-minister-defends-relationship-with-china/, October 30, 2018.
32. Norman Girvan, Foreign Capital and Economic Underdevelopment in Jamaica (Kingston: Institute of Social and Economic Research, University of the West Indies, 1971) page 29.
33. Eric Williams, From Columbus to Castro. A Caribbean History 1492–1968 (London: Andre Deutsch, 1970) page 201.
34. Norman Girvan, Foreign Capital and Economic Development in Jamaica (Mona: Institute of Social and Economic Research, University of the West Indies, 1971).
35. Stephen D. Krasner, Defending the National Interest. Raw Materials. Investments and US Foreign Policy (Princeton: Princeton University Press, 1978).

36. Thomas Farole and Debra Winkler (eds.), Making Foreign Direct Investment Work for Sub-Saharan Africa. Local Spillovers and Competiveness in Global Value Chains (Washington DC: World Bank, 2014).
37. Albert O. Hirschman, The Strategy of Economic Development (New Haven: Yale University Press, 1958).
38. E. Borensztein, J. W. Lee and J. DeGregorio, How Does Foreign Investment Affect Growth, Working Paper No. 5057, National Bureau of Economic Research, (1995).
39. Hollis Chenery and Alan Strout, "Foreign assistance and Economic Development", American Economic Review, Vol. 56, No. 4 (1966) pages 679–733.
40. Richard L. Bernal, "Foreign Investment and Development in Jamaica", Inter American Economic Affairs, Vol. 38, No. 2 (Autumn, 1984) pages 3–21.
41. Foreign Direct Investment for Development. Maximizing Benefits, Minimizing Costs (Paris: Organization for Economic Co-operation and Development, 2002).
42. Richard L. Bernal, The Influence of Small States on Superpowers: Jamaica and U.S. Foreign Policy (Lanham: Lexington Publishers, 2015) pages 91–92. For more on the negotiations see Patrick H.O. Rousseau, Negotiating Change. Pat Rousseau and the Bauxite Negotiations 1974–1977 (Kingston: Heinemann Educational Books (Caribbean) Ltd., 1987).
43. Lloyd G. Waller, Densil A. Williams, Omar E. Hawthorne, and Donavon Johnson, Doing Business in Jamaica. A Qualitative Perspective Discussions of FDI in the Jamaica (Kingston: Ian Randle Publishers, 2018) pages 10–24, Densil Williams and D. Deslandes, "Motivation for service sector foreign direct investments in emerging economies: insights from the tourism industry in Jamaica"' The Round Table, Vol. 97, No. 396 (2008) pages 419–437. Lou Anne A. Barclay, Foreign Direct Investment in Emerging Economies. Corporate Strategy and investment behavior in the Caribbean (London: Routledge, 2000) pages 96–123, Richard L. Bernal, "Foreign Investment and Development in Jamaica", Inter-American Economic Affairs, Vol. 38, No. 2 (Autumn, 1984) pages 3–21 and Norman Girvan, Foreign Capital and Economic Underdevelopment in Jamaica (Mona, Jamaica: Institute of Social and Economic Research, University of the West Indies, 1971).
44. Daniel F. Runde and Christopher Metzger, Fighting Corruption for the U.S. Economic and National Security Interests, April, 2020, page 12.

45. Joan M. Nelson and Stephanie J. Eglington, Encouraging Democracy: What Role for Conditioned Aid? (Washington DC: Overseas Development Council, Policy Essay No. 4, 1992.
46. Jeanne J. Kirkpatrick, "Democratic Elections, Democratic Governments, and Democratic Theory" in David Butler, Howard R. Penniman and Austin Ranney (eds.), Democracy at the Polls (Washington DC: American Enterprise Institute, 1981) page 326.
47. Thomas Carothers, In the Name of Democracy. U.S. Policy in Latin America in the Reagan Years (Berkeley: University of California Press, 1991) page 1.
48. Richard Bernal, "Drugs, Debt and Democracy in the Caribbean: Implications for U.S. Foreign Policy," Trans Africa, Vol. 9, No. 2 Summer, 1992) pages 83–92.
49. Donald Mitchell, Sugar in the Caribbean: Adjusting to Eroding Preferences, Policy Research Working Paper 3802, (Washington DC: World Bank, December 2005) page 5.
50. www.fas.usda.gov/programs/sugar-import-program, Sugar Import Program | USDA Foreign Agricultural Service, Accessed 6 February 2020.
51. Generalized System of Preferences (GSP) | United States ustr.gov/issue-areas/trade-development/preference-programs/g, Accessed 14 February 2020.
52. Richard L. Bernal, The Influence of Small States on Superpowers: Jamaica and U.S. Foreign Policy (Lanham: Lexington Publishers, 2015).
53. ustr.gov/trade-development/preference-programs, Caribbean Basin Initiative (CBI) | United States Trade, Accessed 18 April, 2020.
54. Ustrustr.gov/trade-agreements/free-trade-agreements/c, CAFTA-DR (Dominican Republic-Central America FTA)—Ustr, Accessed 18 April, 2020.
55. Howard French, "Caribbean Exodus: U.S. Is Constant Magnet", New York Times, May 6, 1992.
56. Laurie Gunst, Born Fi' Dead. A Journey Through The Jamaican Posse Underworld (New York: Holt Paperbacks, 1996).
57. "US gives Caribbean failing grade for human trafficking", Jamaica Observer, June 22, 2019.
58. Exploratory Assessment of Trafficking in Persons in the Caribbean Region: The Bahamas, Barbados, Guyana, Jamaica, The Netherlands Antilles, St. Lucia, Suriname (Geneva: International Organization for Migration, 2005) page 2.
59. Richard L. Bernal, "Drugs, Debt and Democracy in the Caribbean: Implications for U.S. Foreign Policy," Trans-Africa, Vol. 9, No. 2 Summer, 1992) pages 83–92.

60. Ivelaw Lloyd Griffith, Drugs and Security in the Caribbean. Sovereignty Under Siege (University Park: Pennsylvania State university Press, 1997).
61. International Narcotics Control Strategy Reports (Washington DC: United States Department of State, 1991–2000).
62. US Department of State 2019 International Narcotics Control Strategy Report (Washington DC: United States Department of State, 2019).
63. Ivelaw Griffith, 2000). The Political Economy of Drugs in the Caribbean (New York: Palgrave Macmillan, 2000) page 100.
64. Cynthia Barrow-Giles and Don D. Marshall, Living at the Borderlines: Issues in Caribbean Sovereignty and Development (Kingston: Ian Randle Publishers, 2003) page 111.
65. US Department of State 2010 International Narcotics Control Strategy Report (Washington DC: United States Department of State, 2010).
66. U.S. Department of State, 2019 Trafficking in Persons Report: Saint Lucia (Washington DC: 2019).
67. Murder rates up in English-speaking Caribbean, The Economist Intelligence Unit, January 8, 2018.
68. Jonathan Blitzer, "The Link Between America's Lax Gun Laws and the Violence That Fuels Immigration", The New Yorker, March 22, 2018 and U.S. guns fuel Jamaica's gang wars—World news—Americas, www.nbc-news.com/world_news-americas/us-guns-f, Accessed 22 April 2020.
69. Calendar Year 2014. Department of Justice, Bureau of Alcohol, Tobacco, Firearms and Explosives, Office of Strategic Intelligence and Information (Washington DC: Department of Justice, As of March 10, 2015).
70. Chelsea Parsons and Eugenio Weigend Vargas, Beyond Our Borders—How Weak U.S. Gun Laws Contribute to Violent Crime Abroad, Center for American Progress, February 2, 2018.
71. Richard L. Bernal, "A Caribbean Policy for the Trump Administration", Center for Strategic and International Studies Policy Brief, April 13, 2017.
72. Kenneth O. Hall (ed.), Integrate or Perish. Perspectives of Leaders of the Integration Movement 1963–1999 (Mona: University of the West Indies Press, 2000) page 220.
73. Didacus Jules and Tennyson S. D. Joseph (eds.), At the Rainbow's Edge. Selected Speeches of Kenny D. Anthony 1996–2002 (Kingston: Ian Randle Publishers, 2004) page157.
74. U.S. Department of State in its March 2017 International Narcotics Control Strategy Report.
75. Richard L. Bernal, "A Caribbean Policy for the Trump Administration", Center for Strategic and International Studies Policy Brief, April 13, 2017.
76. Chiquita Brands to Reorganize Under Bankruptcy Protection—WSJ, https://www.wsj.com/articles/SB1006903294995339000, November 28, 2001.

77. Anthony Depalma, "Citing European Banana Quotas, Chiquita Says Bankruptcy Looms", New York Times, January 17, 2001.
78. Chiquita Brands files for bankruptcy, UPI, https://www.upi.com/Business_News/.../Chiquita...bankruptcy/34891006965690/, November 28, 2001.
79. Chiquita proves to be a slippery takeover target | Fortune, October 24, 2014.
80. Nicholas Stein, "Yes, We Have No Profits The rise and fall of Chiquita Banana: How a great American brand lost its way", Fortune Magazine, November 26, 2001.
81. Nicholas Stein, "Yes, We Have No Profits The rise and fall of Chiquita Banana: How a great American brand lost its way", Fortune Magazine, November 26, 2001.

Bibliography

Books

Acemoglu, Daron, and James A. Robinson. 2012. *Why Nations Fail. The Origins of Power, Prosperity and Poverty*. New York: Crown Business.

Acker, Alison. 1989. *Honduras: The Making of a Banana Republic*. Boston: South End Press.

Adrian, Fraser. 2016. *The 1935 Riots in St. Vincent: From Riots to Adult Suffrage*. Kingston: University of the West Indies Press.

Amin, Samir. 1973. *Accumulation on a World Scale*. New York: Monthly Review Press.

———. 1996. *Imperialism and Unequal Development*. New York: Monthly Review Press.

Arghiri, Emmanuel. 1972. *Unequal Exchange. A Study of the Imperialism of Trade*. New York: Monthly Review Press.

Ashley, Paul. 2018. *Dudus. The Extradition of Jamaica's #1 Drug Don*. Kingston: Paul Ashley.

Baldwin, Robert E. 1988. *Trade Policy in a Changing World*. Chicago: University of Chicago Press.

Baumgartner, Frank R., Jeffrey M. Berry, Marie Hojnacki, Beth L. Leech, and David C. Kimball. 2009. *Lobbying and Policy Change: Who Wins, Who Loses, and Why*. Chicago: University of Chicago Press.

Beckford, George L. 1972. *Persistent Poverty. Underdevelopment in Plantation Economies of the Third World*. New York: Oxford University Press.

Beckles, Hilary M. 2013. *Britain's Black Debt: Reparations for Caribbean Slavery and Native Genocide*. Kingston: University of the West Indies Press.

R. L. Bernal, *Corporate versus National Interest in US Trade Policy*, https://doi.org/10.1007/978-3-030-56950-1

Bentley, Arthur. 1967. *The Process of Government.* Cambridge: Belnap Press of Harvard University.

Berle, Adolpe A., and Gardiner C. Means. 1932. *The Modern Corporation and Private Property.* New York: Harcourt, Brace and World.

Bernal, Richard L. 2015. *The Influence of Small States on Superpowers: Jamaica and U.S. Foreign Policy.* Lanham: Lexington Publishers.

Berry, Jeffrey M., and Clyde Wilcox. 2008. *The Interest Group Society.* 5th ed. New York: Routledge.

Bertrab, Von Herman. 1997. *Negotiating NAFTA. A Mexican Envoy's Account.* Westport: Praeger.

Bertram, Arnold, and Norman W. Manley. 2016. *The Making of Modern Jamaica.* Kingston: Arawak Publishers.

Bhagwati, Jagdish N., and Arvind Panagariya. 1996. *The Economics of Preferential Trade Agreements.* Washington, DC: American Enterprise Institute.

Birnbaum, Jeffrey. 1992. *The Lobbyists: How Influence Peddlers Work Their Way in Washington.* New York: Three Rivers Press.

Bolland, O. Nigel. 1995. *On the March: Labour Rebellions in the British Caribbean 1934–39.* Kingston: Ian Randle Publishers.

Borensztein, Eduardo. 2006. *Living with Debt. How to Limit the Risks of Sovereign Finance.* Washington, DC: Inter-American Development Bank.

Campbell, Charles S., Jr. 1951. *Social Business Interests and the Open Door Policy.* New Haven: Connecticut College and University Press.

Cardosa, Bernando Henrique, and Enzo Faletto. 1979. *Dependence and Development in Latin America.* Berkley: University of California.

Chapman, Peter. 2009. *Bananas: How the United Fruit Company Shaped the World.* Canongate.

Choate, Pat. 1990. *Agents of Influence. How Japan's Lobbyists in the United States Manipulate America's Political and Economic System.* New York: Alfred Knopf.

Chomsky, Aviva. 1996. *West Indian Workers and the United Fruity Company in Costa Rica 1870–1940.* Louisiana State University Press.

Chomsky, Noam. 2016. *Who Rules the World?* New York: Metropolitan Books.

Clarke, Peter. 2008. *The Last Thousand Days of the British Empire. Churchill, Roosevelt, and the Birth of Pax Americanna.* New York: Bloombury Press.

Clegg, Peter. 2002. *The Caribbean Banana Trade. From Colonialism to Globalization.* New York: Palgrave Macmillan.

Cockburn, Alexander, and Ken Silverstein. 1996. *Wasington Babylon.* London: Verso.

Cohen, Rick. 2013. *The Fish that Ate the Whale: The Life and Times of America's Banana King.* London: Picador.

Colby, Jason M. 2011. *The Business of Empire: United Fruit, Race, and U.S. Expansion in Central America.* Ithaca: Cornell University Press.

Coll, Steve. 2013. *Private Empire: ExxonMobil and American Power*. New York: Penguin Books.

Cullather, Nick. 2006. *Secret History: The CIA'S Classified Account of Its Operation in Guatemala 1952–1954*. 2nd ed. Stanford: Stanford University Press.

Dalrymple, William. 2019. *The Anarchy: The East India Company, Corporate Violence, and the Pillage of an Empire*. London: Bloomsbury Publishing.

Davies, Peter N. 1990. *Fyffes and the Banana: Musa Sapientum. A Centenary History 1888–1998*. London: Athlone Press.

Deardorff, Alan Verne, and Robert Mitchell Stern. 1998. *Constituent Interests and U.S. Trade Policies*. Ann Arbor: University of Michigan Press.

Destler, I.M. 1995. *American Trade Politics. 3rd*. Washington, DC: Institute for International Economics.

Dexter, Lewis Anthony, Raymond A. Bauer, and de Sola Pool Ithiel. 2007. *American Business and Public Policy: The Politics of Foreign Trade*. 2nd ed. New York: Aldine Transaction.

Domhoff, G. WIlliam. 2013a. *Mythy of Liberal Ascendancy: Corporate Dominance from the Great Depression to the Great Recession*. New York: Routledge.

———. 1990. *The Power Elite and the State: How Policy is made in America*. New York: Aldine De Gruyter.

———. 1978. *The Powers That Be: Processes of Ruling Class Domination in America*. New York: Random House.

———. 2006. *Who Rules America: Power, Politics and Social Change*. New York: McGraw-Hill.

———. 2013b. *Who Rules America? The Triumph of the Corporate Rich*. 7th ed. New York: McGraw-Hill Education.

Doran, Charles F., and Joel J. Sokolsky. 1986. *Canada and Congress: Lobbying in Washington D.C.* Halifax: Centre for Foreign Policy Studies.

Dosal, Paul J. 1995. *Doing Business with the Dictators: A Political History of United Fruit in Guatemala 1899–1944*. Rowman & Littlefield Publishers.

Dreiling, Michael C., and Derek Y. Darves. 2016. *Agents of Neoliberal Globalization. Corporate Networks, State Structures and Trade Policy*. New York: Cambridge University Press.

Drutman, Lee. 2017. *The Business of America is Lobbying: How Corporations Become Politicized and Politics Became More Corporate*. Oxford: Oxford University Press.

Eisner, Gisela. 1974. *Jamaica, 1830–1930: A Study in Economic Growth*. Westport: Greenwood Press.

Ellis, R. Evan. 2018. *Transnational Organized Crime in Latin America and the Caribbean. From Evolving Threats and Responses to Integrated, Adaptive Solutions*. New York: Lexington Books.

Emmanuel, Arghiri. 1972. *Unequal Exchange. A Study of the Imperialism of Trade*. New York: Monthly Review Press.

Fay, Peter Ward. 1998. *Opium War, 1840–1842: Barbarians in the Celestial Empire in the Early Part of the Nineteenth Century and the War*. Chapel Hill: University of North Carolina.

Ferguson, Niall. 2004. *Empire: The Rise and Demise of the British World Order and the Lessons for Global Power*. New York: Basic Books.

Fraser, Adrian. 2016. *The 1935 Riots in St. Vincent: From Riots to Adult Suffrage*. Kingston: University of the West Indies Press.

Freeman, Milton. 1962. *Capitalism and Freedom*. Chicago: University of Chicago Press.

Furtado, Celso. 1974a. *Development and Underdevelopment*. Berkeley: University of California.

———. 1974b. *Development and Underdevelopment*. Berkeley: University of California.

Gallagher, Peter. 2000. *Guide to the WTO and Developing Countries*. The Hague: Kluwer Law International.

Gardener, Lloyd C. 1964. *Economic Aspects of New Deal Diplomacy*. Boston: Beacon Press.

Gardner, Richard. 1969. *Sterling-Dollary Diplomacy: The Origins and the Prospects of Our International Economic Order*. New York: McGraw Hill Press.

Gibson, Martha Liebler. 2000. *Conflict Amid Consensus in American Trade Policy. American Governance and Public Policy*. Wasington, DC: Georgetown University Press.

Girvan, Norman. 1978. *Corporate Imperialism: Conflict and Expropriation*. New York: Monthly Review Press.

Glegg, Peter. 2002. *The Caribbean Banana Trade from Colonialism to Globalization*. New York: Palgrave.

Goffee, Leslie Gordon. 2006. *When Banana was King: A Jamaican Banana King in Jim Crow America*. Kingston: LMH Publishing Company.

Goldstein, Judith L. 1994. *Ideas, Interests and American Trade Policy*. Ithaca: Cornell University Press.

Gonsalves, Camillo M. 2019. *Climatized Stigmatised*. Kingstown: Strategy Forum Inc.

Graeber, David. 2011. *Debt. The First 5000 Years*. New York: Melville House Publishing.

Grossman, Gene M., and Elhanan Helpman. 2002. *Interest Groups and Trade Policy*. Princeton: Princeton University Press.

Grynberg, Roman. 2012. *WTO at the Margins: Small States and the Multilateral Trading System*. Cambridge: Cambridge University Press.

Hanes, Travis, and Frank Sanello. 2004. *The Opium Wars: The Addiction of One Empire and the Corruption of Another*. Sourcebooks.

Hart, Richard. 2002. *Labour Rebellions of the 1930s in the British Caribbean Region Colonies*. Socialist History Society.

———. 1999. *Towards Decolonisation. Political, Labour and Economic Development in Jamaica 1938–1945.* Kingston: Canoe Press University of the West Indies.

Hartung, William D. 2010. *Prophets of War: Lockheed Martin and the Making of the Military-industrial Complex.* Nation Books.

Harvey, David. 2007. *A Brief History of Neoliberalism.* Oxford: Oxford University Press.

Haughton, Suzette A. 2011. *Drugged Out. Globalisation and Jamaica's Resilience to Drug Trafficking.* Lanham: University Press of America.

Hoekman, Bernard M., and M.M. Kostecki. 2001. *The Political Economy of the World Trading System: The WTO and Beyond.* Oxford: Oxford University Press.

Hoekman, Bernard M., and Petros C. Mavroidis. 2015. *World Trade Organization (WTO): Law, Economic, and Politics.* 2nd ed. New York: Routledge.

Holyoke, Thomas T. 2016. *Interest Groups and Lobbying: Pursuing Political Interests in America.* Boulder: Westview Press.

Hufbauer, Gary Clyde. 1993. *NAFTA: An Assessment.* Washington, DC: Institute for International Economics.

Irwin, Douglas A. 2017a. *Clashing over Commerce: A History of U.S. Trade Policy.* Chicago: University of Chicago.

Irwin Douglas A. 2017b. *Peddling Protectionism: Smoot-Hawley and the Great Depression.* Rev ed. Princeton: Princeton University Press.

James, Lawrence. 1994. *The Rise and Fall of the British Empire.* New York: St. Martin's Press.

Jawara, Fatoumata, and Aileen Kwa. 2004. *Behind the Scenes at the WTO: The Real World of International Trade Negotiations.* London: Zed Books.

Jones, Kent. 2010. *The Doha Blues. Institutional Crisis and Reform in the WTO.* Oxford: Oxford University Press.

———. 2004. *Who's Afraid of the WTO?* Oxford: Oxford University Press.

Kaiser, Robert G. 2009. *So Damn Much Money: The Triumph of Lobbying and the Corrosion of American Government.* New York: Vantage.

Katz, Alyssa. 2015. *The Influence Machine: The U.S. Chamber of Commerce and the Corporate Capture of American Life.* New York: Spiegel & Grau.

Kennedy, Paul. 1989. *The Rise and Fall of Great Powers. Economic Change and Military Conflict From 1500–2000.* New York: Vintage.

Kepner, Charles D., and Jay Soothill. 1935. *The Banana Empire. A Case Study of Economic Imperialism.* New York: Vanguard Press.

Kirst, William. 2013. *Globalization and America's Trade Agreements.* Washington, DC and Baltimore: Woodrow Wilson Center Press and Johns Hopkins University Press.

Koeppel, Dan. 2008. *Banana. The Fate of the Fruit that Changed the World.* New York: Hudson Street Press.

Korten, David C. 2001. *When Corpoations Rule the World.* Hartford: Kumarian Press.

Krueger, Anne. 1995. *Trade Policies for Developing Countries*. Washington, DC: Brookings Institution.

Kuczynski, Pedro-Pablo, and John Williamson. 2003. *After the Washington Consensus: Restarting Growth and Reform in Latin America*. Washington, DC: Peterson Institute for International Economics.

Ledbetter, James. 2011. *Unwarranted Influence. Dwight D. Eisenhower and the Military-Industrial Complex*. New Haven: Yale University Press.

Lewis, Charles. 1998. *The Buying of Congress. How Special Interests Have Stolen your Right to Life Liberty and the Pursuit of Happiness*. New York: Avon Books.

———. 1996. *The Buying of the President*. New York: Avon Books.

Lewis, Patsy. 2002. *Surviving Small Size. Regional Integration in Caribbean Ministates*. Kingston: University of the West Indies Press.

Livingstone, Grace. 2013. *America's Backyard: The United States and Latin America from Monroe Doctrine to the War on Terror*. London: Zed Books.

Lovett, A., Alfred E. Eckles Jr., and Richard L. Brinkman. 1999. *U.S. Trade Policy. History, Theory, and WTO*. New York: M. E. Sharpe.

Lundberg, Ferdinand. 1973. *The Rich and the Super-Rich: A Study in the Power of Money Today*. Lyle Stuart.

Marichal, Carlos. 1989. *A Century of Debt Crises in Latin America. From Independence to the Great Depression 1830–1930*. Princeton: Princeton University Press.

Mark, Fagan. 2015. *Lobbying: Business, Law and Public Policy, Why and How 12,000 People Spend 3 + Billion Impacting Our Government*. Heathrow: Vandeplas Publishing.

Markovits, Andrei S. 2007. *Uncouth Nation: Why Europe Dislikes America*. Princeton: Princeton University Press.

Martin, James W. 2018. *Banana Cowboys: The United Fruit Company and the Culture of Corporate Colonialism*. Albuquerque: University of New Mexico Press.

Matsushita, Mitsuo, Thomas J. Schoenbaum, Petros C. Mavroidis, and Michael Hahn. 2015. *The World Trade Organization. Law, Practice, and Policy*. 3rd ed. Oxford: Oxford University Press.

Maurer, Noel. 2013. *The Empire Trap: The Rise and Fall of U.S. Intervention to Protect American Property Overseas, 1893–2013*. Princeton: Princeton University Press.

Mearsheimer, John J., and Stephen M. Walt. 2008. *The Israel Lobby and U.S. Foreign Policy*. New York: Farrar, Straus and Giroux.

Medvetz, Thomas. 2012. *Think Tanks in America*. Chicago: University of Chicago Press.

Melville, Thomas, and Marjorie. 1971. *Guatemala. Another Vietnam*. Harmondsworth: Penguin.

Mills, C. Wright. 1956. *The Power Elite*. New York: Oxford University Press.

Minsky, Hyman. 2008. *Stabilizing an Unstable Economy*. New York: McGraw-Hill.
Mitchell, James F. 1996. *Guiding Change in the Islands*. Waitsfield, VT: Concepts Publishing.
Mizruchi, Mark S. 1982. *The American Corporate Network, 1904–1974*. Beverly Hills: Sage.
Moberg, Mark. 2008. *Slipping Away: Banana Politics and Fair Trade in the Eastern Caribbean*. New York: Berghahn Books.
Mukherjee, Ramkrishna. 1974. *The Rise and Fall of the East India Company*. New York: Monthly Review Press.
Myers, Gordon. 2004. *Banana Wars. The Price of Free Trade. A Caribbean Perspective*. London: Zed Books.
Nichols, John, and Robert W. McChesney. 2013. *Dollarocracy. How Money and the Media Election Complex is Destroying America*. New York: Nation Books.
Nurse, Keith, and Wayne Sandiford. 1995. *Windward Islands Bananas: Challenges and Options Under the SIngle European Market*. Kingston: Friedrich Ebert Stiftung.
Ocampo, Jose Martin, and Juan Martin. 2003. *Globalization and Development. A Latin American and Caribbean Perspective*. Palo Alto and Washington, DC: Stanford University Press and World Bank.
O'Hefferman, Patrick. 1991. *Mass Media and American Foreign Policy: Insider Perspectives on Global Journalism and the Foreign Policy Process*. Westport: Praeger.
O'Loughlin, Carleen. 1968. *Economic and Political Change in the Leeward and Windward Islands*. New Haven: Yale University Press.
Painter, David. 1986. *Private and Public Policy: Multinational Oil Companies and U.S. Foreign Policy, 1941–1954*. London: I.B. Taurus.
Palast, Greg. 2002. *The Best Democracy Money Can Buy*. London: Pluto Press.
Palmer, Colin A. 2014. *Freedom's Children: The 1938 Labour Rebellion and the Birth of Modern Jamaica*. Chapel Hill: University of North Carolina Press.
Park, Mi. 2018. *The IMF and WTO. How Does Geopolitics Influence Global Finance and International Trade*. Coal Harbour Publishing.
Pastor, Robert A. 1981. *Congress and the Politics of U. S. Foreign Economic Policy*. Berkeley: University of California Press.
Patterson, P.J. 2018. *My Political Journey. Jamaica's Sixth Prime Minister*. Kingston: University of the West Indies.
Petras, James, and Morris Morley. 1975. *The United States and Chile: Imperialism and the Overthrow of the Allende Government*. New York: Monthly Review Press.
Petras, Michael E., Rivkin W. Jan, Mihir A. Desair, M. Gehl Kathrine, William R. Kerr, and Manjari Raman. 2019. *A Recovery Squandered. The State of U.S. Competitiveness in 2019*. Cambridge: Harvard Business School.
Post, Ken. 1978. *Arise Ye Starvelings*. Hague: Martinus Nijhoff.

Prechel, Harland. 2000. *Big Business and the State: Historical Transitions and Corporate Transformations 880s–1990s*. Albany: State University of New York Press.

Reinhart, Carmen M., and Kenneth Rogoff. 2011. *This Time is Different: Eight Centuries of Financial Folly*. Princeton: Princeton University Press.

Robins, Nick. 2006. *The Corporation that Changed the World: How the East India Company Shaped the Modern Multinational*. London: Pluto Press.

Robinson, David, and Paul Cashin. 2006. *The Caribbean: From Vulnerability to Sustained Growth*. Washington, DC: International Monetary Fund.

Robinson, Randall. 1998. *Defending the Spirit. A Black Life in America*. New York: Dutton.

———. 2001. *The Debt: What America Owes to Blacks*. New York: Plume.

Rodney, Walter. 2014. *How Europe Underdeveloped Africa, Eric WIlliams, Capitalism and Slavery*. Chapel Hill: University of North Carolina Press.

Rooth, Tim. 1992. *British Protectionism and the International Economy: Overseas Commercial Policy in the 1930s*. Cambridge: Cambridge University Press.

Rowbottom, Jacob. 2010. *Democracy Distorted: Wealth, Influence and Democratic Politics*. Cambridge: Cambridge University Press.

Sanders, Sir Roland. 2005. *Crumbled Small. The Commonwealth Caribbean in World Politics*. London: Hansib Publications.

Sandiford, Wayne. 2000. *On the Brink of Decline. Bananas in the Windward Islands*. St. George's: Fedon Books.

Schattschneider, E.E. 1935. *Politics, Pressures and the Tariff*. New York: Prentice-Hall.

Schlesinger, Stephen, and Stephen Kinzer. 2005. *Bitter Fruit: The Story of the American Coup in Guatemala*. 2nd ed. New York: Daivid Rockefeller Center for Latin American Studies.

———. 2006. *Bitter Fruit: The Story of the American Coup in Guatemala*. Rev. and expanded. New York: David Rockefeller Center for Latin American Studies.

Schott, Jeffrey. 1989. *Free Trade Areas and U.S. Trade Policy*. Washington, DC: Institute for International Economics.

Schott, Jeffrey J., and Johanna W. Buurman. 1994. *Uruguay Round: An Assessment*. Washington, DC: Peterson Institute for International Economics.

Schott, Jeffrey. 1998a. *Launching New Global Trade Talks: An Action Agenda*. Washington, DC: Institute for International Economics.

———. 1998b. *Restarting Fast-Track*. Washington, DC: Institute for International Economics.

———. 1996. *WTO 2000: Setting the Course for World Trade*. Washington, DC: Institute for International Economics.

Schott, Jeffrey, and Gary Clyde Hufbauer. 1994. *Western Hemisphere Economic Integration*. Washington, DC: Institute for International Economics.

Servan-Schreiber, Jean-Jacques. 1969. *The American Challenge*. Harmondsworth: Penguin.

Shoch, Janes. 2000. *Trading Blows: Party Competition and U.S. Trade Policy in a Globalizing Era*. Chapel Hill: University of North Carolina Press.

Shoup, Laurence H. 2015. *Wall Street's Think Tank: The Council of Foreign Relations and the Empire of Neoliberal Geopolitics, 1976–2014*. New York: Monthly Review Press.

Shoup, Laurence, and William Minter. 2004. *Imperial Brain Trust: The Council on Foreign Relations and United States Foreign Policy*. Authors Choice Press.

Skonieczny, Amy. 2017. *Corporate Lobbying in Foreign Policy, Oxford Research Encyclopedia of Politics*. New York: Oxford University Press.

Smith, Hedrick. 1988. *The Power Game. How Washington Works*. New York: Random House.

Smith, Robert F. 1960. *The United States and Cuba. Business and Diplomacy, 1917–1960*. New Haven: College and University Press.

Sobel, Richard. 1993. *Public Opinion in U.S. Foreign Policy. The Controversy over Contra Aid*. Lanham: Litchfield and Rowman.

Stopford, John, and Susan Strange. 1991. *Rival States, Rival Firms*. Cambridge: Cambridge University Press.

Thomson, Robert, and George I. Brizan. 1987. *Green Gold. Bananas and Dependency in the Eastern Caribbean*. London: Latin American Bureau.

Tilley, Kenneth G. 2009. *Coming of Age. Speeches by Hon. Dr. Denzil L. Douglas*. Kingston: Ian Randle Publishers.

Tirthankar, Roy. 2012. *The East India Company: The World's Most Powerful Corporation* . Allan Lane.

Tivnan, Edward. 1988. *The Lobby. Jewish Political Power and American Foreign Policy*. New York: Touchstone Books.

Useem, Michael. 1984. *The Inner Circle: Large Corporations and the Rise of Business Political Activity in the U.S. and U.K.* New York: Oxford University Press.

Vernon, Raymond. 1998. *In the Hurricane's Eye. The Troubled Prospects of Multinational Enterprises*. Cambridge: Harvard University Press.

Wallach, Lori. 2013. *The Rise and Fall of Fast Track Trade Authority*. Washington, DC: Public Citizen, Inc.

Wallach, Lori, and Michelle Sforza. 1999. *The WTO: Five Years of Reason to Resist Corporate Globalization*. Seven Stories Press.

Wallach, Lori, and Patrick Woodall. 2004. *Whose Trade Organization? The Comprehensive Guide to the WTO*. New York: The New Press.

Wallsvh, Lori, and Michelle. 1999. *Whose Trade Organization?* Washington, DC: Public Citizen.

Welch, Barbara M. 1996. *Survival by Association. Supply Management Landscapes of the Eastern Caribbean*. Montreal: McGill-Queen's University Press.

Wiarda, Howard J. 1995. *American Foreign Policy: Actors, and Processes*. New York: Harper Collins College Publishers.

Widdicombe, Stacey H., Jr. 1972. *The Performance of Industrial Development Corporations: The Case of Jamaica*. New York: Praeger.

Wild, Antony. 1999. *The East India Company: Trade and Conquest from 1600*. New York: Harper Collins.

William, Domhoff G. 1967. *Who Rules America?* Englewood Cliffs: Prentice-Hall.

Wolf, Martin. 2005. *Why Globalization Works*. New Haven: Yale University Press.

Yarrow, Andrew L. 2008. *Forgive Us Our Debts: The Intergenerational Dangers of Fiscal Irresponsibility*. New Haven: Yale University Press.

Zetter, Lionel. 2014. *Lobbying: The Art of Political Persuasion*. Petersfield: Harriman House.

Articles in Journals

Aiello, Francesco. 1999. The Stabilisation of LDC's Export Earnings. The Impact of the EU STABEX Programme. *International Review of Applied Economics* 13 (1): 1–14.

Alleyne, Dillon, and Ian Boxill. 2003. The Impact of Crime on Tourist Arrivals in Jamaica. *International Journal of Tourism Research* 5 (5): 381–391.

Arslanalp, Serkan, and Henry Peter Blair. 2006. Debt Relief. *Journal of Economic Perspectives* 20 (1): 207–220.

Baldwin, Robert E., and Christopher S. Magee. 1990. Is Trade Policy for Sale: Congressional Voting on Recent Trade Bills. *Public Choice* 105 (1/2): 79–101.

———. 2010. Bananas: Geneva Agreement Signed; Bilaterals Cut Tariffs Further. *Bridges* 14 (20).

Barnes, R.C., and E.R. Ritter. 2001. Networks of Corporate Interlock: 1962–1995. *Critical Sociology* 27 (2): 192–220.

Basdeo, Sahadeo. 1992. CARIBCAN: A Continuum in Canada-CARICOM Economic Relations. *Caribbean Studies* 25 (3–4): 189–219.

———. 1993. CARIBCAN: A Continuum in Canada-Commonwealth Caribbean Economic Relations. *Canadian Foreign Policy* 1 (2): 55–79.

Beckford, George L. 1967. The West Indian Banana Industry: The Scope for Rationalization and Regional Collaboration. *Social and Economic Studies* 2 (3).

Bernal, Richard L. 1991. Caribbean Debt Relief. *Caribbean Studies* 4 (2): 45–58.

———. 1988a. The Great Depression, Colonial Policy and Industrialization in Jamaica. *Social and Economic Studies* 37 (1 & 2): 33–64.

———. 2013. The Unimportance of the English-Speaking Caribbean in U.S. Foreign Policy as Told by Presidents and Secretaries of State. *Caribbean Journal of International Relations & Diplomacy* 1 (1): 132–150.

———. 1998a. The WTO Dispute Mechanism: A Developing Country Perspective. *International Lawyer* 33 (3): 871–873.

Birdsall, Nancy, Dani Rodrick, and Arvind Subramanian. 2005. How to Help the Poor Countries. *Foreign Affairs* 85 (4): 136–152.

Boamah, Daniel, and Winston Moore. 2009. External Debt and Economic Growth. *Monetary Affairs* 22 (2): 139–157.

Brenton, Paul, and Miriam Manchin. 2003. Making E.U. Trade Agreements Work: The Role of Rules of Origin. *The World Economy* 6 (5): 755–769.

Bryan, Anthony T. 1989. The International Dynamics of the Commonwealth Caribbean: Challenges and Opportunities in the 1990's. *Journal of Interamerican Studies and World Affairs* 31 (3): 1–7.

Bucheli, Marcelo. 2005. Banana War Maneuvers. *Harvard Business Review* 83 (11): 22–24.

———. 2008. Multinational Corporations, Totalitarian Regimes, and Economic Nationalism: United Fruit Company in Central America, 1899–1975. *Business History* 50 (4): 433–454.

Bunting, David, and Jeffrey Barbour. 1971. Interlocking Directorates in Large Corporations, 1896–1964. *Business History Review* XLV (3): 317–335.

Burris, Val. 2005. Interlocking Directorates and Political Cohesion among Corporate Elites. *American Journal of Sociology* 111 (1): 249–283.

Cardoso, F.H. 1972. Dependency and Development in Latin America. *New-Left Review* 74: 83–90.

———. 1999. Caribbean Nations Warn U.S. on Drug Cooperation after Banana Retaliation. *Inside U. S. Trade* 17 (11).

Dooley, Peter C. 1969. The Interlocking Directorate. *American Economic Review* 59 (3): 314–323.

Dos Santos, T. 1970. The Structure of Dependence. *American Economic Review* 60 (2): 231–236.

Dreiling, Michael, and Derek Darves. 2011. Corporate Unity in American Trade Policy: A Network Analysis of Corporate-Dyad Political Action. *American Journal of Sociology* 116 (5): 1514–1563.

Evans, Robert. 1999a. WTO Approves U.S. Sanctions. *Journal of Commerce* 3A.

Feuer, Carl. 1984. Better Must Come: Sugar and Jamaica in the 20th Century. *Social and Economic Studies* 33 (4): 1–49.

Goldschmied, Nadav, Galily Yair, and Keith Kenneth. 2018. Evidence for Cross-Cultural Support for the Underdog: Is the Affiliation Driven by Fairness and Competence Assessments? *Frontiers in Psychology* 9.

Grossman, Lawrence S. 1994. British Aid and Windward Bananas, The Case of St. Vincent and the Grenadines. *Social and Economic Studies* 43 (11): 151–179.

Hart, Ansel. 1954. The Banana in Jamaica: Export Trade. *Social and Economic Studies* 3 (2): 212–229.

Inoue, Tatsumi. 2010. The British Import Duties Act of 1932 and the Ottawa Preferential Agreements. *The Journal of Political Economy and Economic History* 53 (1): 16–29.

Isaac, Wendy-Ann, Michael Joseph, Wayne Ganpat, Marisa Wilson, and Richard Brathwaite. 2012. The Caribbean's Windward Islands Banana Industry: A Heritage of Dependency. *Journal of Rural and Community Development* 7 (2): 98–117.

Joefield-Napier, Wallace. 1985. External Public Debt and Public Finances in OECS Member Countries and Belize: 1977–82. *Social and Economic Studies* 34 (4).

Knight, Franklin W. 2014. The Struggle of the British Caribbean Sugar Industry, 1900–2013. *The Journal of Caribbean History* 48 (1/2).

Knight, W. Andy. 2019. The Nexus between Vulnerabilities and Violence in the Caribbean. *Third World Quarterly* 40 (2): 1–22.

———. 2000. Lori's War: The FP Interview. *Foreign Policy* 118: 29–55.

Letter to President William Clinton from Newt Gingrich and Trent Lott. 1998, October 9. Inside U.S. Trade. 16 (40).

McFarlene, Dennis. 1964. The Future of the Banana Industry in the West Indies: An Assessment of Supply Prospects for 1965 and 1975. *Social and Economic Studies* 13 (1): 38–93.

Meredith, David. 1975. The British Government and Colonial Economic Policy, 1919–1939. *The Economic History Review* 28 (3): 484–499.

Page, Sheila, and A. Hewitt. 2002. The New European Trade Preferences: Does Everything but Arms (EBA) Help the Poor? *Development Policy Review* 20 (1): 91–102.

Panagariya, Arvind. 2002. E.U. Preferential Trade Agreements and Developing Countries. *World Economy* 25 (10): 1415–1432.

Patterson, Eliza. 2001. The U.S.-E.U. Banana Dispute. *American Society for International Insights* 6 (4).

Prebisch, Raul. 1959. Commercial Policy in the Underdeveloped Countries. *American Economic Review* 49 (2): 251–273.

Ray, Dennis M. 1972. Corporations and American Foreign Relations. *The Annals of the American Academy of Political and Social Science* 403: 80–92.

Roy, William. 1984. Interlocking Directorates and the Corporate Revolution. *Social Science History* 7 (2): 143–164.

Samuels, Michael. 1982. Time for an Activist Export Policy. *Business America* 5 (3).

Spiro, Herbert J. 1988. Anti-Americanism: Origins and Context. *The Annals of the American Academy of Political and Social Science* 497: 120–132.

Sunkel, Osvaldo. 1969. National Development Policy and External Dependence in Latin America. *Journal of Development Studies* 6 (1): 23–48.

———. 1973. The Centre-Periphery Model. *Social and Economic Studies* 22 (1): 132–176.

Useem, Michael. 1979. The Social Organization of the American Business Elite and Participation of Corporation Directors in the Governance of American Institutions. *American Sociological Review* 44 (4): 553–572.

Walker, Fredrick. 1937. Economic Progress of St.Vincent, B. W. I., Since 1927. *Economic Geography* 13 (3): 217–234.

Welch, Barbara. 1994. Banana Dependency: Albatross or Life Raft for the Windwards. *Social and Economic Studies* 43 (1): 123–149.

Wicker, E.R. 1958. Colonial Development and Welfare, 1929–1957: The Evolution of a Policy. *Social and Economic Studies* 7 (4): 170–192.

Williams, Michelle. 2000. Caribbean Shiprider Agreements: Sunk by Banana Trade War? *Inter-American Law Review* 31 (1): 163–195.

Wright, Allan, and Kari Grenade. 2014. Determining Optimal Public Debt and Debt-Growth Dynamics in the Caribbean. *Research in Applied Economics* 6 (2): 87–115.

Chapters in Books

Amo-Yartey, Charles, and Therese Turner-Jones. 2014. Fiscal Consolidation and Debt Reduction in the Caribbean: An Overview. In *Caribbean Renewal. Tackling Fiscal and Debt Challenges*, ed. Charles Amo-Yartey and Therese Turner-Jones, 1–24. Washington, DC: International Monetary Fund.

Anderson, Rachel, Tim Taylor, and Tim Josling. 2003. The Caribbean and the Banana Trade. In *Banana Wars. The Anatomy of a Trade Dispute*, ed. Timothy E. Josling and Timothy G. Taylor, 123–150. Walliford: CABI Publishing.

Barfield, Claude. 2000. The Role of Interest Groups in the Design and Implementation of U.S. Trade Policies. In *Social Dimensions of U.S. Trade Policies*, ed. A.V. Dearorff and R.M. Stern, 271–280. Ann Arbor: University of Michigan Press.

Barriteau, Eudine. 2006. The Economic Philosophy of Eugenia Charles and Dominica's Development, 1980–1995. In *Enjoying Power: Eugenia Charles and Political Leadership in the Commonwealth Caribbean*, ed. Eudine Barriteau and Alan Cobley, 183–213. Kingston: University of the West Indies Press.

Beckford, George L. 1974. Issues in the Windwards-Jamaica Banana War. In *Readings in the Political Economy of the Caribbean*, ed. Norman Girvan and Owen Jefferson, 77–86. Kingston: New World.

Beckford, George. 2000. Origins, Development and Future of the Jamaican Banana Industry: A Century of Revolutionary Struggle of the Peasantry. In *The George Beckford Reader*, ed. Kari Levitt, 352–358. Kingston: University of the West Indies Press.

Bernal, Richard L. 1988b. "Default as a Negotiating Tactic in Debt Rescheduling Strategies of Developing Countries: A Preliminary Note." In *Foreign*

Investment, Debt and Economic Growth in Latin America, Antonio Jorge and Jorge Salazar-Carrillo, 41-58. London: Macmillan Press.

———. 1982. Economic Growth and External Debt in Jamaica. In *External Debt and Economic Growth in Latin America*, ed. Antonio Jorge, Rene F. Higonnet, and Jorge Salazar-Carrillo, 89–108. New York: Pergamon Publishers.

———. 2000a. Globalization and Small Developing Countries: The Imperative for Repositioning. In *Globalization: A Calculus of Inequality*, ed. Denis Benn and Kenneth Hall, 88–128. Kingston: Ian Randle Publishers.

———. 2001. Globalization and Small Developing Economies. The Challenges and Opportunities. In *Small States in the Global Economy*, ed. David Peretz, Rumman Faruqi, and Eliawony J. Kisanga, 39–51. London: Commonwealth Secretariat.

———. 2011. Improving the Participation of Small Developing Countries in the Governance of the Multilateral Trading System. In *Making Global Trade Governance Work for Development. Perspectives and Priorities from Developing Countries*, ed. Carolyn Deere Birkbeck, 231–258. Cambridge: Cambridge University Press.

———. 2006. Special and Differential Treatment for Small Developing Economies. In *WTO at the Margins. Small States and the Multilateral Trading System*, ed. Roman Grynberg, 309–355. Cambridge: Cambridge University Press.

———. 1985. The Vicious Circle of Foreign Indebtedness: The Case of Jamaica. In *External Debt and Development Strategy in Latin America*, ed. Antonio Jorge, Jorge Salazar-Carrillo, and Frank Diaz-Pou, 111–128. New York: Pergamon Press.

Bernal, Richard L., and Winsome Leslie. 1999. Canadian Economic Assistance to CARICOM Countries: Assessment and Future Prospects. In *Canadian-Caribbean Relations in Transition: Trade, Sustainable Development and Security*, ed. Jerry Haar and Anthony Bryan, 190–209. London: Macmillan and New York:St. Martin's Press.

Bernal, Richard L. 2003. Small Developing Economies in the World Trade Organization. In *Agriculture, Trade and the WTO*, ed. Merlinda D. Ingco, 108–122. Washington, DC: World Bank.

Brenton, Paul, and T. Ikezuki. 2004. The Impact of Agricultural Trade Preferences with Particular Attention to Least Developed Countries. In *Global Agricultural Trade and the Developing Countries*, ed. Atamon Aksoy and John Beghin, 55–74. Washington, DC: World Bank.

Brewster, H.R., and C.Y. Thomas. 1967. Trade Between the West Indies and Canada: The Development, Structure and Terms of West Indian Trade with Canada. In *Canada-West Indian Economic Relations*, ed. Kari Levitt and Alister McIntyre, 14–61. Montreal: Centre for Developing Area Studies, McGill University.

Domeland, Dorte, Carlos A. Primo, and Braga. 2009. Introduction. In *Debt Relief and Beyond. Lessons Learnt and Challenges Ahead*, ed. Carlos A. Primo Braga and Dorte Domeland, 1–8. Washington, DC: World Bank.

Freeman, Helen. 2004. Special Trade Arrangements to Improve Market Access. In *Agriculture and the WTO. Creating a Trading System for Development*, ed. Merlinda D. Ingco and John D. Nash, 291–315. Washington, DC: World Bank.

Fullberg-Stolberg, Claus. 2004. *The Caribbean in the Second World War*. In *General History of the Caribbean*, ed. Bridget Brereton, vol. V, 82–140. London: Macmillan Publishers.

Girvan, Norman. 2000. Creating and Recreating the Caribbean. In *Contending with Destiny. The Caribbean in the 21st Century*, ed. Kenneth Hall and Denis Benn, 31–36. Kingston: Ian Randle Publishers.

Grayson, George W. 1998. Lobbying by Mexico and Canada. In *The Controversial Pivot. The U.S. Congress and North America*, ed. Robert Pastor and Rafael Fernandez de Castro, 70–94. Washington, DC: The Brookings Institution Press.

Griffith, Ivelaw. 2003. Security and Sovereignty in the Contemporary Caribbean: Probing Elements of Local-Global Nexus. In *Living at the Borderlines: Issues in Caribbean Sovereignty and Development*, ed. Cynthia Barrow and Don Marshall, 209–225. Kingston: Ian Randle Publishers.

Hall, Douglas. 1964. The Early Banana Trade from Jamaica, 1868–1905. A Descriptive Account. In *Ideas and Illustration in Economic History*, ed. Douglas Hall, 56–79. New York: Holt, Rinehart and Winston.

Knight, Franklin W. 2004. *The Caribbean in the 1930s*. In *General History of the Caribbean*, ed. Bridget Brereton, vol. V, 42–81. London and Paris: Macmillan Publishers and UNESCO Publishing.

Lewis, W. Arthur. 1994. *The Industrial Development of Puerto Rico*. Vol. 1, Caribbean Economic Review, Vol. 1 Nos. 1 & 2 (1949) in *Sir WIlliam Arthur Lewis, Collected Papers 1941–1988*, ed. Patrick A. M. Emmanuel, 793–823.

Maingot, Anthony P. 1999. The Decentralization Imperative and Caribbean Criminal Enterprises. In *Transnational Crime in the Americas*, ed. Tom Farer, 144–170. New York: Routledge.

Monge-Roffarello, Luca, Michael Swidinsky, and David Vanzetti. 2004. Small Island Developing States and Agricultural Trade Liberalization. In *Competitiveness Strategies for Small States*, ed. Lina Briguglio and Cordina Gordon, 307–337. Island and Small States: Institute of the University of Malta and the Commonwealth Secretariat.

Persaud, Bishnodat. 1980. Exporting Earnings Stabilization in the ACP/EEC Convention. In *The Political Economy of EEC Relations with African, Caribbean and Pacific States. Contributions to the Understanding of the Lome Convention on North-South Relations*, ed. Frank Long, 91–106. Oxford: Pergamon Press.

Ramsaran, Dave. 2003. Understanding the Socio-Cultural Dynamic of Globalisation: The Case of St. Lucia and St. Vincent and the Grenadines. In

Living at the Borderlines: Issues in Caribbean Sovereignty and Development, ed. Cynthia Barrow and Don Marshall, 95–117. Kingston: Ian Randle Publishers.

Rasmussen, Tobias. 2006. Natural Disasters and their Macroeconomic Implications. In *The Caribbean: From Vulnerability to Sustained Growth*, ed. Ratna Sahay, David Robinson, and Paul Cashin, 181–205. Washington: International Monetary Fund.

Robinson, Michele. 2014. Does Debt Restructuring Work? An Assessment of Remedial Actions. In *Debt and Development in Small Island Developing States*, ed. Damien King and David Tennant, 207–218. New York: Palgrave Macmillan.

Sahay, Ratna. 2006. Stabilization, Debt and Fiscal Policy in the Caribbean. In *The Caribbean. From Vulnerability to Sustained Growth*, ed. Ratna Sahay, David O. Robinson, and Paul Cashin, 17–57. Washington, DC: International Monetary Fund.

Seepersad, Randy. 2017. Crime, Violence and Public Safety. In *Crime, Violence and Security in the Caribbean*, ed. M. Raymond Izarali, 19–51. New York: Routledge.

Scott, Barfield. 2005. Declining Diplomatic Influence and the Banana Trade Dispute. In *Diplomacy and Developing National Post-Cold War Foreign Policy Making Structures and Processes*, ed. Justin Robertson and Maurice A. East. London: Routledge.

Skidelsky, Robert J. 1976. Retreat from Leadership: The Evolution of British Foreign Economic Policy, 1870–1939. In *Balance of Power or Hegemony? The Interwar Monetary System*, ed. Benjamin M. Rowland. New York: New York University Press.

Tennant, David F. 2014. Debt and Development in SIDS: An Urgent Call for Action. In *Debt and Development in Small Island Developing States*, ed. Damien King and David Tennant, 1–9. New York: Palgrave Macmillan.

Wiley, James. 1997. Dominica's Economic Diversification: Microstates in a Neoliberal Era. In *Globalization and Neoliberalism: The Caribbean Context*, ed. Thomas Klak, 155–177. Lanham: Rowman & Littlefield Publishers.

Williams, William Appleman. 1970. The Large Corporation and American Foreign Policy. In *Corporations and the Cold War*, ed. David Horowitz, 71–104. New York: Monthly Review Press.

Williamson, John. 1990. What Washington Means by Policy Reform. In *Latin American Adjustment: How Much has Happened*, ed. John Williamson, 7–38. Washington, DC: Peterson Institute for International Economics.

Monographs and Working Papers

Acevedo, Sebastian. 2014. *Debt, Growth and Natural Disasters: A Caribbean Trilogy*. IMF Working Paper WP/14/125, Washington, DC: International Monetary Fund.

Addy, David Nii. 1999. *Restructuring the Loss of Preferences: Labour Challenges for the Caribbean Banana Industry.* Working Papers 993341213402676, Geneva: International Labour Organization.

Alexandraki, Katerina, and Hans Peter Lankes. 2004. *The Impact of Preference Erosion on Middle-Income Developing Countries.* IMF Working Paper WP/04/169, Washington, DC: International Monetary Fund.

Arias, Pedro, Cora Dankers, Pascal Liu, and Paul Pilkauskas. 2003a. *The World Banana Economy 1985–2000.* Rome: Food and Agriculture Organization.

Asonuma, Tamon, Gerardo Peraza, Kristine Vitola, and Takahiro Tsuda. 2014. *Sovereign Debt Restructuring in Belize: Achievements and Challenges Ahead.* IMF Wokring Paper WP/14/132, Washington, DC: International Monetary Fund.

Bernal, Richard L. 1998b. *Integration of Small Economies in the Free Trade Area of the Americas.* CSIS Policy Paper on the Americas, Vol. IX, Study No. 1, Washington, DC: Center for Strategic and International Studies.

———. 2009. *Participation of Small Developing Economies in the Governance of the Multilateral Trading System.* Working Paper No. 44, Waterloo: Centre for International Governance Innovation.

———. 1996. *Strategic Global Repositioning and the Future Economic Development of Jamaica.* North South Agenda Paper No. 18, Miami: North-South Center, University of Miami.

Bernal, Richard L., and Steve Lamar. 1996. *Caribbean Basin Economic Development and the Section 936 Tax Credit.* North South Agenda Paper, No. 22. Miami: North-South Center, University.

Borensztein, Eduardo, and Ugo Panizza. 2008. *The Costs of Sovereign Default.* IMF Working Paper WP/08/238, Washington, DC: International Monetary Fund.

Borrell, Brent. 1996. *E.U. Bananarama 1993: The Story Gets Worse.* Canberra and Sydney: Centre For International Economics.

———. 1994. *E.U. Bananarama III.* Policy Research Working Paper, No. 1388. Washington, DC: World Bank.

———. 1995. *EU's Bananarama-Slipping, World Bank Development Brief No. 50.* World Bank.

Borrell, Brent, and Yang Maw-Cheng. 1992. *E.C. Bananarama 1992.* Policy Research Working Paper Series 523, Washington, DC: World Bank.

———. 1992. *E.C. Bananarama 1992: The Sequel.* Working Paper, No. 958. Washington, DC: World Bank.

Brooks, Skylar, and Domenico Lombardi. 2015. *Sovereign Debt Restructuring: Issues Paper.* CIGI Papers No. 64. Waterloo: Center for International Governance Innovation.

Calderon, Cesar, and J. Rodrigo Fuentes. 2013a. *Government Debt and Economic Growth.* IDB Working Paper Series No. IDB-WP-424. Washington, DC: Inter-American Development Bank.

———. 2013b. *Caribbean Small States: Challenges of High Debt and Low Growth.* Washinton, DC: International Monetary Fund.

Cecchetti, Stephen G., M.S. Mohany, and Fabrizio Zampolli. 2011. The Real Effects of Debt. BIS Working Papers No. 352. Basel: Bank for International Settlement.

Chauffour, Jean-Pierre, and Jean-Christophe Maur. 2011. *Preferential Trade Agreement Policies for Development: Handbook.* Washington, DC: World Bank.

———. 1996. Chiquita's Brand of Doing Business in Honduras, COHA Occasional Paper, Vol. 1, No. 3.

———. 2007. *Crime Violence and Development: Trends, Costs and Options in the Caribbean.* Washington, DC: World Bank.

de Melo, Jamie. 2012. *Bananas, The GATT, The WTO and U.S. and E.U. Domestic Politics.* Working Paper No. 45. Fondation pour les Etudes et Recherches sur le Development International.

Domhoff, G. Williams. 2013c. *Interlocking Directorates in the Corporate Community.* Who Rules Amearica. https://whorulesamerica.ucsc.edu/power/corporate_community.html.

Donald, J. 2010. *Jamaica's Debt-Propelled Economy: A Failed Economic Strategy and its Aftermath.* SALISES Working Paper Series No. 1. Kingston: University of the West Indies.

Evenett, Simon J., and Johannes Fritz. 2015. *The Tide Turns? Trade Protectionism and Slowing Global Growth.* 18th Global Trade Alert Report. London: Centre for Economic Policy Research.

Girvan, Norman. 1986a. *Notes on Jamaica's External Debt in Omar Davis (ed), The Debt Problem in Jamaica.* Monographs No. 1. Economics Department, Kingston: University of the West Indies.

———. 2018. *Global Overview of Drug Demand and Supply. Latest Trends, Cross-Cutting Issues.* Vienna: United Nations.

Godfrey, Claire. 1998. *A Future for Caribbean Bananas—The Importance of Europe's Banana Market to the Caribbean.* Oxford: Department, Oxfam, UK.

Greenidge, Kevin, Roland Craigwell, Chrystol Thomas, and Lisa Drakes. 2012. *Threshold Effects of Sovereign Debt: Evidence from the Caribbean.* IMF Working Paper No. 12/157. Washington, DC: International Monetary Fund.

Grynberg, Roman, and Sacha Silva. 2004. *Preference-Dependent Economies and Multilateral Liberalization: Impacts and Options.* London: Commonwealth Secretariat.

Hallam, David, and Steve McCorriston. 1992. *Fair Trade in Bananas?* Agricultural Economics Units, University of Exeter.

Harris, Donald J. 2010. *Jamaica's Debt-Propelled Economy: A Failed Economic Strategy and its Aftermath.* SALISES Working Paper Series No. 1. Kingston: University of the West Indies.

Hoekman, Bernard, and Susan Prowse. 2003. *Economic Policy Responses to Preference Erosion: From Trade as Aid to Aid for Trade.* World Bank Research Policy Paper 2721. Washington, DC: World Bank.

Hornbeck, J.F., and William H. Cooper. 2011. *Trade Promotion Authority (TPA) and the Role of Congress in Trade Policy.* Washington, DC: Congressional Research Service.

Hurley, Gail, H. Minh H. Pham, and Machel Stewart. 2012. *Jamaica's Debt Exchange: A Case Study for Heavily Indebted Middle-Income Countries.* Discussion Paper, New York: United Nations Development Programme.

Inama, Stefano. 2003. *Trade Preferences for LDCs: An Early Assessment of Benefits and Possible Improvements.* Geneva: UNCTAD.

James, Ronald, Jemma Lafeuillee, Mike Xin Li, Gonzalo Salinas, and Yevgeniva Savchenko. 2019. *Explaining High Unemployment in ECCU Countries.* IMF Working Paper, WP/19/144. Washington, DC: International Monetary Fund.

King, Damien, and Anika Kiddoe. 2010. *Achieving Fiscal Sustainability in Jamaica: The JDX and Beyond.* Kingston: Caribbean Policy Research Institute.

Kotschwar, Barbara, and Wilson Hufbauer. 2011. *Trade Policy, Standards and Development in Central America.* World Bank Research Paper 2576. Washington, DC: World Bank.

Lawrence, Robert Z., and Susan Rosegrant. 1999. *Banana Wars: Challenges to the European's Banana Regime.* Cambridge: John F. Kennedy School of Government.

Levitt, Kari. 1991. *The Origins and Consequences of Jamaica's Debt Crisis, 1970–1990.* Kingston: Consortium Graduate School of Social Sciences.

Lewis, W. Arthur. 1977. *Labour in the West Indies - The Birth of a Workers' Movement.* Original Edition Fabian Society, 1939, London: New Beacon.

Limao, Nuno. 2016. *Preferential Trade Agreements.* Working Paper 22138, Washington, DC: National Bureau of Economic Research.

Marie, J.M. 1979. *Agricultural Diversification in a Small Economy: The Case for Dominica.* Occasional Paper No. 10, Cave Hill: Institute of Social and Economic Research, University of the West Indies.

Michaelopoulos, Constantine. 2003. *The Role of Special and Differential Treatment for Developing Countries in the GATT and World Trade Organization.* World Bank Policy Research Working Paper No. 2388, Washington, DC: World Bank.

Mitchell, Donald. 2005. *Sugar in the Caribbean: Adjusting to Eroding Preferences.* Policy Research Working Paper 3802. Washington, DC: World Bank.

Mitchell, Travis. 2015. Debt Overhang and the Challenges of Financing Sustainable Growth and Development. Annual Commonwealth & Francophone Dialogue with G20 Discussion Paper No. 1.

Mlachila, Montfort, Paul Cashin, and Cleary Haines. 2010. *Caribbean Bananas: The Macroeconomic Impact of Trade Preference Erosion*. IMF Working Paper WP/10/59. Washington, DC: International Monetary Fund.

Odel, Maurice. 1987. *Transnational Banks and Problems of Small Debtors*. Adlith Brown Memorial Lecture, Institute of Social and Economic Research, University of the West Indies, Mona, Jamaica, Kingston: University of the West Indies.

Ozden, Caglar, and Eric Reinhardt. 2003. *The Perversity of Preferences: Generalized System of Preferences and Developing Country Policies, 1976–2000*. World Bank Policy Research Working Paper No. 2955. Washington, DC: World Bank.

Page, Sheila, and Peter Kleen. 2005. *Special and Differential Treatment of Developing Countries in the World Trade Organization*. Global Development Studies No. 2. EGDI Secretariat, Stockholm: Ministry of Foreign Affairs, Sweden.

———. 2010. *Peeling Back the Truth on Guatemalan Bananas*. Washington, DC: Council on Hemispheric Affairs.

Pescatori, Andrea, Damiano Sandri, and John Simon. 2014. *Debt and Growth: Is there a Magic Threshold?* IMF Working Paper WP/14/34, Washington, DC: International Monetary Fund.

Prebish, Raul. 1950. *The Economic Development of Latin America and its Principal Problems*. New York: United Nations Economic Commission for Latin America.

———. 2001. Preferential Trade and Developing Countries. Bad Aid, Bad Trade. Prepared for the Cairns Group Farm Leaders Meeting.

———. 1999. *Restructuring and the Loss of Preference. Labour Challenges for the Caribbean Banana Industry*. Geneva: International Labour Organization.

Ruprah, Inder Jit. 2013. *Does Size Matter? Yes, If You are Caribbean!* Inter-American Development Bank Country Department Caribbean Group Policy Brief No. IDB-PB-201. Washington, DC: Inter-American Development Bank.

Ruprah, Inder Jit, Karl Melgarejo, and Ricardo Sierra. 2014. *Is There a Caribbean Sclerosis?* Washington, DC: Inter-American Development Bank.

Stoeckel, Andrew, and Brent Borrell. 2001. *Preferential Trade and Developing Countries: Bad Aid, Bad Trade*. Rural Industries Research and Development Corporation, Publication No. 01/116. Canberra: Australian Governement Publishing Service.

———. 1972. *Subversion in Chile: A Case Study in U.S. Corporate Intrigue in the Third World*. London: Spokesman Books.

Tamon, Asonuma, Gerardo Peraza, Kristine Vitola, and Takahiro Tsuda. 2014. *Sovereign Debt Restructuring in Belize: Achievements and Challenges Ahead*. IMF Working Paper WP/14/132. Washington, DC: International Monetary Fund.

Tangrmann, Stefan. 2002. *The Future of Preferential Trade Arrangements for Developing Countries and the Current Round of WTO Negotiations on Agriculture*. Rome: Food and Agridulture Organization of the United Nations.

———. 1997. *The Economic and Social Contribution of the Banana Industry in the OECS*. Basseterre: Research and Information Department, Eastern Caribbean Central Bank.

Trebesch, Christoph, Michael G. Papaioannou, and Udajbir S. Das. 2012. *Sovereign Debt Restructuring 1950-2010: Literature Survey, Data and Stylized Facts*. IMF Working Paper No. 12/203, Washington, DC: International Monetary Fund.

Magazine

Bartlett, Donald L., and James B. Steele. 2000. How to Become a Top Banana. *Time*, January 30.

Barton, Paul. 1997. Lindners gave widely in Politics. *The Enquirer*, November 12.

Dove, Timothy. 2000. Action Battery, Hit by a $200,000 Bill From the Blue. *Time*, February 7.

Drutman, Lee. 2015. How Corporate Lobbyists Conquered American Democracy. *The Atlantic*, April 20.

Fox, John, and Nancy Fuior. 1988. Bananasplit. *Mother Jones*, November/ December.

Greenfield, Karl Taro. 1999. Banana Wars. *Time Magazine*, February 8.

Inside U.S. Trade. 1996. Latins to seek WTO Panel on E.U. Banana Regime this Month. April 12.

Isikoff, Michael, and Brook Larmer. 1997. And Now, Bananagate? *Newsweek Magazine*, April 28.

Kambhampaty, Anna Purna. 2019. What We Can Learn from The Near-Death of the Banana. *Time*, November 18.

Kaplan, Arthur. 2000. Galaxy Graphics, Goodbye, Art. *Time*, February 7.

Larmer, Brook. 1997. The Banana Wars. *Newsweek Magazine*, April 28.

Musher, Amy. 1999. Letter to Hazel Ross-Robinson. *Time Magazine*, February 18.

The Caribbean Coalition. 1995. Caribbean Nations Ask U.S. to Abandon Harmful Trade Proceeding. March 22.

The Economist. 1999. At Dagger Dawn. May 8.

———. 1997. Expelled From Eden. *The Economist*, December 20.

———. 2014a. Full Circle. Drugs trafficking in the Caribbean, May 24.

———. 2014b. Full Circle. Drugs Trafficking in the Caribbean. *The Economist*, May 24.

Thompson, Derek. 2016. America's Monopoly Problem. How Big Business Jammed the Wheels of Innovation. *The Atlantic*, October.

Weisskopf, Michael. 1997a. The Busy Back Door Men. *Time Magazine*, March 31.

Newspaper

Adams, James, and Jaimie Seaton. 1995. Washington Goes Bananas over Britain's Colonial Fruit Run. *London Sunday Times*, April 9.

Alden, Edward. 2000. U.S. and E.U. Still Split on Beef and Bananas. *Financial Times*, December 19.

Alden, Edward, and Christopher Bowe. 2001. Chiquita Sues Brussels Over Losses Caused by Banana Import Curbs. *Financial Times*, January 26.

Andrews, Edmund. 1999. What Bananas? Tariff Fight Baffles Europe. *New York Times*, March 5.

Archibald, George. 1997. Banana Baron Peeled Off Half a Mil, White House Paid Back in WTO Fight. *Washington Post*, August 25.

Beard, David. 1998. In Jamaica, They'll Have No Bananas. *Sun Sentinel*, March 29.

Bennett, James. 1997. Clinton in Caribbean: No Bananas Today. *The New York Times*, May 11.

Bernal, Richard L. 1997a. Friendly Fire Hits Caribbean. *Journal of Commerce*, April 24.

———. 1999a. Banana Trade Vital to Caribbean. *The Journal of Commerce*, February 3.

———. 1997b. WTO Banana Case, Friendly Fire Hits Caribbean. *The Journal of Commerce*, April 24.

———. 1995. Fighting a Banana Battle now will Mean U.S. will Lose Lots of Trade Later. *Washington Times*, August 24.

Best, Tony. 1997. The Caribbean, Bananas and the OAS. *New York Carib News*, Week Ending, June 24.

Bohning, Don. 1998a. Banana Wars Snag Caribbean Island Nations. *Miami Herald*, December 23: C1.

———. 1998b. U.S. Relations with Caribbean Under Strain. *Miami Herald*, October 27.

Boustany, Nora. 1998. Yes We Have No Banana Pact. *Washington Post*, November 20: A 50.

Constantine, Gus. 1999. Caribbean Nations Hurt by Banana Dispute Threaten to Retaliate. *The Washington Times*, March 9.

Cooper, Helene. 2001. Dole Fails to Find Much Appeal in Accord to End Banana War. *Wall Street Journal*, April 23.

de Jonquieres, Guy, and Nancy Dunne. 1999. A Partnership in Peril. *The Financial Times*, March 8.

De Palma, Anthony. 2001. Citing European Banana Quotas, Chiquita Says Bankruptcy Looms. *New York Times*, January 17.

Eames, Sarah. 2019. Number of Family Farms Continue to Decline. *The Daily Star*, April 14.

Evans, Roy. 1999b. WTO Approves U.S. Sanctions. *Journal of Commerce*, April 20.

Farmsworth, Clyde H. 1983. U.S. Raises Tariff for Motorcycles. *New York Times*, April 2.
The *Financial Times*. 1998. Banana Split. December 18: Editorial.
Financial Times. 2001. Chiquita Shares Halve on Debt Woe. January 17.
———. 2016. Fyffes/Sumitomo: Good Picking. December 9.
———. 1998. The U.S. and E.U. Go Bananas. November 11: Editorial.
Frantz, Douglas. 1998. Chiquita Still Under a Cloud After Newspaper's Retreat. *The New York Times*, July 17.
Gallagher, Mike, and Cameron McWhirter. 1998. Contributions Buy Influence. *Cincinnati Enquirer*, May 3.
Herbert, Bob. 1996. In America; Banana Bully. *New York Times*, May 13: A 15.
Ingraham, Christopher, and Howard Schneider. 2014. Industry Voice Dominate the Trade Advisory System. *Washington Post*, February 27.
Jamaica Gleaner. 2015. Taiwan Writes off Half of Grenada's Debt. January 8.
———. 2019. Drug Trafficking is a Global Problem Foisted upon the Caribbean Countries. June 18.
———. 2012. Grenada Wins Court Judgement in Taiwan Debt Dispute. June 30.
James, Canute. 1995a. Caribbean Lose Patience with U.S. Over Banana Row. *Financial Times*, July 13.
———. 1996a. U.S. Banana Move Shocks Caribbean. *Financial Times*, April 30.
———. 1996b. Caribbean Leaders Ask Canada for Assistance in Banana Dispute. *Journal of Commerce*.
———. 1997a. Caribbean Leaders Want Bananas on the Plate. *Journal of Commerce*, May 7.
———. 1997b. Caribbean U.S. Blame Each Other in Banana Split. *Journal of Commerce*, December 15.
———. 1995b. Clinton Backs Preferences for Caribbean Bananas. *Journal of Commerce*, June 20.
James, Canute, and George Parker. 1999. U.S. Faces Caribbean Threat to Quit Drugs Treaty. *Financial Times*, March 8.
James, Canute, and James Wilson. 1999. The Big Place of the Banana in a Small Part of the World. *Financial Times*, March 19.
Journal of Commerce. 1997. Ending Banana Insanity. April 11.
———. 1999. Importers Go Bananas Over Sanctions on E.U. Trade. March 5.
Knight, Franklin W. 2007. Caribbean Diplomacy in Washington. *The Jamaica Observer*, January 24.
Koppel, Naomi. 1999. Banana Dispute Deadlocks U.S., E.U. *Washington Times*, January 26.
Lamb, Christina. 1999. U.S. Action on Bananas a Nightmare for Islands. *Washington Times*, March 9.
Maggs, John. 1995. In Banana Dispute, Discretion Gives Way to Politics. *Journal of Commerce*, May 2.

Marquis, Christopher. 1996. Bananas or Drugs, Caribbean Tells U.S. *Miami Herald*, June 13.
Martin, Susan Taylor. 1997. Banana War Squeezes Tiny Dominica. *The Washington Times*, April 15.
McWhirter, Cameron, and Mike Gallagher. 1998. Island Economies on the Line. *Cincinnati Enquirer*, May 3.
McWhirther, Cameron, and Mike Gallagher. 1998. Influence: This is Just Money Politics. *Cincinnati Enquirer*, May 3.
Moran, Joe. 2009. Defining Moment: The Banana Returns to Britain, December 30, 1945. *Financial Times*, July 31.
Navarro, Mireya. 1999. Outpost in Bananas and Marijuana Wars. *New York Times*, March 4.
Ogletree, Charles, and Randall Robinson. 1999. The Banana War's Missing Link—Campaign Funding. *The Christian Science Monitor*, March 31.
Olson, Elizabeth. 1999. Banana Talks with Europe Turn Nasty. *The New York Times*, January 26.
Peale, Cliff. 1996. Report Blasts Chiquita's Honduran Links. *Washington Post*, November 21.
Rangel, Charles. 1999. Will Dispute Squash Banana Growers. *Washington Times*, February 16.
Safire, Wiliam. 1997. Bananagate. *The New York Times*, March 26.
Sanger, David E. 1998. U.S.—Europe Trade War Looms Over Bananas. *New York Times*, December 22.
Stewart, Lucretia. 1994. Bananas are Their Only Fruit: The Trade which Sustains the Windward Islands. *The Independent*, September 4.
Sweeney, John P. 1999. The High Cost of Clinton's Trade War with the European Union. *The Heritage Foundation*, March 26.
The Daily Gleaner. 1999. Clinton Lied. March 19.
The Jamaica Gleaner. 1999. E.U. MP Backs Caribbean in Banana Trade Dispute. April 16.
The Miami Herald. 1998. Caribbean Disturbance. August 10: Editorial.
The Washington Times. 1997. Caribbean Growers' Lobby Goes Bananas. April 16.
Thurow, Lester C. 1999. When Trade Partners Go Bananas, Don't Ease Up; Get Tough. *USA Today*, March 31.
Washington Post. 2000. Banana Republic. October 26.
Weisskopf, Michael. 1997b. The Busy Back Door Men. *Time Magazine*, March 31: 40.
Wickham, DeWayne. 1995. Banana Wars: Give Caribbean a Break. *USA Today*, May 15.
Williams, Frances. 1999. Island Growers Spike U.S. Sanctions Move. *Financial Times*, January 26.

Winestock, Geoff. 2000. U.S. Starts a Fight with Dole Food Co. In the Banana War. *The Wall Stree Journal*, October 9.
Wolf, Martin. 1999. Going Bananas. *Financial Times*, March 25.
Yeutter, Clayton. 1995. The Banana Battlements. *Washington Times*, August 7.

Reports

2017 International Narcotics Control Strategy Report on Money Laundering and Financial Crimes. 2018. Washington, DC: Department of State.
Arias, Pedro, Cora Dankers, Pascal Liu, and Paul Pilkauskas. 2003b. *The World Banana Economy, 1985–2002.* Rome: Food and Agriculture Organization.
Caribbean Drug Trends 2001–2002. 2003a. Bridgetown: Caribbean Regional, United Nations Office on Drugs and Crime.
Caribbean Human Development Report, Human Development and the Shift to Better Citizen Security. 2012. New York: United Nations.
Crime, Violence and Development: Trends, Costs and Policy Options in the Caribbean. 2007. Washington, DC: World Bank.
Economic and Social Survey. 1967. Kingston: National Planning Agency.
Economic and Social Survey Jamaica 2018. 2019. Kingston: Planning Institute of Jamaica.
Gill, Henry S., and Anthony P. Gonzales. 1995a. *Economic Consequences of a Banana Collapse in the Caribbean.* Caribbean Banana Exporters Association.
Global Overview of Drug Demand and Supply. Latest Trends, Cross Cutting Issues. 2018. Vienna: United Nations.
Godfrey, Claire. 1998. *A Future for Caribbean Bananas—The Importance of Europe's Banana Market to the Caribbean.* Policy Department, Oxfam, UK.
Organisation of Eastern Caribbean States Systematic Regional Diagnostic, Report Number 127046-LAC. 2018. Washington, DC: World Bank, 3.
Report of Eminent Persons Group Mission to Jamaica, Dominica and St. Lucia. 1997b. The Imapact of the United States' Challenge to the European Union Banana Regime on Political, Economic and Soical Order in the Caribbean and Consequences for U.S. National Interests.
The E.U. Banana Regime: Evolution and Implications of its Recent Changes. 2010. Brussels: Directorate-General for External Policies of the Union, Policy Department.
The Economic and Social Contribution of the Banana Industry in the OECS. 1997. Research and Information Department, Eastern Caribbean Central Bank.
The Impact of Banana Supply and Demand Changes on Income, Employment and Food Security. 1999. Rome: Food and Agriculture Organization.
The World Banana Economy, 1970–84, FAO Social and Economic Development Paper No. 57. 1986. Rome: Food and Agriculture Organization.
World Bank Indicators. 2019. Washington, DC: World Bank.

World Economic Outlook April 2017. 2017a. Washington, DC: International Monetary Fund.

Letters

40 Member of Congress. 1997. Letter to President Clinton. July 31.
Ambassadors of the CARIBBEAN Banana Exporting Countries. 1996. Letter to The Hon. Michael Kantor, Secretary of Commerce. April 16.
Ambassador Bernal, Richard L. 1990. Letter to Ms. Rose Lanam, President, Jamaica Awareness Association in Los Angeles. March 15.
Bernal, Richard L. 1999b. Letter to the Editor, The Washington Post. October 23.
Calamarro, Raymond S., C. Christopher Parlin, and David S. Christy. 1995. Letter to Irving A. Williamson, Deputy General Counsel, USTR. February 10.
Caucus, Congressional Black. 1997. Letter to President William Clinton. October 22.
President Clinton, William. 1997a. Letter to Congressman Peter A. DeFazio. December 12.
———. 1997b. Letter to Congresswoman Maxine Waters. December 12.
Cosby, Bill, Earl Graves, Bob Johnson, Ed Lewis, Jesse Jackson, Joseph Lowery, Susan Taylor, and Danny Glover. 1996. Letter to President Clinton. November 6.
Governor of Guam, Guitierrez, Carl T.C. 1999. Letter to Ambassador Richard Bernal. March 11.
(Name of Letter Writer). 1999. Letter to Mr. Aaron T. Manaigo, Chairman, National Council of Black Republicans. March 11.
President of the Jamaica Volunteers Association Morgan, Donald G. 1998. Letter to President William Clinton. November 13.
———. 1998. Letter to the Editor of the Washington Post. December 3.
Prime Minister Patterson, P.J. 1997. Letter to President William J. Clinton. June 2.
———. 1999. Letter to CARICOM Heads of Government. *E.U. Banana Import Regime*, June 15.
Ross-Robinson. 1999. Letter to Mr. Don. Logan. February 10.
Senator Coverdell, Paul D., and Representative Saxby Chambliss. 1998. Letter to Ambassador Charlene Barshefsky. September 9.
USTR Barshefsky, Charlene. 1997. Letter to Congressman Charles Rangel. June 23.
Walters, Maxine, Nancy Kaptur, Roland V. Dellums, Duncan Hunter, and Roscoe G. Bartlett. 1997. Letter to President Clinton from Representatives. June 9.
Waters, Maxine, et al. 1997a. Letter to President William J. Clinton. July 31.
Waters, Maxine, Ronald Dellums, Marcy Kaptur, Duncan Hunter, and Roscoe Bartlett. 1997b. Letter to President William Clinton. June 9.

Other

A Time to Choose. Caribbean Development in the 21st Century. Washington, DC: World Bank, April 2005.

All Information on the Citizenship—Investment Programme Taken from St Kitts & Nevis Citizenship - Investment Programme - aaa-ii.com. Adwww.aaa-ii.com/St. Kitts & Nevis/Passport.

Allison, Bill. NRA Spent Record Amount Lobbying Congress, With Little to Show. Bloomberg, February 5, 2019. https://www.bloomberg.com/.../nra-spent-record-amount-lobbying-congress-with-littl. Feb 5, 2019.

American Apparel & Footwear Association—Wikipedia. https://en.wikipedia.org/wiki/American_Apparel_%26_Footwear_Association. www.citizen.org › about. About Us - Public Citizen. Accessed 8 February, 2020.

Apply for Citizenship—Dominica Citizenship by Investment. https://cbiu.gov.dm/dominica-citizenship/how-to-apply/.

"Banana Dispute Heats Up." Latin America Data Base, News and Educational Services, November 2, 1995.

Banana Production in the Caribbean—Wikipedia. https://en.wikipedia.org/wiki/Banana_production_in_the_Caribbean.

Bernal, Richard L. NAFTA at Three: The Case for NAFTA Parity. Statement submitted to the House on Ways and Means Trade Subcommittee, House of Representative One Hundred Fifth Congress, First Session, September 11, 1997. Washington, DC: Government Printing Office, 1998. pages 261–263.

Bernal, Richard, ambassador of Jamaica to the U.S. remarked: "Support for continued membership by Caribbean countries in the World Trade Organization is eroding because of the WTO ruling.…Caribbean countries generally have been favourably disposed toward multilateral institutions…They saw these institutions as a protective shield.…but nowadays sentiment is changing following the WTO ruling". Michelle Williams, "Caribbean Shiprider Agreements Sunk by Banana Trade War", University of Miami Inter-American Law Review, Vol. 31, No.1. Spring, 2000. pages 163–195.

Caribbean Drug Trends 2001–2002. Bridgetown: Caribbean Regional, United Nations Office on Drugs and Crime, February, 2003.

Caribbean Human Development Report, Human Development and the Shift to Better Citizen Security 2012. New York: United Nations, 2012.

Caribbean Tourism Overview—Caribbean Tourism Organization. https://www.onecaribbean.org/content/files/TourismOverview.pdf

CARICOM's Intra-Regional Trade, Vol. 1 1990–2000. Georgetown: CARICOM Secretariat, 2992. page 6.

Carla Anderson Hills—Wikipedia. https://en.wikipedia.org/wiki/Carla_Anderson_Hills.

Charlene Barshefsky—Wikipedia. https://en.wikipedia.org/wiki/Charlene_Barshefsky.

"Chinese Mother and Daughter with Antigua & Barbuda CIP Passports wanted by Chinese Gov", Times Caribbean, January 26, 2016.

Crime, Violence and Development: Trends, Costs and Policy Options in the Caribbean. Washington, DC: World Bank, 2007.

Dame Mary Eugenia Charles. A personal reflection on her legacysearchlight.vc › searchlight › features › 2008/10/03 › dame-mary-eug... Oct 3, 2008.

Development—Special and differential treatment provisions—WTO. https://www.wto.org. Accessed 1 September, 2019.

Dominica Offers Citizenship to Chinese Investors for $200,000 ... dominicanewsonline.com/.../business/dominica-offers-citizenship-to-chinese-investors... Apr 1, 2015.

"Dominica: Much Ado about Bananas", The Courier, N°140. July–Aug 1993.

EC Fact Sheet on Caribbean Bananas and the WTO, Memo/97/28. Brussels: European Commission, 18 March, 1997.

Eisenhower, Dwight. The Military–Industrial Complex: The Farewell Address of President Eisenhower, delivered January 17, 1961. See http://www.americanrhetoric.com/speeches/dwightdeisenhowerfarewell.html. and James Ledbetter, Unwarranted Influence: Dwight D. Eisenhower and the Military-Industrial Complex. New Haven: Yale University Press, 2011.

Embassy of Jamaica, Report of the Western Hemisphere Banana Meeting, Coral Gables, Miami, April 9, 1996.

Escaping the Poverty Trap. The Least Developed Countries Report 2002. Geneva: United Nations Conference on Trade and Development, 2002.

"EU's Banarama-Slipping." World Bank, Development Brief, No. 50. March, 1995.

FAO. 1985. *World Banana Economy, 1970–84*. Rome: Food and Agriculture Organization.

For more detail see Gordon Myers, Banana Wars. The Price of Free Trade. A Caribbean Perspective. London: Zed Books, 2004.

ec.europa.eu › sites › agriculture › files › sugar › doc › sugar-faq_en. Frequently Asked Questions The Abolition of EU Sugar ... Oct 1, 2016. Accessed 7 February 2020.

Generalized System of Preferences (GSP) | United States. ustr.gov › issue-areas › trade-development › preference-programs › g. Accessed 14 February 2020.

Gill, Henry S., and Anthony P. Gonzales. Economic Consequences of a Banana Collapse in the Caribbean, Report prepared for the CARICOM Secretariat, May 1995. 62 pages.

Girvan, Norman. 1986. Notes on Jamaica's External Debt. In *The Debt Problem in Jamaica, Monograph No. 1, Economics Department*, ed. Omar Davis. Mona, Jamaica: University of the West Indies.

In Internal E.U. Politics is Well Discussed in Gordon Myers, Banana Wars. The Price of Free Trade. A Caribbean Perspective. London: Zed Books, 2004.

Inter-American Development Bank, Caribbean Region Quarterly Bulletin, Revising Fiscal Challenges, 6 (3), September, 2017.

Intergovernmental Group on Bananas CCP; BA 1991/7. Rome: Food and Agriculture Organization, 1991.

International Narcotics Control Strategy Report on Money Laundering and Financial Crimes Vol. II, 2017. Washington, DC: Department of State, 2018.

"Interview with Edison James, Leader of the Opposition." The Courier N°140. July–Aug, 1993.

Ishmael, Odeen. The Impact of the September 11 Terrorist Attack Against the United States on the Caribbean Political Economy. www.guyana.org/Speeches/ishmael_112801.html. Nov 29, 2001

Lamy Hails Accord Ending Long Running Banana Dispute. Press/591 15 December 2009. WTO: 2009 Press Releases.

Letter to President Clinton from Representatives Maxine Waters, Nancy Kaptur, Ronald V. Dellums, Duncan Hunter and Roscoe G. Bartlett, June 9, 1997.

Lobbying Spending Database Defense. 2019. penSecrets. https://www.opensecrets.org/lobby/indus.php?id.

Main Causes of the Banana War. www.soc.duke.edu/. Accessed 27 March 2020.

Memorandum from the Caribbean Banana Exporters Association. Select Committee on International Development Minutes of Evidence. www.Parliament.UK. Accessed 7 March 2020.

Military-Industrial Complex Speech, Dwight D. Eisenhower. 1961. Public Papers of the Presidents, Dwight D. Eisenhower, 1960. coursesa.matrix.msu.edu/~hst306/.../indust.htm. Accessed 2 November 2014.

Military—Lockheed Martin. https://www.lockheedmartinjobs.com/military.

Multinational Corporations: An Overview. http://www.sharing.org/information-centre/articles/multinational-corporations-overview

Opioid Overdose | Drug Overdose | CDC Injury Center. https://www.cdc.gov/drugoverdose. Accessed 23 December, 2019.

Perry, Dan. Jamaica Criticizes US On Banana War, Associated Press, March 21, 1999. Apply for Citizenship—Dominica Citizenship by Investment. https://cbiu.gov.dm/dominica-citizenship/how-to-apply/.

Report of Eminent Persons Group mission to Jamaica, Dominica and St. Lucia, The Impact of the United States Challenge to the European Union Banana Regime on Political, Economic and Social Order in the Caribbean and the Consequences for U.S. National Interests. January, 1997a.

Report of the CARICOM Secretariat, Caribbean/United States Summit, REP. 97/1/61 CAR/US, Bridgetown, Barbados, November 4, 1997, page 13.

Report of the Sugar Industry Commission 1944–1945. Kingston: Jamaica Sugar Industry Commissions, 1945.

"Report on The Impact of the United States Challenge to the European Union Banana Regime on Political, Economic and Social Order in the Caribbean, and the Consequences for U.S. National Interests", Eminent Persons Group, Mission to Jamaica, Dominica and St. Lucia, January 1997.

Review of United States Foreign Policy, Hearing before the Committee on International Relations, House of Representatives, One Hundred Fourth Congress, Second session, July 31, 1996. Washington, DC: Government Printing Office, 1997.

Sanchez, Ray. Summit's Issue: Bananas/In the Caribbean, Trade Dispute Tops for Clinton, May 11, 1997. https://www.newsday.com/mainnews/rnmi0207.htm

www.fas.usda.gov › programs › sugar-import-program. Sugar Import Program | USDA Foreign Agricultural Service. Accessed 6 February 2020.

The Doha Round Texts and Related Documents. Geneva: World Trade Organization, 2009.

The EU Banana Regime: Evolution and Implications of its Recent Changes. European Parliament, Directorate-General for External Policies, Policy Department, 2010.

The Geneva Agreement on Trade in Bananas (GATB) is reproduced in and explained in Eckart Guth. The End of the Bananas Saga. Journal of World Trade, 46 (1). 2012.

The Politics of the Process is Discussed in Detail in Peter Clegg, The Caribbean Banana Trade. From Colonialism to Globalization. London: Palgrave Macmillan, 2002.

The Report of the West India Royal Commission. The Moyne Report. Kingston: Ian Randle Publishers, 2012.

The US/EU Banana Dispute, European Union News, No. 96/98, November 10, 1998.

The World Banana Economy. 1970–84. FAO Social and Economic Development Paper No. 57. Rome: Food and Agriculture Organization, 1986.

Timeline: Highlights of the 15-year Airbus, Boeing Trade War ... Accessed 7 February, 2020. ustr.gov › policy-offices › press-office › press-releases › october › us-... US Wins $7.5 Billion Award in Airbus Subsidies Case – USTR. Oct 2, 2019.

U.S. EU Sign Agreement Designed to Settle Bananas Dispute ...geneva.usmission.gov › 2010/06/08 › u-s-eu-sign-agreement-bananas. Jun 8, 2010.

"U.S. Official: Changes in Banana Preferences would Not Hurt Caribbean." March 10, 1999. Associated Press. www.reuters.com › article › us-wto-aircraft-timeline › timeline-highlight...

"U.S. Will Not Impose Sanctions On Costa Rican, Colombian Bananas." Latin America Data Base, News and Educational Services, 25 January, 1996.

Union Members Summary—Bureau of Labor Statistics. www.bls.gov › news.release › union2.nr0.htm. Jan 22, 2020.

United States Trade Representative. https://ustr.gov/

US: St. Kitts Citizenship Program is Being Abused | Daily Mail Online. www.dailymail.co.uk/wires/ap/article.../US-St-Kitts-citizenship-program-abused.html. May 22, 2014.

World Development Indicators. Washington, DC: World Bank, 2019.

World Economic Outlook April 2017. Washington, DC: International Monetary Fund, 2017.

World Investment Report, 1998: Trends and Determinants. Geneva: United Nations, 1998.

World Investment Report 2015. New York and Geneva: United Nations, 2015.

"World Trade Organization Sides with Chiquita Brands International Versus European Union Trade Preferences." U.S. News and World Report, May 12, 1997 and Thomas K. Grose, "Two Sides of the Banana Split. Fyffes: Looking for Stability", USA Today, March 3, 1999.

World Trade Report 2011: The WTO and Preferential Trade Agreements: From co-Existence to Coherence. Geneva: World Trade Organization, 2011.

WTO | Regional trade agreements and preferential trade arrangements. https://www.wto.org/english/tratop_e/region_e/rta_pta_e.htm. Accessed 1 June 2019.

WTO Banana Ruling Devastating Blow to Vulnerable Caribbean Economies, Caribbean Community (CARICOM) Press Release Ref #: 12/200504, August 2005.

Index[1]

A

ACP banana exporting countries, 84
ACP EU Sugar Protocol, 83
Adjustment financing, 75
Advisory Centre on WTO Law, 155
Advisory Committee for Trade Policy and Negotiations (ACTPN), 18
Africa, 4, 41, 67, 78, 80, 83–85, 111
African American community, 145, 147, 148
African, Caribbean and Pacific Group (ACP), 7, 80, 83, 85, 89, 95n60, 123, 155, 162, 184, 185
Agricultural employment, 6
Aid, 7–9, 21, 50, 51, 64, 70–73, 75, 77, 81–84, 89, 90, 120, 137, 144, 150, 161, 163, 189–190, 209, 210, 213, 214, 216, 219, 225–227
Albright, Secretary of State Madeleine, 125, 139, 151
American Apparel & Footwear Association (AAFA), 19
American capitalism, 28
American Enterprise Institute, 20, 90n1, 233n46
American Farm Bureau Federation, 149, 173n153
American Federation of Labor and Congress of Industrial Organizations (AFL-CIO), 21
American Financial Corporation, 131
American Financial Group, 100, 128, 228
American Society for International Law, 157
Americas Trade, 22
Anglo-American Commission, 49
Anthony, Kenny (Prime Minister), 180, 225
Anti-dumping activities, 44
Antigua and Barbuda, 42, 186, 197, 208, 212, 213, 216
Anti-trust legislation, 179
Archer, Congressman, 105

[1] Note: Page numbers followed by 'n' refer to notes.

R. L. Bernal, *Corporate versus National Interest in US Trade Policy*, https://doi.org/10.1007/978-3-030-56950-1

Arellano, Oswaldo Lopez (President), 100, 103
Argentina, 45
Arnold, Guy, 111
Arthur, Owen (Prime Minister), 125
Associated Press, 145

B

Bahamas, The, 42, 174n160, 186, 193, 195, 208, 211, 212, 215, 222, 233n58
Baker, Captain Lorenzo Dow, 47, 99, 121
Banana Export Company of Jamaica (BECO), 156
Banana exporting countries, 4, 6, 44, 46, 75, 79, 80, 85, 86, 88, 102, 118, 120, 128, 136, 144, 145, 149, 150, 153, 155, 156, 163, 179, 180, 185, 186, 191, 195, 197, 212, 224, 225
Banana exporting islands, 6, 7, 90, 181, 187, 191, 225
Banana exports, 4, 8, 42, 49, 52, 53, 75, 80, 84, 100, 102, 103, 120, 121, 182–184, 187, 188, 219
Banana farming, 51–52, 182, 189, 223
Banana Framework Agreement (BFA), 86, 87, 144
Bananagate, 130
Banana imports, 7, 78, 81, 85, 108, 117–119, 131, 132, 137, 150, 183
Banana industry, 2, 4, 6, 8, 21, 41, 46–54, 56n25, 83, 84, 106, 119–121, 126, 135, 139, 143, 148, 151, 156, 157, 159, 161, 180–183, 185–187, 189, 190, 200n36, 226, 227
Banana Protocol, 78, 85, 86
Bananarama Report, 137
Banana regime of 1993, 79
Banana Republics, 52, 121, 135, 165n31
Banana Trade Advisory Committee Bankruptcy, 78
Banana war, 51, 107, 109–110, 120, 161, 162
Bankruptcy, 10, 51, 88, 111–112, 162, 228
Barbados, 42, 45, 47, 118, 125, 139, 151, 174n160, 174n162, 180, 186, 189, 193, 195, 208, 209, 213, 215, 225, 233n58
Barbados Accord, 152
Barshefsky, Charlene, 27, 126, 132, 141, 143, 151
Bauxite, 49, 217, 219, 223
Beaupre, Lawrence K., 104, 133
Beef hormones and banana resolution, 132, 149
Beggar thy neighbor policies, 14, 109
Belize, 42, 43, 52, 53, 67, 117, 120, 121, 125, 145, 149, 151, 156, 186, 194, 195, 205n110, 208, 213, 215, 222, 224
Bernal, Richard (Ambassador Dr), 89, 91n6, 93n25, 93n27, 93n32, 94n39, 96n67, 97n74, 134–136, 143, 146, 148, 153, 159, 160, 174n160, 175n177, 192, 198n7, 205n108, 230n9, 232n43
Bilateral development assistance, 72
Bishop, Maurice (Prime Minister), 9, 210, 222
Black, Eli M., 100
Blake, Byron, 151, 157
Boeing, 26, 30
Bolivarian Alliance for the Peoples of Our America (ALBA), 181, 212
Borrell, Brent, 137, 153, 184
Boston Fruit Company, 47, 100, 121

Bowles, Erskine (Chief of Staff), 106
Brazil, 41, 45, 89, 151
Bridgetown Accord, 136, 139, 152, 160, 219
Britain, 5, 14, 15, 28, 44, 46–50, 75–78, 80–82, 85, 89, 110, 111, 120, 122, 123, 150, 162, 181
British banana market, 51
British government, 23, 49–51, 77, 78, 81, 102, 120, 150
British policy in the Caribbean, 77
British trade policy, 75
Brittan, Sir Leon, 88, 128, 140, 156
Brookings Institution, 20, 35n40, 91n10, 137
Burnham, Forbes (President), 210
Bush, George W. (President), 221
Business Week, 145

C

Cabinet, 20, 25–27
Calamaro, Ray S., 118, 145
Campaign contributions, 22, 24, 128–130, 141, 148
Canada, 5, 23, 35n40, 45, 76, 77, 82, 89, 96n66, 151, 173n159, 196, 223
Canada-West Indian Reciprocal Treaty, 82
Canada-West Indian Trade Agreement 1925, 82
Canada-West Indies Agreement, 76
Canary Islands, 47, 79, 85
Capitalism, 28
Caribbean, 2, 21, 41–54, 63, 99, 117–163, 179–197, 207–229
Caribbean Americans, 146
Caribbean and Central American countries, 9
Caribbean Banana Exporters Association (CBEA), 118, 138, 142, 149, 150, 187, 190, 201n61
Caribbean banana exporting countries, 2, 7, 8, 43, 84, 157, 188
Caribbean Basin Economic Recovery Act (CBERA), 5, 7, 9, 90, 189, 221
Caribbean Basin Initiative (CBI), 7, 9, 44, 117, 137, 142, 147, 166n42, 189, 221
Caribbean Basin Security Initiative (CBSI), 224
Caribbean business community, 184
Caribbean-Canada Trade Agreement (CARIBCAN), 76, 82
Caribbean Commission, 49
Caribbean Common Market and Community (CARICOM), 43–46, 117, 126, 136, 139, 148, 150–152, 157, 159, 160, 165n19, 180, 181, 186, 190, 193, 211, 213, 225
Caribbean community in the United States, 123, 146
Caribbean economies, 44, 76, 137, 139, 188, 215
Caribbean Free Trade Association (CARIFTA), 45
Caribbean governments, 6–8, 123, 130, 134, 145, 149–151, 180, 194, 211, 226
Caribbean islands, 2, 4, 8, 46, 47, 84, 112, 191
Caribbean private sector, 149
Caribbean Textiles and Apparel Institute, 160
Caribbean-US relations, 136, 151
Caribbean US Summit Bridgetown, 151
Castro, Fidel (President), 136, 210, 212
Cato Institute, 20
Cavendish bananas, 41
CBERA legislation, 7
Center for Immigration Studies, 222

Center for Strategic and International Studies, 20, 91n6
Centers for Disease Control and Prevention report, 29
Central America, 5, 9, 25, 43, 46, 47, 50–53, 78, 79, 81, 92n15, 99–102, 106, 119, 121, 150, 181, 210, 214–216, 224
Central Intelligence Agency (CIA), 122
Centre for Strategic and International Studies, 219
Chabot, Steve, 129, 141
Chamberlain, Colonial Secretary Joseph, 51
Charles, Eugenia (Prime Minister), 30, 184, 185, 191, 198n19, 201n60
Chavez, Hugo (President), 26, 212
Chile, 25
China, 8, 23, 41, 181, 196, 197, 208, 210, 213–216, 225, 227
Chiquita, 2, 5–10, 25, 30, 31, 42, 79, 84, 86–88, 99–112, 117–163, 183, 185, 191, 225, 226, 228–229
Chiquita Brands International Corporation, 5
Christian Science Monitor, 148
Christopher, Warren, 118, 124, 145, 192
Churchill, Winston, 111
Cincinnati Enquirer, 102, 103, 126, 133, 148, 186
Citizenship by Investment Program, 195, 196
Clinton, Bill (President), 4, 104, 106, 118, 119, 123, 124, 129, 130, 138–141, 147, 151, 152, 157, 159, 161, 163, 192, 210
Clinton administration, 2, 6, 7, 88, 104, 109, 110, 118, 123, 127, 130, 139–143, 162, 191
Clinton-CARICOM Summit, 139
CNN, 131, 135, 145
Cocaine trafficking, 160, 191, 223, 224
Coke, Christopher "Dudus", 192
Cold War, 36n52, 111, 136, 210
Colombia, 41, 42, 79, 85, 86, 89, 99, 102, 104, 106, 133, 144, 190, 191, 227, 229
Colonial Development Welfare Act, 49
Common Agricultural Policy, 85
Commonwealth Banana Exporters Association (CBEA), 149
Commonwealth Secretariat, 45, 67, 92n17, 92n18, 93n28
Commonwealth Sugar Agreement, 76
Commonwealth sugar producers, 77
Communism, 5, 106, 184, 222, 223
Compensatory financing, 74
Compton, John, 130
Congress, 3, 13, 16–19, 22, 24, 35n40, 104–106, 118, 123, 125, 129, 131, 132, 134, 140–146, 149, 151, 157–159, 161, 166n42, 208, 209, 211, 227, 229n2
Congressional Black Caucus, 142, 143, 145, 161, 185
Congressional Research Service, 17, 19
Consultative process, 15, 29, 110, 152
Cooperative socialism, 9
Corporate dominance, 29
Corporate interests, 6, 23, 29–31, 101, 106, 109, 118, 134
Corporate reorganization, 73, 74
Corporations on trade policy, 23–25
Corruption, 191, 208, 219, 226
Costa Rica, 41, 42, 46, 53, 79, 85, 86, 89, 99, 102, 103, 144, 193, 214, 221, 229
Cotonou Agreement, 67, 82

Council on Foreign Relations, 20, 33n26
Council on Hemispheric Affairs (COHA), 21, 138
Cox News Service, 104
Crane, Congressman, 105
Cuba, 8, 25, 43, 47, 51, 166n42, 181, 189, 208–212, 218, 222, 227
Cuban Revolution, 210
Cutrale and Safra Group, 10, 228

D
Daschle, Tom, 106
Debt exchanges, 195
Debt financed growth, 194
Debt problem, 194, 195
Debt relief, 9, 44, 227
Debt restructuring, 194, 195, 216
Decree 100, 101
Defense Department, 24
Defense industry, 26
Del Monte Foods Inc, 42, 144
Del Monte Pacific Limited, 42
Democracy, 1, 2, 9, 21, 28, 43, 102, 117, 118, 140, 157, 161, 188, 192, 208, 209, 216, 219, 220, 225–227
Democratic National Committee (DNC), 104, 131
Democratic Party, 27, 104, 110, 123, 129, 140, 142
Democratic Republic of China, 214
Democratic Socialism, 9, 210
Denmark, 80, 88
Department of Agriculture, 220
Department of Commerce, 18
Developing countries, 5, 7, 9, 13, 21, 23, 44, 45, 63–72, 74, 75, 80, 81, 83, 85, 89, 137, 152, 154, 155, 175n179, 183, 214, 217–220, 225, 226
Development aid, 5, 7, 50, 82, 83, 89, 90, 190, 208, 214
Development financing, 73–75, 215, 216
DeWine, Senator Mike, 129, 141
Diplomatic interests, 15
Discriminatory tariff regimes, 66
Diversification, 70, 72, 83, 138, 142, 143, 161, 163, 188, 227
Doha Development Agenda (DDA), 68
Doha Ministerial meeting, 65
Dole, Bob, 104, 129, 130, 141, 142, 144
Dole Foods, 42, 78, 86, 107, 108, 111, 121, 126, 131, 132, 144, 163, 228
Dominica, 4, 42–45, 47, 52, 90, 120, 125, 126, 148, 149, 151, 156, 180, 182, 184–187, 195, 196, 201n52, 208, 212, 213, 215, 216, 223, 225
Dominican banana industry, 47, 52, 120, 182, 185, 186
Dominican Republic, 42, 43, 149, 160, 209, 211, 212, 215, 217, 221, 222
Dominican Republic-Central American Free Trade Agreement, 221
Douglas, Dr. Denzil (Prime Minister), 52, 120, 189
Dreier, David (Congressman), 105
Drug smuggling, 44
Drug trafficking, 2, 8, 135, 136, 148, 160, 185, 190–192, 209, 216, 219, 223, 224, 226, 227

E
Eastern Caribbean banana exports, 2, 47, 53, 84, 183
Eastern Caribbean banana producing islands, 6

Eastern Caribbean Central Bank, 183
Eastern Caribbean islands, 2
East India Company, 23
Economic collapse, 4, 138
Economic crisis, 8, 14, 183–184, 194, 195, 216
Economic growth, 4, 9, 13, 15, 31, 45, 54, 63, 64, 66, 69, 70, 81, 154, 183–184, 193, 195, 197, 217, 219, 225
Economic Partnership Agreement between the European Union and CARIFORUM, 82
Economist, The, 19, 22, 137, 153, 185
Ecuador, 41, 42, 52, 53, 87, 89, 102, 103, 119, 163, 212, 229
EEC banana market, 78–79
El Salvador, 89, 215, 221
Eisenhower, Dwight D. (President), 24, 26
Elder Dempster, 48
Elders and Fyffes, 48, 51, 81
Employment, 4, 6–8, 13, 30, 49, 54, 66, 70, 75, 120, 163, 180, 182, 185, 218, 223
Enabling Clause, 64, 72
Engel, Elliot, 227
English-speaking Caribbean (ESC), 76, 77, 181, 184, 186, 189, 208, 209, 215, 225
Enhanced Integrated Framework for Trade Related Assistance (EIF), 73
Enterprise for the Americas Initiative, 43
Esquivel, Manuel (Prime Minister), 117
EU agriculture ministers, 162
EU banana and beef hormones ruling, 149
EU banana regime, 2, 4–8, 10, 31, 46, 63–90, 99, 104, 105, 107, 108, 111, 118, 124, 125, 132, 135, 137–140, 143, 144, 152, 153, 157–163, 179, 181, 182, 184–187, 189, 190, 197, 209, 219, 225–229
EU policy, 7
EU preferential banana import regime, 2, 7
European colonies, 4
European Commission, 108, 131, 162
European Common Market (ECM), 78, 79, 82
European Court of Justice, 162
European Economic Community (EEC), 50, 78–79, 85
European Union (EU), 2, 19, 42, 63–90, 99, 117, 179, 209
EU trade policies, 131
EU-US solutions, 132
EU-US Summit of Heads of Government, 161
EU-US trade disputes, 30, 134, 137
Export earnings, 8, 67, 81, 181, 186
Export markets, 31, 44, 53, 121, 156, 208, 217
ExxonMobil, 26

F

FAO banana conference 1998, 107, 126
Federal Bureau of Investigations (FBI), 134
Federal bureaucracy, 3, 27
Federal government, 17, 18, 20, 23, 24, 26, 27, 146
Fiji, 67
Financial aid, 9, 50, 73, 161, 180, 189, 190, 209, 216, 225, 226
Financial crisis 2008, 194, 220, 226

Financial Times, 19, 22, 126, 127, 137, 153, 157
First come, first served (FCFS) system for banana imports, 108, 131
Food and Agriculture Organization (FAO), 41, 87, 107, 126
Foreign Corrupt Practices Act 1977, 103
Foreign direct investments (FDI), 9, 45, 183, 210, 214, 215, 217–219, 227
Foreign exchange earnings, 4, 54, 66, 181, 187, 188
Fortune, 22, 27, 229
France, 5, 6, 43, 78, 80, 81, 85, 89, 110, 155, 162
Franc Zone, 78
Frateli group, 118
Free trade, 14, 15, 29, 31, 43, 75, 84, 90, 126, 135, 137, 138, 152, 153, 184, 185
Free trade advocates, 31, 65
Free trade agreement (FTA), 46, 214, 221
Free trade rules, 129
Fyffes, 42, 51, 78, 108, 120, 150, 183, 228

G

Gallagher, Michael, 103, 104
Gardner, Page S., 118
GATT challenge, 85–87
GATT/WTO system, 79, 84
Geest, 50–52, 78, 120, 155, 183
Geithner, Tim, 26
General Agreement on Tariffs and Trade (GATT), 64, 78, 79, 84–89, 154
General Dynamics, 26
Generalized system of preferences (GSP), 66, 67, 71, 72, 83, 220–221
General Motors, 30, 106
Geneva Agreement on Trade in Bananas (GATB), 89
Gephardt, Richard, 106, 142
Germany, 78, 80, 85, 86, 111, 155
Gill, Henry, 53, 138, 187
Gingrich, Newt, 105, 106, 141, 144
Girvan, Norman, 194
Gleason, Ms., 107, 126
Glenn, John (Senator), 141, 144
Global banana industry, 41
Global economic crisis, 14, 194, 216
Global financial crisis, 184, 194, 220, 226
Global liberalization, 66
Global trade, 14, 69
Global Trade Watch, 21, 148, 185
Golding, Bruce (Prime Minister), 216
Gonsalves, Camillo (Minister of Foreign Affairs), 90
Gonzales, Anthony P. (Dr.), 53, 138, 187
Gore, Al (Vice President), 104
Great Britain, 43, 155
Great Depression, 14, 15, 49, 77, 109
Grenada, 4, 9, 42–47, 49, 52, 120, 125, 145, 149, 151, 184, 186, 194–196, 208, 210, 215, 222, 227
Grenada invasion, 44, 184, 209, 222
Guadeloupe, 43, 78, 79, 85
Guardian, 22, 110
Guatemala, 5, 21, 23, 25, 41, 42, 53, 79, 85–87, 89, 101, 102, 106, 121, 122, 131, 133, 144, 221, 229
Guyana, 9, 26, 42, 44, 67, 118, 151, 159, 186, 195, 208–210, 212, 215, 217, 219, 223

H
Hagin, Joseph, 129, 162
Haiti, 43, 166n42, 186, 191, 209, 212, 215–217, 222
Hall, Marshall (Dr.), 149, 151, 158
Hamilton, Alexander (Treasury Secretary), 14
Harley-Davidson Motor Company, 30
Harvard Business School, 29
Hawaii Banana Industry Association, 87, 123
Heaven, Derek (High Commissioner), 157
Helms-Burton Act, 211
Heritage Foundation, 20, 126, 127
Hills, Carla A, 27, 185
Honduras, 21, 41, 87, 89, 100, 102, 103, 106, 131, 133, 138, 144, 221, 229
Hudson Institute, 20
Human trafficking, 8, 222, 224

I
Illegal immigration, 148
Immigration, 132, 144
Import Duties Act, 75, 77
India, 23, 41, 132
Industrialization, 76
Industrial Revolution, 15
Infant industries, 14, 66
Inside U.S. Trade, 19, 22
Institute for International Economics (IIE), 20, 21, 137
Inter-American Convention against the Illicit Manufacturing of and Trafficking in Firearms, Ammunition, Explosives and Other Related Materials, 224
Inter-American Development Bank, 184, 193–195, 210, 216
Inter-American relations, 21
Interest groups, 2, 3, 13, 18–20, 27, 28, 31
International banana trade, 48, 108, 132
International competitiveness, 15, 31, 64, 73
International economic order, 15
Internationalists *vs.* isolationists, 31
International Labour Organization (ILO), 186
International Monetary Fund (IMF), 6, 74, 75, 160, 183, 195
International Narcotics Control Strategy Report, 196, 225
International Organization for Migration, 222
International Trade Commission, 17, 19
International trade policy, 3, 10, 17, 21, 31, 154
Iran, 106
Isolationism, 14
Italy, 80

J
Jackson Lee, Sheila, 105, 146
Jamaica, 4, 9, 42–54, 77, 78, 81, 99, 102, 112, 118–122, 134, 140, 145–149, 151, 152, 156, 160, 180, 181, 183, 185, 186, 192–195, 208–213, 215–219, 223, 224
Jamaica banana industry, 46–48
Jamaica Banana Producers Association, 47, 48, 119
Jamaica Fruit Importing and Trading Company, 47
Jamaica Marketing Company Limited (JAMCO), 78, 156
Jamaica Producers, 78, 112, 118, 149, 158, 183

Jamaica Volunteers Association, 147
James, Canute, 137
James, Prime Minister Edison, 125, 126, 139, 151, 156, 158
Japan, 23, 132, 217
John F. Kennedy School of Government, 21
Joint Action Plan on China-Costa Rica Cooperation 2016–2020, 215
Journal of Commerce, 135, 145, 153

K
Kantor, Michael, 27
Kennedy, John (President), 21, 210
Koeppel, Dan, 104, 122

L
Labor organizations, 21–22
Labour in the West Indies, 76
Latin America and the Caribbean, 22, 214
Laurent, Ambassador Edwin, 157
Least developed countries (LDCs), 64, 67, 69, 71–73, 154
Lewis, Arthur, 76
Lewis, Dr Vaughn, 139, 151
Liberalization of international trade, 14, 15, 84
Lindner, Carl, 10, 100, 103–106, 110, 121, 122, 125, 128–131, 133, 135, 139–142, 144, 148, 163, 228
Lobbying process, 29
Lobbyists, 19–20, 23, 26–28, 107, 123, 126, 132, 133, 141, 142, 146, 157, 159, 163
Lockheed Martin, 26, 27
Logan, Don, 134
Lomé Convention, 67, 78–80, 82, 83, 85, 86
Lott, Senator Trent, 105, 106, 135, 141–144

M
MacKay, Governor Bob, 125
McNamara, Robert, 26
McWhirter, Cameron, 103
Maduro, Nicholas, 212, 213
Manley, Norman, 102, 122
Manley, Prime Minister Michael, 209, 210, 212
Marijuana, 134, 190, 191, 223, 227
Marrakesh Agreement, 154
Martinique, 43, 78, 79, 85
Maurer documents, 3
Mauritius, 67, 83
Maynard, Minister of Government Charles, 90
Media, 2, 4, 18–20, 22, 118, 123, 131–137, 143, 148, 151, 153, 158, 159, 222
Mellon, Andrew, 26
Mercantilism, 14, 15, 23
Mexico, 23, 87, 89, 131, 219, 222
MFN tariff reductions, 68
Miami Herald, 136
Micro scale manufacturing, 182
Middle-income developing countries, 9, 183
Miller, Dame Billie, 180
Minor, Keith C., 47, 99
Mitchell, Prime Minister James F., 134, 156
Mitchell, Prime Minister Keith, 125
Mnuchin, Steve, 26
Moakley, Congressman, 105
Modern democracy, 1
Money, 16, 20, 26–28, 87, 103, 1t23, 129, 131, 133, 141, 163, 191
Money laundering, 8, 135, 159, 191, 225, 227
Mono-sectoral economies, 2
Montserrat, 42, 186, 208
Moore, Robert, 107, 126
Morgan, Professor Donald, 147
Mossadegh government, 106

Most favored nation (MFN) liberalization, 66
Mottley, CARICOM Chair Mia, 213
Moyne Commission, 49, 77
Moyne Commission Report, 76, 193
Multilateral trading system, 14, 68, 69, 72, 84, 88, 89, 157
Multinational corporations (MNCs), 2, 22–25, 27, 28, 30, 42, 52, 84, 106–108, 131, 132, 136, 149, 185, 217, 219, 225
Multinational enterprises (MNEs), 30
Murder rates in the Caribbean, 193

N

Nader, Ralph, 21, 148
Nano-firms, 73
Narcotics trafficking, 6, 8, 136, 193, 224, 225
National Association of Realtors, 26
National Bureau of Economic Research (NBER), 20
National Coalition on Caribbean Affairs (NCOCA), 146
National Council of Black Republicans (NCBR), 148
National Economic Council, 158
National good, 3, 207
National income volatility, 45, 72
National interest, 1, 2, 6–8, 10, 15, 24, 83, 106–107, 137, 157, 179, 207, 211, 217, 220
National Journal, 145
National Law Journal, 27
National Security Council, 18, 125, 146, 158
National security interests, 2, 6, 8, 9, 208, 219
National trade policies, 1
Natural gas, 213, 217, 223
Neoclassical economics, 15, 24
Neoliberalism, 15
New Deal diplomacy, 25
New Jewel Movement, 9, 210
Newsweek, 22, 129, 133, 135, 148, 159, 180, 192, 209
New York Times, 19, 22, 134, 136, 144
Nicaragua, 9, 79, 86, 89, 102, 210, 212, 221
Noboa, 42, 108
Nongovernmental organizations (NGOs), 21, 184
North American Free Trade Association (NAFTA), 20, 23, 27, 43, 160, 189
North Atlantic Treaty Organization (NATO), 109, 111
Northrop Grumman, 26
North South Center, 137

O

Obama, Barrak (President), 210, 211
O'Brien, Francis, 118
O'Brien, Michael, 107, 126
Odeen, Dr Ishmael, 159
One China policy, 215
Open Door policy, 25
Opioid crisis, 29
Organization of American States (OAS), 44, 151, 181, 211–213
Organization of Eastern Caribbean States (OECS), 184, 186
Ottawa Agreement, 77
Overseas Departments of Martinique and Guadeloupe, 85
OXFAM, 21

P

Panama, 41, 85, 89, 102, 106, 144, 214, 215, 221, 229
Panama Canal, 215, 223
Panama disease, 77, 120, 199n32

Panama-US Trade Promotion Agreement, 221
Parlin, C. Christopher, 118, 145
Partnership for Prosperity and Security, 189
Paterson, Eliza, 157
Patterson, Prime Minister P.J., 4, 118, 119, 139, 151, 152, 156, 159, 180
Paulson, Hank, 26
Pax Americana, 15, 123
Pax Britnnicaa, 15
People's Republic of China, 181, 196, 213, 214
People's National Party, 76
Peterson Institute for International Economics, 20
Petro Caribe, 212
Petro Caribe Development Fund, 212
Philippines, 41, 42
Policy implementation, 16
Political Action Committees (PACs), 28
Political process, 31, 133
Pompeo, Secretary of State Mike, 213, 214
Portman, Rob, 129, 141
Portugal, 85
Preference-dependent countries, 67, 72–74
Preference erosion, 64–68, 70, 73–75
Preferential banana import regime, 2, 7
Preferential market access, 4, 5, 50, 53, 66, 67, 75, 76, 121, 155
Preferential trade arrangements (PTAs), 5, 7, 9, 51, 63–64, 67–69, 76, 82, 84, 89, 90, 90n1, 91n8, 152, 183
Private corporations, 1
Private sector, 1, 13, 26, 68, 73, 74, 118, 149, 150, 216, 218
Private sector modernization, 74
Protectionism, 14, 15, 21, 31, 71, 75, 93n30, 109, 111, 142
Protectionist measures, 14, 71, 72
Protectionist trade policy, 14
Provident Financial Group, 128
Public Citizen, 21
Public opinion, 2, 16, 18, 20, 132

R

Rangel, Congressman Charles, 126, 127, 141, 143, 163
Raw material, 13, 49, 75–77, 216, 217
Raytheon, 26
Reagan administration, 109, 137
Reagan, President Ronald, 109, 137, 184, 211
Reciprocal Trade Agreements of 1934, 17
Regional development banks, 72
Regional law enforcement, 208
Republican party, 104, 128, 141, 142, 148, 162
Restructuring, 70, 72–74, 83, 187, 188, 194, 195, 216
Reuters, 145
Revolving door, 27
Robinson, Prime Minister A.N.R, 45
Robinson, Randall, 110, 126, 129, 135, 140, 145–148, 180, 194
Rodriguez, Manuel, 107, 126
Ross-Robinson and Associates, 145
Ross-Robinson, Hazel, 133, 134, 142, 145, 146
Rubin, Robert, 26
Rules of origin, 66, 67, 71, 214
Ruprah, Inder, 184

S

Safire, William, 130
St. Kitts and Nevis, 42, 186, 189, 196, 208, 222

St. Lucia, 4, 42–45, 52, 53, 67, 120, 121, 130, 139, 145, 148, 149, 151, 152, 157, 162, 180, 182, 184–186, 191, 193, 196, 201n52, 208, 212, 215, 224, 225
St. Lucia Banana Growers Association, 180
St. Vincent and the Grenadines, 4, 42, 53, 90, 134, 149, 156, 182, 184, 186, 208, 212, 213
Sandiford, Prime Minister L. Erskine, 225
Sandinistas, 9, 210
Santer, President Jacques, 140
Securities and Exchange Commission (SEC), 100, 103, 134
Security aid, 209
Shiprider agreements, 180–181
Shower Posse, 192
Simcox, David, 222
Single European Act, 85
Skerrit, Prime Minister, 216
Small businesses, 130–131, 179, 180
Small developing economies (SDEs), 6, 63–65, 67, 76, 82, 183, 194, 216, 217
Small island developing states (SIDS), 5, 6, 192, 195
Smoot-Hawley Tariff Act, 14
Social disturbances, 49, 120
Spain, 85, 155, 156, 219
Special and differential treatment (SDT), 64, 65, 67, 69, 73, 152, 221
Special relationship, 110–111
Standard Fruit, 54, 102, 121
State, 1, 6, 15, 16, 18–20, 22, 23, 25, 26, 28, 29, 38n81, 42, 44–46, 70, 74, 76, 78, 80, 83, 85, 100, 104, 108, 119, 129–131, 140, 144, 146, 151, 152, 154–156, 159–161, 184, 186–188, 190, 192, 195, 207, 208, 210, 211, 213, 215, 219, 220, 222, 224, 225
State-corporate nexus, 100–101
State Department, 18, 103, 124, 125, 136, 146, 151, 158, 159, 196, 219
State-owned enterprises, 25
Structural adjustment, 64, 73, 187–188
Sugar Act 1956, 76
Sugar industry, 6, 46, 47, 49, 50, 119, 196
Sugar Industry Diversification Foundation (SIDF), 196
Sumitomo, 42
Summit of the Americas, 44, 118, 130, 151, 160, 181, 212
Suriname, 42, 139, 149, 186, 195, 213, 215, 217

T

Taiwan, 214, 215
Tate and Lyle, 183, 218
Think Tanks, 3, 20–21, 123, 137–138
Tillerson, Rex, 26
Time for Action, 46
Time magazine, 128, 131, 134, 140
Tourist industry, 187, 217, 218
Trade, 1–5, 8, 9, 14–23, 25, 29–31, 42–44, 46, 48, 50, 51, 63–69, 71–73, 75–77, 79, 81–84, 88–90, 99, 105–107, 109, 111, 118, 120, 123–129, 132–138, 141–143, 148, 149, 151–159, 183–186, 188, 190–192, 214–223, 226, 227, 229
Trade Act 1974, 17, 83, 117, 220
Trade Act 2002, 221
Trade adjustment, 74

Trade and Economic Cooperation Agreement, 82
Trade capacity building, 74
Trade deficit, 16, 31, 214, 215
Trade Integration Mechanism (TIM), 74
Trade legislation, 17, 22
Trade philosophy, 14
Trade policies, 1–3, 5–8, 10, 66, 73, 75, 90, 99–112, 130, 131, 138, 142, 154, 180, 220, 221
Trade policy formulation, 2, 3, 13, 19, 22
Trade preferences, 63–66, 68–71, 78, 82–84, 90, 152, 184, 185, 220
Trade Promotion Authority (TPA), 17, 20
Trade sanctions, 17, 87
Trade unions, 21, 29
Trade war, 2, 5, 30, 107, 109, 127, 132, 140, 161
Trans-Africa, 110
Transatlantic nexus, 155–157
Transnational crime, 6, 8, 191, 192, 223–226
Treasury, 18, 26
Treaty of Basseterre, 186
Treaty of Chaguaramas, 186
Treaty of Rome, 78, 79, 85
Trinidad and Tobago, 42, 44, 45, 47, 83, 118, 151, 186, 208, 209, 211, 213, 215, 217, 224
Trump, President Donald, 26, 211, 213
Turf wars, 193

U
Unemployment rates, 6
Union of Banana Exporting Countries (UBEC), 102, 103
United Brands, 78, 100, 102, 103, 122, 183
United Fruit Company (UFC), 5, 9, 10, 23, 47, 48, 50–52, 78, 81, 99–102, 106, 120–122, 228
United Kingdom (UK), 6, 53, 54, 76–78, 82, 156, 157, 184, 190, 196, 223
United Nations (UN), 44, 107, 126, 210
United Nations General Assembly (UNGA), 125, 152, 159
United Self-Defence Forces of Colombia, 104
United States (US), 2, 26–27, 42, 80, 99–112, 117, 179–197, 207–229
University of Exeter, 138
Uruguay Round, 79, 141
USA Today, 133, 145
US banana policy, 107, 123–126, 131, 133, 136, 137, 140, 147–150, 157, 179–197
US-Caribbean Basin Trade Partnership Act (CBPTA), 221
US Caribbean relations, 136
US-Caribbean Strategic Engagement Act, 227
US-CARICOM Summit, 152
US Chamber of Commerce, 25, 26
US Constitution, 17
US corporate interests, 2, 8, 23, 30–31, 101, 118, 134
US Department of Agriculture, 18, 82, 220
US Drug Enforcement Administration, 160
US-EU bilateral trade, 2
US Financial Crimes Enforcement Network, 196
US foreign policy, 3, 5, 15, 18, 21, 23, 26, 43–45, 100, 145, 166n42, 181, 189, 208–210, 217, 219, 223

US government, 2, 5, 8–10, 22, 25, 27, 30, 31, 49, 82, 84, 86, 87, 99–101, 106–109, 118, 121–123, 125, 131, 143–145, 150, 151, 163, 180, 184, 220, 228
US international trade policy, 3, 10
US invasion of Grenada, 44, 184
US national interest in the Caribbean, 8, 10, 207–229
US national interests, 2, 207–229
US national security, 2, 6, 135, 137, 179, 208
US oil companies, 106
US policymaking, 19
US political process, 31
US political system, 13, 22, 28
US public policy, 3
US Trade Act, 188
US trade policy, 2, 3, 5, 7, 8, 13–32, 90, 99–112
US Trade Representative's (USTR) office, 13, 17, 143

V
Venezuela, 8, 26, 79, 86, 89, 181, 191, 197, 208, 210–213, 223–225, 227

W
Wage rates, 53, 121
Wallach, Lori, 21, 148, 185
Wall Street Journal, 19, 22, 163
Washington Consensus, 9, 182
Washington DC, 19, 105, 118, 125, 134, 142, 145, 149, 156, 159, 162, 163, 185, 210, 214, 215, 222
Washington Post, 19, 22, 105, 134, 135, 138, 147
Washington Trade Daily, 22
Waters, Maxine, 105, 126, 129, 140, 143, 147, 159, 185, 192
Weisskopf, Michael, 104
West India Committee, 184
West Indian Commission, 46
West Indian Welfare Fund, 77
West Indies Fruit Company, 101
Whipple, Harry M., 133
White House, 3, 13, 16–18, 88, 105, 106, 118, 123, 125, 130, 132, 140, 147, 151, 152, 158, 162, 163
Williams, Eric, 212
Wilson, Charles E. Wilson, 30
Windward Island Banana Development Company, 158
Windward Island Banana Growers Association (WINBAN), 78, 118, 156
Windward Islands, 49–53, 78, 120, 121, 158, 182, 183, 186
Windwards-Jamaica banana war, 51, 120
Winthrop, Stimpson, Putman and Roberts, 118, 145
Wolf, Martin, 153
World banana trade, 42
World Bank, 45, 72–74, 137, 151, 184, 187, 193, 210
World Trade Organization (WTO), 6, 16, 17, 20, 21, 31, 52, 64, 65, 68, 69, 71, 72, 74, 79, 80, 83–89, 97n74, 104, 105, 107, 109, 110, 119, 120, 125–128, 130–132, 141–144, 148, 152–157, 159, 161, 179, 183, 185, 188, 220, 228
World War II, 15, 31, 51, 77, 79, 120, 217, 218
WTO Challenge, 87–88
WTO dispute settlement system (DSS), 155

WTO Members Dispute Settlement Understanding (DSU), 155
WTO Trade Policy Review, 73
WTO Understanding on Rules and Procedures Governing the Settlement of Disputes, 155

Y
Yaounde Convention, 78
Yeutter, Clayton, 137

Z
Zemurray, Samuel, 100, 102, 122

The manufacturer's authorised representative in the EU is Springer Nature Customer Service Centre GmbH, Europaplatz 3, 69115 Heidelberg, Germany. If you have any concerns regarding our products, please contact ProductSafety@springernature.com

Printed and bound by CPI Group (UK) Ltd, Croydon, CR0 4YY
28/09/2026
02224088-0001